Germans as

Germans as Victims

Remembering the Past in Contemporary Germany

edited by

BILL NIVEN

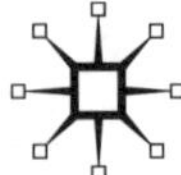

Published by
PALGRAVE MACMILLAN
Houndmills, Basingstoke, Hampshire RG21 6XS and
175 Fifth Avenue, New York, N.Y. 10010
Companies and representatives throughout the world

PALGRAVE MACMILLAN is the global academic imprint of the Palgrave Macmillan division of St. Martin's Press, LLC and of Palgrave Macmillan Ltd. Macmillan® is a registered trademark in the United States, United Kingdom and other countries. Palgrave is a registered trademark in the European Union and other countries.

ISBN–13: 978 1–4039–9042–6 hardback
ISBN–10: 1–4039–9042–5 paperback
ISBN–13: 978 1–4039–9043–3 hardback
ISBN–10: 1–4039–9043–3 paperback

This book is printed on paper suitable for recycling and made from fully managed and sustained forest sources.

A catalogue record for this book is available from the British Library.

A catalog record for this book is available from the Library of Congress.

10 9 8 7 6 5 4 3 2 1
15 14 13 12 11 10 09 08 07 06

Printed in China

Contents

Notes on the Contributors

Pertti Ahonen is Lecturer in History at the University of Edinburgh, Scotland, UK.

Andrew H. Beattie is Lecturer in German Studies at the Institute for International Studies, University of Technology, Sydney, Australia.

Stefan Berger is Professor of Modern German and Comparative European History at the University of Manchester, England, UK.

Paul Cooke is Senior Lecturer in German at the University of Leeds, England, UK.

Andreas Huyssen is The Villard Professor of German and Comparative Literature at Columbia University in New York City, USA

Robert G. Moeller teaches modern German and European history at the University of California, Irvine, USA.

Bill Niven is Professor of Contemporary German History at the Nottingham Trent University, England, UK.

Karoline von Oppen is Lecturer in German at the University of Bath, England, UK.

Helmut Schmitz is Senior Lecturer in the Department of German Studies at the University of Warwick, England, UK.

Stuart Taberner is Professor of German at the University of Leeds, England, UK.

Ruth Wittlinger is Lecturer in Politics at the University of Durham, England, UK.

Stefan Wolff is Professor of Political Science at the University of Bath, England, UK.

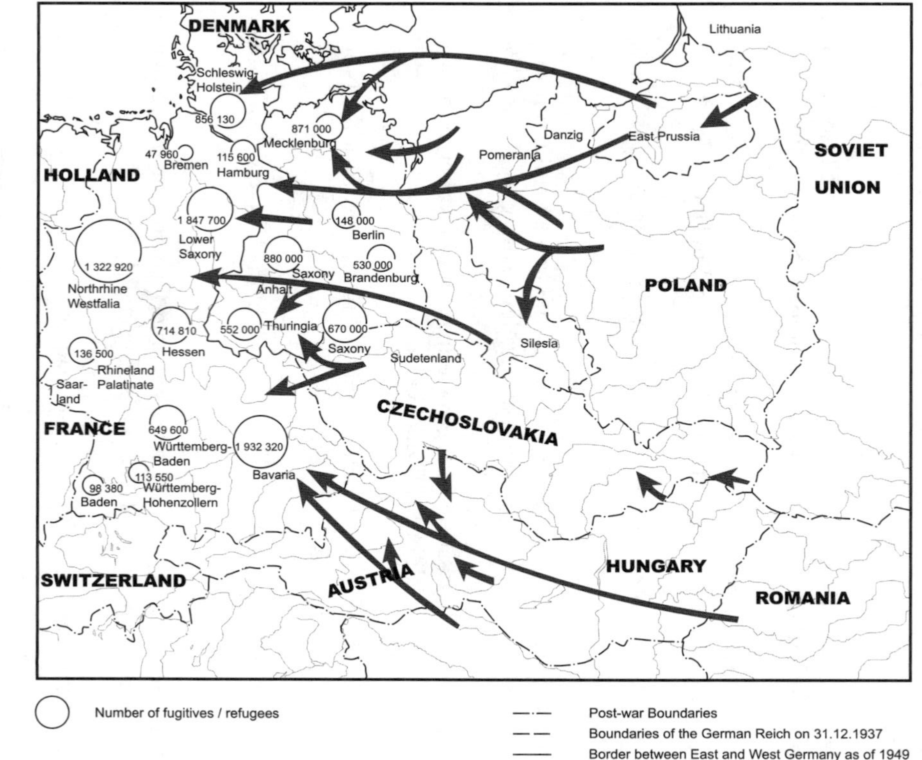

Map 1 Movements of German fugitives and expellees, 1945–1950. Adapted from: Arno Surminski et al., *Flucht und Vertreibung: Europa zwischen 1939 und 1948* (Hamburg 2004), p. 274.

Map 2 United Germany showing the *Länder* and the former German–German border. From J. K. A. Thomaneck and Bill Niven, *Dividing and Uniting Germany* (London and New York: Routledge, 2001), p. ix. Reproduced courtesy of Taylor & Francis Books.

Introduction: German Victimhood at the Turn of the Millennium

Bill Niven

The end of the Cold War

The geopolitical redrawing of the map of Europe between 1989 and 1992 had, without doubt, a significant effect on the culture of memory of the Nazi past that evolved in the united Germany. Even in the 1970s and 1980s, when West Germany at least began to face the Holocaust, it had still been the case that the existence of two Germanies worked against, rather than in the interest of, coming to terms with National Socialism. According to a system of mutual self-exculpation and inculpation, East Germany understood itself as an anti-fascist and West Germany as a neofascist state, while West Germany understood itself as democratic and East Germany as but the continuation of dictatorship, this time in socialist guise. Blame for the Nazi past was thus frequently passed over the border to the 'other' Germany. The collapse of the German Democratic Republic (GDR) in 1990 necessarily brought this interstate moral rivalry to an end. It finally became possible for Germany as a whole to own responsibility for Nazism. This possibility was not realised without opposition. The post-1990 period was characterised in Germany by a number of often embittered debates on Nazism, most of which focused on the degree and extent of German involvement in crimes against Jews and others during the Second World War. In general, it can be said that these debates resulted in a wider recognition and acceptance of this involvement.

Particularly important in this regard was the 1996 debate surrounding Daniel Jonah Goldhagen's book *Hitler's Willing Executioners*, a book which suggested that anti-Semitism had been a typical characteristic of 'ordinary Germans' under Hitler, and that such Germans had killed Jews quite willingly, rather than under constraint. Despite the fact that Goldhagen's book appeared to resurrect the collective guilt theory of the 1950s, and despite the hostility of historians world-wide to Goldhagen's sweeping thesis, many Germans reacted to his arguments with understanding and what seemed to be a genuine sense of contrition. Also very important was the *War of Annihilation: Crimes of the Wehrmacht, 1941–1944* exhibition shown in cities throughout Germany and Austria as of 1995; it sought to demonstrate that there had been widespread participation by the regular German Army in the murder of Jews, Soviet POWs and supposed partisans in Eastern Europe. Millions visited this exhibition or read about it in the media, shocked at its message – namely that crimes against humanity had been committed not just by the SS in concentration and annihilation camps, but also by run-of-the-mill soldiers hitherto thought by many post-war Germans to have been fighting a 'clean' war quite unrelated to the Holocaust. As plans for the construction of a central Holocaust Memorial in Berlin gathered pace throughout the 1990s, Germans seemed increasingly committed to making memory of German shame a pivotal point for reflection on the past and a point of orientation for conduct in the present and in the future. With the dedication of that memorial in 2005, the Holocaust finally appeared to move to the very centre of German cultural and commemorative memory. Moreover, much has been done in united Germany to bring to public attention, commemorate and memorialise the suffering of other, non-Jewish minorities under Hitler – in each case with a concern for the specific nature of their persecution and suffering. Homosexuals, Jehovah's Witnesses, Sinti and Roma, and even deserters from the *Wehrmacht* have all moved from the fringe towards, if not into the centre of public memory since 1990.

This book is not concerned, however, with memory of the suffering *caused* by Germans, but rather with that *endured* by Germans. Memory of the latter, like memory of the former, had also been strongly influenced by the Cold War. Just as East Germans in the GDR were encouraged to understand the Holocaust as a result of capitalist machinations, so they were invited by SED (East German Socialist Unity Party) propaganda to view the bombing of the beautiful city of Dresden by the British and Americans in February 1945 as symptomatic of the destructive force of Western imperialism. The strident political functionalisation of the theme of the bombing of Dresden, and indeed of Allied bombing generally in the GDR, contrasts considerably with the more complex reception of the theme in West Germany. But this reception nevertheless also had a strongly politicised dimension. Thus in 1961, the Interministerial Committee for East/West Film Questions passed the Polish film *Dresden, the Vanished City* by Jan Rypkowski for showing in West German cinemas on the proviso that it was preceded by a short text: 'this film shows the chaos and senselessness of wars into which peoples have been plunged by political dictators and into which such dictators can plunge them again at any time.' The Committee counteracted the anti-Western implications of Rypkowski's film on the bombing of Dresden by framing it as a warning against the consequences of dictatorships past and present, such as that in the Soviet Union.[1]

The situation in respect of memory of the plight of German fugitives and expellees from Eastern Europe was different, yet comparable. Between 12 and 14 million Germans either fled the eastern territories in advance of the Soviet army in 1944/45, or were expelled from there as part of the geopolitical and ethnic reorganisation of Eastern Europe at the end of the war. Treatment of the theme was very low-key in official GDR discourse. Many of these expellees had benefited from post-1945 land reforms in eastern Germany. Generally the GDR prided itself on how well it had integrated its 4 million expellees or 'resettlers' (*Umsiedler*) as they were officially called.[2] But there was little scope in this official success story for the public articulation of the past sufferings of the ethnic Germans at the hands of the Poles and Czechs – who were, after all, the GDR's neighbours in the socialist Eastern bloc – and even less scope for criticism of the Russians. In West Germany, the expellees had their own political party (until the late 1950s), and their own individual and collective organisations with which to lobby the West German parliament on subjects such as the non-recognition of the Oder-Neiße line as Poland's western border. The perceived injustice of the expulsions was a prominent political theme in the Federal Republic of Germany (FRG). But as historian Pertti Ahonen has shown, West Germany's first Chancellor, Konrad Adenauer, while appearing to sympathise with the interests of the expellees, was committed mainly to Western integration and not to German reunification, and certainly not to reunification within the borders of 1937.[3] With the advent of Willy Brandt's *Ostpolitik*, the expellees' intransigent attitudes towards the East became anachronistic. They were regarded as – and to an extent were – died-in-the-wool revisionists. With the collapse of the Eastern bloc and the confirmation in the 2 + 4 Treaty of 1990 of the Oder-Neiße line as Poland's western border, the political heat was taken out of the theme of expulsion. There was a chance for Germans to take an interest in it without fear of being branded right-wing or backward-looking.

The end of the Cold War thus made possible not just a more open and frank confrontation with the Holocaust, it also prepared the ground for a less politicised confrontation with the theme of Allied bombing, and of expulsion. The collapse of the GDR also paved the way for a much clearer articulation of the suffering experienced by eastern Germans at the hands of the Red Army in 1945 (over a million women were raped), the NKVD (the Soviet secret police who oversaw the internment of Germans in the course of Stalinist-style denazification), the SED and the *Stasi* – indeed the suffering arguably only stopped with the implosion of these latter two organisations in 1989/90. The discovery in 1990 of shallow mass graves of some of those thousands of German internees who died in Soviet internment camps of disease and malnutrition between 1945 and 1949 also contributed to an intense public discourse on the injustices of Stalinism and socialism. Before 1990, such East German suffering – including the shooting of East German fugitives at the German–German border – could not be publicly expressed in the GDR, but was instrumentalised in anti-GDR campaigns in the FRG, or, by contrast, played down by Western politicians so as not to damage the policies of *Ostpolitik*. Now, after 1990, it could be – and was – strongly articulated by former persecutees, who organised themselves into interest groups demanding compensation and justice.

The political functionalisation of memory in the GDR and the FRG resulted in the distorted and manipulative representation of themes such as bombing and expulsion; in some cases, it resulted in silence, particularly in the GDR, where subjects such as the rape of women by the Red Army could not be addressed because to do so would have been to contradict the official history, according to which the Soviet soldiers who entered eastern Germany in 1945 were liberators and socialist patriots. 1990 thus represented a significant moment of depoliticisation, a chance, indeed, for an articulation of German suffering *as suffering*, as an existential experience. That moment of depoliticisation offered a chance for empathy, and in some areas it also offered a chance for self-critical reappraisal. Thus the demise of the GDR and the state-imposed view of the bombing war as an act of Western aggression provided east Germans with the opportunity to reconsider whether that bombing war might not, to a significant degree, have been legitimate. However, as I set out to demonstrate below, the potential represented by 1990 was not realised, certainly not in the years of Christian Democrat (CDU) government between 1990 and 1998. With the advent of a Red–Green government in 1998, the theme of German suffering did at last recede from the political agenda; but it did so in a way which caused it to emerge resurgent, as if it had been suddenly unchained, in the public realm. This resurgence, at times, has been so strong as to represent a serious challenge to the primacy of memory of the Holocaust and undermine awareness of German perpetration.

Repoliticisation

Shortly after becoming the first government of united Germany in October 1990, the CDU–Liberal coalition set about repoliticising the theme of German suffering for its own purposes. It is often claimed that Helmut Kohl was the 'Chancellor of unity' because he was in power when unification was achieved and certainly did much to make this unification possible. Kohl's commitment to unity went beyond the political and economic to embrace the spiritual; he sought to bring about an 'inner unity' between east and west Germans on the basis of a common understanding of history. According to this understanding, the Germans had suffered at the hands of two comparable forms of totalitarian rule: National Socialism (1933–45) and Soviet-imported socialism in the Soviet-occupied zone and the GDR (1945–90). In 1993, a historical building known as the New Guardhouse (*Neue Wache*) in east Berlin was officially dedicated as united Germany's central national memorial. Centrepiece of the memorial was a massively inflated reproduction of a sculpture by Käthe Kollwitz, *Pieta*, which shows a mother grieving over her dead son. The choice of this sculpture and idea for the national memorial were Kohl's. More than anything, it was the New Guardhouse which epitomised Kohl's appropriation of the topos of German victimhood for building a post-unification national identity.

A brief consideration of the dedication mounted on the outside of the building bears this out. It begins with a generalised commemorative gesture towards 'the victims of war and the rule of violence'. There follows a reference to the 'peoples who suffered through war' and their persecuted citizens. The text then commemorates the fallen of two world wars, and the 'innocent people' who lost their lives not just in war, but also as a result of war 'in the homeland', 'in captivity' and 'when being driven out of their homeland'. There follow references to the murdered Jews, Sinti and Roma and homosexuals. Certainly it is laudable that the text explicitly mentions these. Nevertheless, implicit within the dedication is a problematic memory hierarchy: first to be cited are those who died in the war and 'in the homeland', not the

Jews. Given that text is necessarily sequential, it is difficult to avoid saying one thing before another. In a famous 8 May speech in 1985, the then Federal President of West Germany Richard von Weizsäcker also placed a reference to the Jews after one to 'all the dead of war and the rule of violence'. But he did so *immediately after*, such that the listener is invited to understand Jews as the prime victims of war and violence. Kohl's 1994 dedication, however, suggests that civilian casualties, soldiers and the victims of expulsion were its prime victims. That these casualties and victims are not to be understood as including Jews is implied by the distinct reference to Jewish deaths which follows. If they don't include Jews, they must largely consist, so the reader is meant to infer, of Germans and perhaps other nationals who died in war. Thus the explicit referencing of Jewish deaths serves not to highlight Jewish suffering, but to rank Jews outside the memorial's prime focus: the Germans.

The New Guardhouse exhibits Kohl's proclivity for transforming Germans retrospectively into victims of war, of Hitler, of expulsion by the Poles and Czechs – and also of Stalinism and socialism after 1945. The reference to 'violence' is as much one to the supposedly totalitarian GDR as it is to National Socialism. Thus Kohl sought to replace the German–Jewish perpetrator–victim relation with one in which Germans appeared, historically speaking, to be victims in the same measure as the Jews. Given the conflicts between east and west Germans following unification, this form of memory politics was clearly designed to reconcile Germans not just with their history, but also with each other; in short, it was a memory politics of national conciliation. There are other examples of such a memory politics from the 1990–98 period, particularly in respect of coming to terms with the East German past. In 1992, for instance, a parliamentary Enquete Commission was set up to investigate and overcome the 'history and effects of the SED dictatorship in Germany'. Judicial measures were set in motion to bring to justice those East Germans who had ordered and carried out the shooting of East German fugitives at the German–German border, while 'laws for the cleansing of SED injustice' were introduced for compensating victims of socialist repression. In addition to implying a moral equivalence between socialism and National Socialism so as to discredit the former, such measures were clearly designed to cast East Germans, retrospectively, in the role of victims. *Me miserum*, or rather *nostrum miserum*, was to become the glue to hold together Germany's new national identity, at least in its historically derived elements.

For all Kohl's universalising approach to victimhood, and as pointed out at the start of this introduction, the 1992–98 period was characterised by widespread historiographical, media and public interest in the issue of German perpetration and guilt, and Jewish victimhood – as shown by the popularity of the critical *Crimes of the Wehrmacht* exhibition. Generally speaking, the CDU's tendency to seek to delegitimise the GDR in retrospect by equating SED socialism with Nazism was never accepted by the public at large. Indeed, the positive public response to Goldhagen's book, which in its own way asserted the incomparability of the Holocaust, can be interpreted as a rejection of such dubious equations. As long as German victimhood, whether before or after 1945, remained a focus of instrumentalisation by the CDU and the political Right in general, that potential for a more judicious and widespread public interest in the topos created in 1990 remained unfulfilled. The theme was still widely regarded with some suspicion.

Red–Green

With the shift to a Red–Green government in September 1998 – the Social Democrat Party (SPD) and Greens had largely welcomed the *Wehrmacht* exhibition – one would have expected the political culture of memory to shift away from Kohl-style universalisation. And indeed it did. The SPD–Green parliamentary coalition largely consisted of Germans born after the war, many of them members of what is known as the '1968 generation' – that generation of students in Germany which had done so much to promote in West German society a more open confrontation with the Nazi past. Gerhard Schröder, Chancellor from 1998 until September 2005, regularly sought in his commemorative speeches to place German perpetration and Jewish victimhood in the foreground. Thus in a speech in May 2002, following the ritual reference to those who died in war and under dictatorship, Schröder said: 'we commemorate the six million Jews murdered by Germans. We commemorate the millions of victims of the war unleashed by Germans among the peoples of Europe and in the Soviet Union.' Only after this is there a reference to the 'unspeakable suffering which this war brought upon our own people'.[4] More recently, in a statement on 8 May 2005, Schröder explicitly spoke out against attempts to transform 'the perpetrator discourse' into 'a victims' discourse'.[5] For Schröder, then, while he acknowledged German suffering, the particular role of the Germans between 1933 and 1945 was one of perpetration; where they were victims, then, of a war of their own making.

Because German suffering was not a significant component of post-1998 memory politics, the shift to Red–Green represented, as it were, a 'handing over' of the theme to the public realm. It could be talked about without that fear of high-level political instrumentalisation which had obtained before. In fact, the advent of Red–Green, to put it metaphorically, seemed to open the flood gates: since 1998, countless television programmes, popular history books, novels and films have thematised German victimhood during and after the war. This has not escaped international attention. Tony Blair recently told Germany's *BILD* newspaper that while it was right for the Germans to commemorate those who were expelled from the eastern territories, that 'should not mean nurturing a culture of victimhood'.[6] Blair's words of warning reflect a concern that recent interest in German suffering has taken on an obsessive dimension. This concern is not without justification. The theme of German suffering may not have played a significant part in the Red–Green government's political and commemorative agenda, but at the same time Gerhard Schröder and other SPD/Green politicians sought to cultivate an image of themselves and of contemporary Germany which invited the German public to approach the topic of German suffering much less critically and judiciously than it might otherwise have done.

At the core of this image was an overweening democratic self-confidence. Not that the national sentiment of Red–Green could have been confused with traditional ethnic nationalism. Under Schröder, citizenship laws in Germany saw a significant shift away from ethnic concepts of identity to one based on *ius soli*. Schröder himself conceived of the nation as a 'voting community' centred around Western values such as democracy, freedom, justice, solidarity and participation; he did not think of it in terms of a 'community of descent'.[7] But this awareness of Germany's democratic character itself constituted a source of national pride. In his speech opening parliament on 10 November 1998, Schröder waxed almost lyrical in his praise for Germany: 'we are proud of this country, proud of the older people who built up this country after the war and created a place for it in a peaceful Europe.' He went on to stress 'the self-confidence of a nation which has come of age, which does not need to feel superior to anyone, nor indeed inferior to anyone'.

Some might see the historian Heinrich August Winkler as providing the historiographic framework for this self-assertive view of united

Germany as a model of Western democracy in his book *The Long Route to the West* (*Der Lange Weg nach Westen*, 2001). Certainly the political scientist Hans Jörg Hennecke believes that Winkler's concept of reunited Germany as a 'democratic, post-classical national state among others' was shared by Red–Green politicians, who, according to Hennecke, distanced themselves from the traditional left-wing idea that Germany should define itself as a post-national democracy.[8] In more general terms, too, Red–Green appeared to abandon or at least compromise on traditional left-wing values following its accession to power in 1998. The journalist Richard Meng has argued persuasively that Schröder's commitment was not to such values, but to principles of 'good governance' in attempting to support the process of modernisation and globalisation in Germany.[9] That a supposedly left-wing coalition, populated to a large extent by former members of the 1968 generation, should have taken to celebrating the health of German democracy certainly represented a break with previous traditions. The very generation which insisted in the 1960s and 1970s that West Germany must face its Nazi past was suddenly given to implying, if not exactly stating, that this past had been faced, and that Germany could move on. Precisely because Red–Green coalition members appeared to have such moral authority in matters of coming to terms with Nazism, their declaration of Germany's achievement of 'normality' was arguably interpreted by many as implying that there was no longer any need to focus largely on German perpetration when remembering the Third Reich and its aftermath. Freed of a sense of guilt-ridden obligation, Germany could develop a vigorous interest in German victimhood that, at times at least, seemed and still seems to border on the self-pitying.

It could even be suggested that this vigorous interest was to a degree fostered by a tone of casualness among Red-Green politicians when commemorating the victims of Nazism and reiterating the need to remember Nazi crime. For all Schröder's verbal rejection of attempts to foreground German victimhood, he also made headlines through his rather relaxed and at times coolly pragmatic attitude to issues pertaining to Nazi perpetration. Witness his oft-cited remark that the Holocaust Memorial should be a place where the Germans 'like to go'. This remark is usually quoted out of context – Schröder actually said that he wished for a memorial where the Germans 'like to go to remember and take issue'.[10] Nevertheless, Schröder seemed to be suggesting that remembering the Holocaust should somehow be a pleasant experience – and the Holocaust Memorial a theme park for the enjoyment of the masses. Witness, too, his unabashed insistence that any compensation for forced labourers paid out by German firms must go hand in hand with the guarantee of legal closure – *Rechtsfrieden* is the German term, literally 'judicial peace'. Michel Friedman, at the time vice-president of the Central Council of Jews in Germany, accused Schröder's government of sending out signals 'which nourish a fatal longing for normality', and he noted the dominance of a 'superficial attitude of irritability' along the lines of 'we won't allow ourselves to be disturbed by history any more'.[11] The critic Reinhard Mohr, moreover, identified in Red–Green politics an 'end of humility'.[12] A casual tone towards the Nazi past was felt by many to be a facet of this 'end of humility'.

Germans as victims in the present

It needs to be stressed, however, that the recent focus on German victimhood, in some cases, results from *protest* against the left-wing tradition of coming to terms with Nazism (*Vergangenheitsbewältigung*) associated with the 1968 generation – however one then conceives of Red–Green's relationship to this tradition. On receipt of the 1998 Peace Prize of the German Book Trade in Frankfurt in October of that year, the German author Martin Walser delivered a speech in which he appeared not only to criticise the supposedly *left-liberal* instrumentalisation of memory of the Nazi period for political purposes, but also to imply that there had been an inflation of such instrumentalised memory in recent years that was detrimental to the health of the nation. The ensuing debate between Walser and the then head of the Central Council of German Jews, Ignatz Bubis, about whether or not Walser's speech constituted an act of 'intellectual arson' preoccupied the media for some months.[13] Whatever Walser's intentions, his speech was often interpreted as expressing the need for a 'scaling down' of the focus on Nazism, and as casting today's Germans in the role of victims – not so much of events in the past, as of constant reminders of German historical guilt by left-wing or liberal intellectuals determined to check any post-unification shift towards German nationalism. Walser's critique of the supposed taboo placed by the Left on patriotism was very much part of a general attack on the 1968 generation, and left-wing intellectuals generally, that has been gathering pace in Germany since 1990. This generation stands accused of having institutionalised a doctrine of politically correct memory which led directly to the marginalisation and indeed exclusion of all memory of German suffering, thus making it impossible for the Germans to mourn their losses. Walser's speech undoubtedly triggered in many Germans the feeling that they were victims of a memory politics which forbade them from remembering they had been victims. Victimisation in the present obstructed empathy with victimhood in the past.

The accusation that the Left was manipulating memory of the Nazi past was not new.[14] In the event, too, Walser's attack on the Left proved rather obsolete, if not redundant, given the 'relaxed' position towards the Nazi past subsequently adopted by Red–Green. But it was not only the Left which came in for criticism. While it would seem unfair to accuse Walser of anti-Semitism, his novel *Death of a Critic* (*Tod eines Kritikers*, 2002) appeared to depict a German writer suffering from victimisation at the hands of a possibly Jewish critic.[15] Klaus Rainer Röhl, a former communist turned nationalist, expressed the view in a book with the significant title *Forbidden Mourning: German Taboos at an End* (*Verbotene Trauer: Ende der deutschen Tabus*, 2002) that the post-war re-education programme in Germany, as well as the Frankfurt School and the ethical rigorism of the 1968 generation were strongly influenced by Jews.[16] The Jews, in other words, were instrumental in seeking to keep the Germans down by instilling in them an inappropriate feeling of collective guilt for Nazism. (Former) representatives of the Left such as Walser and unreconstructed representatives of the Right seemed to join together in objecting to supposed moral and financial pressure from the 'American east coast'. Even Rudolf Augstein, at the time left-liberal editor of the prestigious weekly *Der Spiegel*, suggested that the Berlin Holocaust Memorial, which he described as a 'monstrosity', would be built out of 'respect for the New York press and sharks in lawyers' clothing'; while he does not cite Jews, it is certainly possible to infer that Jews are meant.[17]

Without doubt, the idea that the Left, in cohoots with the Jews, stands to benefit from any German culture of contrition reproduces the conspiracy theories of the Nazis, who argued that the Jews and the socialists were committed to undermining German political strength and national feeling. One or two German politicians, admittedly of the more maverick variety, have made explicit what is certainly implicit in this contemporary conspiracy theory – namely that Jews, given their propensity for imposing victimhood on others, must necessarily be classified as perpetrators, such that they are hardly qualified to take the high moral ground by passing judgment on the Germans. Two examples will suffice here. In a speech in October 2003, the CDU parliamentarian Martin Hohmann claimed that there would be 'some justification' in describing the Jews as a 'perpetrator people'. He supported this claim with reference to the role played by Jews in the Russian revolution and the Soviet secret police; whatever the actual role of Jews in these – and Hohmann certainly exaggerated it enormously – it would hardly provide evidence that the Jews are a perpetrator people.[18] Hohmann's purpose in his speech was to place the Jews on a par with the Nazis; just as most Nazis were Christians who had turned against their religion, he claimed, so the Jewish Bolshevists had dissociated themselves from Judaism.[19] In May 2002, Jamal Karsli, a former member of the Green Party and prospective member of the Free Democratic Party (FDP), caught the headlines in a similar fashion when he accused Israel of 'Nazi methods' and referred to a 'Zionist lobby' in Germany.[20] Despite these remarks, the FDP leader of Northrhine Westfalia at the time, Jürgen Möllemann, supported Karsli's admission as member of the FDP, and was himself not averse to provocative remarks directed against Jews. Following criticism of Karsli by Michel Friedman, Möllemann accused the latter of fomenting the very anti-Semitism he sought to criticise.[21]

Since 1998, then, there have been those in Germany who have sought to discredit the moral authority of Jews whether in America, Israel or in Germany itself.[22] This has accompanied the discrediting of the Left, and it almost certainly represents a reaction against the focus on German perpetration in the public realm in the 1995–98 period. There are some Germans who clearly believe that this focus was only possible because of a moral inferiority complex on the part of the nation, a complex ruthlessly exploited by Jews and left-liberals; by exposing the latter, then, as morally no better than those upon whom they ostensibly presume to pass judgment, the inferiority complex informing national contrition can be overcome. The obsessive focus on German perpetration might give way to a view of history which also takes into account Germans as *victims*; for if Germans are no worse than anyone else, why should they prioritise, in memory, the deeds they committed over those committed against them?

Germans as victims in the past

There is a noticeable correlation in the contemporary preoccupation with German suffering between constructions of victimhood in the present, and constructions of victimhood in the past. Thus while today's Germans are sometimes perceived as victims of a left-wing and Jewish campaign of guilt immersion, the Germans of the Third Reich era are understood to have been victims either of the Allies, or of Hitler. In order to transform the Germans retrospectively into absolute victims, some writers and historians pursue one, and most commonly both, of two related strategies – related in the sense that one is implicit in the other. Differences are often simply a question of emphasis.

The first strategy is to exculpate Germans living at the time of the Third Reich. Thus the Wartberg publishing house has published a series of books chronicling the Allied bombing of German cities (e.g., Hamburg, Kassel, Krefeld, Solingen, Dortmund) which focus centrally on the terrible impact of the bombing on German urban communities.[23] Often these communities are portrayed as innocent collectives untouched by Nazism – composed not of Nazis or fellow-travellers, but simply of 'ordinary citizens'. Such portrayals, as one critic observed, retrospectively denazify the Nazi people's community.[24] As a result, the connection between Allied bombing and the fight against Nazism is erased. Such moral whitewashing of the German urban collective enhances their claim to an absolute status as victims; they did not 'deserve' to be bombed. Other methods of enhancing this claim include pointing out that the bombs that rained down on Germany killed Jews and forced labourers as well as German civilians; the *post hoc* creation of a victim collective in which Jews and Germans rank side by side serves to erase the essential difference between the status of these two groups. The multi-volume collective diary *Echolot* (*Soundings*), compiled from a variety of sources by the German writer Walter Kempowski, places side by side perspectives on the war of, for instance, 'ordinary Germans', Jews, Nazis, Americans, Russians and the British.[25] In that part of his collective diary which focuses on the bombing of Dresden, Kempowksi includes reactions to the bombing by German artist Otto Griebel, the German Jew Victor Klemperer, and a German fugitive from Silesia.[26] And in his 1995 novel *The Boy with the Bloody Shoes* (*Der Junge mit den blutigen Schuhen*), the German writer Dieter Forte describes the district of Oberbilk in Düsseldorf as a place where civilian Germans, Jews and forced labourers are linked by acts of solidarity into a collective which is then ruthlessly bombed from the air.[27]

If the first strategy emphasises a commonality of victim status linking Germans and Jews, the second emphasises rather a commonality of perpetrator status linking Nazis and the Allies – while at the same time implying as a corollary of this that the fate of Germans at the hands of the Allies was every bit as terrible as that of the Jews at the hands of the Nazis. A key example of such a strategy is provided by Jörg Friedrich's book *The Fire* (*Der Brand*, 2002) about the Allied bombing war against Germany. Friedrich describes it throughout in vocabulary generally used in reference to the Holocaust. He writes, for example, of 'mass killing' and of an 'annihilation attack on Kaiserslautern'.[28] To be sure, Friedrich points out that the term 'exterminating attack' was once used by Churchill himself.[29] But Friedrich surely knew that the consistent use in his book of the German word *Vernichtung* (annihilation) would evoke the term *Vernichtungskrieg* (war of annihilation) conducted by the Germans in Eastern Europe mainly against Jews, Bolsheviks and supposed partisans; it also evokes the annihilation of Jews at the extermination camps. Friedrich suggests that the British and Americans, towards the end of the war, sought to eradicate Germany's national cultural and architectural heritage by striking at 'militarily irrelevant shrines such as Hildesheim, Magdeburg, Dresden, Würzburg [and] Nuremberg'.[30] This implies that the Western Allies were somehow seeking to liquidate all traces of Germany's national history as well as bombarding its urban populations, just as the Nazis sought to remove from Europe not only the Jews themselves, but their cultural heritage. And in claiming that Churchill had long harboured ideas of destroying civilian populations, Friedrich implied a similarity to Hitler, who is also known to have expressed destructive thoughts about Jews long before he came to power in 1933.[31]

Friedrich's strategy is one of historical decontextualisation: only by ignoring the basic sequence of cause and effect, and by playing down the military importance of certain German cities bombed by the Allies, can he sustain the view of the Western Allies as gratuitous aggressors. He is not the only historian to write in this way. Thus Hubertus Knabe, in his recent book depicting the end of the Second World War in eastern Germany, describes Soviet post-war internment camps there as 'new Soviet concentration camps' – a conscious linguistic equation of the worst kind.[32] The Germans held in Soviet internment camps were, for the most part, small-time Nazis; unlike the Jews held at Nazi camps, most of the internees were held for a legitimate reason. And they were not tortured, worked to death or murdered. Certainly many died of disease and malnutrition; that, indeed, is an appalling fact and a severe indictment of the Soviets. But this still does not justify such equations. Knabe's aim is to place the Soviets and the Nazis on an absolute par; thus he suggests that the Second World War was started as much by Stalin as by Hitler, a claim which certainly needs more scrutiny than Knabe is prepared to devote to it.[33]

There are even occasional suggestions in contemporary Germany that German victimhood may have been *greater* than that of Jews, and, consequently, that acts of perpetration against Germans may have been worse than acts of perpetration *by* Germans. The most tangible expression of this trend is the proposed exhibition for the Centre Against Expulsions (*Zentrum gegen Vertreibungen*) planned by the League of Expellees (*Bund der Vertriebenen*) for Berlin. While the foundation committed to building the Centre repeatedly claims it wishes to portray ethnic expulsion as a twentieth-century phenomenon, its main focus, as the draft for the exhibition demonstrates, is on the German expellees driven out of Poland and Czechoslovakia at the end of the war. They are to serve as the supreme example, whereas the deportation of Jews is to feature among a catalogue-like presentation of other expulsions in the second half of the exhibition.[34] Even more problematic is the fact that the draft plan for the first half of the exhibition, which is to provide a history of the expulsion of Germans from Eastern Europe at the end of the war, fails totally to contextualise this expulsion within the history of the Nazi deportations of Poles and Jews which preceded it.[35] Like it or not, the expulsion of Germans by the Poles and Czechs in 1945 was in large part a reaction to such brutal policies. By failing to provide such contextualisation, the exhibition aims to construct a view of the German expellees as absolute victims. It also aims to present the Czechs, Poles and Russians as the villains of history.

It could reasonably be argued, then, that some in today's Germany are seeking to undermine the established classification according to which the broad mass of Germans, during the Third Reich, are understood to have formed a 'perpetrator collective'. Equally under attack is the classification according to which the Allies are understood as a 'liberator collective'. At the same time as the boundaries of the 'perpetrator collective' are being shifted to embrace the Allies, those of the 'victim collective' are being altered to encompass the Germans. What this amounts to is a complete reinterpretation of the Second World War. In a sense, it is as if some Germans would like to appropriate the status of absolute victim generally attributed to the Jews. Nowhere is this more the case than in those depictions of the Third Reich in which the German people are presented as the victims of Hitler. In a television talk-show of 10 May 2005, the widow of the former

Social Democratic Chancellor Willy Brandt, Brigitte Seebacher, even claimed that the first victims of Hitler were the Germans themselves – not the Jews, nor the communists, but the Germans as a whole – 'on the night of 30th January 1933'.[36] Thus although a third of those who voted in the November 1932 elections had voted for Hitler (11.7 million Germans), Seebacher preferred to see the Germans as victims of what she clearly believes to have been an unwelcome *coup d'état*.

In Oliver Hirschbiegel's 2004 blockbuster feature film *Downfall* (*Der Untergang*), which reached millions of viewers in Germany and abroad, the German people are presented as Hitler's *last* victims.[37] Focusing on the last days of the war in Berlin and particularly on life in Hitler's bunker, the film does treat the audience to the Führer's tirades against Jews, but increasingly and predominantly it emphasises his dismissive attitude to the near-defeated German people itself, for whose suffering he has nothing but scorn. In fact, he appears quite prepared to see the Germans wiped out. The viewer leaves the auditorium with the sense that Hitler's genocidal will, at least in those final weeks, was directed against his own people. In Hirschbiegel's deeply problematic film, perpetration and victimhood are played out within the national collective, between evil Nazis and good Germans, thus (almost) excluding memory of Jewish suffering. The German people, in the final analysis, have become the Jews, thus eliminating any need for the viewer to reflect on the complicity of millions of Germans in Hitler's regime.

German victimhood in perspective

The post-1990 preoccupation with German wartime victimhood, then, is at times characterised by a *post hoc* construction of absolute victimhood which depends for its viability on ignoring issues such as historical context, processes of cause and effect, action and reaction, and questions of the moral responsibility of those upon whom reactions impinge. It can also be characterised by a construction of Allied, Polish and Czech perpetration which, equally, only functions by ignoring the self-same issues. One can argue as to whether the firebombing of German cities such as Hamburg and Dresden was an *appropriate* reaction to German aggression; but it was, beyond all doubt, an attempt to bring the war to an end, not a gratuitous act of violence visited on innocent people. One can also argue as to whether the expulsion of ethnic Germans from the eastern territories was fair, and one can certainly question the humanity of its execution, but this expulsion was an attempt to solve a problem which had given rise to Hitler's war in the first place – namely the non-contiguity of ethnic and state boundaries. Besides, the ethnic Germans were hardly innocent of responsibility for Nazism. Thus the Sudeten Germans in Czechoslovakia were strongly pro-Nazi before the Sudetenland was occupied by Hitler's troops; indeed 90 per cent of Czech Germans voted for Konrad Henlein's Nazi-style Sudeten German Party in the last free communal elections of May and June 1938.[38] And while the Soviets undoubtedly used their internment camps in eastern Germany to incarcerate a number of innocent Germans and, increasingly, political opponents, these camps nevertheless in the main constituted an admittedly brutal form of denazification, not a form of persecution.

It would be wrong, however, to argue that portrayals of German suffering since the late 1990s are *always* committed to transforming the Germans into absolute victims. There are many examples of a more differentiated and judicious interest in the theme – evidence, perhaps, that the potential opened up by depoliticisation in 1990 has not gone entirely unrealised. This is particularly the case with literary treatments. One only needs to think of Günter Grass's bestselling novella *Crabwalk* (*Im Krebsgang*, 2002).[39] While *Crabwalk* does focus on the terrible fate of thousands of civilian German refugees drowned on the *Wilhelm Gustloff* when it was struck by a Soviet torpedo in 1945, it also carefully depicts the Nazi prehistory of the ship, the Nazi biography of its dedicatee, and the fact that there were non-civilian Germans on board. Grass's novella is in some ways a critique of this very kind of over-cautious contextualisation, yet it also appears to defend the necessity of it. An equally judicious assessment of the fate of expellees is provided by the east German novelist Christoph Hein in his novel *Landgrab* (*Landnahme*, 2002). Hein shows that Germans from the eastern territories were often treated as outcasts in the GDR, a theme also taken up by Reinhard Jirgl in his novel *The Incomplete* (*Die Unvollendeten*, 2001). What is argued here, then, is that the expellees were as much victims of Germans in their new homeland as of Poles and Czechs before that. Such works warn against contemporary tendencies towards creating *post hoc* a kind of German victim collective with which all can identify; the reality is that this collective never existed in the competitive and prejudice-ridden environment of post-war Germany.

One could cite a number of works of recent historiography, moreover, which approach the bombing theme from a perspective that consciously eschews false comparisons and equations. Thus Martin Heinzelmann in his monograph on the (relatively light) bombing of

Göttingen explicitly rejects Friedrich's use of Holocaust-related vocabulary in *The Fire* as 'disgraceful', and Heinzelmann also distances himself from the presentation of Allied bombing as a war-crime.[40] Equally, some recent history books on the expulsion treat the theme from what might be termed a *productively* comparative perspective. Notable here are works by Thomas Urban on the expulsion of Germans and Poles in the twentieth century,[41] by Gregor Thum on the post-war history of the Polish–German city of Breslau,[42] and Philipp Ther's monograph on German and Polish expellees.[43]

These works, all of them written with lucidity and empathy, but not with false sentimentality, document the expulsion of the Germans against the background of Nazism as well as of post-war Allied and Polish politics. Ther and Urban draw attention to a fact that Germans, in their obsession with their own expellees, often forget: namely that Poles were expelled from eastern Poland to western Poland at the end of the war as eastern Poland officially became part of the Soviet Union. In many ways, the twentieth century was indeed the 'century of expulsions'. Structured comparisons of these and of their interconnectedness is the stuff of history writing. And it is possible, as Ther and Urban demonstrate, to examine connections without attempting to create victim hierarchies, or seeking to relativise. There is, it is true, the danger of universalisation; but this is avoided in the above cases by an awareness of the specific circumstances and conditions of each process of expulsion. For all the tendency towards uncritical empathy with German victimhood, then, the theme is nevertheless subject to a genuine *discourse* in Germany in which different views compete for public attention. Some, such as the historian Norbert Frei and the philosopher and sociologist Micha Brumlik, have taken eloquent and reasoned issue with such uncritical empathy.[44] Frei's views have circulated widely – if not quite as widely as those of Jörg Friedrich.

One might, moreover, contend that some Germans, at least, *were* absolute victims of war, not least children (who were also, certainly, victims of Hitler's indoctrination and exploitation).[45] And a degree of relative victimhood is undeniable in many other cases. That some Germans can be regarded as victims is surely borne out by the fact that Czechs and Poles themselves have begun to acknowledge this. In September 2002 in the Czech town of Teplice (formerly Wekelsdorf), a 'cross of reconciliation' was unveiled. It was dedicated to the memory of 22 Sudeten Germans and one Czech woman shot by Czechs on 30 June 1945.[46] Also in September 2002, the Polish town of Lambinowice (formerly Lamsdorf) consecrated a graveyard containing the bodies of 1137 Germans who died in a work-camp run by Poles with Soviet permission in 1945. Most of these Germans were women, children and older people.[47] Most recently, the town of Ustí nad Labem, formerly Aussig (Sudetenland), dedicated a memorial plaque to the 'victims of violence of 31 July 1945' on the bridge where Czech militia and civilians threw Germans into the river and opened fire on them, killing over 50 people.[48] A process of historical reconciliation between Germany, Poland and Czechoslovakia – alongside continuing tensions deriving from the Nazi past –[49] has accompanied Germany's support of the entry of these countries into the European Union. Clearly, any reconciliation in the present depends on reciprocal acknowledgement of past abuses. In Britain, there has also in recent years been a cautious trend towards empathising with the German victims of the bombing of Dresden. It was in response to the erection of a memorial in honour of Bomber Harris in London in 1992 that the Dresden Trust was set up; it contributed to the rebuilding of Dresden's *Church of Our Lady*.[50] Admittedly such gestures have been overshadowed by the recent row surrounding the Queen's visit to Germany in November 2004, when the *BILD* newspaper and some British newspapers became embroiled in a rather unsavoury dispute as to whether Her Majesty should apologise for the bombing of Dresden.

In the final analysis, it is the case that quite a number, but by no means all of the reasons for the contemporary interest in the theme of German suffering are problematic. Certainly this interest not infrequently derives from a desire to recast the Germans as absolute victims in order to challenge the conventional wisdom that Germans were perpetrators. The quite desirable depoliticisation of the theme at the end of the Cold War was immediately followed in the post-unification Kohl era by a repoliticisation in which German victimhood was to become the glue of united Germany's new national identity. Under Schröder the politicisation appeared to stop; nevertheless, the post-1998 political emphasis by a left-wing government on Germany having become a 'normal' democracy was undoubtedly understood in sections of the public realm as a sign that Germany, morally, had come of age, and was therefore 'entitled' to focus on German suffering just as any other 'normal' nation mourns its own dead. In some cases it is erstwhile or supposed left-wing intellectuals such as Martin Walser and Jörg Friedrich who have helped to foment an in part self-indulgent, emotionalised and unreflecting fascination. One wonders to what degree, certainly in Friedrich's case, the belated verbal attacks on Allied morality are not a form of directing anger away from the self; if the 1968ers, decades after having condemned their parents' generation for their part in Nazism, now discover the suffering of this generation, then they should, one might think, have the honesty to critically confront their own neglect of the theme. Friedrich prefers to vent his spleen on the Western Allies.

The conclusions reached by the German research project 'The Passing Down of Historical Consciousness' (*Tradierung von Geschichtsbewußtsein*), namely that family memory in Germany has consistently tended to focus on the suffering of family members during the war rather than on their contribution to Nazism, would seem to contradict the view that the 1968 generation had overcome such uncritical memory.[51] Mona Sue Weissmark's study into generational memory suggests a similar long-standing preoccupation with German suffering.[52] The depressing corollary of such conclusions is that memory of German perpetration, guilt and the suffering of Nazi victims, however intensely cultivated in school education or in acts of commemoration in the 1980s and the 1990s, did not percolate down to the level of family memory. Equally depressing is the thought that the current explosion of memory of German victimhood in the public realm might represent the triumph of the private over the public, of emotion over enlightenment, and of uncritical empathy over pedagogy. In the past, how memory of German suffering was remembered (or not) was determined by politics; now, perhaps, how it is remembered is determined by an 'invasion' of the public realm by private memory.

This would, however, be a very pessimistic reading, and there is little evidence that any such 'invasion' has in turn (re)contaminated German politics. In today's Germany, national identity and foreign policy – for all the increased public focus on German victimhood – still seem firmly based on awareness of German perpetration in the past, and on commitment to democratic ideals as a result. The new CDU–SPD coalition government under Angela Merkel (CDU) is unlikely to seek to change this. Besides, memory of German suffering need not always be a strategy of guilt avoidance; it can serve to sensitise to expulsions and bombing wars in the present, as was evidenced by German reactions to the tragedy in Kosovo, and by the public protests against the bombing of Iraq. Moreover, memory of one's own national suffering need not eclipse memory of national perpetration and the victimhood it caused. 'Self-empathy' can, to a degree, generate empathy for the suffering inflicted on others.

That, of course, is the ideal scenario. But however we evaluate the current preoccupation with German victimhood, it is only fair to point out that Germany is not the only country faced with the problem of finding the right balance in national memory. Forced as members of the Eastern bloc to remember the Second World War in terms of Soviet victory and liberation, Eastern European countries such as Poland, Latvia and Lithuania found little opportunity to reflect publicly on the degree of suffering they endured at the hands of the Soviet Union during the war and subsequently. Since the beginning of the 1990s, this has changed. Driven to a degree by their desire to align themselves with Western countries, several European countries have begun to cast themselves in the role of victims of the Soviet oppressor. While recognition of Jewish suffering in the Holocaust is also, increasingly, a feature of Eastern European memory, it would be true to say that Eastern Europeans are still in part reluctant to acknowledge their historical role in this genocide. This is especially true of Germany's Allies during the war such as Slovakia; but it is also true of Lithuania. Germany's debates on the past are therefore part of a more widespread memory struggle. But of course Germany will also remain a particular case because it was in Germany that the Holocaust was conceived and it was Germans who launched it and, by and large, carried it out.

The present book

One of the characteristics of the current discourse on German victimhood is the insistence in some sections of the media that the theme of such victimhood was, for a long time, 'taboo' in Germany – not just in literature, as Sebald seemed to be suggesting in his volume of lectures *On the Natural History of Destruction* (*Luftkrieg und Literatur*, 2003), but generally. 'That the Germans in the bombing war and in the course of expulsion were also victims is no longer taboo', proclaimed the weekly *Der Spiegel* in 2003.[53] While this introduction has shown that there has indeed been an enormous preoccupation with the theme of German victimhood in recent years, it has also pointed out that the theme was prevalent in pre-unification Germany. It therefore seems extraordinary that some should be claiming it had long been 'taboo'. Thus it was that the idea for the current volume came about. All of its contributors test the relative validity of the 'taboo' claim in the case of political, social and cultural discourse in both Germanies; to date, there is no book in English which offers a comparable consideration – or in German for that matter.[54] While some of the contributors have placed the emphasis of their chapters on the 1950s, others examine more the

1960s, 1970s and 1980s. In most, though not all cases, they come to the same conclusion: namely that discourse on German victimhood was always a feature of memory of the Second World War in West and East Germany alike. This being the case, contributors have sought to understand what has changed about the nature of this discourse over time – especially since unification – and how it related and relates to 'perpetrator' discourse, which places German crime more in the foreground.

The book's opening chapter, by Robert Moeller, examines the role played by victim discourse in both West and East Germany in the 1950s. In the GDR, the cult of memory focused on the victims of fascism (*Opfer des Faschismus*), a concept which, in time, effectively became synonymous with Communist victims of Nazism. In German, the word *Opfer* means both 'victim' and 'sacrifice', and in the GDR the communists persecuted by Hitler were regarded as heroic victims who had sacrificed themselves for the socialist Germany of the future. The GDR thus drew its legitimacy from their victimhood. In the FRG, as Moeller shows, the preferred victims on which official memory focused in the 1950s – despite some attempts to acknowledge Jewish suffering – were those Germans who had suffered or were still suffering as a result of expulsion, bombing, and imprisonment in Allied prisons or Soviet POW and internment camps. In the West, the cult of memory therefore focused more on the victims of both Nazism and Stalinism. Their victimhood served to legitimise West Germany's anti-communism in the present. Moeller follows his opening chapter with a discussion, in Chapter 2, of West German films of the 1950s which propagated a view of German soldiers as victims of Nazism and, in some cases, of communism, thus helping to create the myth of the 'clean' *Wehrmacht*, a myth not shattered until the mid-1990s.

Generally, the 1960s are regarded as a time when, in West Germany at least, there was a shift from the 'culture of German victimhood' examined by Moeller to a greater awareness of the need to remember and reflect on German perpetration. In Chapter 3, Ruth Wittlinger explores this move towards 'perpetrator memory'. But she also sets out to demonstrate that it was a move which had its limits. Wittlinger is sceptical of the degree to which the 1968 student generation really did contribute to facing the Nazi past, and shows how its representatives tended towards a view of themselves as victims, thus continuing the tradition with which they sought to break. In the following chapter on New German Cinema – traditionally thought of as marking a break with the kind of filmic tradition discussed by Moeller – Paul Cooke explores the way in which concepts of German victimhood also found their way into films of the 1970s and 1980s by directors such as Rainer Werner Fassbinder, Helma Sanders-Brahms and Margarethe von Trotta. In Chapter 5, Helmut Schmitz in his discussion of the West German 'Historians' Dispute' (*Historikerstreit*) of the 1980s argues that in the area of historiography, too, a preoccupation with German victimhood was never really off the agenda in West Germany. In Chapter 6, I examine representations of the bombing of Dresden in East German political and cultural memory; here, too, continuities characterise these representations over decades, despite shifts within the discourse.

To a degree, understandings of German victimhood evolved to encompass more than a focus on the Second World War. The 1968 generation felt itself to be victims of their parents' generation, which had passed down responsibility for confronting Nazism; the 68ers also, in a manner reminiscent of GDR propaganda, saw themselves as victims of the 'fascist' West Germany's measures against what it regarded as left-wing extremism. In his chapter on the shootings at the German–German border, Pertti Ahonen shows how West German politicians and media had little hesitation in comparing the killing by East German border-guards of East German fugitives with acts of Nazi terror; victims of Nazism and of socialism were equated. Ahonen's chapter is followed, in Chapter 8, by Andrew Beattie's detailed examination of the evolution of totalitarian thinking in West Germany. Both Ahonen and Beattie, however, also demonstrate how in East Germany, too, a sense of continuity was written into notions of German victimhood. Thus the GDR sought to blame the deaths of East German border-guards on West German 'fascism'.

A general observation of these first eight chapters is therefore that, despite a greater focus on awareness of crimes committed under Nazism as of the 1960s in West and as of the 1980s in East Germany, the theme of German victimhood remained a strong component of both political and cultural memory, such that the explosion of interest in the theme in the 1990s at the very most represented a reprise, at the very least an intensification. But it was not *simply* a reprise or an intensification. Cooke points out that post-unification German cinema, in its portrayal of German victimhood, in many ways seeks to create a view of the Nazi era which synthesises the cinematic response of the 1950s with that of New German cinema; Beattie argues that, in many ways, the totalitarian West German model of memory has been tempered since 1990 to allow for a recognition of the centrality of the Holocaust. In his contribution on post-unification German literature, which makes up Chapter 9, Stuart Taberner argues that several key post-1990 works seek to remember German victimhood within the greater context of German perpetration – a path of careful inclusiveness, however, which is not pursued by all German writers.

It also becomes clear from Andreas Huyssen's contribution (Chapter 10) that the rhetoric of the German peace movement in the post-unification period has been characterised in its protest against various forms of perceived political violence both by traditional slogans such as 'Never again Auschwitz' and newer ones unthinkable in 1960s' or 1970s' West Germany such as 'Never again Dresden'. Thus it is that German suffering becomes a reference point for memory-based protest in the present, not just German crime. Huyssen's chapter also makes clear that the contemporary interest in German victimhood also has its own specific set of triggers which are quite new. Notable in this respect is not just the bombing of Serbia and Iraq, which stimulated a surge of media interest in the bombing war against Germany, but also the ethnic cleansing in the former Yugoslavia, in the context of which countless newspaper articles appeared in the German press on the expulsion of Germans in 1945. In Chapter 11, Karoline von Oppen and Stefan Wolff explore this and other specific triggers – such as the eastward expansion of the EU – to the revival of the role of the German expellee organisations since the late 1990s. Thus while the theme of German victimhood is not new, the parameters within which it is articulated are constantly changing and feeding it new impulses. In the final chapter, Stefan Berger considers the perhaps surprisingly low-key role played by professional historians in contemporary discussions of German victimhood; the key figures in these discussions, it seems, are writers, publicists and journalists such as Sebald, Grass and Friedrich. This is evidence, surely, of how much the 'Germans as victims' topos has become part of Germany's public culture in the new millennium.

The aim of this volume is to introduce readers in the English-speaking world to a controversial topic whose importance cannot be overestimated when seeking to understand contemporary Germany's relationship to its history. It aims not just to provide coverage of the most important aspects of this topic, and of the debate surrounding these, but also to explore the key areas in which this debate was and is played out. Thus the volume discusses the significance of the 'Germans as victims' theme in Germany's political, social and cultural development since 1945. It also seeks to understand the interrelationship between these areas of reception. For reasons of space, however, a certain concentration of focus was required. For instance, while contributors address the 'Germans as victims' theme as it was articulated in literature, film and art, the most important cultural areas of reception, the volume only makes occasional reference to areas of recent popular reception, areas that include internet websites, or video and computer games. While the volume is designed to be wide-ranging and interdisciplinary, it cannot be exhaustive in its coverage. To a degree, it represents 'work in progress'. Currently, a major AHRC-funded research project on perceptions of 'Germans as victims' is being undertaken by the University of Leeds, with input from The Nottingham Trent University. This project will run during the chancellorship of the new German Chancellor Angela Merkel (CDU), who will have been in office for about a year when this volume appears. How will the reception of the theme of German victimhood, one wonders, develop during her four years in office?

A final word on the intended readership for the volume. The contributors have set out to write chapters which include the results of original scholarship. Several of the contributions are in part archive-based, while others explore films and works of literature which, while important at the time of their release or publication, have now been largely forgotten. The media landscape of a divided Germany, a still-neglected subject, is also examined in the volume. At the same time the contributors have turned their attention to works of historiography, novels and films on the subject of German victimhood which have been much discussed in recent years, and not just in Germany; one thinks in this connection, for instance, of Jörg Friedrich's book *The Fire*, addressed in several of the contributions. Here, it was the aim of the contributors both to provide a lively overview of debates thus far, and to take those debates further. The book is thus designed to appeal both to a specialist and student audience, *and* to the general reader. Each of the contributions is self-contained and provides the necessary background information for an understanding of its contents; at the same time all the contributions, taken together, constitute a detailed overview of related aspects of a complex subject – a subject which is likely to remain a focus of discussion in Germany for years to come.

1

The Politics of the Past in the 1950s: Rhetorics of Victimisation in East and West Germany[1]

Robert G. Moeller

This chapter takes as its starting point the 'politics of the past'[2] in the present and the overwhelming evidence that many Germans are seeking ways to mourn German victims of the Second World War. That is the subject of most of the contributions in this volume. In order to understand the present calls for an acknowledgment of German loss and suffering, however, we should first look back at the forms that the rhetorics of victimisation have taken since the shooting stopped in May 1945. What interests me is how the trauma of the mass death, loss and suffering of millions of Germans has entered German public memory, history and politics since the war ended and how representations of that past have changed over time.

The part of this story with which most historians of post-1945 Germany are familiar begins with the 1960s, when an era of silence about the crimes of National Socialism gave way to a public commemorative culture and historical analyses in which not German loss, but the Holocaust emerged as the defining moment of twentieth-century German history. Since the mid-1980s, many argued that this was an incomplete account. They emphasised that histories of National Socialism failed adequately to describe the suffering endured by millions of Germans during the war. But in the mid-1980s calls for Germans to remember their losses triggered vehement negative responses from those who claimed that any attempt to tell the story of German victims would inevitably lead in the direction of apologia and the false equation of German suffering with the crimes committed by Germans. They feared a tendency toward *Aufrechnung* – a reckoning up or settling of accounts – and charged that creating such moral balance sheets allowed Germans to avoid guilt and responsibility by drawing a line below the ledger of moral accountability and laying the past to rest. When Ronald Reagan joined West German Chancellor Helmut Kohl at Bitburg to commemorate the fortieth anniversary of the war's end in 1985, he honoured soldiers of the Waffen-SS buried there, 'victims of Nazism also ... They were victims, just as surely as the victims in the concentration camps'.[3] But many rejected this symbolic act. And when the historian Andreas Hillgruber proposed the juxtaposition of 'Two Demises: The Destruction of the German Reich and the End of the European Jewry', he found himself in the midst of a 'Historians' Dispute' (*Historikerstreit*) and was roundly criticised for presenting tales of German suffering and the suffering caused by Germans in the same book.[4]

I will address these parts of the history of the representation of Germans as victims of the Second World War, but I will focus in greater detail on a chapter of this history that is less familiar, the first decade or so after the war's end. In these years, Germans – East and West – devoted considerable energy to assessing their losses and incorporating their victim status into public memory and politics. It is worth remembering how extensive those losses were. The bombing war left as many as 600,000 civilians dead and wounded 900,000 more. About 12 million Germans from Eastern Europe and the eastern parts of the Reich survived the flight ahead of the Red Army at the war's end or forced expulsion from their former homes after May 1945. The best data available indicate that another 500,000 were killed in the process. Estimates of rapes of German women committed by Red Army soldiers are inexact but range to as high as a million and a half. More than 5 million more Germans in uniform lost their lives before the shooting stopped, well over half of them on the eastern front. When deaths of German POWs in Soviet captivity are added to this total, the war on the eastern front accounts for almost 75 per cent of all German military casualties. At the end of the war, more than a million German women were widows.[5]

These numbers are staggering, and they can only begin to give a sense of the physical and emotional wasteland that Germans confronted in May 1945. However, the search for ways to come to terms with these traumatic pasts did not begin in the mid-1980s or 1990s. In the 1950s, there was not silence about this past; rather, in the political arena and forms of commemoration, stories of German loss and suffering were ubiquitous. When Germans demanded the right to mourn their victims in the 1990s, many claimed to be breaking the 'taboos' that had surrounded this past of loss and suffering, but my thesis is that there is a long 'history of memory' of German victimisation. Those who have not stopped to study *this* history may, as it were, be condemned to repeat it, constantly claiming to break a silence that, I argue, has never really existed.[6]

The politics of the past in the post-war years

When the leaders of the newly created German Democratic Republic (GDR) went in search of a national anthem in 1949, they turned to the poet and prose writer Johannes R. Becher. A member of the Communist Party since 1923, Becher fled Germany for Moscow in 1933. He returned to Berlin in June 1945. A little over four years later, he was charged with finding the words for the music that would celebrate a new nation. The Germany that Becher invoked was 'arising out of the ruins, turned to the future', on a journey toward socialism that led away from the rubble of the fascist regime and a Germany devastated by Allied bombing and the extraordinarily brutal fighting that had accompanied the war's end on German soil. East Germans should look ahead, but this past of loss, devastation and suffering should be incorporated into the foundations of the future they were setting out to construct.[7]

When it came to ascribing responsibility for the ruins, the East German state left no doubt that the 'Hitler gang' had started the Second World War and was guilty for whatever Germans had suffered. To be sure, the German people should have known better than to follow the 'band of criminals', but beginning almost as soon as the shooting stopped, the official position of the Communist Party and its successor, the Socialist Unity Party of Germany (*Sozialistische Einheitspartei*, SED), was that Germans had been deprived of their rights, deceived and victimised by the 'Hitler clique' that had waged an aggressive war against its European neighbours and was responsible, claimed East German President Wilhelm Pieck, for the deaths of 'millions of Germans' who 'had been driven into death on the battlegrounds and on the home front' as well as the millions who had died in concentration camps.[8]

According to this version of the past, those who best understood the origins of Germany's woes were anti-fascists who had struggled against Hitler from the start, often falling victim to the regime, some remaining in Germany, others, like Becher and Pieck, surviving the Third Reich in exile in the Soviet Union. Elevated to the level of a foundational ideology of the East German state, 'anti-fascism' became a way to describe what was noblest about the German past – its socialist traditions – and also to identify what differentiated East from West where one form of fascism had allegedly succeeded another in the post-war period. Those who had died in the anti-fascist resistance struggle or in Nazi concentration camps claimed pride of place in the commemorative practice of the GDR, but the designation *Opfer des Faschismus* (victims of fascism) was interpreted far more broadly to include Jewish victims of Nazi persecution as well.[9]

In the official version of the war that circulated in the GDR, Germans could also claim victim status because of the destruction that American and British bomber pilots had dropped from the skies. Beginning in 1950 annual ceremonies commemorated the February 1945 bombing of Dresden, where the 'civilian population' had fallen victim to the 'use of weapons of mass destruction' (*Massenvernichtungswaffen*) unleashed by the 'Anglo-American gangsters in the skies'.[10] In the context of the emerging Cold War, the SED equated the bombs of Western imperialists falling on Dresden in 1945 with the bombs of Western imperialists dropped on Korea in the early 1950s. Elsewhere, remembering the war meant overcoming its legacy, clearing away the rubble and constructing a different sort of Germany based on positive socialist traditions that the Nazis had sought to eliminate.[11]

Counted among Hitler's victims in East Germany were also those who had put on uniforms to fight the war. They too had been led astray by the Nazis, the agents of 'reactionary militarism', and the 'imperialist agents' of German fascism, particularly heavy industrialists and bankers. 'Criminal leaders' had started the war, and virtually any resistance to the overwhelming power of the 'reactionary Prussian military caste or against the German monopoly capitalists' was pointless.[12] Redemption lay in an anti-fascist education, available to many in Soviet prisoner-of-war camps, where German soldiers were transformed into 'pioneers of a new Germany' whose labour rebuilding the Soviet Union had paid off some of the debt owed by Germans to their liberators. As Frank Biess has demonstrated, the process of conversion also brought with it forgiveness of all past sins,[13] and former soldiers emerged in popular memory not as members of a criminal organisation but as men who had learned from their mistakes.[14]

This past of German victimisation and anti-fascist struggle registered in public ceremonies, political speeches, history books and the socialisation of youth. New recruits to the *Jungpioniere*, the communist youth organisation, dedicated themselves to the memory of Ernst Thälmann, the communist leader who had been imprisoned by the Nazis in March 1933 and killed in Buchenwald in August 1944. The quintessential victim, or, as the historian Dorothee Wierling put it, a 'communist saint', Thälmann's sacrifice could represent the losses of all *Opfer des Faschismus*, and his example was offered as a source of inspiration to the next generation.[15] East Germans of all ages could also see Thälmann's story at the movies, and films that underwrote the ideology of anti-fascism offered didactic tales in which soldiers came to understand the perfidy of National Socialism, or martyrs spilled their blood in the struggle against the Hitler regime.[16]

Not all forms of mourning victim fates were so carefully orchestrated by the state. In interviews with East Germans collected before and after the fall of the Wall, Wierling finds evidence of stories of loss and suffering passed along from parents to their children, which were not collapsed into the framework of official accounts and in which the Red Army did not appear as a liberator.[17] And a mass gravesite for German soldiers established near the village of Halbe around 1950 expressed a sober sense of grief, not the triumphalism of the monuments constructed by the East German regime to celebrate the anti-fascist struggle or by the Soviet forces of occupation to commemorate the sacrifices of the Red Army.[18] But in the restricted public sphere of the German Democratic Republic, there was little space in which to tell stories of the war's end that diverged from the accounts put in place by the state.

The past of National Socialism and the Second World War was also quite present across the border in the Federal Republic of Germany, and in a public sphere not so constrained by the state, an even greater range of stories of suffering and loss emerged. When the first Chancellor of the Federal Republic of Germany (FRG), Konrad Adenauer, addressed the West German parliament in September 1949, he too left little doubt that Germany must acknowledge what Germans had suffered during the war. The 'highest objective' of the new state, Adenauer promised, was 'to strive for social justice and the alleviation of misery'. Germany was a nation of victims. Economic recovery was the essential prerequisite to achieve the 'distribution of burdens'

(*Lastenausgleich*) among those who had suffered enormous losses and those whom fate had spared.

The legacy of the war took many forms. Adenauer alluded to families shattered by the deaths of the soldiers killed in the war when he acknowledged the women who might not find marriage prospects and youth who had been robbed of a stable family. The 'social and ethical healing' of the German people would be possible only when housing stock, levelled by the bombs, was replaced. In West Germany, where only a handful of communist parliamentarians portrayed the Red Army as liberators, the state pledged to restore the losses of those whose livelihoods and homes had been 'liberated' as Soviet forces advanced into Germany in late 1944 and early 1945. Expellees, a group missing entirely from the East German victim role call, were high on Adenauer's list. Some 8 million found themselves in the Federal Republic in 1949. According to Adenauer, millions more had died, victims of communist barbarism. Of great concern as well were the '1.5 to 2 million German prisoners-of-war' who were not accounted for, assumed to be languishing in Soviet camps.[19]

The post-war West German state also acknowledged that Jews and others had suffered extraordinary losses, and in a historic statement before parliament in September 1951 Adenauer announced that 'the Federal Government and with it the great majority of the German people are aware of the immeasurable suffering that was brought upon the Jews in Germany and the occupied territories during the time of National Socialism ... unspeakable crimes have been committed in the name of the German people, calling for moral and material indemnity'.[20] But Germans had suffered too, and it was the political and moral responsibility of the West German state to address the needs of German victims who were not Jewish and whose losses had been inflicted by Allied bombs and the Red Army.

From the perspective of most West Germans, the Allied forces of occupation had done little to alleviate the suffering of the immediate post-war years, constructing moral balance sheets according to which what Germans had suffered was just retribution for the suffering Germans had caused. Adenauer's remarks in 1949 left no doubt that his government would make up for lost time, meeting the needs of German victims. Some 18 million West Germans counted themselves among the 'war-damaged' – victims of falling bombs, expulsion from their homes by the Red Army, or a currency reform that had wiped clean the huge debt that the Nazi state had accumulated during the war, obliterating the savings of millions of Germans. The 'Law to

Aid Victims of War', passed in 1950, was only a prelude to the 'Law for the Equalisation of Burdens' of the war which followed two years later. As Michael Hughes's study of the *Lastenausgleich* demonstrates, the public discussions of this 'moral accounting for Hitler's war' tell us much about how West Germans calculated the costs of the war and processed the past.[21]

Those calling for just treatment also included returning veterans, whose organisations demanded compensation for injuries and time spent in POW camps. As Frank Biess's work demonstrates, the counterpart to the 'pioneers of a new Germany' in the East were the 'survivors of totalitarianism' in the West, representatives of a German *Kulturnation* that had lived to tell the tales of Soviet captivity and who could serve as the source of the 'spiritual renewal' of post-war society. In political speeches, the language of social policy, and the popular press, returnees appeared as courageous men who had been victimised twice, once by Hitler, then by the Soviets. No other group had done more penance for National Socialism's defeat in war. Their redemption for past crimes became the redemption of all Germans.[22] Post-war public opinion polls revealed that only a handful of those Germans questioned believed that most soldiers had done anything but their duty. By the early 1950s, the Allies agreed, and less than six years after the end of the war, they too affirmed that Hitler, not the Army, was the culprit. In the context of the Cold War, it was more important to forge an alliance against a common enemy than to revisit the complicated past of the *Wehrmacht*'s involvement in criminal acts.[23]

Clearing away 'marriage rubble' left by the war was also key to reconstruction. Families at risk – robbed of a 'provider' by the war or strained by the exigencies of long separations and post-war shortages – were classified by contemporary observers among the 'unknown victims of the great tragedy of our people'.[24] There was a broad political consensus supported by a substantial sociological literature that the war had placed particularly great strains on the family. Falling bombs and the war's end on German soil had completely dissolved the boundary between front and homefront, and in ranking the war's victims, some commentators claimed that 'more than any other societal institution, the family had fallen into the whirlpool created by the collapse', making the family 'the central problem of the post-war era'.[25] Solving that problem involved measures to ensure the construction of new housing that would replace the temporary hovels still occupied by many West Germans, instituting policies that would encourage women to bear the children who would fill the gaping demographic hole left by the war, and addressing the problems of young people, robbed of their youth and 'morally endangered' by families at risk.[26]

Rhetorics of victimisation were central parts of the civic culture of the early Federal Republic. The annual meetings of the *Landsmannschaften*, the regional organisations of expellees, became occasions to mourn the 'lost *Heimat* in the German East', and special monuments were constructed in 'memory of those who died in the *Heimat*'.[27] The legacy of falling bombs became part of local histories and of school atlases which carefully documented the extent of destruction, and monuments memorialised those whom the bombs had killed.[28] The losses of bombing victims were also the stuff of annual ceremonies, and when in August 1952 the president of the West German parliament, Hermann Ehlers, dedicated a memorial to those killed in the bombing of Hamburg, he acknowledged that 'all regions of Germany have their share of the wounds that the air war inflicted on the property and blood of our entire nation'.[29] A decade after the war, Dresden had also been added to the calendar of commemorative events in the Federal Republic, and the *Kassler Post* reflected on a destructive history that was 'worse than Hiroshima . . . one of the biggest destructive undertakings of history'.[30]

The 'People's Day of Mourning' (*Volkstrauertag*), first introduced in the 1920s and converted to the 'Hero's Day of Commemoration' under the Nazis, once again belonged to people, not heroes, when it was reintroduced in the Federal Republic in 1950. On a Sunday in November, hundreds of thousands of West Germans participated in ceremonies that affirmed that 'when a people in one of the greatest and most horrible wars in history has fought for its life for six long years, when millions of soldiers fell on all fronts, millions of women and children at home and on the flight from the East – then it is spiritually impossible for this people to go right back to everyday work and pleasure as if nothing of importance has happened.'[31] Remembering what had happened was also the job of community organisations that constructed war memorials and took on responsibility for maintaining the gravesites of those who had fallen in the war. Memorials typically bore Christian religious motifs that emphasised suffering and the senselessness of war, associating all the dead – whether in concentration camps, from bombing raids or in battle – and identifying them as victims of a general period of wartime destruction and terror. This pattern of commemoration paralleled the general post-war emphasis on West Germany's membership in the 'Christian occident', implicitly marking off the Federal Republic from the 'godless East'. Unlike the monuments to the anti-fascist struggle in the GDR, they offered little explicit political gloss on the death of the 'victims of fascism', and the most common message was a general exhortation to ensure that war would never come again.[32]

A shared past of loss and suffering also figured prominently in the pages of illustrated magazines and on movie screens. 'Rubble films' of the early post-war years – featuring the levelled urban landscape – were superseded by movies that allowed West Germans to relive the 'flight from the East', the reunion of parents and children divided by the chaos of war, the struggles of POWs held somewhere 'behind the Urals', and the defeat of the Sixth Army at Stalingrad. The past of German victims – who in most tellings survived to overcome adversity and contribute to post-war reconstruction – sold papers, provided grist for the mills of pulp fiction authors, and made for good box-office well into the latter part of the 1950s.[33]

Those seeking more objective versions of the past needed to turn only to the massive documentation projects undertaken by the West German state to provide detailed accounts of the 'expulsion of Germans from the East', the POW experience, the effects of the bombing war, and the history of the 'Law to Equalise the Burdens'. Rich compilations of individual testimonies, ministerial records and newspaper accounts, these volumes filled bookshelves. Although it is impossible to know how many people actually read them, their production was a clear indication of the ways in which the West German state sought to incorporate a past of loss and destruction into the 'contemporary history' of post-war Germany.[34]

Not everyone accepted accounts of the war in which Germans appeared primarily as victims. Writing in 1946, for example, the philosopher Karl Jaspers acknowledged that 'virtually everyone has lost close relatives and friends, but how he lost them – in front-line combat, in bombings, in concentration camps or in the mass murders of the regime – results in greatly divergent inner attitudes'. Jaspers insisted that 'suffering differs in kind', and he was concerned that 'most people have a sense only for their own kind'. 'It is unjust', Jaspers lectured his readers, 'to call all equally innocent. On the whole, the fact remains that we Germans – however much we may now have come into the greatest distress among the nations – also bear the greatest responsibility for the course of events until 1945. Therefore we, as individuals, should not be so quick to feel innocent, should not pity ourselves as victims of an evil fate, should not expect to be praised for suffering.'[35] Communists, only a marginal presence in West Germany, and German Jews who had survived in hiding or returned to Germany after the war were also not inclined to equate the suffering of all the war's victims.[36] But such critical voices were in a distinct minority, not silenced, but certainly heard infrequently in a political environment in which victims who were neither Communists nor Jews received the most attention.

The list of those claiming victim status in the early history of the Federal Republic diverged from that outlined in East Germany in important ways that reflected how the Cold War structured public memory of the war's consequences. The same Red Army that 'liberated' East Germans prosecuted a brutal war against West Germans. The victim of rape by the Red Army soldier was absent from the account of the war's end promoted by the SED in which Soviets were liberators, not perpetrators.[37] 'Resettlers' in the East were 'expellees' in the West, and responsible for their fate was not Hitler's war but the Soviet Union and a post-war boundary settlement that the Western Allies had sanctioned.[38] The POWs who were the beneficiaries of an enlightened anti-fascist education in the East were the survivors of communist brutality in the West. For the West German state, war widows and waiting wives deserved compensation, while the East German regime sought to mobilise women for the labour force and paid little attention to the needs of women left 'standing alone' by the war.[39]

But there were also images of the past that East and West shared. In both states, there was a clear distinction between a small group of Nazi leaders who were responsible for Germany's woes and the mass of good Germans who had been betrayed and were ready to learn from the past. East and West German victims alike established their identities as survivors, and survivors became the shapers of their own destinies, able to return Germany to the proper path – whether that path pointed toward a 'Christian occident' and the 'social market economy' or towards communism. On both sides of the Cold War divide success was measured in reconstructed cities, economic recovery, the provision of adequate housing, and a sense of security. The East German 'resurrection from the ruins' found its counterpart in the West German 'emergence out of nothing' (*Aufstieg aus dem Nichts*), the title of a large-format, richly illustrated book published in 1954 that began with devastation and ended with renewal.[40] Clearing away the rubble did not mean forgetting; recovery and reconstruction were measures of how successfully Germans, East and West, had overcome the misery of the war.

In both German states, the past was also remembered selectively. At least on an official level, the Federal Republic acknowledged that crimes against Jews had been committed 'in the name of the German people', but criminals remained largely faceless, and the focus on the consequences for Germans of 'Hitler's war' meant that what had brought Hitler to power and allowed the Nazi state to prepare for war received relatively little attention. In East Germany, Jews persecuted by the Nazi regime found a place only with difficulty in an undifferentiated mass of the 'victims of fascism'. And in both Germanies other victims of Nazi persecution, so-called 'asocials,' Sinti and Roma, homosexuals and foreign workers forced to labour in Germany during the war were denied victim status altogether. In West Germany, this list of exclusions also included communists, who were charged with maintaining their allegiance to a totalitarian regime.[41]

The acknowledgment of German 'crimes against humanity' was also sometimes paralleled by claims that German victims had endured no less than what Germans had inflicted on others. When an East German account of the bombing of Dresden published in 1955 referred to Germans immolated in that city's fiery 'hell', it established the equivalence of the crimes of the Allies and the crimes of the Nazis.[42] In public commemorative events that lumped together all *Opfer des Faschismus* (victims of fascism), the East German regime also erased distinctions between victim fates. Such tendencies were even more pronounced in the Federal Republic. In early public opinion surveys of the US occupation forces, at least some of the returning POWs interviewed about their responses to Allied films depicting concentration camps voiced the opinion 'that all the dead bodies "were all killed by Anglo-American bombs and anti-aircraft shells"', and 'conditions in concentration camps were no worse than those imposed on refugees from the east'.[43] A former officer, denied his claims to a pension by the Allied forces of occupation, compared his fate to that of the Jews. Indeed, if anything, he was worse off, because 'the Jews had been able to count on the support of world-wide Jewry', while no one cared about the woes of former officers. Thirteen years later in 1961, in a popular movie about POWs who remained in the Soviet Union long after the war's end, the German protagonist told the camp's Jewish translator – an Austrian in service of the Soviets – the same thing: 'Yes, you were under arrest, but all over the world people were fighting for you; that was right, I know, but what of us?'[44] In their testimonies, at least some expellees also settled on the same powerful analogy to describe their fate: the war's end confronted Germans in Eastern Europe with circumstances comparable to those in Nazi concentration camps.[45]

Comparisons of German and Jewish suffering were by no means the exclusive preserve of the political right, and when the Social Democrat Carlo Schmid called for the release of the last remaining POWs in the Soviet Union, he charged that the Soviets had turned German POWs into 'modern slaves', subjecting them and civilians hauled eastward to 'inhumane treatment that deserves its own Nuremberg'.[46] And in 1950, addressing parliament on the occasion of West Germany's first 'People's Day of Mourning', Konrad Adenauer recalled POWs and others deported and forced to work in the Soviet Union after the war and asked whether 'ever before in history millions of people have been sentenced with such chilling heartlessness to misery and misfortune?' The point of reference in Adenauer's comparison could remain implicit.[47] Comparisons of different victim fates were not all the same. In some cases, mentioning Jews and Germans in one breath reinforced interpretative frameworks according to which a war and a reign of terror unleashed by Hitler had claimed many victims, some German, some Jewish. In others, there were clear overtones of a negative response to a victors' justice imposed by the Allies, whose crimes were deemed no less serious than those committed by Germans. And in still others, German suffering became a form of atonement and collective penance, an acknowledgment of what Germans had done that became the basis for simultaneously making amends and demanding that others recognise what had been done to Germans.

Public memories that emphasised tales of overcoming adversity and moving beyond the past to create a new future left little room in the West for the psychologically disturbed veteran who continued to relive the trauma of a war of mass death, the disabled soldier whose family bore the burden of rehabilitative services not adequately covered by the state, or the expellee who by the late 1950s was still living in substandard housing.[48] In the East, the complete exclusion from public discourse of expellees and those POWs not converted by their anti-fascist education left them only private spaces in which to attempt to heal their physical and mental wounds. Germans, East and West, also drew selectively on the past in ways that reflected the geopolitical alliances in which they were enmeshed. The memory of the war and its legacy was instrumentalised to explain and justify the Cold War that had followed; for the West, the Soviet Union was the enemy before and after 1945; and for the East, the imperialists who had bombed Dresden now threatened Korea.

In 1983, at a conference to commemorate the fiftieth anniversary of the Nazi seizure of power, Hermann Lübbe argued that in the post-war era West Germans had of necessity maintained a 'certain silence' (*gewisse Stille*) around memories of National Socialism. For Lübbe, keeping silent about the past was essential for permitting West Germans to construct a functioning civil society after 1945, a virtue, not a vice.[49] Without much effort, it would be possible to extend this thesis of a necessary post-war silence to include East Germany as well. There, far more attention was devoted to the anti-fascist resistance than to fascist criminals, and those fascists who were identified were located in the other Germany. This brief review of the representations of the war's end in the first decade or so after the end of fighting suggests that maintaining the 'certain silence' around Nazi crimes was, however, a noisy business. Germans, East and West, were able to say relatively little about their responsibility for the crimes of National Socialism, at least in part because they talked so loudly about their own status as victims. On both sides of the border, Germans made the transition from the racially defined 'community of the people' of the Third Reich to the community of victims of a war for which they accepted no responsibility, to the community of survivors that gradually emerged from the ruins, ready to preserve and rebuild what remained of the 'good' Germany. In 1997, the novelist W. G. Sebald, referring to the victims of the bombing war, described 'the well-kept secret of the corpses built into the foundations of our state'.[50] A look back at the record of social policy, the construction of public memory and the emergence of forms of public commemoration in East and West suggests that the dead helped to define the bases of both post-war German states in ways that were anything but secret.

In neither East nor West was there evidence that rhetorics of victimisation fueled a politics of resentment similar to that promoted by many Germans after defeat in the First World War. There was no 'Stalingrad syndrome', no lost war for which Germans must seek revenge. The public commemoration of mass death, loss and suffering was accompanied by the exhortation to avoid all future wars, not to redeem loss at the end of a gun, as the Nazis had proposed after 1918.[51] The German word *Opfer* can denote both passive victimisation and sacrifice or suffering in service of a higher cause. The pre-1945 emphasis on the latter meaning of the term, celebrated by the Nazis, gave way in the late 1940s and 1950s to the former. Death yielded no answers, and the primary lesson it offered was that future wars should be avoided. In official pronouncements and public commemorations, the past enabled Germans to admonish, not threaten. Indeed, seen from the perspective of the 1920s and 1930s, the success of both German states at confronting the past of the Second World War – and moving beyond it – was remarkable.[52] The war stories post-war Germans told were incomplete, but they did define usable pasts, outlining paths that allowed both German states to move from war to post-war and from post-war to a Cold War in which East and West sought 'peaceful coexistence'.

'The post-war years are over': the shifting contours of the past, 1960s-1980s

By the late 1950s and early 1960s, Germans, East and West, knew that they were moving into a new phase of post-war history. When Adenauer's Christian Democratic successor Ludwig Erhard announced in 1965 that 'the postwar years are at an end', he expressed widely held sentiments that it was time to focus on the future. The proclamation by Walter Ulbricht to the Socialist Unity Party congress two years earlier that the 'new era, the era of socialism has begun in Germany'[53] made clear that in the East, too, the time had come to outline a future that was less directly shaped by the past. As they set out to enter the 'era of socialism', East German leaders continued to offer the vision of the past that had emerged clearly in the 1950s. Official accounts emphasised that the conditions that had brought about fascism in 1933 still flourished across the border in the West, but these were variations on established themes, not a new version of the politics of the past.

In the West, however, the end of the post-war years opened a space in which a more critical examination of National Socialism was possible. In the process, a focus on German crimes eclipsed discussions of German victimisation. The literature on the emergence of this critical confrontation with the past in the Federal Republic is vast and constantly growing. Here, I will suggest only some of the highlights of the developments that shaped the complication of public memory in West Germany.[54]

By the late 1950s, the West German state began systematically to collect evidence that could be used in prosecuting German citizens who had carried out acts of murder and violence in German uniforms, a clear departure from the 'amnesty lobby' that had prevailed in the early 1950s. The trial of Adolf Eichmann in Jerusalem in 1961 received extensive coverage in the Federal Republic and was followed by the 1963 prosecutions of 20 Auschwitz personnel in Frankfurt. And throughout the 1960s, when a majority of the legislators in the West German parliament voted to extend the statute of limitations for murder, they were particularly concerned with murders of a very specific sort – those committed by Nazis in the service of the Third Reich.

In the early 1960s, Adenauer's cabinet – dotted with a number of high-ranking officials whose Nazi pasts delivered evidence to support East German charges that Adenauer's Germany was tied to Hitler's – became a political liability for the aging Chancellor and led to the resignation of a cabinet minister. The emergence in 1964 of the National Democratic Party, a right-wing organisation that contained explicit neo-Nazi tendencies, was further cause for concern and provided additional grounds for intensified efforts to analyse why Germans had followed Nazi leaders in such large numbers. By the late 1960s, a majority in the parliament was ready to elect as Chancellor the Social Democrat Willy Brandt, who had spent the war fighting Germans in the Norwegian resistance. In May 1970, as the West German parliament commemorated the end of the Second World War for the first time, Brandt called officially for a sober confrontation with the past, not only for those who had experienced National Socialism, but also for those born since the end of the war because 'no one is free from the history that they have inherited', a history of German crimes, not crimes against Germans.[55]

A cohort of historians and political scientists more likely to have experienced Nazism as adolescents than as young adults added to this mix, seeking to write a 'contemporary history' of Germany that focused far less on the Second World War's consequences for Germans who had met the racial, religious, sexual and political criteria of the Third Reich, and far more on its causes and consequences for German Jews and other Europeans.[56] By the late 1960s their message found a receptive public among radical students, children of the rubble who had been raised on tales of a suffering Germany. They charged that the failure of their parents' generation to resist National Socialism was tantamount to complicity. By the 1980s this intensified scrutiny of a past of Nazi crimes led to the acknowledgment of more and more victims, particularly homosexuals, Sinti and Roma, Jehovah's Witnesses and 'asocials', and to historical analyses of why this 'mosaic of victims' had been denied victim status in the past.[57]

The new version of the German past began to make its way into the politics of public commemoration, foreign relations with Germany's East European neighbours and Israel, and history books. Television also did its part to influence public opinion, and the 1979 broadcast in the Federal Republic of the American mini-series *Holocaust* had an enormous impact. Of West Germans aged over 14, nearly half saw at least part of the series.[58] Comparisons of German victims and victims of Germans did not vanish from public discourse, but on the left-liberal side of the political spectrum, it was widely accepted that what Germany had lost was the price Germans had to pay for the crimes of National Socialism. A critical perspective relegated to the margins in the 1950s was by now widely held by a broad spectrum of politicians, religious leaders, intellectuals and journalists. Addressing the parliament on 8 May 1985, Richard von Weizsäcker, the president of the Federal Republic insisted that German 'crimes against humanity', particularly the 'breach of civilisation' (*Zivilisationsbruch*) of the Holocaust, must remain at the centre of public memory and commemoration in West Germany. They have.[59]

By now, we have arrived in the 1990s, the point at which many of the other contributions to this volume begin, reflecting on the calls for a unified Germany to make a place for other memories of the war. The 'silence of victims', however, has never been complete, and as Bitburg and the 'Historians' Dispute' made clear, patterns of public memory put in place in the first post-war decade have continued to circulate with variations for over 40 years. In both East and West, rhetorics of victimisation laid the groundwork for analyses of the past in which victims could not be guilty, and the only real perpetrators were a handful of fanatics. Part of the problem lay – and continues to lie – in the very categories of analysis. Victims and perpetrators appear as mutually exclusive categories. In the 1950s Germans were innocent victims of fanatical Nazis in both Germanies, and of the Red Army in the West and imperialist bombs in the East. The story of the German past that emerged in the Federal Republic in the 1960s, 1970s and 1980s was one in which 'no one was free from history', and if not collectively guilty, Germans were certainly collectively accountable for their past. For many on the left-liberal side of the political spectrum, acknowledging the horror of what Germans had done closed off the space in which it was possible to discuss the expulsion, bombed cities or other forms of German loss.

In an article about the memory of the bombing war in the 1950s, Thomas Neumann asks what it would have required to tell a story of loss and destruction in which it was possible to 'process one's own guilt' while accounting for the 'terror of war that one had suffered'. In the 1950s no one had an answer.[60] Fifty years later the question remains the same, and many of the other essays in this volume explore how successful Germans have been in providing answers since unification. As we revisit the past of German suffering at the war's end, we should remember, however, that this is precisely what we are doing – *re*visiting a history that has been discussed endlessly since 1945. Studying this history – the history of how German victimisation has been represented – can help us to understand why in some moral and political environments it was possible for historians to ask some questions and not others; how memory can block historical understanding and impede an open discussion of the past; and why over 60 years after the Second World War, calls for Germans to mourn their dead do not involve 'breaking the silence', but do possibly offer new perspectives from which we might begin to write a history of National Socialism in which some Germans were victims, some Germans were perpetrators, and some Germans were both.

2

Victims in Uniform: West German Combat Movies from the 1950s

Robert G. Moeller

Before Germany's defeat in the Second World War, over 15 million men – some Austrians, some from those parts of Europe incorporated into the 'Great Reich', and most from Germany – would serve in the military. Of these, over 5 million were dead in May 1945. For every man in uniform, there were wives, lovers, mothers, fathers, siblings and children at home who were touched by the experiences that men had at the front. Where in post-war Germany was there a place to bury the war dead and heal the physical and psychological wounds of returning veterans? Could Germans in uniform who had engaged in organised killing on a massive scale also be victims? In post-war years, there were a range of answers to these questions, and in this chapter, I focus on those offered in West Germany. Immediately after the war, the Allies offered one definitive response by putting German military leaders in the dock at Nuremberg, holding them responsible 'in large measure for the miseries and suffering that have fallen on millions of men, women, and children'.[1] Although the *Wehrmacht* was not found guilty as a 'criminal organisation', some individuals did come to trial and were sentenced to jail terms. Not surprisingly, most veterans and their families – that is, most Germans – had difficulty accepting that German military men belonged in jail. They openly resisted Allied charges that some Germans in uniform had committed crimes of war and favoured a version of the past in which soldiers were not killers but victims, defenders of the Fatherland who had served with honour.[2]

When we talk about the 'unmastered past' (*unbewältigte Vergangenheit*) of post-war Germans, we are most likely to mean the past of German crimes against others, particularly Jews. But in the first decade or so after the war, the past most Germans sought to master was one of the traumatic impact of war and defeat on Germans, among them, millions of soldiers. In the early 1950s, the theme of German soldiers as victims of 'Hitler's war' resounded in the halls of the West German parliament, where returning veterans were guaranteed the 'thanks of the fatherland' in the form of pensions and programmes to reintegrate them into civil society. There was also a place for dead comrades in the 'national day of mourning', a time to remember *all* the victims of the war, including those who had died in uniform. The drive of the Western Allies to get Germans back into uniform – as participants in the North Atlantic Treaty Organisation (NATO) – meant that they too were ready to see German soldiers as victims of 'Hitler's war'.[3]

The work of cleaning up the *Wehrmacht* and confronting the 'unmastered past' also took place in a space visited by millions of West Germans in the 1950s and studied very little by historians – the cinema. Indeed, the steady pressure of the West German state to put some men back into military uniforms in the mid-1950s paralleled a boom in movies that offered representations of the conflict that had ended only a decade earlier. West Germany's formal entry into NATO, the proclamation of West German sovereignty in May 1955, and the military rearmament that followed seem to have convinced the West German movie industry that it was all right to fight the war a second time. In the decade where more Germans went to the movies than ever before – or ever since – some 10 per cent of the movies they could see were about the war.[4] Movies, all made in black-and-white, recalling wartime newsreels, wrote one film reviewer in 1955, were finally ready to present the war in ways that 'approached reality' and were 'believable'.[5]

In part, the war conquered West German film production because American imports had proven that Germans had a taste for combat films. The Field Marshal Erwin Rommel who entertained West German audiences in the early 1950s spoke dubbed German and was played by James Mason (*The Desert Fox*, Henry Hathaway, 1951). *Damned in All Eternity* (*Verdammt in aller Ewigkeit*) was known first to American audiences as *From Here to Eternity* (Fred Zinnemann, 1953), and the German version of *The Caine Was Their Fate* (*Die Caine war ihr Schicksal*) (Edward Dmytryk, 1954) replaced mutiny with destiny but still featured a deranged Humphrey Bogart. Eager to make money where money was to be made, West German movie producers and directors began to churn out films in which the actors spoke German. In 1954 and 1955, West Germans could see the ace fighter pilot General Harras, based on Ernst Udet, a First World War hero who was charged with expanding the *Luftwaffe* under the Nazis, go head to head with his superiors in Helmut Käutner's *The Devil's General* (*Des Teufels General*, 1955), a film version of Carl Zuckmayer's popular play. They could applaud Admiral Wilhelm Canaris, the head of military intelligence, who nobly sought to maintain his dignity and honour even as he served the Third Reich. They could reflect on those military men who had attempted to bring an end to the war by assassinating Hitler in *It Happened on July 20* (*Es geschah am 20. Juli*) (Georg Wilhelm Pabst, 1955). And in *Children, Mothers and a General* (*Kinder, Mütter und ein General*) (Laslo Benedek, 1955), they could follow a ragtag collection of women who pushed their way to the eastern front in the spring of 1945 to bring home their sons, victims of a Nazi ideology that had exhorted them to fight to the bitter end. And by the end of the decade, they followed German POWs into Soviet captivity in movies like *The Doctor of Stalingrad* (*Der Arzt von Stalingrad*) and *Taiga* in which soldiers, first victimised by Hitler's war machine, now sought to survive another variety of totalitarian rule. Mass-mediated war stories were extremely popular.[6] Memories, not just markets, were, however, at stake in this mini-boom of war movies. The cinema was another place where West Germans could think about the 'unmastered past'.

In this chapter, I focus on four of the best-known war movies from the second half of the 1950s. *08/15* is a trilogy that follows the path of the character Herbert Asch from basic training to the war in Russia, and from there to the war's end in the West. *Star of Africa* (*Stern von Afrika*), a 1956 movie, tells the story of Hans Joachim Marseille, a legendary fighter pilot. *Dogs, Do You Want to Live Forever?* (*Hunde, wollt ihr ewig leben*), a 1958 movie, depicts the 'incineration of the Sixth Army' at Stalingrad. And finally, in the 1959 film *The Bridge* (*Die Brücke*), it is late April 1945 as seven schoolboys are mustered to fend off oncoming Americans. The selection of these four movies is not completely arbitrary. All four did extremely well at the box-office. They offer a range of perspectives on the 'unmastered past'. They were all widely reviewed, and critical commentaries constitute an intriguing 'public sphere' in which the meanings of the war were discussed. And finally, for anyone who wants to see them, they are only a mouseclick away at 'the American video store for German movies' (www.germanvideo.com), equipped with subtitles, or, for those who have some German, at amazon.de. In a volume committed to reaching not just an academic audience, but also the elusive 'literate public', I wanted to write about movies that millions of Germans saw and that millions (maybe thousands) of those interested in German history – armed with a credit card and a VCR or DVD player – can still see.

'Everymensch' goes to war: the story of Gunner Asch

As West German military planners and politicians debated what shape a new military should take in the mid-1950s, Paul May's *08/15*, based on a novel of the same title by Hans Hellmut Kirst, revealed that the soldier for a reformed army, advertised by military reformers as the 'citizen in uniform' could be found in the old. Such good Germans, defined by their obligations to friends, family, and community, not blind loyalty to any higher powers, were marching on the parade grounds of the new *Bundeswehr*. In the person of Herbert Asch (Joachim Fuchsberger), the hero of *08/15,* they were also marching across the silver screen in the uniform of the *Wehrmacht*. In Part I of this trilogy, Asch spends most of his time outsmarting a sadistic drill sergeant whose methods occasion only disdain. When it becomes obvious that the humiliation of a dehumanising routine has led Asch's best friend, Johannes Vierbein (Paul Bösiger), a sensitive misfit, who would rather pick out a Beethoven piano sonata than clean his rifle, to consider suicide, Asch intervenes, saving his friend and skewering their taskmasters by revealing their incompetence. Called in to sort things out, Major Luschke (Wilfried Seyferth), tough but fair, the embodiment of what's best about a still vibrant military tradition, sides with Asch. 'I hear that recently you have had thoughts about how to improve the ranks of the junior officers – great, good, terrific', Luschke enthuses, promoting Asch so that 'now you can translate your theories into practice'.

In Part II, Asch moves eastward to fight the war in Russia. 'General Winter' rules, a solemn voice-over intones, and the war has come to a standstill in the ice and snow. Commanding the German forces is Captain von Plönies (O. E. Hasse), cut of the same cloth as Luschke, but Asch's new nemesis is Captain Witterer, a Nazi careerist who is ready to send his men on impossible missions if it will get him an Iron Cross. Asch outsmarts him too, though Part II ends in tragedy as Vierbein, sent by Witterer to face unequal odds, is ground to a pulp by a Russian tank.

By the spring of 1945 – and Part III – the credits roll as we hear 'Yankee Doodle', announcing that the Americans are coming. Nazi war crimes have hardly been at centre stage so far in this drama, but in Part III, they loom large. The crimes Nazis commit, however, are not against Jews or other civilians, rather, they are against the notions of honour that Asch and Plönies embody. The culprits are an SD officer and his SS accomplice who seek to escape ahead of the Americans with a truckload of plundered war booty. Before he surrenders to the Americans, Asch will bring these evildoers to justice, and Plönies, now a general, sentences one to be hanged. When the Americans arrive, they get it all wrong, believing that Plönies has killed a resistance fighter, that he, not the Nazi, is the real 'war criminal'. The good general is shuffled off behind barbed wire. Asch and his mates plot to facilitate his escape from American custody, but the general makes clear that he is not about to abandon his men. The 'representation of the better Germany', as one reviewer remarked,[7] the general also confesses that he did not do enough to stop the Nazis; now he must pay the price. Asch joins the general to await American justice, but the wry smile on his face as the movie ends indicates that he is already looking forward to a brighter future.

More than any of the other movies discussed in this chapter, *08/15* echoed the debates over German rearmament and the moves to muster the first recruits for the newly created *Bundeswehr.* Although some historians have interpreted the movie as grist for the mill of opponents of West Germany's entry into NATO, contemporary reviewers emphasised that May offered a critique not of the military but of militar*ism* and provided a sober cautionary tale about how *not* to organise an army. May claimed that he had sought to provide 'optical evidence' that would show how bad things really were but would also honour 'our best in uniform', because 'a people which does not respect its past has no future'.[8]

For many critics the movies delivered an answer to the 'question of what face a future German military should have'.[9] As military planners in the newly created West German Ministry of Defence puzzled over how best to recruit and train soldiers, on display in the movies were precisely those values that they wanted to promote. When Theodor Blank, the Minister of Defence, and some of his staff – including former generals – went to see the film, one press account recorded, they left promising that the 'new army will be different',[10] though the values embodied by Asch, his mates and his commanding officer suggested that reform need not mean jettisoning the entire past. The film was an invitation, remarked one reviewer, to overcome the 'neurosis' that prevented some Germans from seeing anything positive in military tradition.[11]

The 'optical evidence' that *08/15* delivered was as much of how post-war memory had evolved as it was of the war itself. Praised by one reviewer as the 'surgeon of German consciousness',[12] May's scalpel did not cut into certain bits of gray matter, and *08/15* offers little evidence of the death and destruction that dominated the visual landscape of the war and immediate post-war years. Within the midst of 'the darkest chapter of German history' – how *08/15* characterised the Nazi era – there were as many signs of 'spiritual restoration' as there were of loss and suffering. The intact town to which Asch and his mates return testifies to their success at defending the Fatherland. Gone from the visual landscape – of newsreels and movie melodrama – were the beaten, bedraggled men who had returned in 1945, and in their place was a revived masculinity that could contribute significantly to post-war West German recovery.

Praise for *08/15* was not universal, and what some critics found lacking suggests that not all West Germans agreed about how best to locate the Second World War in their history. Critics expressed their disappointment that the film in no way illuminated why Germans had gone to war. As one commentator put it in the Social Democratic Party's periodical, *Die neue Gesellschaft*, the trilogy 'attacked the dictator and his helpers', but was silent about the fact that 'a significant part of those who were depicted as victims were actually guilty and had believed in the dictator right up to the last moment.' Viewers could go home 'relieved, because [the film] confirmed the lie that they bore no responsibility for what happened'. Another reviewer remarked that by starting the story in 1939, *08/15* failed to ask when the 'darkest chapter in German history' had actually begun.[13] Even in answering the question it most directly posed – how the military should be structured in a democratic society – *08/15* trivialised a vitally important subject, presenting the *Wehrmacht* as an 'amusing bunch of complete idiots', not the 'horrifying machine' that it had been.[14] Part III could leave audiences with the feeling that 'World War II [was] mostly merry'. 'We really had a nice little defeat', quipped one critic. 'In any case, there's never been so much laughter about the catastrophe of 1945.'[15]

Siegfried in the desert or born 'to fly and shoot'

Reviewers who wanted more critical confrontations with the past found no satisfaction in Adolf Weidenmann's 1956 film, *Star of Africa*. Weidenmann had won acclaim for his movie *Canaris* that presented the tortured tale of the admiral who headed military intelligence during the war but ultimately joined resistors among the highest ranks of the military, costing him his life. In *Star of Africa*, his hero is no resister. Instead, Hans Joachim Marseille, a youthful fighter pilot, is a 'blonde Siegfried', who like Wagner's hero in the *Ring* Cycle knows no fear.[16] Critics noted that Weidenmann and his screenplay writer, Herbert Reinecker, had a collaborative past as exuberant propagandists of the Third Reich, and they had teamed up in 1944 to make *Young Eagles* (*Junge Adler*), a movie in which youthful Germans did not fly planes, rather, they built them.[17] More than one reviewer commented on the similarities between *Star of Africa* and films made under the Nazis. 'Flying is a piece of religion', a line from *Young Eagles* spoken by a young worker who clearly hoped one day to climb into the machine he was building, resounded in the movie that Reinecker and Weidenmann made only a little more than a decade after this piece of propagandistic melodrama premiered.[18]

Flying is definitely a religion for Marseille, and it is apparent that he lives for nothing else. Square-jawed, flashing a million-DM smile, he dances on the edge of discipline and dismissal in a *Luftwaffe* training facility before the war, part daredevil, part overachiever, all German. But newsreel footage reminds us what war will really mean, and a voice-over tells us that after September 1939, 'the tragedy of the German youth began, as they ran blind and believing toward their ruin.'

Before ruin comes to Marseille, he will establish his credentials as Germany's best fighter pilot. He will make it to Africa eventually, but he and his best friend Robert and his comrades get there via Paris, a city that seems to have welcomed Germans with open arms as tourists, not occupiers. Once at his post, Marseille is part of a decent, fun-loving group of comrades whose job it is to bring down their British opponents. The death of some of Marseille's mates injects a moment of sobriety, and in a late-night tête-à-tête a paternal commanding officer reminds Marseille that war is hell. Marseille, however, continues to claim that he fears nothing, and reflections on death are drowned out by Dixieland jazz and the high spirits of a makeshift cabaret. At centre stage is a relentlessly cheerful African, Matthias, the 'little mascot' of the regiment, who leaps on to the crudely fashioned stage, whips off his shirt, and performs the dance the men have requested. As Matthias works up a healthy sweat, his body glistens, and the camera pans over the faces of transfixed Germans. Danger follows pleasure, as Marseille once again takes to the skies, and his continued string of successes wins him not only the Iron Cross but also Matthias as a 'personal servant', described in publicity materials as a 'maid for all work' in this homosocial family.

Marseille continues to triumph, and in the *Vaterland*, he's the darling of the illustrated press. Back in Berlin to receive special recognition from the Führer, he also meets Brigitte, a teacher. Impulsive about more than flying, Marseille convinces Brigitte to accompany him to Rome where he will meet Mussolini. They spend a few glorious days together, and Marseille now knows that there is more to life than planes. Brigitte wants to make love and babies, not war, but Marseille rejects her counsel that he desert, flying to England rather than back to Africa. Loyalty and honour trump a heterosexual resolution. Brigitte senses that Marseille will die in the desert, but still cheerfully fearless, he is taken by surprise when his plane malfunctions, and his fate is sealed when his parachute catches on the wing of his machine.

Viewed from the perspective of the early twenty-first century, *Star of Africa* is more than a little hard to believe. Many critics in 1957 found it no more credible. Although a handful of reviewers praised it as a tribute to youth, sacrificed to Nazi insanity,[19] far more common were views like those expressed by the critic for the *Süddeutsche Zeitung*, aghast that 'now they're flying again, they're winning again, and they're falling again, they do it most discreetly and no blood flows'. Where was National Socialism in a movie that claimed to mourn the death of youthful innocence and innocent youths? How could the movie offer young Germans role models who never questioned their actions?[20] Critics noted the 'teutonic glorification' of the film, reminiscent of a style perfected by Goebbels, and had the Nazis won the war, they speculated, the movie Weidenmann and Reinecker would have made about Marseille would have looked little different. If there were heroes to celebrate, then why not Dietrich Bonhoeffer or Anne Frank?[21] If the movie did not endorse the Nazis or war, it explicitly opposed neither, concluded Karena Niehoff, the reviewer for *Der Tagesspiegel*.[22] The headline of a review that announced 'Undefeated in the Skies of the Silver Screen' echoed the post-First World War mythology that the German army had remained 'undefeated in the field of battle'. And another reviewer remarked on the irony of Weidenmann's use of Spanish planes that had originally been given by the Nazis to Franco's fascist regime.[23] In an interview, Weidenmann claimed that with the film, he was attempting an act of 'spiritual cleansing', reminding audiences that 'in history there are no completely new beginnings, only continuations.'[24] Critics all but universally agreed that the history Weidenmann presented evoked dangerous continuities and sought to clean up a past that was stained a permanent brown.

It is fascinating to see how much troubled critics of *Star of Africa* in 1957, but it is no less interesting to consider what escaped their critical commentary. Race was at the centre of the Third Reich. Although they were never subjected to the level of persecution reserved for Jews, blacks were systematically marginalised in the Nazi state, discriminated against, and subjected to an aggressive programme of sterilisation. Yet in the midst of *Star of Africa* frolics a black African, enthusiastically embraced by Marseille and his comrades. The film did not capture racial attitudes that were dominant in the Third Reich – when Matthias would doubtless not have figured in an Ufa film – and the past of the Nazi persecution of blacks drew no comment from reviewers of Weidenmann's film.[25]

Critics had as little to say on the subject of sex as they did about race, and it raised no critical eyebrows that Marseille swept Brigitte not only off her feet but in short order into bed. Intimacy takes place off-screen, but when the two young lovers reflect on their future progeny lying about half-dressed, there is no doubt about what they have been up to. In Dagmar Herzog's important work on sexuality in the Third Reich, she describes how Nazi propaganda advocated the 'emancipation of sexual life', including pre- and extramarital sex; Marseille and Brigitte seem to have got the message.[26] If sex has led to talk of a family, it also has apparently not led to reproduction. At the movie's end, when she learns of Marseille's death, Brigitte is gently weeping, not rushing for the bathroom to deal with morning sickness.[27] The complete silence of critics on the film's sexual content suggests ways in which Nazi attitudes toward sexuality and procreation were other parts of an 'unmastered past', about which film reviewers had nothing to say.

The 'incineration' of the Sixth Army

Critical commentaries on *Star of Africa* emphasised that an 'honest war movie' would choose for its subject matter not the daring antics of one-on-one combat above the African desert, but rather the stories of 'the foot soldier in the Russian quagmire at Stalingrad'.[28] Frank Wisbar's 1959 film *Dogs, Do You Want to Live Forever?* was one response. What it shared in common with *Star of Africa* was its star, Joachim Hansen, who had portrayed Marseille. Two years later he was in the snow drifts of the Russian winter, encircled by Russian troops. However, *Dogs* begins not in Stalingrad but Berlin, with Nazi newsreel footage of Hitler watching a military parade. A sober voice-over intones: 'it is magnificent to watch a parade. To the tune of stirring music, brightly polished boots hit the asphalt.' But the narrator fast forwards to where the story will end 'when snow and wind blow away the shrouds and cover up what at first was so radiant and certain of victory'. At Stalingrad, Hitler's order to fight on, the narrator explains, 'would be the death sentence for the Sixth Army', the path that will lead to the 'gravestones on the hill of Calvary in Stalingrad'.

Although historical scholarship has subsequently established that the turning-point in the war came not at Stalingrad but when the Red Army turned back the *Wehrmacht* at Moscow in 1941, for most West Germans the battle on the Volga marked the moment when they understood how bleak their future might be. In the 1950s, it became the quintessential symbol of the victim status of German soldiers, driven to their death by Hitler or, for those who survived, driven into Soviet prisoner-of-war camps where they confronted another face of totalitarianism.[29] Wisbar told his audiences a story they already knew.

Wisbar had emigrated to the United States in 1938, because, he explained to the *Frankfurter Rundschau,* 'I'd had it. Then, with the "Night of Broken Glass", it was really too much.'[30] What he chose not to tell the reporter was that before he reached this weighty conclusion, he had divorced his Jewish wife at the behest of Goebbels and that some of the films he made for Ufa had pleased the Führer. Still, he fell from favour with his boss, and by the late 1930s he was ready to leave. In 1956, he came back to Germany from the United States where he had worked, churning out TV shows, convinced that 'it was senseless to make senseless movies', a category that doubtless included *08/15* and *Star of Africa.* He hated 'nothing more than war',[31] and he was driven to Stalingrad by his 'need to investigate the truth about one of the greatest tragedies of our time'.[32]

In *Dogs*, Hansen starts out as the same bright-eyed enthusiast that he portrayed in *Star of Africa*, but the film's invocation clues us in to the fact that before the movie ends, his character, Gerd Wisse, will have learned a thing or two. In German, Wisse is close to *wissen* – to know – and Gerd will come to understand the truth about the Nazis' war. The movie charts his steady descent into disillusion as he realises that the most enthusiastic Nazis are cowards, and the worst Nazi of all sits in Berlin, consistently refusing the requests of the commanders at the front to be allowed to 'break out' of the circle of Red Army troops that surrounds them. When in the midst of a firefight in the ruins of the city the shooting briefly stops, an exasperated Wisse rhetorically asks:

'whatever are we doing in this part of the world?' If he thought he once knew, he now has no answer.

The Sixth Army surrenders. Some officers, lined up to be marched off by the Soviets, attempt to shift all the blame to their generals, triggering a cynical tank commander to remind them, 'don't fool yourselves. Everyone is guilty who could have prevented this disaster and cooperated anyway.' Newsreel footage of Germans trudging off to Soviet POW camps is interspersed with a final benediction from a military pastor. His faith has also been tested, but he is still hopeful that 'perhaps we can learn something from all this'. Wisse has the last word: 'or perhaps not'.

Many Germans saw *Dogs,* among them, Franz Josef Strauss, the Minister of Defence. He rejected Wisbar's request to provide *Bundeswehr* soldiers for battle scenes in the movie, arguing that the 'time is not yet ripe for a convincing representation of this fateful event'. Seconding Strauss's refusal to cooperate with Wisbar, Adolph Heusinger, the commander in chief in the Defence Ministry, questioned whether it was 'in the general interest once again to dig up this greatest tragedy of the German military'.[33] Strauss's refusal even led to a debate in the West German parliament, where the Defence Minister insisted that prudence was particularly important with films that addressed 'the still unmastered past of our most recent political and military history'.[34]

Most reviewers strongly disagreed. Judged the second most popular movie of 1959, the film won a National Film Award,[35] and critics joined in praising it. *Dogs*, reviews concluded, was as an anti-war movie that 'represented a monument to the innocent victims of the war'. Even critics who had become sceptical about 'militaristic . . . still quite brown movies of rehabilitation' gave Wisbar high marks for making a movie that 'honoured not war, but the dead, constructing a monument that was not gold-coated'.[36] The film identified Stalingrad as a symbol of the 'crimes of Hitler's war'.[37] A review in the influential *Frankfurter Allgemeine Zeitung* concluded that it was an 'objective presentation of the front, the common soldier, and his horrifying suffering', an important contribution to 'the theme of our unmastered [*unbewältigte*] past of the war'.[38]

A review in the *Frankfurter Rundschau* echoed the pastor's closing words and praised *Dogs* as a 'new chance to learn' from the defeat.[39] Some critical reviewers, however, emphasised that Wisbar would not teach audiences 'why in fact the Germans marched to Stalingrad',[40] and the Social Democratic Party's weekly, *Vorwärts*, questioned whether it was possible to understand the 'crazed and criminal plans of the brown "master race" to conquer the world' without critically examining the origins of the war.[41] Wisbar had not, added the critic of the *Süddeutsche Zeitung*, done anything to illuminate the 'laws of war'.[42] Other parts of the curriculum the film had to offer were long since familiar in 1958, and the clear-cut distinction between good Germans and bad Nazis was not one that Wisbar introduced. The film also offered reassurance to domestic critics of rearmament that Germans who once again put on uniform in the 1950s were sadder but wiser, changed, like Wisse, by their experience. Still, reviewers lauded Wisbar's success at communicating the 'meaning of war' to West Germany's youth, and for 'today's young soldiers' it offered invaluable lessons about the 'naked horror of the character of war'.[43] Although Strauss might argue that the film inadequately illuminated the 'moral bases for defensive preparedness',[44] Wisbar's defenders argued that his message was precisely what the soldiers of the new *Bundeswehr* needed.[45]

As one reviewer emphasised, what the film illuminated was not only the face of battle, but the faces of fathers, too often buried beneath the 'prosperity of the years of the economic miracle [that] has drawn a layer of fat over our hearts so that we have forgotten the victims'.[46] *Dogs* was a reminder to sons of their fathers' pasts. Concerns about 'rebellious youth' in the second half of the 1950s focused on the fact that for many post-war young people, there were no adequate role models, and Alexander Mitscherlich employed the categories of a popularised psychoanalysis to describe the 'invisibility of the father'. Fathers no longer had work that allowed them to demonstrate their abilities, leading to the 'removal of the father' (*Entväterlichung*) from society. Distant or altogether absent fathers produced rebellious sons.[47] *Dogs* made fathers present, heroes, capable of exerting an influence, even from the 'mass grave' of Stalingrad.

Critics concluded that the film's 'resonance with the public' was a clear indication that West Germans should move beyond the 'shameful silence' that had too long surrounded this 'perfect example of the horrible, final consequence of the authoritarian principle, built on the bases of absolute power and slavish obedience', the 'greatest tragedy of German history'.[48] As one reviewer put it, perhaps Germans still shared with the Führer an inability to come to terms with 'defeat, guilt, and fate'; perhaps 'the ghost of Hitler still survives within us'.[49] Wisbar returned from America to serve as the exorcist of this German past. Packed movie houses, noted one reviewer, were a clear indication that 'even movie audiences were now ready to contribute to the so-called "mastering of the past"',[50] a past in which the victims wore *Wehrmacht* uniforms.

A bridge to another 'unmastered past'?

Writing in 1959, Enno Patalas disagreed. He complained that 'war movies – particularly German war movies – offered little occasion for approval'. Patalas, a film critic who was an outspoken critic of 'Papa's Kino', the cinematic work of 'fathers' tainted by their Nazi past, bemoaned the fact that war movies invariably presented battle as something glorious. 'Genocide' (*Völkermorden*), he continued, appeared only in the most stylised form, and death could became transcendent. In this blanket condemnation, Patalas left room for one exception, Bernhard Wicki's 1959 *The Bridge*, a film that went 'furthest in its denunciation of war ... [that] rejected all compromises; [and in which] war appeared as the complete horror that it is'.[51]

Patalas was not alone in his praise for the movie, and other critics who did not endorse his global indictment of virtually all other war films agreed that this one stood in a class by itself. No other war movie received a more universally favourable treatment by reviewers for whom it 'was something completely new in the film history of the post-war period', 'a political and moral act'.[52] Even East German critics who typically wrote off West German war movies as thinly veiled propaganda for the *Bundeswehr* applauded Wicki, and when the movie made it to Moscow, it received rave reviews there too. It was no less successful on the other side of the Cold War divide, and from New York to Los Angeles, it was critically acclaimed.[53] A movie that had been turned down by several production companies and directors, fearful about the public's willingness to see anti-war stories, was a completely unexpected box-office hit, and its success continued to resound as it accumulated more prizes than any another film of the post-war period.[54]

What set Wicki's film apart? *The Bridge* begins in the quotidian of a small south German town in late April 1945, still spared from the direct impact of war. The conflict registers in the presence of Polish and Russian POWs (involuntarily filling in as agricultural workers), rationing and a general sense of dread about the future. What adult men remain are not worth much – psychologically and physically disabled – or, like the local Nazi boss, preparing to cut and run. Seven teenage boys are at the centre of the film. Sigi, a washerwoman's son, is not the blonde Siegfried of *Star of Africa*. Rather, this Sigi naively celebrates the Reich's teutonic past by naming his rabbits Alberich and Wotan, and he knows plenty about fear. Jürgen Borchert is the son of an estate owner whose father has died in the war. Karl Horber's father runs a hair salon, unimpeded by the prosthetic hand that suggests a war injury. His mother is absent, and filling the void is a good-looking assistant. His father's lover, she also occupies his fantasies, and when he catches her with his father *in flagrante delicto*, he flies into a rage, dismissed by his father as 'only a kid' who belongs in kindergarten. Albert Mutz's father is at the front, and his good-hearted mother has taken in Hans Scholten, evacuated from Berlin to avoid the bombs. The Nazi boss's son, Walter Forst, is disgusted by his father's political and moral corruption, the clear evidence that he is about to flee, and his none too discreet affair with a beautiful blonde who works for him. Klaus Hager has also fled the bombs for the quiet of the small town, and in the process has found romance with Franziska, the only girl in their class.

Still in short pants, stumbling with embarrassment over *Romeo and Juliet* in front of their English teacher – freed from military service by a medical deferment – the boys experience the war as a romanticised adventure. Their adolescent fantasies, however, are suddenly called into question once they receive orders to report for duty. Overnight they go from short pants to oversized uniforms and helmets so big that they obscure their faces. The barracks scenes echo Part I of *08/15*, as the boys hit the dirt, get up and sprint, clumsily holding on to their rifles; but there is no comic relief. Twenty-four hours after their arrival, the barracks are in turmoil as all men are roused from bed to face the oncoming Americans. The boy's English teacher has appeared at the barracks to petition the commanding officer to see if they can be exempt from combat, and he discovers that the gray-haired officer is a former colleague, a schoolteacher too. When the English teacher begs that 'these children should not be sacrificed for no reason right at the very end', the commanding officer shoots him a withering glance, and reminds him that if the boys are enthusiastic about warfare, it's only because they've believed the patriotic ideals that teachers have pumped into their heads. Still, as the troops prepare to head out, it is obvious that he will not send the boys to their death, and in a rushed conversation, he counsels their drill sergeant to leave them guarding a bridge, already scheduled for demolition as the Americans appear. No harm will befall them.

When the boys realise how close to home they have landed, their disappointment is palpable. Defending the bridge where once they played 'Indians' does not qualify as the war they set out to fight, but the brusque NCO convinces them of the seriousness of their task. When he fails to return from his foray into the town to find them coffee – victim of a paranoid local gendarme who mistakes him for a deserter and shoots him – it becomes apparent that this will not be a story with a happy ending. The boys look on as convoys of the injured and scared, even bearers of the Iron Cross, hurry by in retreat. When American tanks approach, creaking monstrosities that the boys hear long before they come into sight, they open fire and hit two. In the battle that ensues as American reinforcements appear, carnage fills the screen for over 20 minutes. When an American approaches their position, gun pointed heavenward, not at them, he shouts: 'Hey, hey, stop shootin', c'mon' give up, we don't fight kids, go home, go home, Kindergarten, Kindergarten', words that enrage Karl who machine guns the GI. He stumbles toward Karl, his guts in his hands. But by the time the shooting stops and the Americans retreat to regroup, Karl is dead too, and only Klaus and Albert are standing. As they stagger across the bridge, they run into two members of the detonation team, there to blow it up. The revelation that their friends have died for no purpose at all, defending a bridge long since doomed to destruction, leaves them incredulous. Albert shoots one member of the bomb squad, and as the other retreats, he shoots Klaus. Albert alone will survive to tell this tale as the movie ends.

As reviewers noted, *The Bridge* broke with many of the conventions that defined other war movies. There are no heroes. Germans kill the enemy, but Germans also kill Germans, and when the enemy dies, it is off-camera. In Wicki's April 1945 – the same spring bursting with trees in bloom in Part III of *08/15* in a Germany on the verge of renewal – Germany is marked by the 'complete disruption of the ethical order'.[55] Death redeems no one. Writing in general of war movies from the fifties, the film historian Gerhard Paul concludes that they sought to make a 'civilised act' out of the 'catastrophic, chaotic, primal experience of war, conforming [war] to a visual, narrative, and moral order that a war does not possess'.[56] *The Bridge* was the exception that proved the rule.

Although some critics noted that Wicki provided no sense of the war's origins, others commented that his film nonetheless included a clear indictment of a generation of parents who had abdicated all moral responsibility, offering their children no alternative to National Socialism. In the movie, some adults know this. When the boys' schoolteacher pleads on their behalf with their commanding officer, he blames the 'forgers' who have perverted their youthful idealism, but his confession that once the war is over, he will abandon his profession indicates that he also feels a sense of shame for the part he has played. Karl's father mistakes his son's confused sexual longings for impertinence, and Walter's father fearfully flees responsibility. Other models of masculinity – the heroes who wear Iron Crosses around their necks – are in flight. The boys are victims, but Hitler and Nazis in Berlin are not the only ones who carry responsibility for their fate. They race enthusiastically into uniform because they think it will allow them to grow up, and no one is telling them how else to achieve that goal.[57] To be sure, the regime is at fault, but 'guilt lies also with adults who did not fulfil their responsibilities as educators'.[58] In this sense, *The Bridge* moved beyond films that discriminated neatly between the Nazis and Germans, making Germans victims of 'Hitler's war'. The overwhelming consensus among movie critics was that if young viewers mistakenly saw the film as yet another glorification of militarised masculinity, such misunderstanding reflected on their parents and teachers who – like the parents and teachers in the film – were not doing their part to educate the next generation.[59] The film's exhortation – 'never let this happen again' – was addressed to the parents of 1945 *and* the parents of those turning 16 fourteen years later.[60]

When critics compared *The Bridge* with other war movies, it was most frequently to emphasise that Wicki had broken the mould. And if any war movie could be placed in the same league, it was an American film, Lewis Milestone's *All Quiet on the Western Front*, based on the novel by the German author Erich Maria Remarque that had appeared nearly 30 years earlier. But reviewers were quick to add that while Wicki's movie was universally praised, Milestone's had been met by rowdy SA (storm) troops who disrupted showings of the film. The movie thus became evidence of how Germans had learned to deal with defeat far more successfully a second time around, and the film's international circulation allowed West Germans to send this message to the rest of the world.[61]

'What does coming to terms with the past mean?'

In 1959, the year in which millions of West Germans viewed *The Bridge*, the philosopher Theodor Adorno sharply criticised West Germans for failing to accept responsibility for the crimes of National Socialism; he took them to task for their inability to 'come to terms with the past'.[62] Adorno's past was that of a devastating war and a racist campaign to 'cleanse' Europe of Jews and other groups considered subhuman. He concluded that 'the much-cited work of the reprocessing of the past has not yet succeeded, and has instead degenerated into its distorted image – empty, cold, forgetting'.[63] However, Adorno's reflections do not adequately capture how West Germans remembered and processed other pasts in the post-war years. Commenting in 1959 on *The Bridge* in a letter to a magazine aimed at West German youth, Andreas Burger reflected that 'fifteen years after the end of the war, we speak of the "unmastered past" – it's almost become a catchphrase',[64] a catchphrase that appeared throughout critical receptions of the movies discussed in this article. Burger's past was not Adorno's. It was one in which Germans were victims, not perpetrators.

To be sure, the movies discussed here presented a highly selective version of the past. Only in *The Bridge* does the enemy bleed. For the most part, the movies distinguished neatly between bad Nazis and good Germans, and it is easy to tell heroes from villains. Many of the war stories they told were classic narratives of male heroism, valour, bravery and courage leavened with pathos, suffering and even tears, narrative elements that doubtless could be found in the post-1945 cinemas of many other nations that participated in the war. With the exception of *The Bridge*, West German films depicted good-natured enlisted men who often reluctantly put on the uniform, whose first loyalty was to their loved ones and each other, and whose worst enemies might often be superior officers who were supposed to be on their side. They showed men who had been filled with a belief in Führer and Fatherland, but quickly learned that they and their country had been betrayed by the Austrian upstart. And they portrayed men of principle who were caught between their dislike – even hatred – of National Socialism and a sense of honour that prevented them from questioning even those orders they knew to be bad. Movies alone did not create this version of the war at the front, and the selective past that they represented had already taken shape in public policy debates, commemorative practice, official histories, and the pages of the daily press and illustrated magazines that serialised the stories on which some of the films were based. I discussed in Chapter 1 how this past took shape, and key parts of it had long since become part of West Germany's public memory before Gunner Asch marched across the silver screen.

Because of what they did *not* represent, some critics saw combat films as little more than propaganda for West German rearmament and vehicles to allow German men to reprise the war with more positive outcomes the second time around.[65] Writing in 1959 of *Dogs, Do*

You Want to Live Forever?, Erich Kuby – who by the early 1960s would assume a role as a precursor of the West German 'new left' – acerbically noted that movies filled with heroic survivors offered a means to retell war stories with different outcomes. Reflecting specifically on *Dogs* – but in terms that could easily be applied to *Star of Africa* and *08/15* – he commented that 'our life in West Germany since 1950 can only be comprehended if we understand that this time around every single German wants to win the war he lost. The German man cannot tolerate having a lost war in his past.' For Kuby, *Dogs* delivered the message that armed with only a few more anti-tank weapons, air power and a division or two, Germans could have trounced the Soviets at the city on the Volga: 'Every German man who leaves this movie can feel that he has been exculpated. He can tell himself, right, if they had only given us more, we were really pretty terrific guys.'[66]

But West German movies that presented the war at the front were not about winning the war the second time around; they were about winning the peace. They established the moral high ground on which Germans could look back on National Socialism as part of a community of victims, offering cautionary tales about the horrors of modern warfare and the totalitarian menace, and narrating a version of the past in which men in uniform were compassionate, courageous and caring – not killers. These movies were first and foremost about how to 'master' one version of the 'unmastered past'.[67] As West Germans overcame the traumatic experience of the Second World War, National Socialist rule and complete defeat, it is perhaps not surprising that they flocked to the movies to see such versions of the Second World War. Indeed, far more remarkable is that a subset of critical reviewers – one possible stand-in for a West German 'public sphere' – was consistently asking for more, insisting on war stories that talked not just of endings but also origins, and not only of German victims but those Germans had victimised. And West German audiences indicated how ready they were for more complex accounts of the past when they turned out in droves to see *The Bridge*, an account in which Germans, not just Hitler or Nazis, bore responsibility for the war.

The work of mastering Adorno's past, one in which most Germans had enthusiastically embraced the National Socialist regime and many in uniform had murdered Jews and other non-combatant civilians, would begin in earnest in the 1960s, but not in popular movies that depicted men in uniforms.[68] Indeed, they more or less vanished from the movies as West Germans retreated into their living rooms and went less often to the cinema. When the war returned to the big screen in forms intended for a mass audience – in Wolfgang Petersen's *Das Boot* (1981) and Josef Vilsmaier's *Stalingrad* (1993) – crazed Nazis were pitted against innocent Germans in ways that were not unfamiliar. When other pictures – this time photographs – went on tour nationally in the mid-1990s in the *War of Annihilation: Crimes of the Wehrmacht, 1941–1944* exhibition, providing staggering evidence of the army's participation in the murder of Jews and other civilians on the eastern front, they triggered a massive negative response that suggested how difficult it was to revise the vision of the 'clean' *Wehrmacht* to which movies like *08/15*, *Star of Africa*, and *Dogs, Do You Want to Live Forever?* contributed. The evidence from the 1950s suggests that most war stories – particularly those that are produced for mass consumption – remained trapped in melodramatic narratives that divide the world neatly into good and bad, guilt and innocence.[69]

Several of the chapters in this volume focus on the 'politics of memory' in the late 1990s and the first part of the twenty-first century. But as I suggested in my comments in Chapter 1, the pasts that circulate in the present are in many instances variations of the pasts that circulated in the early post-war years. To understand which pasts those were, we would do well to take seriously a medium through which memories of the Second World War were mediated for millions of post-war Germans, and to follow them to the movies.

3

Taboo or Tradition? The 'Germans as Victims' Theme in the Federal Republic until the mid-1990s[1]

Ruth Wittlinger

As early as in the first half of the twentieth century, Maurice Halbwachs made the case that memory is shaped by the attitudes and objectives of the present and therefore a social construct. He argued that the past 'does not recur as such, that everything seems to indicate that the past is not preserved but is reconstructed on the basis of the present'[2] so that 'collective memory is essentially a reconstruction of the past in the light of the present'.[3] Debates about Germany's Nazi past make the constructed nature of the past and collective memory according to the needs of the present particularly obvious. At various stages, Germans have chosen to remember the Third Reich and its immediate aftermath through a variety of discursive practices and often in fundamentally different ways. In other words, collective memory is also selective memory. Remembering certain aspects always automatically implies neglecting and maybe even forgetting others. Accordingly, memories which cultivate victimhood and those which address the issue of responsibility and guilt for the crimes of the Third Reich have competed for dominance at different stages of West Germany's post-war development.

Although there are different ways to determine the various phases since 1945,[4] the most typical way is a division into three main phases illustrating how either one of these two strands has clearly managed to present itself as the dominant paradigm of each period.

Whereas the early post-war period was characterised by a remembering of German victimhood, the period from the 1960s onwards is traditionally seen as having concentrated on German perpetrators. Since the latter half of the 1990s – gaining momentum with the beginning of the new millennium – the victim theme has re-emerged. That there is a link between the two discourses in the sense that the enhanced collective concentration on one potentially leads to neglecting the other has been suggested by various scholars. Robert G. Moeller, for example, has pointed out that during the early post-war period, West Germans were able to dismiss charges of 'collective guilt' and even claim the status of 'heroic survivors' by 'telling stories of the enormity of their own losses'.[5] More specifically, Aleida Assmann has identified 'the victim syndrome' as one of three strategies (silence and anti-communism being the other two) employed by Germans to suppress an acknowledgement of guilt and an acceptance of responsibility.[6]

Similarly, the renewed focus on victimhood which became apparent in the 1990s has been accompanied by what has been referred to as the 'Walserisation of the Berlin Republic',[7] which – in reference to the Walser-Bubis Debate –[8] suggests another trend towards suppressing questions of responsibility regarding Germany's National Socialist past.

However, in contrast to the division of the West German culture of memory into three more or less distinct phases, some have suggested that the 'victims' theme has never really been absent from this culture. Julia Kölsch, for example, has argued that German memory culture consistently draws on a concept of victimhood with which everybody can identify – especially the Germans – and on a concept of perpetrator which is positioned *outside* of the collective.[9] Others have claimed that the notion of German victimhood has enjoyed an even longer continuity. Thus Ole Frahm argues that the theme is not limited to the post-war period, but can in fact be traced back to the lifetime of the Third Reich.[10] In stark contrast to this is the fact that every time the victims' theme has received some public attention, it has been accompanied by claims that 'at last' the taboo of remembering German suffering has been broken. Accordingly, the renewed focus on Germans as victims in the 1990s has been greeted with the customary declaration that the expulsions of ethnic Germans in and after 1945 constituted 'an unresolved chapter of contemporary European history'[11] and that these events had been 'a taboo' for the most part of the two Germanys' post-war history.[12]

In this chapter, I wish to argue for a more differentiated view of the post-1960 period which questions the 'three-phase' division. For all the supposed dominance in this period of questions of German responsibility and guilt, and while the Nazi past certainly became the central reference point of the political culture of the Federal Republic,[13] the 'Germans as victims' theme remained a feature of the culture of memory. I begin with a brief overview of the 1950s period in order to set the context for my analysis of the post-1960s.

The early post-war period until the late 1950s

In contrast to earlier suggestions that the 1950s in West Germany were characterised by silence and negation, a persuasive case has been made more recently which suggests that the widespread amnesia only applied to the crimes committed in the period between 1933 and 1945.[14] There did indeed exist a collective memory, but one that focused largely on German victimhood. What was missing, in particular, were feelings of guilt, shame and a culpable conscience.[15] It was the Germans themselves who felt they had been victims of a dictatorship with a criminal group at the top which had led the German population astray.

The Nuremberg trials encouraged this early interpretation that Germans were victims by sentencing those 'supposed mainly responsible' and, as a result, opened the flood gates for mass exculpation, thereby allowing the majority of Germans to perceive themselves as having been 'Hitler's first victims'.[16] The war became a central reference point, with public memory soon being reduced to 'war stories' of fighting and imprisonment, evacuation and expulsion and stories of loss and rape.[17] As Robert G. Moeller has pointed out '[i]n this abbreviated account of National Socialism, all Germans were ultimately victims of a war that Hitler had started but everyone lost'.[18]

Although there were exceptions to the German victimisation discourse in the 1950s – represented, for example, by Eugen Kogon and Karl Jaspers – the past constructed around German victimhood and suffering represented what Moeller called a 'usable past' for the Federal Republic (FRG) with the stories of expellees and POWs becoming 'the stories of all West Germans'.[19] Based on the needs to which the moral and material post-war chaos gave rise, a common identity founded on this selective past started to emerge. As Aleida Assmann has pointed out, the paradigmatic case of collective memory is the memory of victimhood: 'nothing unites as much as the historical trauma of a collective experience as victims'.[20]

From the early 1960s until the mid-1990s

The dominance of the theme of German victimhood in the immediate post-war period started to come under challenge at the end of the Federal Republic's 'formative decade', when a whole range of events and developments contributed to a change of focus from victimhood to culpability. In terms of domestic politics, the post-1960 period saw the final years of the Adenauer chancellorship, the consolidation of the 'economic miracle', the Grand Coalition, the first left-of-centre coalitions led by Brandt and Schmidt, the movement of 1968, the extra-parliamentary opposition, Red Army Faction (RAF) terrorism and finally, at the beginning of the 1980s, the advent of Helmut Kohl and his promise of spiritual and moral change (or *geistig-moralische Wende*). In terms of intra-German relations, the period was demarcated at its beginning by the erection of the Berlin Wall, saw the emergence of Willy Brandt's *Ostpolitik*, and came to an end with the fall of the wall and German unification.

In terms of the Federal Republic's relationship to its Nazi past, this period is characterised by one central tenet: much more widespread and open discussion, and an acknowledgement of responsibility for crimes committed by Germans which was in clear contrast to the late 1940s and 1950s when the emphasis was on German victimhood and, as Wilfried Mausbach has pointedly put it, 'the Holocaust did not exist'.[21] This phase is also significantly different from the late 1990s when the discourse on Germany's past became more diverse again, with renewed calls for a 'line' to be drawn under Germany's Nazi past, an emerging trend towards the globalisation of the Holocaust and – with the thinning out of the war generation – a growing and increasingly more institutionalised commemorative culture.

In the early 1960s, generational change among the political elite as well as the 'commercial revolution'[22] contributed to the widespread perception of having reached 'the end of the post-war period' – as announced by Ludwig Erhard in 1963 and again in 1965. At the same time, the political culture of West Germany started to become more democratic, more liberal and more pluralist in nature with a 'critical public' emerging. Although the political system of the FRG was fundamentally questioned by some sections of society towards the end of the 1960s, data show that the early 1960s were characterised by increasing satisfaction with democracy and a basic approval of political, social and economic institutions.[23] Even during the last third of the 1960s and the first third of the 1970s, large sections of society showed a fundamentally optimistic view of the future as at no other previous time in West German history.[24]

Considering this general picture of the 1960s, it is hardly surprising that a focus on German victimhood was neither necessary nor suitable any longer for large sections of society. In terms of foreign policy, the discourse of victimisation with the Soviets as the perpetrators did not fit into the picture any more either. The 1960s constituted a significant step away from Adenauer's 'politics of strength' in the 1950s, with Egon Bahr (SPD) articulating in 1963 what was to become the core of a new foreign policy approach towards the East aimed at gradual change – namely 'change through rapprochement' (*Wandel durch Annäherung*). These developments in both foreign policy as well as domestic politics helped to create a different environment; as the theme of German victimhood became increasingly marginalised, German culpability received more and more attention. Already in the late 1950s, at the end of the FRG's 'formative decade', criticism was made of the preceding decade in terms of the moral as well as the material shortcomings of reconstruction.[25] In addition to this, knowledge about the Third Reich increased, with several documentations finding widespread distribution even though the topic still played a very marginal role in television coverage.[26]

Furthermore, as Edgar Wolfrum has argued, historiographical revisions were an important catalyst in starting to transform the interpretation of recent history. These were put forward by Fritz Fischer and Ernst Nolte, for example, and also included the attempt of Golo Mann to overcome the 'ahistoricity' of the 1950s and face the legacy of National Socialism. Thus Golo Mann prepared the ground which enabled later discussions regarding responsibility and guilt to take place.[27] Most importantly, however, there were a number of trials of former Nazis, such as the Eichmann trial in Jerusalem in 1961, and the Auschwitz trial in Frankfurt between 1963 and 1965. These increased public awareness and stimulated more interest. To some extent, this process had already started in 1958 with the SS 'task force trial' in Ulm which led – much too late – to the setting up of a central authority in Ludwigsburg which was in charge of collecting evidence for use in prosecutions of crimes committed by German citizens during the Nazi era (*Zentralstelle für die Verfolgung von NS-Verbrechen*).[28]

In addition, there were a number of developments which made the past appear very present indeed. An increase in far-right activities and an anti-Semitic wave at the end of the 1950s, as well as scandals involving government ministers and high-level civil servants with a Nazi past, suggested a worrying continuity with the Third Reich. Such racism and political continuities made the threat posed by a past that West Germany had not yet dealt with seem more real. Accordingly, '[m]ore than a decade after the war's end, West Germans showed a willingness to confront both German responsibility in past and present, *and* the facts of Jewish suffering – a significant move toward an expanded discussion of the Nazi past and its consequences.'[29]

In spite of all this, however, discussions in the critical mass media did not necessarily reflect the opinions of the majority. Opinion polls conducted between 1958 and 1965 suggest that there was not only a significant but also an increasing majority which wanted to draw a line under the discussions about the crimes committed during the Third Reich.[30]

Whereas the 1960s largely served to establish the discourse on German guilt, the period from 1970 onwards saw an increasing institutionalisation of it. A very clear and unambiguous acknowledgement of responsibility and culpability set the tone at the beginning of the decade when, in 1970, Chancellor Brandt fell to his knees before the monument of the Warsaw Ghetto uprising. In the same year, 8 May was for the first time commemorated in the *Bundestag* (although significant acts of commemoration of the end of the war subsequently only occurred at five-year intervals). Furthermore, at the end of the 1970s the first 'big' commemoration of the Shoah and of 9 November 1938 ('Night of Broken Glass') took place, with German politicians participating.[31]

The very different atmosphere of the 1960s and 1970s can be well illustrated by the fate of a federally funded project which was supposed to complement Theodor Schieder's *Documentation of the Expulsion of Germans from East-Central Europe* by recording the experience of the other major group of German victims: the POWs. By 1970, when the project reached completion, the official response to it showed much more sensitivity and caution with regard to the issue of German suffering in view of the suffering *caused by* Germans. This has led Robert G. Moeller to conclude that, by this time, the West German state had recognised the need to acknowledge the complications of its past.[32]

The contribution of the 1968ers

Although there is a more general dispute with regard to the influence of the 1968 student generation on the development of the Federal

Republic,[33] in terms of dealing with the Nazi past, it needs to be stressed that the changes had started to occur earlier. Detlef Siegfried, for example, argues that the critical students of the late 1960s did not trigger the debate on Nazism, but merely radicalised an already intensive discourse which had preoccupied West German society for the previous ten years.[34] With hindsight, even members of the APO (extra-parliamentary opposition) – formed at the time of the Grand Coalition of the Christian Democratic Union (CDU) and the Social Democratic Party (SPD) (1966–69) – have come to the conclusion that they did not engage adequately with the complexity of the Nazi past.[35] In this context, Axel Schildt has argued that the extra-parliamentary opposition's reductionist view of the West German state as one only marginally different from a fascist regime contributed to a 'de-concretisation and trivialisation' of the Nazi regime.[36] In his view, it was the period around 1960, not that around 1968 which brought about a change with regard to debates about Germany's Nazi past. What had previously been individual voices had turned into a coherent force discussing in increasingly concrete terms the criminal character of the National Socialist regime, and the problems of integrating the political elite which had been part of it. In contrast to this, Schildt claims, the movement of 1968 'de-realised' the Third Reich again through its abstract discussions of the relationship between the state, the economy and fascism.[37]

The Nazi past played an important role in providing *the* demarcation line between the generations. As Gerd Koenen, a former activist of the protest movement, has pointed out, the first important reaction was an angry desire to dissociate oneself from those who were responsible for it all.[38] At the same time, however, the Nazi past of the parent generation provided the '68ers with the opportunity to position themselves in 'militant innocence and moral superiority'.[39] Comments such as 'You can't talk to people who did Auschwitz' and 'We only needed to say Dachau ... to throw them' clearly show that references to the Nazi past were not only made to express moral indignation but also to discredit and silence the parental generation and push through one's own agenda.[40]

The enormous burden of the historical legacy of the period between 1933 and 1945, coupled with the '68ers' alienation from their parents' generation paradoxically produced a new and very different category of 'German victims' among the protest generation. The theme of victimhood entered the debate from a very different angle when members of the protest movement started to identify with the victims of the

Third Reich and frequently called themselves the 'new Jews'. As one member of the movement of 1968 described it in retrospect:

> We were also 'victims of the Nazi-regime!' Rudi Dutschke, who as an adolescent had fantasised that he was in reality the son of a Jew in hiding, frequently claimed during his time as a leader of the student movement that the ruling elite were trying 'to turn the students into Jews' but – he asserted – the students were not prepared to play the role of helpless victims.[41]

This feeling of being 'something like *survivors*, victims of the persecution of the Nazi regime' as Koenen later described it,[42] adds an – at first sight – very unlikely clientele to the discourse on German post-war suffering.

In *The Imaginary Jew*, the French philosopher Alain Finkielkraut comments on events in May 1968 when thousands of demonstrators chanted 'We are all German Jews!' as a reaction to the refusal of the authorities to let Daniel Cohn-Bendit return to France. He expresses his dismay that all of a sudden the role of the victim seemed open to everyone who desired it:

> Yet for all the sincerity the demonstrators possessed, their indignation tells only half the story. The improvised march was also a festival: Jewish identity was no longer for Jews alone. The event taking place put an end to such exclusivity. Every child of the post-war era could change places with the outsider and wear the yellow star. The role of the Just now belonged to whoever wished to assume it; the crowd felt justified in proclaiming its own exceptional status, which largely explains the exuberant cheer of its members.[43]

Since then, various other positions adopted by the generation of 1968 have further called into question the extent of their confrontation with the Nazi past. Karl Wilds, for example, has pointed out the paradox created by the fact that the 'critical milieu which during the 1980s insisted upon the historical singularity of the Holocaust and considered the relativisation approach a threat to the enlightened political culture of the Federal Republic' is now 'at the forefront of identifying "Holocausts" in process around the globe'.[44] To Wilds, this appears as 'a much more perfidious form of relativisation' and in fact 'effects a de-historicisation of the NS period and ultimately denigrates the unique experience of the victims of the Holocaust'.[45]

What the new climate from the 1960s onwards meant for the 'traditional' victims, I will illustrate in the following section by examining the theme of the expellees and the role of their organisations.

From victimhood to disruptive influence: the expellees

At 16 per cent, the group of expellees constituted a considerable section of the total population of West German post-war society.[46] In the early post-war period and initially against the wishes of the Allies, they founded regional organisations, the Homeland Societies (*Landsmannschaften*), which were to become very active not only in terms of representing the interests of the expellees politically, but also in terms of preserving a common cultural heritage and providing a support network in the new environment. After all, the suffering of the expellees was not over on their arrival in West Germany. Apart from their personal fate of being expelled, and in addition to having lost their homeland (*Heimat*), they had lost most material goods in the process and therefore had in many cases a more difficult start in West Germany than local Germans. Moreover, because the local population had also experienced considerable hardship, they did not extend much of a welcome to the expellees on their arrival, a fact pointed out by Richard von Weizsäcker in his speech to mark the fortieth anniversary of the end of the war. Weizsäcker referred to the expellees' experience of 'bitter hardship and deep injustice well beyond 8 May 1945', with local Germans often lacking the necessary understanding and empathy.[47]

The Allies as well as the German governments did, however, recognise the expellees early on as an important group whose integration would be vital to the success of the newly founded state and who needed to be wooed for their votes. In addition to this, they provided living examples of German victimhood which – as mentioned earlier – was an important factor in terms of creating a new identity for the West German state. The expellees and their cause received formal recognition and representation through the Ministry of Expellees, Refugees and the War-Damaged. Furthermore, a 'law to equalise the burden' (*Lastenausgleichsgesetz*) was passed in 1952 which supported the expellees financially. The expellees received further recognition of their special status and an acknowledgement of their suffering through a series of projects which were to document their experience, the most extensive of which was commissioned by the ministry itself.[48]

With the onset of the 1960s, however, the status of the expellees and their organisations within the political life of the Federal Republic started to change significantly, both as a result of internal developments, and of shifts in the way they were perceived by the political elite and large sections of West German society. Their diminished importance became very apparent at the end of the 1960s when the Ministry of Expellees, Refugees and the War-Damaged was abolished, with its functions being transferred to the Ministry of the Interior. This clearly signalled 'that it [the government] viewed the expellee problem as a matter of domestic policy alone'.[49] This was made even more explicit in 1970 when Brandt declared that the Federal Republic did not have any territorial claims on Eastern Europe.[50] Interest in the history of expulsion also seemed to subside within the group of expellees itself, as evidenced by the reduced appeal of the specialist expellee press and the diminished circulation of the expellee organisations' own newspapers.[51]

There are a number of reasons which account for the change in status of the expellees and their organisations, and for their reduced impact. Very important factors were *détente* and the new *Ostpolitik* which had fundamentally changed the approach towards the East, and which turned the expellees and their demands into relics of a bygone age. In terms of political propaganda, their experience at the hands of the Russians had been a useful example of Soviet aggression at the height of the Cold War. Now, with a thaw in relations between East and West, their concerns were undesirable and unsuitable for the new age, and were likely to hinder progress in terms of the new agenda. However, instead of adjusting their agenda away from 'foreign-policy preoccupations to a focus on the preservation of the cultural heritage of the former Eastern provinces', the expellees 'stuck to their traditional cold-warrior stances'.[52] The result, as Ahonen has pointed out, had severe consequences: 'this refusal to face reality cost the expellee lobby dearly. It was the main reason for the movement's increasing isolation from the mainstream of West German society.'[53] In the domestic arena, a significant reason for the start of the demise of the expellee organisations can be found in the largely successful integration of the expellees into West German society. As Benz has pointed out, at the end of the 1960s it was very obvious that 'one of the greatest post-war miracles' – the integration of the expellees – 'had become a reality'.[54] Increasing economic prosperity and affluence also added to a waning of interest in the victims' theme. Generational change and the lack of a homogenous group identity of expellees, furthermore, started to affect their status and erode their significance.[55] In the end, it was unification with its official recognition of the post-war border settlement that 'marked the terminus on a long road of political decline' of the expellee organisations.[56]

The victims' discourse of the expellees between the 1960s and 1990s

However, in spite of the continuous demise of the expellee organisations from the 1960s onwards, there is clear evidence that their discourse of victimhood did not wholly disappear between the 1960s and the 1990s. In addition to the detailed documentations compiled in the early years,[57] there is an abundance of academic literature on the topic. In his literature review, Hellmuth Auerbach has emphatically rejected claims made in the context of the fiftieth anniversary commemorations of the expulsions that these events, their causes and their consequences had long been suppressed and even deliberately concealed by historians.[58] His review clearly illustrates that there was a steady flow of publications on the topic from the 1950s right through to his cut-off date in the mid-1990s. Although there might have been a slight drop in interest in the topic in the 1960s, the 1980s with their renewed interest in the immediate post-war history – probably encouraged by the revisionism of the *geistig-moralische Wende* – was characterised by an intensive revitalisation of the academic discourse on the fate of the expellees.[59] A bibliography published in 1989 by Gertrud Krallert-Sattler counted nearly 5000 titles on the topic.[60] This increased interest continued in the 1990s after the collapse of communism made the eastern territories more accessible, while simultaneously making them less retrievable than ever as a result of the final, official recognition of Germany's borders in the East.

In spite of frequent claims that the novella *Crabwalk* (*Im Krebsgang*, 2002) by Günter Grass has broken a taboo, there is plenty of evidence to suggest that literature had long made a considerable contribution to the discussion of the fate of expellees.[61] At a conference organised by the Cultural Foundation *Stiftung Ostdeutscher Kulturrat* in 2003 on the topic, the extent as well as the diversity of literature on expulsions and the expellees were emphasised. Bodo Heimann, one of the speakers, pointed out that around 100 German authors had dealt with the theme in approximately fifty novels, stories, short stories, poems and plays. He divided the authors into three groups. The first group included those authors who were already established writers before the Second World War (e.g., Agnes Miegel and Gottfried Benn), whereas the second group consisted of those who experienced the war as young adults (e.g., Ilse Langer, Ruth Storm, Günter Grass, Siegfried Lenz and Christine Brückner). Authors who experienced the expulsion as children or were not even born when it happened constituted the third group (e.g., Ursula Höntsch and Monika Taubitz).[62]

One particular genre, the *Heimatbuch* (regional historical accounts) has also made a significant contribution to the preservation of memories of life in the lost homelands. Between 1945 and the beginning of the new millennium, nearly 500 such expellee publications appeared in the Federal Republic, representing 20 per cent of all regional history accounts published in German.[63] Furthermore, there are numerous popular history books and eyewitness accounts which have kept the topic of German expellee suffering alive.

The theme of German suffering has also been present beyond the 1950s in the popular press and on television, even if the official discourse dictated an acknowledgement of a different past. In 1972, for example, the magazine *Quick* published a series of articles on the fates of German POWs in the Soviet Union.[64] In 1981, there was a three-part TV series entitled *Flight and Expulsion* (*Flucht und Vertreibung*); and in 1985, a television broadcast entitled *The German Post-War Miracle: Suffering and Achievements of the Expellees* (*Das deutsche Nachkriegswunder. Leid und Leistung der Vertriebenen*) also dealt with the topic.[65]

Hence, official documentations, academic as well as literary works and representations in the media ensured a continued presence of the victims' theme throughout the period from the 1960s onwards even though the expellee organisations themselves experienced a decline in influence. This clearly shows that collective memory is not homogeneous, and that different memory discourses can easily coexist. Although the dominant theme of this period was clearly responsibility and guilt for German crime, a clear counter-discourse existed which continued to keep the 'Germans as victims' theme alive. Thus the period is characterised by a remembering of the *victims of the Germans* without completely forgetting *German victims* at the same time. There are several reasons for the continued presence of the German victimhood theme. The personal experience of the expulsions and the loss of the *Heimat* no doubt continued to have a considerable impact in the lives of individuals, and it is hardly surprising that this experience fed into academic as well as literary works. Organisations like the Homeland Societies, moreover, fostered and institutionalised the collective regional identity of the expellees, thereby ensuring that their past suffering did not fall into oblivion. The physical absence of *victims of the Germans* also made it easier for the 'Germans as victims' theme to persist, not least since it continued to be a popular strategy to offset guilt.

National Socialism and the Holocaust in German family memory

Moreover – and this applies not just to the suffering of the expellees – recent research has shown that German victimhood by far outweighs German culpability in German family memory. A study by Harald Welzer, Sabine Moller and Karoline Tschuggnall into the way historical consciousness is passed on to the next two generations suggests that the 'victimisation discourse' has always been very prevalent in Germany, even outside the boundaries of specific victims groups such as the expellees and the prisoners of war.[66] One of the most striking results of the study is the discovery of the way in which victimhood is constructed, with the roles of victims and those of perpetrators being reversed.[67] The authors compare the process of intergenerational communication with what happens in Chinese whispers, when a story is continuously passed on to the next person until its content and main message are hardly recognisable.[68]

Their qualitative study was complemented by a quantitative study which was carried out in 2002. Its results underpin those of the earlier study and suggest that there is a dominant perception in the population that relatives were not Nazis; in fact 'anti-Semites and perpetrators seem to be basically non-existent in German families'.[69] The results from both studies have led the authors to conclude that there is a vast discrepancy between the official commemoration culture and private remembering: 'whoever is to blame for the Holocaust, whoever committed the crimes in the war of extermination, the forced labour system and in the camps – one thing seems to be clear to nearly all citizens of the Federal Republic: Granddad was no Nazi!'[70]

The persistence of the victims' theme in family memory can be explained in terms of the different ways in which the past is processed. Welzer and his fellow authors distinguish between an 'encyclopedia', which stores knowledge-based information about the Third Reich, and an 'album' which is an emotionally more significant reference system that includes specific people such as parents, grandparents and other relatives, as well as letters, photos and other personal documents. It is the 'album' that is full of pictures of 'war and heroism, suffering, sacrifice and victimhood, fascination and fantasies of grandeur' – unlike the 'encyclopedia', which contains 'crime, exclusion and destruction'.[71] The task of reconciling the vastly different contents of the two books is very often managed by assigning the parents or grandparents a role that is not included in the 'encyclopedia'.[72] Given generational change and the imminent disappearance of the war generation, this trend is likely to continue.

Conclusion

In contrast to suggestions that the victims' discourse which emerged in the 1990s – possibly with the 'Appeal against Forgetting' (*Aufruf gegen das Vergessen*)[73] and the Walser-Bubis Debate as key turning points – and gained momentum in the new millennium with a multitude of publications and TV programmes broke with a taboo, a clear continuity of the victims' theme in the post-war history of the Federal Republic can be established. The early post-war period, especially, was dominated by a collective memory which focused on German victimhood rather than on crimes committed by the Germans. Although the period between the early 1960s and the 1990s was largely devoted to the process of coming to terms with the past (*Vergangenheitsbewältigung*) by addressing questions of responsibility and guilt, the victims' theme was never fully eclipsed by this process. As the case study of the expellees shows, the theme of German suffering continued to show a strong presence. The publication of a multitude of historical and literary material and the broadcasting of TV programmes ensured that the theme did not fall into oblivion even though the expellee organisations themselves became marginalised during the period.

Another important dimension of the victims' discourse can be found in the way that historical consciousness of the Third Reich and the Holocaust is passed on to the next generations. As the study conducted by Welzer and colleagues has shown, family memory reverses the roles and magically attributes victim status to family members who lived through the Third Reich. This also contributes significantly to a continued presence of German victims rather than perpetrators in the collective memory of the Federal Republic. Considering that it was the acknowledgement of guilt and responsibility rather than any preoccupation with victimhood that allowed German heads of government to join the victors in the celebrations to mark the end of the war in the new millennium, the renewed focus on German suffering is not necessarily to be welcomed. Memory of the Third Reich and the Holocaust still plays a considerable part in shaping the views that other countries hold of Germany.[74] It is therefore unlikely that what increasingly looks like an obsession with German victimhood will make a positive contribution to Germany's image abroad.

4

The Continually Suffering Nation? Cinematic Representations of German Victimhood

Paul Cooke

In recent years German films have provoked a level of international interest not seen since the 1970s and 1980s, when filmmakers of the New German Cinema, such as Rainer Werner Fassbinder and Wim Wenders, enjoyed great acclaim with their searing indictments of the state of society. A key topic for this older generation had been the question of dealing with the legacy of National Socialism. However, for those filmmakers responsible for this new interest in German cinema, it appeared, initially at least, that the National Socialist period was losing its relevance, with films such as Tom Tykwer's hugely successful *Run Lola Run* (*Lola rennt*, 1998) owing more to MTV and computer game culture than any specifically German historical legacy.[1] But after the release of Caroline Link's Oscar-winning story of Jewish refugees in Kenya during the war, *Nowhere in Africa* (*Nirgendwo in Afrika*, 2001), and Oliver Hirschbiegel's highly controversial film about the final days of Hitler, *Downfall* (*Der Untergang*, 2004), as well as numerous other productions, it became clear that this is far from the case.[2] Indeed, if anything its significance seems to be on the increase.

This new surge of cinematic interest in the legacy of National Socialism coincides, of course, with a time when culture generally seems to be particularly preoccupied with the question of German wartime suffering, and the extent to which Germans might be seen as victims of, rather than having to accept responsibility for, the events of history, a context which was, to a degree, responsible for much of the criticism of Hirschbiegel's film. The *Daily Mail*, for example, saw it as the product of Germany's new tendency to 'wallow in a victim role', in order to avoid accepting culpability for the past, even going so far as to suggest that the film seems intent upon forgiving Hitler himself.[3] Of course, as is evident throughout this volume, present debates about the issue of German wartime suffering can hardly be considered new. Robert G. Moeller, for example, makes the point that in the early post-war years 'a past of German suffering was ubiquitous' across German culture, with the discussion of topics such as the Allied air war, the treatment of German POWs, the plight of the expellees, and the relationship of the indigenous population to the occupying powers commonplace, the specific emphasis being, to a degree at least, contingent on the ideological system articulating them.[4] Any perceived novelty regarding present perspectives on history can be largely related to the events of the 1960s, when attitudes towards the war and the Third Reich began to change radically, particularly in West Germany. The trial of the SS officer Adolf Eichmann in 1961, the Auschwitz Trials of 1963–5, along with seminal studies such as *The Inability to Mourn* (*Die Unfähigkeit zu trauern*, 1967) by Alexander and Margarete Mitscherlich started to create an image of Germany not as a society that had suffered during the war, but as one that had allowed the mass murder of the Holocaust to take place and that, moreover, had done little to atone for its complicity, however passive, in such events. This view of Germany as a nation of perpetrators was then compounded towards the end of the decade when those that had grown up after the war started to question the older generation, taking to the streets in order to force them to account for their relationship to the National Socialist regime. Gudrun Ensslin, soon to become a member of the terrorist organisation The Red Army Faction (RAF), spoke for many activists at the time when she stated bluntly that those currently in charge of German society belonged to 'the generation of Auschwitz', which had not only *not* dealt with its past, but had also allowed pre-war fascistic structures to flourish in a West German state that for some was only superficially democratic.[5] Thus, from the 1960s until at least the 1980s, a perpetrator discourse was dominant, a focus intent upon forcing Germany to accept its guilt for the past, and with that to overcome the legacy of National Socialism. As such, might it not be better to view contemporary representations of German victimhood not as breaking previously held taboos, but as simply showing that attitudes have come full circle?

Through an examination of developments in German film, however, I wish not only to question the view that wartime suffering is being discussed now for the first time, but also the idea that events in the 1960s marked a clear break with earlier discussions of victimhood and, further, that present debates mark a wholesale return to earlier attitudes. I focus on three key moments in post-war German cinema, in order to suggest a more complex relationship between victimhood and guilt in the changing ways that German society has sought to come to terms with its history. First, I examine films of the 1940s and 1950s, looking at how the notion of victimhood was used, both implicitly and explicitly, as a focal point, around which an inclusive sense of community could coalesce. Second, I turn to the film production of the New German Cinema, a high point in post-war German film that came in the wake of events in the 1960s. Here I suggest that while there were clearly major shifts in attitudes towards the past during this period, it is nonetheless still possible to find images of Germans as victims, even if such images are often used for radically different ends than they had been previously. Finally, I look at recent cinema. I argue that, rather than simply marking a return to views held in the 1940s and 1950s, the current representation of German victimhood in film is often best seen as a synthesis of *both* this period's views *and* those found in the New German Cinema. Indeed, I argue that at times they say as much about the legacy of the social ruptures that the events of the 1960s themselves set in train, as they do about the issue of coming to terms with National Socialism. In so doing, such films may well at times revisit old motifs, but always from a very different perspective, specifically suggesting that the now unified Germany might at last see itself as a 'normal' nation which can put its past behind it.

The post-war years on film: victimhood and nation-building

While images of German suffering were indeed widespread in the immediate post-war period, this is not to say that the question of culpability for the events of the recent past was ignored. However, when it was addressed in film it tended to be used to confirm the status of ordinary Germans as victims twice over, of the Hitler dictatorship on the one hand and of the Allied campaign and subsequent occupation on the other. The first films to be made in the immediate aftermath of the war were so-called 'rubble films' (*Trümmerfilme*), many of which were produced with the support of the newly formed DEFA (*Deutsche Film-AG*) in the Soviet zone. These films addressed Germany's recent past directly, identifying the criminals of the previous regime, in order that the masses might be exonerated, a process of exoneration to which the representation of victimhood was central. While the Americans where concerned to build a market for the backlog of Hollywood films not released during the war (often re-edited or dubbed in such a way as to remove any reference to the National Socialist era), and so were initially often sceptical towards supporting domestic productions, the Soviets saw film as a key weapon in their propaganda campaign to re-educate the German nation in the ways of anti-fascism and socialism.[6]

In Wolfgang Staudte's *The Murderers Are among Us* (*Die Mörder sind unter uns*, 1946), the first rubble film to be made, for example, the bombed-out ruins of Berlin provide the *mise-en-scène* for the story of former army doctor Hans Mertens (Ernst Wilhelm Borchert), who faces the task of coming to terms with his harrowing war experience. He is aided in this endeavour by the beautiful Susanne Wallner, played by Hildegard Knef. Returning home to her derelict apartment, Susanne finds it occupied by the doctor, who does not accept her right to live there. Susanne refuses to be intimidated, insisting that she is the rightful owner, that she has a 'gültigen' ('valid') rental agreement. However, as the camera's gaze moves slowly to the room's broken window, where we see the couple staring out on to the destroyed buildings of the surrounding area, the man reminds us poignantly that these buildings' inhabitants too all had a 'gültigen' agreement, an agreement which, he goes on, turned out to be 'endgültig' – that is, their final agreement, the Allied bombing campaign having pronounced a death sentence on the entire city.

Mertens castigates the woman, accusing her of a lack of solidarity with her fellow Berliners, suggesting that she ran away from the city to safety while the bombs were falling. The spectator, however, knows that Susanne, too, is a victim, in her case wholly of the Nazis, having just been released from a concentration camp where she was imprisoned due to her father's socialist credentials. Indeed, while the film dramatises the devastation caused by the Allies, it also never lets us forget that it is the National Socialist warmongers who are ultimately responsible for recent events. The root of Mertens's trauma lies in his witnessing of the murder of innocent Polish civilians during the war, on the orders of his superior officer Ferdinand Brückner (Arno Paulsen), a clear-cut example of just such a warmonger. Brückner is quick to make the most of peace. When the two men eventually make contact back in Berlin, he is already successfully running a factory and is eager to put the past behind him. Mertens, on the other hand, is consumed by this event, leading him to attempt to kill his former commanding officer. This he is prevented from doing by Susanne, with whom he has now fallen in love, and who explains to him that it is not the place of individuals to pass judgement. It is their duty, rather, to bring charges 'on behalf of millions of innocent murdered victims'. It is clear that these innocent victims include those gassed at Auschwitz, reported in Brückner's newspaper which lies unread on his breakfast table, as well as the other victims of Nazi concentration camps such as Susanne and her father. However, crucially, while Brückner sits in prison insisting in vain upon his innocence, the film cuts to a string of images of suffering women, children, German soldiers and finally to a shot of the graves of the German war dead. Thus, Jewish and socialist victims are joined by the masses of 'ordinary' Germans who, it would appear, have suffered just as much in the recent past, thereby creating a unified front of German victimhood, out of which, it is implied, a new society can develop.

Although Staudte was not a communist, and only made the film in the East because this was where he gained funding, the film fits what would become the GDR's official anti-fascist line. It is, for example, clear that the German people, particularly in the Soviet Zone, should 'face the future' rather than the past, as the national anthem of the German Democratic Republic (GDR) would declare some three years later. Susanne returns to Berlin intent upon 'living, finally living'. While the criminals of the previous regime must be brought to justice, for ordinary individuals to dwell on the past undermines this imperative, preventing the population from taking the step into a happier tomorrow. The world of the past is still alive and well in the ruins of the city, where the doctor wallows self-destructively in an environment populated by black-marketeers fuelled by American jazz and alcohol, the reincarnation of the most decadent aspects of Weimar culture, suggested by the film's obvious evocation of Josef von Sternberg's *The Blue Angel* (*Der blaue Engel*, 1930). However, this is a world, the film seems to assure us, that will be cleared away, by the state's efforts to bring war criminals such as Brückner to justice, and by the hard work of right-minded people such as Susanne and other 'rubble women' (*Trümmerfrauen*), those much mythologized figures of the post-war period we see clearing the bombsites and who are here unequivocally cast as the innocent victims of fascism.

During the 1950s, the 'rubble films', like Germany's bombed-out landscapes, began to disappear. While films continued to be made in both the East and West German states that dealt explicitly with the legacy of the past, such as Bernhard Wicki's *The Bridge* (*Die Brücke*, 1959), a film that examines the exploitation of German youth by the Nazis in the last days of the war, much popular cinema seemed to take a 'holiday from history' as historian Heinrich Heimpel puts it.[7] This is most obviously the case with the *Heimatfilm*, a highly popular genre that dominated film production in 1950s' West Germany. *Heimat* is a notoriously difficult word to translate into English. Literally meaning 'home' or 'homeland', the word also carries with it nostalgic connotations, evoking a sense of the 'traditional values' of 'the good old days', when life was ostensibly less complicated and more 'natural'. Examples of the *Heimatfilm* can be found as early as 1921 in, for example, Ewald André Dupont's *The Geierwally* (*Die Geierwally*). However, it is in the 1950s that the genre reached its zenith, as West German audiences flocked to cinemas to watch escapist, brightly coloured images of Germany as a rural idyll, where dirndl-clad women and warm-hearted men fell in love and married to a soundtrack of German *Volksmusik*, providing a cinematic embodiment of traditional German family values.[8]

Although the *Heimatfilm* is a uniquely German film genre, it is often compared in terms of its ethos with the American western, since both use an imagined space to reflect a nationally inflected set of idealised characteristics. However, as Elizabeth Boa and Rachel Palfreyman note, an important difference between the two genres is that 'the bulk of the [*Heimatfilm*], in contrast to the western, is set in the present day and included contemporary motifs'.[9] As such, although these films offer audiences an entertaining moment of escapism, they nonetheless tell us a great deal about the society from which these same audiences wished to escape. On the one hand, many of the films self-consciously negotiate the pace of modernisation in contemporary society, integrating the consumer culture of the post-war 'Economic Miracle' into a traditional notion of German national identity.[10] On the other, and of particular interest for this present chapter, far from ignoring history, we in fact often find the idealised resolution of the legacy of the recent past and, specifically, the need to overcome a sense of German victimhood, provoked for instance by the Allied bombing campaigns (already a feature of the 'rubble films'), the plight of those expelled from the eastern regions, or by tensions between the indigenous population and foreign occupying forces.

Typical of the genre is Hans Wolff's *The Spring before the Gates* (*Am Brunnen vor dem Tore*, 1952). The film opens with three travelling minstrels walking in the beautiful rolling hills of the German countryside, the bucolic setting providing a perfect counterpoint to the bombed-out cityscapes of Staudte's film. The minstrels themselves might be read as an idealised image of the eastern expellees, who are welcomed with open arms into village life. Early on we see the men break into the home of one of the villagers in search of food and shelter. Rather than having them arrested, the homeowner arranges for the men to find work at the local hostelry, *The Spring before the Gates*, which is about to reopen having just been vacated by occupying British soldiers. The man even allows the musicians to take part in the village's annual festival, although, we are told, 'really only long-time residents of the town are allowed to join in'. The integrative atmosphere of the *Heimat* is then further reinforced on the opening night of the same hostelry, where we see two *Volksmusik* groups enter into good-natured competition with each other, the one dressed in Cossack garb and playing balalaikas, the other an accordion and mouth organ group, dressed in Western European shirt and tie. Interestingly, however, the 'eastern' group plays western folk tunes, such as 'A Hunter from Kurpfalz', whereas the western orchestra chooses music from the lost eastern regions, such as 'Little Annie from Tharau', a song from Samland in East Prussia. The competition is finally resolved when our three migrant musicians, along with Inge, the hostelry's beautiful landlady, join forces and sing the song 'The Spring before the Gate' (after which both the hostelry and the film are named) to the rapturous applause of all assembled. Thus, far from being traumatised by their status as migrants, or being seen as a problem that the inhabitants must deal with, the travelling minstrels, the film's symbolic expellees, become the adhesive that glues the rest of the party together. Consequently, the spectator is left with the impression that the world of the *Heimatfilm* is the home of all Germans wherever they are from, and that the culture of the lands east of the Oder-Neisse line is alive and well and has a place in the hearts of all its inhabitants.

This feeling of harmony is not only directed at the expellees. The heroine Inge is the epitome of the *Heimat* woman, her inn providing a hearth for the entire village, offering food, work and companionship to anyone who needs it. At the start of the film Inge is engaged to a British soldier. Although she has heard nothing from the man since he left for England, he soon returns to claim his bride. As such, and as Boa and Palfreyman point out:

> The alluringly wealthy English suitor screens out darker aspects of occupation when many women suffered rape and when the borderline between rape and prostitution was fluid; soldiers who gave away cigarettes and chocolate for sex did not usually return with offers of marriage and life in an English mansion.[11]

Yet the 'screening out' of the often exploitative sexual relations between German women and the occupying forces, as well as the replacement of bomb-torn cities with chocolate-box fantasies of the countryside, and of the reality of expulsion with the romantic life of the troubadour clearly point implicitly to the very traumas of wartime suffering they explicitly cover over and assuage. Thus the film ultimately highlights the continued sense in the 1950s of Germany as a nation of victims, albeit one that had now overcome the pains of its past experience.

The New German Cinema: from victims to perpetrators?

Although hugely popular at home, the *Heimatfilme* did very little for the nation's international cultural reputation. By the 1960s, West German cinema was generally considered to be in a poor state of health, reaching its nadir in 1961 when the Federal Minister of the Interior announced that no Federal Film Prize would be awarded as no film had been made that year worthy of it. This low point, however, ultimately led to the emergence of what became known as the New German Cinema, one of the most artistically productive periods of post-war German film-making, artistic production that is rooted in the social upheavals of the late 1960s.[12] As such, many of the films made during this period reflect broader social debates on the question of dealing with the National Socialist period, highlighting the shift of emphasis from Germans-as-victims to Germans-as-perpetrators. As Anton Kaes suggests, unlike the makers of the *Heimatfilme*, figures such as Fassbinder and Wenders, as well as Alexander Kluge, Margarethe von Trotta and Helma Sanders-Brahms, who were to dominate German cinema from the late 1960s until the 1980s 'no longer considered German history taboo'. Instead, such artists 'subjected contemporary West German society to critical scrutiny', specifically calling on their parents' generation to accept responsibility for their past.[13] While this is undoubtedly the case, this does not mean that images of Germans as victims disappeared from the screen. On the contrary, we often see such images simply re-contextualised, in order that they might be used in the filmmakers' project of holding society to account not only for the specific crimes of National Socialism, but also for the perceived relationship between attitudes from the past and a range of contemporary issues, including the victimisation of women under patriarchy, and what were believed to be the 'fascist' tendencies of present-day American 'imperialism'.

Turning first to the legacy of National Socialism, Fassbinder's *The Marriage of Maria Braun* (*Die Ehe der Maria Braun,* 1979), for example, one of the internationally most successful films to come out of the New German Cinema, opens to the sound of an Allied bombing raid. The film's first shot sees a portrait of Adolf Hitler blown aside by an explosion to reveal the marriage ceremony of the film's eponymous heroine, played by Hanna Schygulla. The main body of the film explores Braun's attempts to leave the war years behind her and to negotiate life in the 'Economic Miracle' of the 1950s, showing how she sacrifices her emotional and psychological well-being to build a prosperous life for herself and her husband. In so doing, Fassbinder's protagonist acts as a metaphor for Germany's post-war development. This reaches its climax when, at the end of the film, we see her blow herself up in a gas explosion to a soundtrack of Herbert Zimmermann's famous commentary on the German football team's 1954 World Cup win in Bern. This victory was understood by many at the time as the moment when Germany had at last put its past behind it and could once again see itself as a normal nation. However, its juxtaposition in Fassbinder's film with the fatal gas explosion undermines any early declaration of German normalisation. Moreover, by beginning and ending the film with an explosion, Fassbinder aligns himself with the broader critique of his generation, suggesting a strong sense of continuity between the Federal Republic of Germany (FRG) and the National Socialist era. This continuity is then confirmed in the film's closing sequence, which presents a series of shots of the Federal Republic's post-war Chancellors, thereby recalling the portrait of Hitler with which the film opens.

Maria Braun is accusatory in tone. At the same time, it is hard not to have some sympathy with the film's central protagonist, sympathy which is evoked not least by Fassbinder's starting point for his presentation of continuities between the past and present, namely the experience of living through an Allied bombing raid. This suggests that at the core of what the filmmaker sees as the nation's post-war crisis is not simply the need for the population to accept guilt for the past, but also to accept and face the very real trauma of what they themselves also suffered, rather than to gloss over it, as had been the case in the *Heimatfilme*. The importance of addressing the fact that the older generation, although culpable for the past, might also be traumatised by it is highlighted even more clearly in Sanders-Brahms's 1979 film *Germany Pale Mother* (*Deutschland, Bleiche Mutter*). Here we similarly find a woman used as a symbol for the state of the German nation that draws heavily on images of German wartime suffering. Set during and after the National Socialist period, the film tells the story of a young woman, Lene (Eva Mattes) whom we see fall in love, marry and have a daughter, Anna (Anna Sanders). The narratorial perspective of the film is that of Anna, who is trying to understand how her mother has become the woman she knows as an adult. Again, the Allied bombing campaign is a dominant aspect of the film's presentation of the war. Anna, for example, is born amidst a particularly heavy air raid, the sound of the falling bombs and original footage of Allied bombers punctuating the close-up shots of Lene suffering the pains of labour. The traumatic situation of Anna's birth is, however, only the beginning of their problems. The nightly bombing raids profoundly affect both Lene and her child's early life, eventually leading to the destruction of their home and belongings, leaving them with nothing. At the end of the war their victim status becomes even more profound, when we see Lene brutally raped by two American soldiers, an event which the woman accepts with disturbing stoicism, explaining to her small daughter, 'That's the victor's right little girl. They take the loot and the women.'

This graphic invocation of female victimisation at the hands of the invading armies, normally particularly associated with the behaviour of Soviet soldiers, here takes on a broader symbolic significance, in turn showing how the concept of victimhood begins to be recontextualised in these films to address other important contemporary issues that exercised activists from the late 1960s onwards. On the one hand, the rape sequence clearly suggests an image of Germany as the victim of aggressive US imperialism, often seen by the demonstrators in the late 1960s and 1970s as a new form of fascism, particularly in the wake of the war in Vietnam. One thinks, for example, of the demonstrations in front of 'America House' in Berlin, where the crowds made this link explicit in their chants of 'USA – SA – SS'.[14] On the other, Sanders-Brahms, one of a number of feminist filmmakers to emerge from the New German Cinema, points to what she views as the fascistic nature of patriarchy itself. As in Fassbinder's film, the level of continuity between pre- and post-war Germany is emphasised. While it is apparent that Lene has some measure of culpability for her passive complicity in Nazi crimes (we see her, for example, draw the curtain and turn away as her Jewish neighbour is rounded up), it is the male members of society in *Germany Pale Mother* who are most obviously to blame for National Socialism and its continued place within present attitudes. In the aftermath of the war we once more see an idealised image of the 'rubble women' as women come together to form a harmonious community, clearing the rubble and beginning the process of building a new society. This female community is then fatally ruptured when men such as Lene's husband, Hans (Ernst Jacobi) return home. The man is viewed by his daughter Anna as a destructive interloper who has no place in the female space of the domestic sphere. And the legitimacy of Anna's suspicions are confirmed in the father's violent attitude towards his daughter. We see him beat her for going along with a harmless joke played on him by an old friend, and see her quake under her father's oppressive glare as he chides her for producing sloppy school work. Although it is made clear that the soldiers themselves have been traumatised by the war, the key point in the film is that post-war patriarchy has still to break with the violent authoritarian structures that existed under National Socialism.

'The war started inside whilst outside there was peace', the narrator explains to the spectator in an attempt to capture the mood in her home after her father's return. As such, the film's presentation of family life differs significantly from that of the 'rubble films' discussed above. Yet it is one that is found in many accounts of this younger generation's description of their home. In his study of the New German Cinema, for example, Eric L. Santer cites the findings of the journalist Peter Sichrovksy, who examined the experience of the children and grandchildren of the National Socialist generation. He cites an interview with the 29-year-old son of a former SS officer, who complains:

> There's all that talk about [the] Jews being the victims of the war. But for those ... who survived, the suffering ended with Hitler's death. But for us, the children of the Nazis, it didn't end. When their world collapsed in ruins and ashes, the heroes of the Third Reich staked out another battleground – the family.[15]

As well as a confirmation of an image of the domestic sphere as battleground, we find here the startling suggestion that the younger generation had somehow taken over the role forced upon the Jews under the Nazis, becoming the new victims for those who are left over from the war. This is clearly a highly problematic position to take. Nonetheless, as John E. Davidson notes, it is not uncommon amongst those who were critical of the post-war state.[16] Indeed, in Margarethe von Trotta's *The German Sisters* (*Die Bleierne Zeit*, 1981), another very successful film from the period, we find the expression of just such points of correspondence between the post-war generation and the victims of National Socialism, as well as the notion of the domestic sphere as a battleground, which in von Trotta's case is used as a means of exploring the causes of the terrorist violence that emerged in the aftermath of upheavals in the 1960s. Specifically, the film examines the fraught relationship between two sisters, Marianne and Juliane, a relationship based loosely on that between Gudrun Ensslin and her sister Christiane, both of whom are products of the period's radicalism. Marianne, recalling Gudrun Ensslin's biography, becomes part of a terrorist group, a decision that finally leads to her imprisonment and death. Juliane, like Christiane, decides to stay within the realm of law and to attack the state through her journalism.

In the film's depiction of the two sisters' early life during the 'leaden times' of the 1950s, as the film's German title describes them, we find ample evidence for the continued existence of the authoritarian traditions within the domestic sphere identified by Sichrovksy's interviewee, and which, as Marc Silbermann notes, continually foreground the sisters' victim status.[17] The girls are brought up in a family dominated by a draconian father figure, a protestant pastor, who is an obvious product of traditional German patriarchal bourgeois values, against which the older sister, Juliane, constantly rebels, suggesting the shape of things to come a decade later. Although most people in authority refuse to discuss the past, the one notable exception is their father, who is the only person they encounter that is willing to break the silence on history and expose them to the reality of National Socialist crimes, a stance which would seem to contradict his unreconstructed authoritarianism. However, in confronting the past, the father in fact only adds to the girl's victimisation. We see him show their school class Alain Resnais's disturbing documentary about concentration camp victims, *Night and Fog* (*Nuit et Brouillard*, 1955). The film has a profound effect on both Marianne and Juliane, their disgust manifesting itself physically when we see them leave the auditorium in order to vomit in the toilets. Here it becomes clear that the girls are victims of the past twice over. On the one hand, through the attitude of their father at home, they are shown to suffer a National Socialist authoritarianism that continues to flourish. On the other, their reaction to the film highlights the fact that it is this generation which is paying the price for its parents' crimes, being forced to shoulder the burden of guilt and come to terms with a past for which its members had no responsibility. *The German Sisters* then goes on to suggest that it is this historical double bind which has led to the present cycle of terrorist violence, violence that has, in turn, provoked a further fascistic response by the state, implied in the film's representation of prison life in 1970s' Germany. We see, for example, the highly intrusive nature of the search Juliane is forced to undergo when visiting her sister. This, along with the suspicion that Marianne's eventual death was not the suicide it was claimed to be, seems to give at least some credence to the RAF's suggestion at the time that their treatment in Stammheim was as bad as that of Nazi prisoners in the death camps, a claim that, of course, provides a rather extreme example of the tendency identified by Davidson, namely of those who were critical of the West German state to identify with the Jews under Hitler.[18]

As we have seen, throughout the films of the period there is a strong emphasis on Germany as a perpetrator nation that has failed to break with its past. However, it should finally be noted that, as in both Fassbinder and Sanders-Brahms's films, at the heart of *The German Sisters* lay not an image of the post-war generation as the victims of an unbroken fascist tradition, but, once again, an image of German wartime suffering. Thus the film, like the others examined here, appears to contradict the notion that this period unambiguously rejected all discussion of the kind of victimhood discourse typical of the 1940s and 1950s. The film is punctuated with a series of flashbacks. In the earliest of these, we see the children being woken by their mother during an air-raid. We observe the fear on the faces of the children and their mother as they huddle in the shelter, shuddering at the sound of the bombs exploding above their heads. The film has an almost archaeological structure, the narrative present being interspersed by excavations into the sisters' memories, as von Trotta probes the reasons why each sister took the path she did. We are never given a satisfactory answer to this. However, it is clearly significant that the temporal starting point of this examination, or the deepest moment of excavation, is the experience of wartime suffering, an experience that begins a chain reaction, the results of which continue to dominate society in the film, and which, it would appear, show little sign of finding a resolution.

Contemporary German cinema: German history resolved?

In *The German Sisters*, we find a shift away from an examination of the past that focuses solely on the legacy of National Socialism to one that also begins to address the ramifications of the social upheaval of the 1960s and 1970s. In recent German film we see this tendency continue. This is evident in films that address the legacy of the period directly, such as Hans Weingartner's *The Edukators* (*Die fetten Jahre sind vorbei*, 2004). It is also evident in the apparent return to the attitudes of the post-war decade in recent films that discuss the issue of National Socialism. To conclude this chapter, I wish to examine one such recent hit film, Sönke Wortmann's *The Miracle of Bern* (*Das Wunder von Bern*, 2003), which shows this tendency particularly clearly, drawing together many of the themes already discussed and showing their development in the now unified Germany. Moreover, like Hirschbiegel's film *Downfall*, it also provoked a degree of outrage amongst critics for its representation of history, albeit on a smaller scale.[19] The film tells the story of the former *Wehrmacht* soldier Richard Lubanski (Peter Lohmeyer), who returns to his home and family in the Ruhr in 1954 after having spent twelve years in a Soviet POW camp. We see the difficulties Richard faces trying to find a place in a family that has learnt to manage without him and in a society that he does not recognise. Central to the film is the relationship between Richard and his youngest son, the football-obsessed Matthias (Louis Klamroth).

Echoing the type of familial relationship we find in *Germany Pale Mother*, the father has a destructive impact on the family. Alienated and traumatised by this new society, he lashes out at his children, attempting to reassert the discipline he feels they lack, but which for the spectator smacks of Germany's authoritarian past, a connection not lost on Richard's eldest son Bruno (Mirko Lang), a figure who, like Juliane in von Trotta's film, prefigures the confrontational attitudes that would dominate in the 1960s. Yet there is a further dimension to this film which returns us more obviously to the representation of wartime suffering as it was presented in the 'rubble films' of the 1940s. Richard, like Mertens in *The Murderers Are among Us*, is a damaged man. This is most evident in a sequence showing his attempt to return to work as a coal miner. We see Richard collapse, overwhelmed by memories of his experiences in a Soviet salt-mine, an image that highlights his trauma to a far greater extent than was the case, for example, in Sanders-Brahms's film. Here we are strongly encouraged to understand the world from Richard's point of view. This is made explicit when, after yet another altercation between the youngest son and his father, Richard's wife intervenes, explaining to Matthias that he should try and understand his father's perspective. She asks him to imagine how it was for him to suffer being away from his family for 12 years. 'But it's not my fault', interjects the boy, to which his mother responds 'is it your dad's?'. At the same time the mother has words with her husband, making him realise that he must reform his ways, that he can no longer attempt to rule his family through intimidation and fear. Consequently, the film tempers the accusatory position of New German Cinema. It echoes its critique of post-war society, but, through the intervention of female reason it suggests a position of compromise, thereby pointing to a possible *rapprochement* between the generations and a resolution to any inherent violence within patriarchal society such as that suggested in *Germany Pale Mother.*

The developing relationship between Matthias and Richard is mirrored in the relationship between the German football team's coach, Sepp Herberger, and his high-spirited striker Helmut Rahn during the team's successful World Cup campaign in Switzerland. Frustrated by their defeat at the hands of the Hungarians in the opening round, Rahn breaks his curfew and gets drunk, much to the annoyance of Herberger. However, just as the coach is about to discipline his player, he is given a lesson in wisdom from an old cleaning lady in their hotel. In a further female intervention in the film, the woman stops the coach from confronting Rahn, asking him not to cross her freshly mopped floor. As he laments the fact that the player will have to be punished, she responds, 'Rubbish. You're not in Germany now. You don't always have to punish 'em.' In the words of the woman we find the final message of the film. Unlike the 'rubble films', which were intent upon finding the 'murderers' in order to exonerate the masses, or the films of the New German Cinema that wished to take these very masses to task, this contemporary film addresses not only the question of culpability, but also the issue of German victimhood, in an attempt to suggest that while the accusations of the 1960s were important, they have now perhaps gone far enough, and that the nation might at last be permitted to move on from this period of history.

It is at this point that the relevance of the football setting becomes very clear. Unlike its evocation in the final explosion sequence of Fassbinder's film, the World Cup win is here re-enacted very much as a celebration of German normality. It would seem that the headline of

1954, 'We are someone again!', is in 2003 at last allowed to come to fruition. Crucially, however, this is not to be understood as a statement of a problematic version of German nationalism. Interestingly, for example, the film does not show the crowd singing the outlawed first verse of the national anthem, as the actual crowd in Bern famously did. Instead, this is an image of a harmonious, mature German nation that has put its authoritarian ways behind it, and where the population now very much has the 'ability to mourn'. This is most obviously evidenced in Robert's tears as he sits with his son after the final game, overcome with emotion both for the present moment and for the weight of the past, and where, most importantly, the generational conflicts of the 1960s have been overcome. Indeed, it is not only generational divisions that can be resolved. This is also clearly a nation where splits between East and West need not be overstated, since we see shots of the whole of German society, both FRG and GDR, unified in the act of watching the final match on the television and in their appreciation of the West German team. As such, and as Stuart Taberner notes, *The Miracle of Bern* ultimately recalls most clearly the mood, and particularly the look, of the *Heimatfilm.*[20] While the cool tones of von Trotta's version of the 1950s in *The German Sisters* are also echoed in many of the sequences set in the Ruhr, in Bern we see a return of the vibrant chocolate-box Technicolor of *The Spring before the Gate*, as the German team, along with Robert and Matthias, who have managed to sneak on to the team's train, travel off into the sunset through an idyllic rural landscape populated by happy country folk waving their team on their way.

In *The Miracle of Bern*, we see an articulation of German victimhood which does not return wholeheartedly to the position of the 1950s, since it very much takes account of the question of German culpability. Nonetheless, it also rejects the accusatory glare of the New German Cinema, presenting us with an unambiguous example of the type of 'Cinema of consensus', which, as Eric Renschler suggests (with a good deal of dismay), has come to dominate post-unification film production.[21] As such, we see a return to some aspects of earlier sensibilities in the film's re-enactment of the integrative atmosphere of the *Heimatfilme*, albeit from a new perspective that also accounts for the perpetrator discourses that came about in the 1960s. With the question of German wartime suffering able to be articulated, and the issue of guilt and responsibility accepted, in *The Miracle of Bern* we see the clear declaration of German normalisation. The nation, it would appear, can at last begin to leave its past behind it, not because this past is to be ignored, but because it has now been dealt with. However, if the present surge of films examining National Socialism and the legacy of the war is anything to go by, even if Germany is indeed learning to have a less tortured relationship to its history, the fascination of German filmmakers with the period seems far from being on the wane, nor, it should be added, is the ability of the films produced to attract audiences and, what is more, controversy.

5

The Birth of the Collective from the Spirit of Empathy: From the 'Historians' Dispute' to German Suffering

Helmut Schmitz

As pointed out in the introduction to this volume, the legacy of National Socialism was integrated in the course of the 1990s into the official self-image of the 'Berlin Republic' through a series of controversial public debates: debates prompted by the planned Berlin Holocaust Memorial, Daniel Jonah Goldhagen's book *Hitler's Willing Executioners* (1996), the Walser-Bubis debate (1998), and the travelling exhibition *War of Annihilation: Crimes of the Wehrmacht, 1941–1944*. This process has been described as a progressive 'institutionalisation' of the memory of Nazism, the outcome of which is a form of national 'ownership' of this memory from a perspective of historical responsibility.[1] However, over the last few years there has been an increasing shift in German memory discourse away from a commemoration of the Holocaust to a focus on the German experience of National Socialism, the air war and the expulsion from the eastern territories. One of the triggers of this shift was W. G. Sebald's 1997 lectures *On the Natural History of Destruction* (*Luftkrieg und Literatur*, 2003), in which he put forward the thesis that post-war German literature had omitted to inscribe the experience of the Allied bombing campaign into literary memory. Sebald's lectures about a *historical* failure resulting from the complex post-war emotional landscape of guilt, denial, traumatisation and continuities in Nazi mentality were received by the German press as lifting a taboo on public discourse about German wartime suffering and as legitimising a *present* debate. The same response greeted the publication of Günter Grass's novella *Crabwalk* (*Im Krebsgang*, 2002).[2]

German suffering, a topic which for a long time had been accompanied by the odium of revisionism, was suddenly present in the mainstream media as never before since the 1950s. Guido Knopp's five-part TV documentary series on the flight and expulsion of Germans from the eastern territories in 1944–45, *Die große Flucht* (2001), had a viewing audience of 5 million or 16 per cent.[3] Jörg Friedrich's book about the bombing raids, *The Fire* (*Der Brand*, 2002), and his subsequent book of photographs *Sites of Fire* (*Brandstätten*, 2003) enjoyed critical and public success, *The Fire* selling over 200,000 copies in hardcover alone (the 2004 paperback edition sold over 25,000 copies in the first two months), and *Sites of Fire* selling over 30,000 copies in the first year. The most contentious public issue is the Centre Against Expulsions, which the League of Expellees (*Bund der Vertriebenen*) wants to build in Berlin, housing permanent exhibitions on the expulsion of Germans from eastern Europe and twentieth-century expulsions in general.

In what follows, I would like to problematise the recent public discourse on German suffering by setting it in the context of considerations on historical trauma, loss, mourning and melancholia, victims and perpetrators and the question of empathy and representation. While individual suffering has an unquestionable right of expression and acknowledgement, the public representation and commemoration of collective historical suffering usually serve collective purposes and underwrite a collective narrative. The question, then, is why 60 years after the end of the war the undoubtedly traumatic suffering of the Germans should become an object of compulsive public representation, and what the rhetorical forms of these representations are. One of the recurrent features of the representation of German suffering is the claim to the status of victim. This is in itself not unproblematic. While suffering is ethically neutral, with respect to the history of National Socialism the concepts of victim and perpetrator are ethically coded, victims being the objects of an act of morally reprehensible victimisation. The status of Germans as victims (of the Allied bombing raids, of Stalin's expulsions, of Hitler's politics) appears to be at odds with their status as perpetrators. Despite the frequent insistence that to commemorate German suffering does not mean to equate it with the suffering of Nazi victims, one of the central rhetorical operations in the current allocation of victim status to the Germans is the employment of images and *topoi* otherwise familiar from Holocaust discourse.

In exploring part of the argumentative trajectory of the current concern with German suffering, I want to focus on what appears to me to be the common denominator in most of the debates around the memory and legacy of National Socialism from the 'Historians' Dispute' onwards – namely the shift from a memory discourse that focuses on the victims of Nazism to a discourse that focuses on the suffering of the German collective. The former I will refer to as 'victim-centred memory', the latter as 'perpetrator-centred memory'. Connected to this shift are discursive attempts to 'contain' the Holocaust within a nationalised memory discourse. The ultimate purpose of these is to relegitimise a German perspective on National Socialism from the vantage point of empathy, a perspective which had been de-legitimised with the increasing focus on Nazi atrocities in the course of the 1960s. I will trace these discursive attempts through the arguments of Ernst Nolte and Andreas Hillgruber in the 'Historians' Dispute', through the exchange of letters between Martin Broszat and Saul Friedlander on the historiography of the Nazi everyday, and the Walser-Bubis debate. Finally, I will link them to recent representations of German suffering. Before I engage with the various debates, I wish to set up a framework for thinking about the problem of empathy with respect to the Holocaust, victims, perpetrators and (national) communities.

Victim-centred memory

One of the main points of contention in the 'Historians' Dispute' was the centrality of the Holocaust, both for any understanding of National Socialism as well as its position in European history. As Avishai Margalit and Gabriel Motzkin have argued, in the course of the 1950s and 1960s the perception of the Holocaust shifts and it becomes the 'negative myth of origin' of the Western world.[4] In other words, the Holocaust attains the status of a foundational narrative for the present. Connected with this is an interpretation of the Holocaust as a rupture in European civilisation, which necessitates a review of the belief systems that our society is based on. Originating in Max Horkheimer's and Theodor W. Adorno's *Dialectic of Enlightenment* (*Dialektik der Aufklärung*, 1947), the idea of the Holocaust as historical rupture was taken up in philosophy, social theory and historiography.[5] For the historian Dan Diner, 'the break with civilisation carried out in Auschwitz becomes the actual universal starting point from which to measure the world-historical meaning of National Socialism.' The conviction that the Holocaust represents the essence of National Socialism leads to a strong victim-centred approach. For Diner:

> the approach oriented towards the perspective of the victim in no way represents either a purely subjective or even a complementary way of viewing things. Rather it is the more comprehensive perspective and the more appropriate to the totality of the phenomenon, because it proceeds from the absolute extreme case.[6]

According to Diner, then, the victim perspective represents the total experience of National Socialism, whereas the perpetrators have no 'experience' in this sense, due to the division of labour that was the administrative principle of the Holocaust. For Marx, the division of labour in the factory produces the alienation of the worker from the product over which he has no control. The same holds true for the division of labour in Nazi Germany's 'death factories': it bars the perpetrators from having any experience of the truth of their actions. However, such an understanding of the Holocaust runs the risk of invalidating any German 'experience' of National Socialism that is not placed within the context of the gas chambers. This fundamental difference in perspective between Nazi victims and Germans is a problem for everyone seeking to relegitimise *German* experience of National Socialism and the war. Those Germans who lived through Nazism largely as bystanders are faced with the problem of how to address and represent their own suffering and losses during the war legitimately, while at the same time having to come to terms with the legacy of guilt and responsibility for Nazism and the Holocaust. One problem of what Saul Friedlander has described as the different traumatisation of the victim and perpetrator collective is that, in the highly politicised memory discourse of the Federal Republic, the demand for and necessity of working through the perpetrator past appears incompatible with the memory of German suffering.[7]

The 'Historians' Dispute'

The attempt to relativise the centrality of the Holocaust and to relegitimise a German perspective from the vantage point of empathy were central to the 'Historians' Dispute'. The debate was triggered by Jürgen Habermas's polemical article on Ernst Nolte and Andreas Hillgruber, two conservative historians who had challenged the historiographical and public consensus on the centrality of Auschwitz for the assessment of National Socialist Germany.

Nolte's article 'Between Historical Legend and Revisionism?', an abbreviated version of which was published in the *Frankfurter Allgemeine Zeitung* on 24 July 1980, opens with the assertion that the Third Reich continues to exert a dominating influence on the contemporary German imaginary. Nolte observes that, in contrast to the image of Napoleon's reign 50 years after his defeat in 1815, the image of the Third Reich is purely negative, due to Hitler's war of extermination and the dimensions of the Holocaust. Nolte makes two assertions that have bearing on the issues we are concerned with here. First, that the public focus on Nazi atrocities has led to a victim-centred perspective on Nazi history. Second, that the persistently negative image of the Third Reich is a threat to the discipline of historiography, with the demonisation of Nazism giving rise to constructs resembling those of myth. Both these assertions are interrelated, as the victim-centred perspective essentially produces the negative image of the National Socialist era. The first assertion will return in the Walser-Bubis debate, and the second in the exchange of letters between Martin Broszat and Saul Friedlander. Most importantly, Nolte's claim that 'in "published opinion" the facts have appeared with such exclusivity that only the voices of the victims have been audible' implies a hegemony of victim perspective in public discourse that bars any different imaginary from emerging. Nolte argued for a 'revision' of the position of the Third Reich in German and European history, calling for an end to the historical isolation of the Nazi era, and for a rebuttal of the instrumentalisation of its image in public discourse. His own contribution to a 'historisation' of the Third Reich was to attempt to integrate the Holocaust into a European continuum of exterminatory fantasies and policies. In his view, the annihilation of social classes and groups was the answer of the respective societies to the traumatic experience of European modernisation and its ruptures. Nolte identifies Stalin's extermination of the Soviet bourgeoisie as the 'original' annihilation to which the Nazi genocide responded as a 'copy': 'Auschwitz is not primarily the result of traditional anti-Semitism and was not just one more case of "genocide". It was the fear-borne reaction to the act of annihilation that took place during the Russian Revolution.'[8]

Two issues are at stake here. First, Nolte's attempt to read the Holocaust as Hitler's copy of Stalin is essentially an attempt to relativise its historical singularity in a reversal of cause and effect. The same rhetorical manoeuvre can be seen in Nolte's argument that, because of Chaim Weizman's proclamation in September 1939 that the world's Jews would fight with England, Hitler had 'good reason to be convinced of his enemies' will to annihilate long before the first reports about the events in Auschwitz became public'. He thus would have been justified in interning them as prisoners of war.[9] This reversal of cause and effect, in which the Jews appear either as the original aggressor or as the originators and proprietors of a victim-centred discourse that is holding the articulation of a specific German memory of National Socialism in check returns with vigour in the Walser-Bubis debate.

Second, central to Nolte's argument is the allegation that the negative image of National Socialism is being instrumentalised for political interests, which hinders historiographical research. Nolte implied that German memory and historiography of National Socialism are dominated by two interest groups: the 1968 generation on the one hand and, on the other, the survivors with their interest in 'having a permanent special status and the privileges that go with it'.[10] The focus on Auschwitz in both groups, he suggested, creates an obsession with German collective guilt which essentially replicates in inverted form the Nazis' stigmatisation of the Jews as guilty. Nolte's argument thus moves the accused Germans into the structural position of the Nazi victims, with the '68ers and survivors in the position of aggressor.

The second publication at the centre of the 'Historians' Dispute' was a brief book consisting of two essays by Andreas Hillgruber, *Two Kinds of Demise* (*Zweierlei Untergang*, 1986). As its subtitle indicated, Hillgruber's book focused on the 'destruction of the Third Reich' and the 'end of European Jewry'. In it, he attempted to parallel the 'catastrophe of the German East' with the Nazi Holocaust, and to validate the experience of German suffering during the last stages of the war from a position of empathy. Hillguber argued that the only possible form of identification for the German historian was with the 'concrete fate of the German population in the East and with the desperate and sacrificial efforts of the German Army in the East and the German Marine in the Baltic sea'.[11] For Hillgruber, in the context of the events in the East the concept of 'liberation' was only justified from the perspective of Nazi victims; it was to be rejected with respect to the 'fate of the German nation as a whole', since it implied an identification with the Red Army. According to Hillgruber, then, there were two valid but incompatible perspectives on certain areas of National Socialism: that of the victims and that of the Germans. Hillgruber's attempted validation of the German perspective on the events in the East in a tragic-heroic historical narrative – he depicts the *Wehrmacht* holding out against the attack of the Red Army – was deeply problematic in its suggestion of a victim status for the German population of the East that was equal to that of Hitler's victims.[12] Furthermore, it excluded Nazism's German-Jewish victims from the 'nation as a whole'.

According to Charles Maier, Hillgruber's explicit particularist empathy with the fate of the German Army and the German population in the East violated the historicist ethos of empathy with a plurality of perspectives.[13] Hillgruber later conceded that his plea for empathy with the German war experience was made in the interest of a national historiography.[14] Dan Diner has criticised German-centred historiographical approaches that remove the Holocaust from the centre as producing a double history, that of the Germans and that of the victims, essentially replicating the Nazi division into Germans and 'others'.[15]

Martin Broszat and Saul Friedlander

The issue of a double and incompatible perspective on National Socialism returned in the exchange of letters between Saul Friedlander and Martin Broszat. The trigger to this exchange was Broszat's essay 'A Plea for the Historisation of National Socialism' (1985). There he argued that the dominant *a posteriori* perspective on Nazism, originating in the shock at its atrocities, remained too focused on systemic and ideological aspects, thereby obscuring the inherent contradictions and tensions within the regime. Furthermore, Broszat argued, the *a posteriori* perspective reduces Nazism to an 'all encompassing rule of force', keeping the period in a 'moral quarantine' which results in a 'routinised conceptual and linguistic apparatus'. It is thus blind to the hidden continuities between National Socialism and post-war West Germany. Moreover, Broszat lamented, the cold and distant approach to the Nazi era undermines 'the ability to feel one's way empathetically into the web of historical interconnections' as well as 'the pleasure of historical narration'.[16] What Broszat calls for is thus a reversal in perspective, from the end of National Socialism to its beginnings. While some of Broszat's arguments may sound close to Nolte's – such as the allegation that a moralising perspective on Nazism obscures historical vision and leads to stereotyped public phraseology – Broszat's purpose is essentially a historical appropriation of the Nazi era from the perspective of responsibility. Rather than just an 'objectification' of the

Third Reich, it combines the historicising effort with 'a comprehending, subjective appropriation and empathetic reliving (*Nachvollzug*) of past achievements, sensations, concerns and mistakes'. The objective of this, rather than just historical understanding, is 'insight' – which in German carries the implicit meaning of having reviewed one's errors of judgement.[17]

Broszat explicitly distinguishes this historicising approach from the perspective of Nazi victims. While acknowledging the necessity to respect the perspective of living memory, he refers to it as mythical, believing it might represent a 'coarsening' of 'historical recollection'. In contrast to Nolte's relativising polemic, Broszat's arguments are presented with scholarly seriousness. Nevertheless, central to the approach of Nolte, Hillgruber *and* Broszat is the overcoming of the historian's moral distance from the object of historical understanding. Not only is the historicist method ultimately empathetic. Both Nolte's and Broszat's allegations that historiography is too much in the grip of a mythologising victim perspective conflates survivor experience with scholarship. By setting 'rational' German historicisation against victim 'mythology', the Third Reich is put at an *historical* distance in order to undercut the *moral* distance introduced by the Holocaust; it is moved historically further away in order to bring it emotionally closer. This is effectively the result of the focus on Nazi 'everyday history' championed by Broszat which, he argues, has been obscured by the centrality and the moral imperative of the Holocaust in previous historiography. In his reply to Broszat, Saul Friedlander expressed the suspicion that the 'blockage' on the historian's imaginary that Broszat desires to remove is rather the 'negative central position' of National Socialism as a whole. He points out that a return to the 'pleasure of historical narration' can only be achieved at the price of removing the Holocaust from the centre of Nazism.[18]

Martin Walser and the Walser-Bubis debate

The Walser-Bubis debate can be described as the dialectic switching-station from commemoration of Nazi atrocities to a collectivised memory of German experience that is conceived of in emphatic difference to that of Nazi victims. In 1998, Walser used his acceptance speech for the Peace Prize of the German Book Trade to polemicise against the continuous representation of what he referred to as 'our disgrace'.[19] Walser repeats central arguments of the 'Historians' Dispute' in condensed fashion. He criticises public commemorative language of

Nazism as ritualised and sterile, and as being in the interest of contemporary politics. This combines Broszat's reservations against conceptual routine with Nolte's belligerent allegation of an intellectual left-wing opinion-machine that hegemonises the image of Auschwitz for the continuous shaming of Germany. Walser alleges that this 'routine of accusation' serves the interest of producing 'good conscience', as it creates distance between the accusers and any association with the guilty party, and it aligns them with the Nazi victims. This argument returns, as we will see, in the debates around German suffering. Against this public rhetoric of 'intimidation', Walser argues in favour of the privacy of conscience. Alleging that the ultimate function of symbolic public representation is exculpatory, Walser privileges individual conscience because it is not representable and thus not in danger of being instrumentalised.

Walser's opposition of public rhetoric and private conscience creates a binary in which the authentic private conscience is conceived of as constantly under siege from inauthentic public forms of address that are perceived as 'accusatory'. The inauthentic public memory of National Socialism is ultimately in the hands of a non-specified 'other'. The vacant position of the 'other' can be filled at various points with whomsoever assumes the position of perceived aggressor. While in the Peace Prize speech, it is the left-wing German intellectuals who are allocated this role, in Walser's discussion with Ignatz Bubis, it is the Jews. Ignatz Bubis, then President of the Central Council of German Jews, had conspicuously remained seated during the standing ovation which greeted Walser's speech. A few days later he accused Walser of 'spiritual arson'. On 14 December 1998, both men met in the offices of the *Frankfurter Allgemeine Zeitung* to discuss the matter.

The encounter between Walser and Bubis was a struggle about who owns the discourse on the Holocaust – a struggle in which Walser increasingly allocated Bubis the position of the outsider who, however unjustifiably, is in charge of terminology. According to Walser, public jargon serves to regulate German memory of Auschwitz with its 'frozen, routine use of language ... victim-centred, perpetrator-centred'. Against the inauthentic outsiders who dominate public memory, Walser invokes the privacy of conscience of a German collective that wishes to deal with the memory of Nazism 'in our way': 'our conscience is our conscience, and we will not let others stipulate the rules'.[20] The 'others' who are prescribing the uses of memory and conscience are thus the Jews who are seen by the 'we' of the German collective as hitherto being in possession of the discourse on the Holocaust.

Walser's rhetoric of 'us and them' creates an inside–outside economy that claims sole representational power for the German collective with respect to their experience of National Socialism. Alleging that the concepts of victim and perpetrator are socially divisive, Walser's plea for 'a new language' that includes everybody contains a desire for a homogenised perspective that suspends the radical division of victim and perpetrator experience. However, this collective German experiential perspective necessitates breaking with the perceived hegemony of the victim perspective. Turning Diner's argument on its head, Walser alleges that the victims' perspective is inauthentic to the Germans. Nazi victims, having no choice in the matter, are excluded from the experience of the ethical ambiguities of Nazism. Their experience does not fall within that of the German collective.

The Walser-Bubis debate is significant for two reasons. First, Walser's privileging of private conscience and personal memory over public commemoration in the interest of 'his soul's peace', exposes a rift between official public representation and private memory.[21] While the official commemoration of the National Socialist legacy has increasingly focused on the regime's atrocities, private and family memory has been dominated by the experience of hardship and suffering.[22] What happens in the Walser-Bubis debate is thus a switch in public representation from the dominance of images of Nazi crimes to images dominant in German family memory. This essentially presupposes the sidelining of the Holocaust as well as the rejection of the interdependence between German experience and the experience of Nazi victims. In this framework, Jewish-German citizens become excluded from the German experiential collective at the moment they insist on their necessarily different experience and perspective. What is thus created is a two-track history whose origins in Nazi racial politics are all too easily overlooked – yet it is ultimately underpinned by the Nazi-like distinction between the German *Volk* and those who do not belong to it.[23]

Re-establishment of a commemorative community as a community of victims

The reconceptualisation of the German collective as one of victims is central to a series of literary and non-literary representations over recent years. In Dieter Forte's autobiographical novel about the firebombing of Düsseldorf, *The Boy with the Bloody Shoes* (*Der Junge mit den blutigen Schuhen*, 1995), the collective personnel appear as double victims, both of Hitler and of the Allies.[24] This narrative, in which the German collective appears as Hitler's hostage, is also central to Jörg Friedrich's *The Fire*. One of the most striking features is the collectivisation of victims. In both Forte and Friedrich the Germans, POWs and Nazi workslaves all appear as the victims of the Allies' will to total destruction. Ulla Hahn's novel *Blurred Images* (*Unscharfe Bilder*, 2003) overwrites the image of the German soldier as an integral part of Hitler's war of extermination in Eastern Europe with the image of the suffering soldier. To make this work, the narratives have to rely on a radical distinction between ordinary Germans and fanatical Nazis, a strategy that can be observed in nearly all recent visual and literary representations of German experience. This simplistic dichotomy circumvents recent insights into the complex processes of mediation between political and social structures, ideology and consent – and it is the best indicator that the Nazi era in German popular culture is turning into a heritage site.

Moreover, the Centre Against Expulsions, planned by the League of Expellees, is to house a permanent exhibition about the 'fate of the German expellees and the expulsion of other European peoples in the twentieth century'.[25] The outlined plan for the exhibitions both incorporates the 'fate of the German expellees' into a narrative of expulsions on the twentieth century, and gives it a special status by separating it from the other expulsions in the exhibition. This double framing both erases the political distinctions between the various expulsions *and* effectively turns the Centre into a national memorial. What is being created here is a cathartic narrative in which members of a national collective are imagined as subjects of atrocities and suffering. This cathartic process can also be observed with respect to the exhibition *War of Annihilation: Crimes of the Wehrmacht, 1941–44*. Despite its critical and controversial nature, the exhibition triggered communication between the generations, engendering a process of reconciliation through 'empathy with the perpetrators'. Hannes Heer, original curator of the exhibition has welcomed this 'cathartic process' as one of its outcomes.[26]

Competition with Auschwitz

One of the most striking features of recent representations of German suffering is that they appear to be in competition with the legacy of the Holocaust. That is to say, they frequently borrow from Holocaust imagery and tropes in order to attain gravity and legitimacy. Through this rhetorical operation, German victims are allocated a status similar to that of Holocaust victims. The charging of depictions of German suffering with Holocaust imagery recurs with such regularity that one is reminded of a reflex, emanating, perhaps, from the collective unconscious. A few examples will suffice.

Both Guido Knopp's TV series on the flight of the German expellees, *Die große Flucht*, and Friedrich's *The Fire* were accompanied by a series of articles in the German weekly *Der Spiegel*. One article contains a photograph of the former East Prussian town of Nemmersdorf (now Majakowskoje), whose population was massacred by the Russians in October 1944 before the village was subsequently recaptured by SS units.[27] The photograph shows a line of dead townspeople stretching towards the horizon, with a number of SS officers at the far end of the line, an image otherwise familiar from SS killings in Poland and Russia. Another *Spiegel* article features a photograph of a mass grave after the firestorm in Hamburg that is virtually indistinguishable from mass graves of Nazi victims.[28] Jörg Friedrich's book of photographs *Sites of Fire*, finally, contains a photograph of corpses piled up into a pyre for incineration after the bombing of Dresden. As Heinz-Peter Preußer has commented, 'all these images seem to have one original image: the Holocaust'. Such photographs enable contemporary Germans to equate the fate of their dead predecessors with that of Nazi victims, while forgetting the context in which the latter became victims namely German perpetration.[29]

Friedrich may claim that there can be no analogy between the Holocaust and the Allied fire bombing. Nevertheless, in *The Fire* he frequently draws just such a parallel when he uses vocabulary that is otherwise associated with Nazi atrocities to refer to the effect of the bombing, such as 'massacre' or 'extermination';[30] and, according to Friedrich, the German victims do not simply die in the fumes, they are 'being gassed'.[31] In what can only be described as an inversion of the roles of victims and perpetrators, Friedrich turns the British into the 'older master race with more practice' whose nineteenth-century colonialist policies are re-enacted by the Nazis in the heart of Europe and whose exterminatory will is directed against the Germans.[32] One might add in this context that the Centre Against Expulsions planned for Berlin will be modelled on the Washington Holocaust Museum. There is thus a competing desire to move the suffering Germans into the structural position of the Jews. This might be due to the fact that the Holocaust has become a global signifier for extermination, victimisation and suffering. However, with respect to the German national imaginary, it appears rather to be the case that the Holocaust is felt to represent an obstacle to German narratives of suffering. The obsessive concern with atrocities in the evocation of German wartime experience can thus be read as a stylistic device to validate the German position by allocating it the same traumatic status as the Holocaust.

Blocking (collective) empathy?

Over recent years, a reassessment of the student movement has taken place in Germany. Increasingly, the student movement is seen as having collectively withdrawn empathy from their parents' generation. Shocked by the realisation of the latter's implication in Nazism, the student generation came to see their parents exclusively as perpetrators. The result, according to this reassessment, was a polarisation in the discourse of memory. This view can be found in any number of contemporary literary depictions of the relationship between the student generation and their elders.[33] It was reiterated by Hannes Heer in his speech on reception of the Carl-von-Ossietzky medal,[34] and by Peter Schneider with respect to his generation's attitude to their parents' experience of the Allied bombing: 'more radically than the generation of Günter Grass, the '68ers excised from their vision of history all images of Germans that did not fit the frame of "perpetrator generation"'.[35]

The implicit argument in contemporary critiques of the student generation's avoidance of empathy is that it is now possible to end the polarised memory discourse of German perpetrators and Jewish victims, and to see Germans as both perpetrators *and* victims. However, what is more often than not at stake is the replacement of the image of perpetrator with that of victim for the purpose of collective and national commemoration. This intention is visible in Günter Franzen's polemical condemnation of Uwe Timm's *In My Brother's Shadow* (*Am Beispiel meines Bruders*, 2002). According to Franzen, the German Left's inability to empathise with German suffering is the consequence of a 'strict division of the world into . . . perpetrators and victims', resulting from the emotional pressure the second generation experienced in the face of the moral complexities of historical reality. This led, Franzen argues, to a 'decree of abstinence with respect to national commemoration'.[36] The ultimate objective of Franzen's call for an end to the victim/perpetrator dichotomy is the unproblematic commemoration of Germans as victims in a national community.

It is thus possible to describe the current mass representation of German suffering as a form of 'belated' or displaced collective empathy in which the children and grandchildren of the 'perpetrator collective' empathise with their suffering ancestors. The turning point here is the issue of guilt. With the institutionalisation of the memory of the Holocaust as a national responsibility and the shift from second to third post-war generation, the question of guilt and repression that determined so much of German memory discourse is no longer central to the historical imaginary. This, together with the historical distance, opens up the potential for empathising with the 'German experience'.

Trauma and collective identity

The re-establishment of a collective of sufferers depends on a political decontextualisation of individuals and groups, whereby the political is substituted with the immediacy of suffering. The undeniable immediacy of trauma, in which all social and political categories are shattered and the pure creature appears, facilitates this. However, one difference remains: in all representations of Nazi atrocities, whether they emanate from the Nazis themselves, from Allied documentation or from survivor testimony, the victims appear directly as objects of a (collective) political and ideological will to exterminate them. The political quality of their victimhood is an irreducible part of the experience and status of Nazi victims – an experience of heteronomy, of being designated a member of a group destined for extermination. From the perspective of the victim/perpetrator dichotomy, the traumatised survivor of Nazi policies remains the individual subsumed under a category destined for death, while the perpetrator remains a member of a murderous 'people's community' (*Volksgemeinschaft*). To legitimise an image of German suffering, to appear as an 'ordinary' individual, the German subjects first have to be stripped of their political character as members of this Nazi collective. However, their representation as victims of the Allies, or indeed Nazism itself, reconfigures them as a collective on a different axis. This is eminently visible in Friedrich's *The Fire* and *Sites of Fire*. Both text and photographs rely on a rhetoric of excess to illustrate the transgressive nature of the fire-bombing, documenting the atrocities of the bombing raids in painful detail. In the firestorms, national and ethnic differences are lost, for the bombs make no distinction between German adults, POWs, mental hospital inmates and children; all that remains is the human creature, faced with death in the flames. While Friedrich is ostensibly at pains to avoid losing sight of historical context, by combining a portrayal of individual suffering with one of the loss of German cities, the beauty of which is continuously evoked, he retrospectively collectivises and nationalises the catastrophe. In contrast to Sebald, who has remarked that any engagement with the true nature of the horrors has an element of voyeurism, Friedrich's determination to recount the intensity of the experience in word and image produces a narrative of national and collective trauma in which the scenes of atrocities are the absolute cornerstone.[37] *The Fire* tells the same story over and over again, of the extinction of a centuries-old urban environment in the greatest act of destruction since the Thirty Years War.

Both *The Fire* and *Sites of Fire* operate with a narrative in which German cities appear as an intact cultural heritage that is destroyed in the firestorms. The photographs of destruction in *Sites of Fire* are framed by two chapters 'Then' ('Früher') and 'Now' ('Heute'), in which images of predominantly old German towns with their medieval facades and small, crooked alleyways are juxtaposed with the ugliness of post-war reconstructions and contemporary urban spaces. Friedrich's books function therefore as both narratives of trauma and narratives of loss, narratives that meet in a configuration of the present as originating in the experience of bombing. Friedrich stresses the 'exterritoriality' of the traumatic intensity of the experience, the 'exit from country and time'. By interpreting the firestorms as an arrest of time, not just on an individual but also on a collective level, Friedrich aligns them with the Holocaust, which is generally understood as constituting a radical rupture and the traumatic origin of the present. Thus Friedrich's representation of German suffering becomes a foundational narrative of mythic proportions. In the juxtaposition of 'Then' and 'Now', the pre-war German towns are retrospectively idealised as spaces of a 'whole' collective cultural heritage, generally a sign of melancholia rather than mourning.[38]

Conclusion

It is possible to describe the German nation's current concern with its own victim status as a dialectic shift away from an obsessive concern with the Holocaust. In other words, the issue of German suffering has become prominent at precisely the moment the legacy of the Holocaust is becoming part of the official memory of the Berlin Republic, and the matter of coming to terms with the past seems to be settled. In the current climate of German concern with images of their own wartime suffering, the issue of mourning must be distinguished from the flood of images in the media that turn the Nazi era into a form of heritage industry.

It seems appropriate to question whether Germany ever mourned its own traumatic losses during the war – with respect to the cultural heritage that was destroyed, the territories that were lost and the lives that were extinguished.[39] From the end of the war to the present day, any articulation of suffering has been immediately incorporated into a politicised memory discourse, be it in the form of the exculpatory soldier (*Landser*) films and literature of the 1950s, the claims of the League of Expellees for restitution and compensation, or the post-1968 mistrust of German narratives of suffering. It is doubtful, however, whether the current empathy of the nation with the suffering of its ancestors during the war actually does constitute a belated act of mourning. If the wartime generation's failure to come to terms with Nazism effectively displaced the task on to the post-war generations, the same can be said for the task of mourning German losses. This displaced task, however, is now being undertaken as one of identity building. The form of empathy at stake here relies on emotional identification with the collective suffering of one's ancestors. This produces a national collective, an 'imagined community', in Benedict Anderson's sense, which is concerned with the 'transformation of fatality into continuity, contingency into meaning'.[40] The problem is not so much that this happens at all – after all, many nations affirm their sense of collective identity by commemorating their war dead – but rather that it largely happens at the expense of, and in competition with, the remembrance of Nazi victims.

6

The GDR and Memory of the Bombing of Dresden

Bill Niven

Introduction

Dresden, it would seem when looking back over its 800-year-old history, has experienced more than its fair share of fires. In July 1491, a terrible conflagration engulfed and destroyed half the city, including the famous *Church of the Holy Cross* (*Kreuzkirche*). During the Seven Years War, in the summer of 1760, following the occupation of Dresden by the Austrians, Frederick the Great ordered its bombardment; two-thirds of the old part of the city or *Altstadt* were destroyed, including the *Church of the Holy Cross* again. It was razed to the ground in one of the many fires set off by the cannons; Bernardo Bellotto, the pupil and nephew of Giovanni Canaletto and a court painter in Dresden in the mid-seventeenth century, painted the ruined *Church of the Holy Cross* as a skeletal frame standing deep in a pile of rubble.[1] Gottfried Semper's famous opera house burnt down in 1869. Between 1935 and 1938, the Dresden artist and communist Hans Grundig, despite a painting ban imposed on him by the Nazis, secretly painted a triptych entitled *The Thousand Year Empire* (*Das Tausendjährige Reich*) in which he portrayed *inter alia* the ruins of a city, above which he has painted in a line of bombers. Grundig, it seemed to later commentators,[2] had with uncanny accuracy predicted a further destruction of Dresden – one that duly followed on 13/14 February 1945, when British and then American planes launched upon the city a devastating attack which laid waste to large parts of the *Altstadt* and parts of the suburbs.

Reading books such as Jörg Friedrich's recent *The Fire* (*Der Brand*, 2002), one might be tempted into thinking that the preoccupation with the bombing of Germany is a new phenomenon. Certainly the degree of media and public interest seems new, as does the fact that this interest can be felt across Germany, not just in cities generally associated with heavy destruction through bombing, such as Cologne, Hamburg or Dresden. However, as this chapter will set out to show by example of Dresden, the topic of the bombing was certainly not taboo in East Germany. In fact, well-orchestrated commemorations of the destruction of Dresden played a central role in state memory in the German Democratic Republic (GDR). In the following, I shall explore the character and function of this official commemoration, as well as examining the portrayal of, and significance attached to, the bombing of Dresden in East German art and literature. I argue that inherent to the official, artistic and literary discourse, despite shifts over time and occasional tensions within and between these discourses, was the same fundamental pattern: self-pity on the one hand, and indignation towards the Western Allies on the other. The more intense the sense of Allied blame, the greater the sense of German victimhood. My analysis is preceded by a brief overview of the motivation for the British and American bombing of Dresden. I conclude with some thoughts on the differences and similarities between the contemporary culture of remembering the bombing of Germany, and the GDR's at times obsessive culture of remembering the bombing of Dresden.

Reasons for the bombing of Dresden

There is evidence that the British had been considering launching a devastating knockout bombing attack on Berlin, codenamed 'Thunderclap', as of July 1944. The idea behind such an attack, according to the chief of Air Staff, Air Marshal Portal, was to produce a massive number of casualties, some 50 per cent fatal (about 110,000). 'It is suggested', continued Portal, 'that such an attack resulting in so many deaths, the great majority of which will be key personnel, cannot help but have a shattering effect on political and civilian morale all over Germany.'[3] The saturation-bombing of Hamburg in July 1943 with the subsequent firestorm and massive loss of life was certainly a prelude to the development of plans for Operation 'Thunderclap'. In the event, the bombing of Dresden, while to a degree the result of the 'Thunderclap' idea, cannot simply be understood as its realisation. Nor, as the historian Frederick Taylor has shown, can the decision to bomb Dresden be attributed to the notion of 'moral bombing' alone.

In the circumstances of early 1945, the British were looking for ways to support the Russian advance into Germany. When Portal's deputy, Norman Bottomley, issued orders to Bomber Command on 27 January 1945, he stressed that Portal had approved the idea for 'one big attack on Berlin and related attacks on Dresden, Leipzig, Chemnitz or any other cities where a severe blitz will not only cause confusion in the evacuation from the East but will also hamper the movement of troops from the West'.[4] According to historian Mark Connelly, Dresden became a target because the city 'contained an important railway line which could be used to transfer troops from one front to the other'. It was also full of refugees, displaced people and wounded soldiers, such that 'a blow against Dresden would cause unbelievable chaos and terror in an already tottering Germany'.[5] From Bottomley's note to Bomber Command it is also clear that any attack on Berlin, Dresden or Leipzig was not to be on the scale envisaged by 'Thunderclap', given the need to continue bombing oil plants and other 'approved target systems'[6] – in the end, though, the British and American raids on Dresden over the course of 13 and 14 February 1945 certainly constituted the most concentrated short-period bombing of a German city in the Second World War.

While Taylor shows that there was no formal mention of Dresden in the transcript of the Yalta Conference in early February 1945 – when Stalin, Churchill and Roosevelt met primarily to discuss redrawing the map of Eastern Europe after the war – he points out that one of the British interpreters from Russian to English distinctly remembers that the Soviets brought up the subject of bombing Dresden, indeed called for the city to be bombed. In other words, while the idea may have originated with the British, and been carried out by the British and the Americans, at Yalta it became agreed Allied policy.[7] At the very least the Russians were more or less informed of the intention to bomb Dresden and raised no objections. After all, the deputy Soviet Chief of General Staff, Antonov, had at Yalta expressed concerns that the Germans might seek to move troops from Norway, Italy, central Germany and the western front to the eastern front.[8] Any bombing of cities such as Dresden, Berlin and Chemnitz could only hinder German redeployment. It would therefore not be judicious to attribute sole responsibility for the destruction of Dresden to the Western Allies. Nor would it be fair to place the burden of responsibility as far as Britain's key role is concerned entirely on the shoulders of the chief of

Bomber Command, Sir Arthur Harris, even if the idea of bombing Dresden, Leipzig and Chemnitz might first have been his.[9] 'Butcher' Harris has come in for much criticism for his commitment to the area bombing of German cities; and there can be little doubt that Harris did, at times, think he could win the war by laying waste to German cities, and that he did not always follow Air Staff briefs to focus bombing mainly on strategic goals such as oil plants.[10] Nevertheless, the idea of area bombing was not his invention; the Air Ministry had issued an area bombing directive as early as 14 February 1942 – a few days before Harris took over at the head of Bomber Command.[11] And the bombing of German cities in February 1945, including that of Dresden, was hardly Harris's responsibility alone; the Joint Intelligence Committee, Air Staff, and indeed Churchill himself all played their part in bringing it about.

The process by which Dresden came to be bombed, and the motives for it, will have meant little to the population of the city which suffered its impact. The degree of destruction was huge. The historian David Irving notoriously claimed that the number of those killed was in the order of 135,000, a hugely inflated figure.[12] Irving inflated the figure even further when he claimed to have traced a document which proved the actual number might be over 200,000. In fact, Irving fell victim to a propaganda trick. The document concerned was a copy of a forgery which emanated from the Nazi Propaganda Ministry; Goebbels had exaggerated the numbers of dead in order to shock the world and engender indignation at the bombing.[13] Most historians put the number of dead at 35,000–40,000, which is dreadful enough. Many were killed outright by the effect of the bombs. As Dresden's *Altstadt* was consumed by a ferocious firestorm that sent billowing piles of smoke several miles up into the sky, many others 'died in the streets as they tried to flee – burned, asphyxiated, dragged into the hot, hungry mouth of the firestorm', as Taylor graphically puts it.[14] Others were cooked alive as they took what they thought would be refuge in Dresden's various water reservoirs, such as that at the 'old market' (*Altmarkt*). Those who survived the ordeal later described the horrors they had witnessed.[15] In the bombing and subsequent fires, many historic buildings in a city rich with cultural and architectural heritage were destroyed, such as the *Zwinger*, Gottfried Semper's opera-house and the *Church of Our Lady* (*Frauenkirche*). In the light of this human and cultural carnage, it is easy to forget that 'Dresden was . . . a functioning enemy administrative, industrial, and communications center that by February 1945 lay close to the front line.'[16] However extreme the bombing might have been – and the second wave of British bombs in the early hours of 14 February, when Dresden was already ablaze, was extreme – there were military reasons for bombing the city.

The bombing of Dresden in official GDR commemorative discourse

For all the horror of the destruction of Dresden, then, it was not a gratuitous act. It was designed, regardless of its effectiveness in this respect, to aid the Soviet advance. But this was not the view taken in the GDR's official discourse. From about 1950 onwards, the Socialist Unity Party (SED) attributed to the Western Allies a range of devious, scheming, and even quite blatantly murderous motives for the bombing of Dresden. A short summary will suffice here to encapsulate the views typical of GDR historiography, official pronouncements and commemorative statements. These views, it should be noted, were always predicated on the basic assumption that there was *no* tenable military motive for the bombing, an assumption underpinned by a constant denial that the old parts of Dresden could possibly constitute a legitimate target. Thus it was claimed, perhaps less frequently in the 1970s and 1980s than earlier, that the bombing was the expression of sheer destructiveness, a propensity the Western Allies were seen as having in common with the Nazis. More consistently, it was stated that Dresden was destroyed in order to promote American and British imperialist or at least territorial interests. In other words, the Western Allies did not want to accept the provisional post-war zonal boundaries drawn up at Yalta, but wished to push the boundaries of their own zones further east.[17] Quite why the bombing of Dresden would usefully serve such a purpose was never adequately explained. The most common claim of all was that the bombing of Dresden was a show of sheer might designed to intimidate the Soviets and thereby strengthen the bargaining hand of the Western Allies in future negotiations with Stalin. Other claims included the assertion that the Western Allies – who also bombed other east German cities early in 1945 – wished to cripple what was to become the Soviet-occupied zone so that it would not recover as quickly as the Western-occupied zones. This list of motives is far from exhaustive. Walter Weidauer, for instance, Dresden's mayor from 1945 until 1958, peddled the view that Operation 'Thunderclap' originally envisaged dropping an atom bomb on Dresden; because the atomic bomb was not yet ready, Weidauer argued,

Churchill decided to bomb Dresden anyway – and prepare the way for a separate peace with the Germans and an assault on the Soviets.[18]

As the historian Gilad Margalit has pointed out, this strongly anti-Western reading of the bombing of Dresden was not so typical of the immediate post-war years in eastern Germany; it was only as the Cold War increased in intensity, as of the early 1950s, that it became a standard part of SED rhetoric. Thus the East German politburo, Margalit writes, took a decision in 1950 to transform the fifth anniversary of the bombing of Dresden into a public campaign against the 'Anglo-American warmongers'.[19] The arguments outlined above thus developed entirely in line with a general propaganda drive aimed at discrediting the British and Americans and rallying the East German populace behind the Soviet Union and its ostensible commitment to peace and indeed the peaceful reunification of Germany. Effectively, the bombing of Dresden was interpreted as part of the developing conflict between the Western Allies and the Soviet Union, with the former perceived as the aggressor. As a result of this projection of the Cold War into the World War, the purpose of Allied involvement in the latter, namely the defeat of Hitler, was lost from view. The German population of Dresden were cast in the role of victims of British–American aggression, the Soviets in the role of defenders of the Germans against this aggression. Moreover, the victimhood status of Dresden's population was enhanced, and differences between Germans and their victims elided by suggesting that 'imperialist forces' were as much to blame for the bombing of Dresden as they were for Auschwitz. This is just one example of the way in which the creed of anti-fascism in East Germany came to mean opposition to Nazism *and* 'Western imperialism'. Such historiographical sophistry removed the need for any sort of acknowledgement that the bombing might have represented an attempt by the Western Allies to help the Soviet advance against the real aggressor at the time – namely the Germans themselves. The perpetrator role of the latter was conveniently side-stepped. Ironically, as Margalit has argued, the GDR's condemnation of the British and Americans for having launched what was termed a 'terror attack' against Dresden more or less reproduced Nazi propaganda.[20]

This interpretation of the bombing of Dresden, and indeed of other cities such as Berlin offered a kind of psychological deal of exchange, a deal which many GDR citizens will have found attractive: in return for the promulgation of a view of their past which cast them as victims of the Western Allies, they were asked to re-imagine the Soviets as liberators. While the Soviets did of course liberate the eastern Germans from Nazism, many of the latter experienced the liberation more as an act of rape, plunder and pillaging – not to mention the imposition of a new form of dictatorship.[21] That there was a need to convince particularly Dresden's population that the Soviets were not plunderers and art-thieves is clear from a number of publications in which the Soviets are praised either for their role in feeding the populace and rebuilding the city's administrative and political structures,[22] or for restoring and returning many of the works of art which had previously hung in Dresden's art galleries.[23] In 1945, the Soviets carried off a vast booty of these works of art. They returned some of them, duly restored, in 1956 for display in the reopened Semper gallery – including Raphael's *Sistine Madonna.* But the official pomp and ceremony surrounding this ostensible act of generosity masked the fact that the Soviets did not return everything they had taken, and indeed have not returned it to this day.[24]

Regular commemorative occasions to mark the anniversary of the bombing of Dresden helped, over decades, to drive home and reinforce the official SED view, as did corresponding interpretations in school textbooks.[25] Pro-Soviet propaganda alternated in official speeches with anti-Western statements, which were updated over the years to reflect the latest form taken by the supposed Western – particularly American and West German – threat to world peace. Whether it be the Korean War, West Germany's entry into NATO, Western deployment of nuclear weapons, the war in Vietnam or Ronald Reagan's 'Star Wars' programme or some other form of Western military activity, the SED was always able to find examples of Western aggression to compare to the bombing of Dresden. Thus it was that the German dead of Dresden became the prototypical victims of imperialism in the GDR, evoked in warning against present trends – far more so than the victims of Auschwitz, who were less memorable for the SED because they were victims of Nazism rather than the United States and Britain. To impress upon the population of Dresden and the GDR as a whole just what they stood to lose, official commemorations often set the socialist post-war reconstruction of Dresden in relation to Western destructiveness. In 1952, for instance, the GDR's German Peace Committee (*Deutsches Friedenskomitee*) orchestrated a massive commemoration in Dresden in which the city became symbolic of the will to rebuild, and an inspirational example to follow for the reconstruction of East Berlin. However, this 'will to rebuild of the whole German people' was seen as threatened by the 'Anglo-American warmongers'.[26] The bombed-out Germans, particularly those in the

GDR, were in danger of becoming victims again. In commemoration and books on Dresden in the GDR, the celebration of Dresden's reconstruction followed on from drastic evocations of its ruins and dead.[27] But this sense of having overcome the past was precarious. It was made clear that the Western threat remained. In the 1950s, the SED also tried to make West Germans aware of this threat in the hope that they would support the idea of peaceful German unification under socialist auspices. The German Peace Committee sent out, or at least planned to send out, 'hundreds of thousands' of postcards with this message to West Germany as part of the 1952 Dresden commemoration campaign.[28]

Over time, the SED's interest in the propagandistic commemoration of the bombing dwindled. With the advent of *Ostpolitik* and the signing of the Basic Treaty with West Germany in 1972, improved relations to the Federal Republic became a political goal which would have been endangered by too much explicit retrospective emphasis on 'Anglo-American imperialism'. Accordingly, the state-orchestrated commemorations to mark the twenty-fifth anniversary of the bombing in 1970 were the last large-scale commemorations for more than a decade. But when, on 13 February 1982, a group of 1000 young people with candles gathered in a silent vigil at the ruins of the *Church of Our Lady* (which served as an official memorial against 'war and fascism'), the SED responded by reintroducing large-scale commemorations in 1983.[29] Clearly, officialdom was concerned that the official discourse on Dresden, which remained anti-Western even if it had become less strident, would be displaced by an alternative, grass-roots peace movement discourse in the GDR which would seek to draw attention to the danger of miltarism at home, as well as to human rights' abuses in East Germany. But the resumption of official commemoration did not stop the peace movement, which attempted to interfere with it. During the official commemorative march on 13 February 1989, one individual held up a placard declaring 'Dresden warns no excuses for NATO strategists no military parades on the Republic's birthday'. This was a protest both against NATO *and* the military parade planned for East Berlin in October to celebrate the GDR's fortieth birthday. In the evening of the same day, 500 people gathered at the ruins of the *Church of Our Lady*, one of whom petitioned the GDR for the right to leave by holding up a placard calling for human rights and basic freedoms.[30] However, while turning the message to be learnt from the bombing of Dresden against the SED, the peace protesters did little to challenge the basic perception of those who had suffered in the bombing-raid as victims, and, like the SED, used Dresden as a warning against future victimhood. While there was clearly a tension between official and unofficial acts of commemoration in the 1980s, the positions underpinning these were only in part irreconcilable.

Remembering the bombing of Dresden in art

While official commemoration of the bombing of Dresden in the GDR only became typical as of the early 1950s, the theme found drastic expression already in artistic representations in 1945. In fact, the ruins of Dresden were one of the most frequent motifs in German post-war art. Most famous of all depictions is the series of ink sketches by Wilhelm Rudolph, *Dresden Destroyed* (*Das zerstörte Dresden*, 1945/46), a cycle of 150 drawings showing different parts of the devastated city.[31] Rudolph's sketches are executed with stark strokes, they are dark and threatening, haunted and haunting; the often diagonal cross-hatched lines drawn across the skies above the skeletal buildings recall the trajectory of the bombs. Theodor Rosenhauer's oil-paintings *View of the Japanese Palace in Dresden after the Attack* (*Blick auf das Japanische Palais in Dresden nach dem Angriff*, 1945) and *View of the New Market in Dresden after the Attack* (*Blick auf den Neumarkt in Dresden nach dem Angriff*, 1945) are similarly bleak evocations of the ruins; human figures, small and forlorn, move through the rubble. While Rudolph and Rosenhauer allow the ruins to speak for themselves, Willy Wolff's ink-drawings are a mixture of realism and symbolism, and introduce a note of bitter irony into the depiction. *Entrance to No. 5* (*Eingang Nr. 5*, 1946/47) shows a twisted gateway behind which only a narrow fragment of wall is left standing, while *Parking Lot* (*Parkplatz*, 1946/47) portrays a bent parking-sign, with a wasteland behind it and the ruins of the city in the background. In the context of destruction, signs in the semantic system which regulates urban living would seem to have become meaningless, indeed absurd. But not all of the earliest representations of Dresden's destruction are without hope. Two self-portraits are notable in this regard. In Erich Gerlach's *Self-portrait in front of Ruins* (*Selbstbildnis vor Trümmern*, 1945), the artist looks towards the viewer, with reproach and anger, but also with defiance. Otto Griebel's famous oil-painting *Self-Portrait in front of Dresden Burning* (*Selbstbildnis vor dem brennenden Dresden*, 1945) shows the painter, the flames of the burning city visible over his shoulder, holding an ear of corn – symbol of fertility and rebirth – in his left hand.[32] Individual survival, with an accompanying tenor of determination and orientation towards the future, is set in both Gerlach's and Griebel's self-portraits in contrapuntal relation to destruction.

If there is one motif which recurs again and again in artistic and sculptural reflections on Dresden's destruction, then it is that of mother and child. The preoccupation with this motif reflects, of course, the reality that women and children often suffered most when German cities were bombed. This was particularly the case with Dresden, which was crammed at the time of the February bombings with German evacuees and fugitives from Eastern Europe: many of these were women and children. But the focus on mother and child also represents a contemporary reflection on Raphael's world-famous painting *Sistine Madonna*, which had been acquired for Dresden in 1745. Raphael's sublime painting expresses the strength of maternal protectiveness, the powerful union of mother and child, and yet it also expresses the vulnerability of that bond, and there is concern and sadness in the Madonna's gaze. These ideas were taken up by post-1945 painters when addressing the destruction of Dresden. Some of these mother–child paintings are bleak in the extreme, none more so than Werner Reifarth's ink-sketching *Mother and Dead Child* (*Mutter und totes Kind*, 1945/46). It depicts the agonised pain of a mother at her loss in part expressionist, part surrealist style. Wilhelm Lachnit's moving painting *The Death of Dresden* (*Der Tod von Dresden*, 1945) shows a mother sitting amid glowing red ruins, her face covered by her hand; to her left, in the background, death itself sits with head in hands. The despair of this painting is mitigated by the figure of a child with its arms over the mother's knees, looking towards the viewer. The child's facial expression is one of helplessness, yet in looking up, out and away from the ruins, it would also seem to symbolise the future.

As time passed and the reconstruction of Dresden proceeded apace, the image of women in Dresden paintings and drawings changed. Now, the focus was on that icon of post-war reconstruction in both West and East, the 'Trümmerfrau'. 'Rubble women', a term connoting the enormous contribution made by women not just to clearing away bricks, but also to the whole process of rebuilding, feature in Dresden paintings such as Rudolf Bergander's *Rubble Women* (*Trümmerfrauen*, 1954), Erich Gerlach's *How the Rebuilding of Dresden Began* (*So fing in Dresden der Aufbau an*, 1948) and Josef Hegenbarth's *Rubble Woman* (*Trümmerfrau*, 1949). Hegenbarth's distemper painting of a robust, thick-armed, chubby-lipped rubble woman resting momentarily on her spade as an equally powerful woman thrusts her spade into the ground behind her is a far cry from Lachnit's *The Death of Dresden*.

In Hegenbarth, women are anything but overcome; they have become the overcomers, turning their hand with vigorous self-confidence to the healing of the city's wounds – in the background of the painting, a man looks on as if in deference to the active women in the foreground. The image of the 'rubble woman' was set in stone and became part of Dresden's memorial landscape with the dedication in 1952 of Walter Reinhold's identically named sculpture on the square in front of the Town Hall.

While many paintings from the 1950s onwards focused on Dresden as a symbol of energetic reconstruction and construction – one thinks in this connection of Theodor Rosenhauer's *Reconstructed Elbe Bridge* (*Wiederhergestellte Elbbrücke*, 1953) and Paul Michaelis's *The Building of Dresden's Palace of Culture* (*Bau des Kulturpalastes Dresden*, 1968) – it never lost its association with destruction. Increasingly, however, as that act and state of destruction receded in time, it was its symbolical significance as a historical warning to future generations, rather than its own specific horror that came to interest artists. That symbolical significance was evoked again and again in paintings which were, essentially, reactions to present dangers, such as the Cold War and the nuclear threat. Dresden was quoted in these paintings and drawings as an example of the kind of devastation which many feared was likely to recur. Accordingly, in these 'anti-war' GDR paintings the ruins of Dresden form the background rather than the foreground; the foreground is occupied most frequently by human figures, who were in many cases absent from the bleak townscapes of the post-war representations. In Christian Hasse's *Women Seeing Dresden Burn* (*Frauen sehen das brennende Dresden*, 1957), women, their backs to the viewer, regard the conflagration in despair, while Theodor Rosenhauer's *After the Attack* (*Nach dem Angriff*, 1955) depicts a group of people who have escaped the flames, seeking to console each other as they huddle together. Thus the inferno is communicated through its impact on people, with whose emotion the viewer identifies; as the burning Dresden is only hinted at in these two paintings, its metaphorical significance is highlighted. It stands for *any* destruction and conflagration – past and future.

As GDR painters moved away more and more from socialist realism, paintings with a thematic link to Dresden developed a more symbolic and abstract language. Rudolf Nehmer's *The Ball* (*Die Kugel*, 1971) shows what appears to be a glass ball balancing on the thinnest of wires over rubble, a rusting tin-can, shards from broken bottles and wilted sunflowers; buildings reminiscent of university buildings in

Dresden and Leipzig loom in the background. Nehmer's oil-painting thus sets the ruins of Dresden in relation to environmental pollution and consumerism, rather than the nuclear threat; the future of mankind, like the glass ball, hangs in a slender balance – and depends, perhaps, on the impact of youth, enlightenment and education. The threat of East–West conflict, however, remained a dominant motif. In direct reaction to news of the building of a neutron bomb, Christian Hasse painted a series of paintings among which is *Ash Wednesday* (*Aschermittwoch*, 1982), in which ghostly, carnivalesque figures, escorted by a skeletal, death-like apparition disguised as a military commander, drift skywards from the valley below. Here the reference to the bombing of Dresden is in the depiction of carnival; it was on Shrove Tuesday and Ash Wednesday that Dresden was bombed in February 1945. Carnival is traditionally imagined and acted out as a ritual for driving out the spirits of the night; but here, the dressed-up figures are plucked away from their festivities by the darkest spirit of all – death. With the dread at the prospect of renewed conflict, images of mother and child, as a symbol of life but also of life's vulnerability, returned to paintings referring to Dresden. Erich Gerlach's *The End (Terrible Vision)* (*Ende (Grauenvolle Vision)*, 1983/84) depicts a downcast mother, her child on her knee, in fragmented form against a nightmarish backdrop of Dresden's destruction. Equally pessimistic is Heinz Drache's *The Powerless Angel* (*Der machtlose Engel*, 1981), in which a stiff, almost petrified angel makes its way over the burning city.

Do the paintings and drawings described above show Germans as victims? Art, because it does not use words, can often be more universal in its statements. The artistic depictions of Dresden's destruction in the GDR, give or take a few more obviously politicised paintings, can be read as general comments on the destructiveness of war, acts of mourning and laments for the loss of architectural glories; later, they become warnings against future war. Nevertheless, there is seldom in these depictions an awareness of cause and effect; and they are often characterised by uncritical empathy. Moreover, as any visitor to an art gallery or temporary exhibition in the GDR would know, the official political view was that the bombardment of Dresden was a totally indefensible act of imperialist British–American aggression against innocent German civilians. The reception of these paintings as expressions of indignation, accusation and justifiable German self-pity was thus to a degree predetermined, whatever their artists intended. Equally, while not many artists concerned about the Cold War gave their admonitory paintings titles such as *Say No to NATO Rockets!*

(*Nein zu NATO-Raketen*, the title of a 1984 oil-painting by Gerhard Bondzin), such paintings will often have been interpreted as anti-Western in sentiment even where their anti-war message was not clearly one-sided. Such interpretation was encouraged by exhibitions such as that titled *Dresden: Confession and Duty* from 1985. The catalogue for this exhibition brings together anti-war Dresden paintings in a section called 'Artists for Peace', which is introduced by a text stressing the commitment of the Warsaw Pact to peace, while the United States and its allies are accused of posing a threat to peace.[33] In this context, it is exclusively *East* Germans who are the victims – the *West* Germans, by contrast, are cast in the role of potential perpetrators.

Remembering the bombing of Dresden in literature

The city of Dresden has always been associated with art and architecture; unsurprisingly therefore, perhaps, it was mainly in painting and to a lesser extent sculpture that the theme of the bombing and destruction of the city found expression after 1945. But this does not mean that the theme did not also become a literary one. One of Germany's most famous dramatists, Gerhart Hauptmann, provided what was probably, in the GDR, the most frequently quoted comment on the bombing when he remarked in 1945 that the sight of Dresden's destruction would bring tears again to the eyes of anyone who has forgotten how to cry.[34] But in the 1950s and 1960s, it was lesser literary lights such as Max Zimmering and Hildegard Maria Rauchfuß who took up the theme of this destruction and/or its aftermath, principally in novels.

Max Zimmering was a German-Jewish communist who spent the years of the Third Reich in exile (and internment on the Isle of Man and in Australia) before settling in Dresden after 1945. Initially, he seems to have regarded the destruction of Dresden as the price that had to be paid – as he put it in a poem of 1946 – for 'the numb stupidity' of the German people.[35] But his view was to change, as his 1954 novel *Phosphorus and Lilac* (*Phosphor und Flieder*) demonstrates. *Phosphorus and Lilac* was probably the most widely read of all GDR novels on the bombing of Dresden and its aftermath; it ran to several editions in the 1950s and sold tens of thousands of copies. Essentially, it replicates, in its shape and choreography, the structure and tone of official socialist, anti-Western post-1950 GDR commemoration. It begins with an extremely graphic description of the bombing of Dresden, and of the casualties caused by the supposed strafing of civilians on the banks of the Elbe by low-flying American planes.[36] 'Why are we being punished like this', asks Anna Bergius repeatedly as she flees the flames with her husband [*PL*, 18 and 22]; she receives no answer. Nevertheless, the novel does provide explanations for the bombing, particularly through the dynamic figure of Reichhold, a communist. Far from blaming the bombing on the 'stupidity' of German loyalty to Hitler, Reichhold blames it on the destructive energies of Western imperialism. As he clears away the charred and shrivelled-up bodies from the ruins of Dresden, loading them on to carts, he draws a direct comparison between the Nazi camps and the British–American bombs: 'how few had understood that death in the German concentration camps was but the brother of death from the Anglo-American flying fortresses'. Reichold goes on to interpret the 'flame of Auschwitz' in which millions were burnt as the 'sister of the flame which suffocated and burnt hundreds of thousands of Dresden citizens'. For Reichhold, both the Nazi camps and the destruction of Dresden show the 'true face of imperialism', namely 'the annihilation of human beings' [*PL*, 59]. That Dresden's citizens are comparable to Jewish victims is a point apparently emphasised in the novel by one of the men helping Reichhold to load up bodies. He points out that the Margrave of Meißen had Jews burnt alive during carnival time in 1349 because he owed them money. 'When innocent people are to be burnt to death, our masters apparently prefer to do it at this time – or are we to believe it was pure chance that the Americans and British chose Shrove Tuesday to send down their rain of phosphorus?' [*PL*, 63]. It seems extraordinary that Zimmering, a Jewish victim of Nazism and a regional president of the League of Those Persecuted by Nazism in the GDR (*Vereinigung der Verfolgten des Naziregimes*) until 1952, should so comfortably equate Dresden with Auschwitz. It is also telling. In the GDR, it was not advisable to argue for the special status of Jewish victimhood under Nazism, at least not in the 1950s.

If the British and Americans, as Zimmering's novel suggests, are mass murdering imperialists who bomb Dresden out of destructiveness or the wish to extend their influence into the proposed post-war Soviet zone, then it follows that the citizens of Dresden are *pure* victims – of both the Allies and the Nazis, who are described in the novel as hounding harmless citizens [*PL*, 48]. Upon the absolutely criminal image of the Allies, and the separating out of the evil Nazis from the bulk of the people depends Zimmering's reinvention of the 'people's community' (*Volksgemeinschaft*) as a collective of innocents: 'ordinary folk always have to pay a bitter price', as Reichhold puts it [*PL*, 51]. Yet *Phosphorus and Lilac* is not all bleak. On the contrary: most of the novel is in effect a panegyric to reconstruction after the war. Its principal characters – a former Social Democrat, a former professor, communists, an artist and a writer all persecuted under Nazism – become part of a larger reconstruction collective, namely Dresden's population, who, untainted by Nazism, give themselves over to the task with intact ethical elan. The novel depicts contributions made by its characters to the reconstruction of the Albert Bridge over the Elbe, the *Zwinger* and the Playhouse; towards the end of the novel, the rebuilding of the Semper Opera House is envisaged. While providing accommodation for bombed-out civilians is also a theme in the novel, the focus is clearly on the rebuilding of Dresden's cultural heritage. This might seem surprising, given the aristocratic nature of such heritage. But in *Phosphorus and Lilac* it is made clear that the process of rebuilding by 'the people' represents a socialist reappropriation 'for the people' of elite buildings. When the Playhouse is reopened, Reichhold tells Professor Bergius that, while the facade has remained the same, the auditorium has changed. 'Our basic aim was to get away from "bourgeois court theatre", and create a theatre for the people' [*PL*, 334]. The destruction of Dresden thus also represented a chance to remould that cultural heritage along socialist lines. Dresden's history is similarly remoulded in the novel by stressing its proto-socialist artistic legacy, visible in the participation of Richard Wagner, the singer Wilhelmine Schröder-Devrient and the architect Gottfried Semper in the 1848/49 revolution [*PL*, 61 and 350ff].[37]

Zimmering may seem to shift the emphasis from victimhood to reconstruction, but the two remain connected. His novel implies that the German people have long been the victims of imperialism and capitalist exploitation (in all its forms and historical manifestations), and that only after 1945, in an act of regenerative self-assertion, were they able to take control of their own fate and finally realise the aims of Dresden's suppressed socialist tradition. Their historical victimhood enables us, as readers, to appreciate their right to now become *actors*. In the novel, it becomes inappropriate as the reconstruction proceeds to dwell too much on past victimhood (and indeed perpetration). Thus the artist Jochen Riemeyer follows his oil painting representing 'the face of fascism' [*PL*, 214] with a painting of a 'youthful rubble woman' [*PL*, 307]. The writer-figure in the novel, Wallner, similarly feels inspired to praise rubble women in his poetry, while distancing himself from a pessimistic preoccupation in painting with townscapes showing ruins [*PL*, 241]. The very same sense of need to turn away from the destruction of the past to the construction of the future informs Hildegard Maria Rauchfuß's novel *To Whom the Stones Give Answer* (*Wem die Steine Antwort geben*, 1953). Rauchfuß's novel sets in at the end of the war, and describes a love affair between the sculptor Manfred Rohloff, who is spearheading the rebuilding of the *Zwinger*, and Karla, a fugitive from East Prussia now living in Dresden. Karla's integration into the reconstruction collective under Manfred's tutelage symbolises the integration of the expellees into East German society – a common topos in GDR literature.[38] That she, without herself ever having been a rubble woman, should inspire Wallner's sculpture of the same name confers upon her the right to be considered a true Dresdner, despite her origins in Allenstein.

Yet while Zimmering and Rauchfuß impress on the reader a dynamic sense of national rebirth in pseudo-emancipatory symbols such as the 'rubble woman',[39] this does not mean they believe German victimhood to be definitively a thing of the past – for both novels depict the ever-present threat posed by West Germany and its allies. Thus the character Horrn in Rauchfuß's novel orchestrates the theft of material from the ruins of Dresden for sale over the border: that his shamelessness knows no bounds becomes clear when he considers pilfering supplies reserved for rebuilding the *Zwinger*. In Zimmering's novel, the danger posed by the West is military in nature; at one point, concerned women in a maternity ward discuss the American atomic threat. One fugitive from Upper Silesia (now Poland) reflects on how she has lost everything including her homeland, only now to be faced with the prospect of another war, issuing this time from the United States [*PL*, 414–15]. The dynamic of rebirth and regeneration is thus a precarious one. Zimmering particularly implies a continuity in the narrative of perpetration and victimhood past and future; the 'imperialist' Americans bombed innocent Dresden in 1945, and now they are threatening the peaceful socialist bloc with an even worse scenario of bombing.

Not all Dresden reconstruction literature is as manifestly pro-socialist and anti-Western as the above novels. Karl Otto's cycle of sonnets *Shining Legacy* (*Leuchtendes Erbe*, 1956) celebrates the restoration of the *Zwinger* in altogether more broadly humanist terms. Nevertheless, one of the sonnets laments the 'annihilation' of Dresden and 'the absurdity, the deceitfulness, the treachery' which the poet believes to have triggered it;[40] and another contains the verse: 'And there came men and women, unbidden, / The wounds of annihilation on their faces, / To rebuild what violence destroyed.'[41] Here too, then, the

Dresdener are victims turned actors; that they have the strength for *construction* after facing *destruction* redounds to their moral credit. A work which certainly eschews direct politicisation of the theme of the bombing is Eberhard Panitz's *The Fires Subside* (*Die Feuer sinken*) of 1960. In fact Panitz's novel, while set during and after the bombing, only uses it as a backdrop to his real interest: the search among the ruins for a young boy who has made off with an SS pistol and dog, and for an escaped communist prisoner. Panitz's interest is also in the witch-hunt atmosphere in Dresden in the final weeks of the war, as well as in the mood of suspicion and betrayal among SS men as the Soviets approach. The devastation of Dresden is but a physical manifestation of moral disarray and general chaos. Not that Panitz abandons the theme of victimhood so common in 1950s literature; only here Andreas (the boy) and Franke (the communist) are clearly the victims of the increasingly neurotic Nazis.

In time, literary references to the bombing of Dresden in the GDR certainly became more personalised in tone. Of no work is this more true than of Panitz's story *My Father's Tram* (*Meines Vaters Straßenbahn*, 1979), in which a now adult narrator recounts his childhood experiences in Dresden during and after the war (Panitz was himself born in Dresden in 1932). Here, the bombing is but one of a series of events which impact on the narrator; it is given no greater weight than these other events, any more than the theme of the ruins is dwelt upon. Panitz does not shy away, in his description of the post-war period, from describing hunger, black marketeering, hoarding, the rapid discarding of past identities and the merciless way schoolchildren make fun of a schoolteacher of Jewish background who had been incarcerated by the Nazis in Hohnstein. Panitz's story thus appears to offer a more honest and differentiated appraisal to that provided by Rauchfuß and Zimmering. It also seems to offer a less positive message. While the narrator's father joins the communist party after 1945, he is soon thrown out. And while he does contribute to the reconstruction by helping to lay tram tracks, his refusal to be treated for gallstones – which leads to his death – appears as a wilful act of self-destruction, flying in the face of the reconstructionist ethos. The most remarkable aspect of the story is that Panitz depicts the father as weakened and probably traumatised by his spell in a Soviet POW camp.[42] The theme of the rape of German women by the Soviet occupiers is also, albeit briefly, referred to in the story – if only in the form of a rumour.[43] Panitz does not criticise the Soviets directly, but that his book got past the GDR's censors is still surprising. For all this, Panitz's

My Father's Tram still generates a view of the Germans as victims – explicitly of Nazi fanatics determined to defend Dresden at all costs after the bombing, implicitly of the Soviets.

The 1960s, 1970s and 1980s saw the publication of many poems in which the bombing of Dresden was a theme. Several important GDR poets, not least Heinz Czechowski (1935), Volker Braun (1939), Bernhard Tragelehn (1936) and Karl Mickel (1935) were born in Dresden (as were Thomas Rosenlöcher (1947) and Durs Grünbein (1962), poets whose reputations have been established since unification in 1990). Each of these poets approached Dresden's past in their own, personal way, and developed a discourse different to that of official SED Dresden commemoration. Yet in some ways poetic and official discourse were not so far apart in the post-1960s' era; the theme of German victimhood was never far away. Examples from the work of one key poet, Heinz Czechowski, will illustrate this.

In a perhaps paradoxical mixture of optimism and pessimism, official GDR commemorative discourse on Dresden was often characterised by a forward-looking emphasis on peaceful socialist reconstruction after the bombing on the one hand, and condemnation of the West for its past and present aggressiveness on the other. Czechowski's poetry is more uniformly pessimistic. In one of his earliest poems, 'Early Morning' ('Frühe', 1963), the poet writes: 'so that we don't forget/ Where we came from,/ The day will not accept lies:/ Between burnt stones/ The gorse blooms yellow in the wind.'[44] Here, as throughout Czechowski's poems over several decades, the destruction of Dresden recurs as a traumatic experience which the poet is unable to overcome. Nowhere is this trauma more succinctly and bitingly captured than in his most famous poem, 'To a City Lost in the Flames' ('Auf eine im Feuer versunkene Stadt'). Czechowksi evokes here the contrast between the cheerful atmosphere of Shrove Tuesday in February 1945, and the sudden plunge into destruction, as the masked celebrants of carnival are forced 'down into the cellar, breathing in/ The mouldering smell of their own/ Decay'.[45] The bombing is experienced as a cynical shattering of a pre-lapsarian idyll. It is precisely this dystopic devastation that renders Dresden, for Czechowski, a symbol of the naivety of faith in progress. Certainly the poet, for himself, expresses a tension in 'To a City' between the future coming towards him, 'worked out in all its details', and the fact that he still sees the city in flames, while 'the time I have left behind me,/ Cries'. The dead of the bombing of Dresden reappear in Czechowski's poems; no degree of reconstruction, it seems, can lay the ghost of the past.[46]

Not only does Czechowski undermine the official optimistic reconstruction rhetoric by showing how thinly it conceals the backward pull of traumatic memory, he also has the temerity to suggest that the threat to Dresden's present and future comes not necessarily (just) from the West. In 'Down by the River' ('Auf den Plätzen am Fluß'), the poet expresses the fear that the message of Dresden's dead is one he will carry with him into oblivion, 'like the river carries its phenol and/ The dying fish which/ No longer have a name'.[47] Thus the dead of the bombing are set in relation to the fatal effects of pollution. The threat in the present which Czechowski identifies in 'Down by the River' is one of industrialisation, not Western aggression, and given the antiquated state of much GDR industry, it is clearly a domestic threat.

Yet Czechowski's poetry also conformed to official discourse in its view of the bombing itself and the destruction of Dresden, which it condemns often through sarcasm, irony and graphic imagery. Word coinages such as 'Shrove Tuesday freight'[48] encapsulate the perceived incongruence of carnival and destructiveness, and come close to accusing the Allies of cruel cynicism and even sacrilege, while expressions such as 'The streets./ Desecrated with corpses' certainly do imply an act of sacrilege.[49] Thus while Czechowski's poetry avoids forward-looking SED rhetoric, it partakes of official anti-Western discourse in the indignation of its language, an indignation underyling which is a view of Dresden's citizens as victims of an act of supreme barbarism.[50]

Conclusion

The above discussion of the reception of the bombing of Dresden in the GDR is not meant to imply that West Germans did not have occasion to remember that city's destruction. David Irving's book on the bombing, in which he vastly inflated the number of victims (135,000), appeared in West Germany in translation in 1964 as *Der Untergang Dresdens* (English: *The Destruction of Dresden*, 1963). According to Matthias Neutzner, it led to a view of Dresden in West Germany as a unique catastrophe worse than any other aerial attack – including the ones on Hiroshima and Nagasaki – in history.[51] Thus in the West, too, memory of Dresden was associated, not least thanks to Irving's figures, with memory of German suffering. By and large, at least, western memory of the bombing of Dresden remained free of anti-Americanism. Often, however, it was combined with anti-socialist regret that the city now lay in the GDR. The Saxon

Homeland Society (*Bundeslandsmannschaft Sachsen*), an organisation representing Saxons living in West Germany, regularly remembered the bombing, but it particularly liked to recall the fact that Dresden was now an 'unfree' city in an aggressive socialist zone. The TV and radio correspondent and producer Peter von Zahn, for instance, delivered a lecture to the Homeland Society in 1965 in which he stressed that the peoples who bombed Dresden and London were now working together to prevent a renewed war, this time emanating from the socialist east.[52]

The memory of the bombing war against Germany in contemporary Germany generally, and of the bombing of Dresden specifically is, I would therefore argue, an extension and broadening of a long-existing trend. In many ways, Jörg Friedrich's *The Fire* represents a radicalisation of GDR anti-Western rhetoric.[53] Far from being the first commentator to apply words such as 'annihilation' or 'massacre' to the bombing of Germany, Friedrich is following in the footsteps of authors like Max Seydewitz, General Director of Dresden's State Art Collection from 1955 till 1968, whose 1955 book on the bombing of Dresden abounds with terms such as 'massacre', 'murder', 'annihilation', 'barbaric', 'criminal', 'violation of human rights' and the like.[54] Friedrich thus seems to be welding together the anti-Americanism of the 1968 generation with the anti-Westernism of SED propaganda. Certainly every 'rediscovery' of German suffering has specific roots, and Friedrich's book is rooted in the self-confident approach to the Nazi past cultivated by Red-Green (see the introduction), historiographically underpinning as it does the 'right' of Germans in the present to refuse to go along with the American–British bombing of Afghanistan and Iraq. The most significant aspect of *The Fire*, however, is probably its contribution to emotionally reuniting a still-divided nation. The message of his book is that east and west Germans have a common history of victimhood at the hands of the Americans and British, for the bombers dropped their loads all over the country. Friedrich applies SED Dresden rhetoric to the fate of *all* German cities in the bombing war, creating a tapestry of national suffering. Hence his chapter on the bombing of Dresden juxtaposes it with the bombing of the western town of Darmstadt.[55] The mushrooming of publications over the last five years detailing the bombing of individual cities in east and west Germany indicates that Friedrich's book is expressive of a trend.[56] Also indicative of this trend was the recent TV film *Dresden*, broadcast on Second German Television in two parts on 28 February and 7 March 2006. In this sentimental tale, a British bomber-pilot is redeemed from the sin of bombing Germany by the love of a German woman. After ten years of bitterly debating the legacy of the GDR, the Germans can agree that, as far as the bombing war against German cities was concerned, Ulbricht and Honecker got it right: it was a crime.

7

Victims of the Berlin Wall

Pertti Ahonen

Debates about German victimhood and suffering in post-unification Germany have focused primarily on the Nazi period and its aftermath. Two groups of Germans in particular have stood in the limelight: expellees forced from their homes in the East and civilians sucked into the maelstrom of Allied bombing raids against the Reich. Other kinds of German war victims have also attracted extensive public attention, before and after unification, including *Wehrmacht* soldiers brutalised by military campaigns, especially on the eastern front; POWs detained as a result of those operations, particularly by the Soviets; and women raped and otherwise victimised by Allied forces, primarily by the much-dreaded Red Army. As other contributions to this volume show, such victim discussions are no post-unification novelty. Most key elements of the recent discourses were present in earlier decades as well, although there have, of course, been various changes and adjustments over time.

But not all public narratives of German suffering in the post-1945 period were rooted in the Nazi years alone. German victimhood also possessed a more contemporary visage reflective of the bitter rivalry between the two German states during the Cold War. Both the Federal Republic and the German Democractic Republic (GDR) were eager to play up the suffering inflicted on their citizens by the rival regime beyond the Iron Curtain. An accentuation of the sins and savagery of the 'other side' promised major potential benefits for each polity: propaganda points at home and abroad, gains in domestic identity-building, and diversion of public attention from more mundane problems closer to home. Although several different victim groups played a role in these efforts at political point-scoring and mud-slinging, both countries assigned special significance to a particular site of suffering, prominent both as a symbol of the traumatic division of the nation and, even more importantly, as an incubator of one very concrete human tragedy after another: the inter-German boundary in general and its highest-profile segment – the Berlin Wall – in particular. Among the myriad tragedies associated with this border, it was the violent deaths that drew the most attention and became the focal point of extensive victimisation discourses in both states.

This chapter analyses the prominent – but hitherto largely overlooked – position occupied by victims of violent deaths at the Berlin Wall in public discussions of German suffering during and after the Cold War. As the pages below will show, prior to 1989, both German states publicised and instrumentalised killings at the Wall for political gain. The Wall's victims remained a salient issue after unification too, particularly during the early 1990s, as trials of East German border-guards, military commanders and politicians charged with ordering and carrying out killings at the Wall captured public attention. Although novel in some ways, this post-unification discourse of deaths at the Wall also had many links to its Cold War precedents, to which we shall now turn.

Narratives of the Wall in West Germany

During the Cold War, the narrative of the Wall and its victims that held the most sway, within and without Germany, was the version constructed in the Federal Republic. It was a highly politicised narrative, propagated primarily by the country's political elites and mass media, which highlighted the very real suffering caused by the barrier in the middle of the former capital and sought to extract maximum propaganda advantage from it. The starting point was to denounce the Wall as an abomination and living proof of the depravity of Communism. Predictably, such censure peaked during the first half of the 1960s, in the aftermath of the Wall's construction. At the time, the press and broadcasting media in West Germany and West Berlin seized every opportunity to condemn the 'Wall of Shame' (*Schandmauer*) and to contrast the vitality of 'the modern Berlin' west of that line with the subdued, brooding mood of terror and oppression allegedly prevalent on the other side.[1] A particularly effective propaganda clip, shown to millions of movie-goers as part of a cinema news trailer, highlighted the abnormality of the situation with footage of a group of young

West Berlin boys whose joyful round of football practice ended in tears once one of them accidentally kicked the ball over the Wall.[2] Another representative trailer juxtaposed dramatic scenes of the building of the Wall with rousing political commentary: 'We cannot accept ... the fact that people in Berlin and in the Soviet zone are condemned to lose their freedom. ... We simply refuse to recognise barbed wire as the ultimate political value.'[3]

A similar tone prevailed in the pronouncements and publications issued by governmental authorities in Bonn and West Berlin. According to declarations by the West German government shortly after the Wall went up on 13 August 1961, the East German actions had caused 'indescribable ... human distress' and thereby exposed the 'brutal inhumanity' of the underlying system.[4] Bonn's broader conclusion from this evidence was that the erection of the Wall had amounted to a 'declaration of bankruptcy' by the Communist rulers. According to the Minister for All-German Affairs, a regime compelled to 'install a dividing line of barbed wire, concrete walls and bayonets' possessed 'no legitimacy' – in obvious contrast to the democratic system of the Federal Republic.[5]

Although the very existence of the Wall gave the West Germans a powerful propaganda tool *vis-à-vis* the GDR, the numerous violent deaths of westbound refugees at that barricade provided an even stronger trump card, which the country's political and media elites played to their advantage consistently and effectively. The typical pattern of representation started to emerge as soon as the first two victims perished on 22 August 1961, barely a week after the East German authorities had begun to construct the line of barbed wire and concrete across the city. The two earliest deaths were typically gruesome: Ida Siekmann, a 58-year-old woman, jumped from the window of her third-floor apartment, located directly on the border between East and West, suffered serious injuries as she hit the ground, and died in a West Berlin ambulance. An even crueller fate befell the 21-year old Günter Litfin, who was shot in the head by a GDR transport police officer while trying to swim to the western shore of the River Spree near the city centre. Both cases received immediate and extensive attention in the West German and West Berlin media, which expressed admiration for the courage of the victims and dismay at the brutality of the East German authorities.[6] More deliberative reflection and commemoration quickly ensued: governmental commentary that portrayed the two cases as representative 'refugee tragedies' expressive of the 'hopelessness and desperation' rampant within the 'oversized prison' of the Soviet Zone; candlelight vigils held in memory of the victims; crosses and floral wreaths deposited at or near their places of death to admonish others to reflect on these human tragedies and their political background.[7]

Many other deaths soon followed, with similar public responses. But on the western side one tragedy in particular stood out as the paradigmatic, highly publicised and instrumentalised narrative of suffering at the Wall: the shooting of 18-year-old Peter Fechter near the Checkpoint Charlie border-crossing in the heart of Berlin on 17 August 1962. The tragedy occurred as Fechter, a construction worker, tried to flee to the West together with a friend and colleague, Helmut Kulbeik. The two young men, who had grown frustrated with their lives in the GDR and resolved to turn their backs on the system, dashed into the border strip in the middle of the afternoon and got within a few meters of the Wall before coming under intense fire from East German border-guards. Kulbeik managed to scale the barrier and land in West Berlin uninjured, but his friend was not so lucky. Fechter was struck by a single bullet in the back that caused massive injuries. He fell to the ground just short of the Wall and lay there for the next 50 minutes, groaning in pain and pleading for help. West Berlin authorities were unable to reach the fatally wounded young man, and East German border guards also failed to react, apparently in part because of disorganisation and in part because they feared possible retaliatory action by the West Berlin police. By the time GDR officials emerged to carry the wounded youngster away, nearly an hour after the shooting, it was too late: the unconscious Fechter was pronounced dead on arrival in a hospital.[8]

Although the circumstances surrounding Peter Fechter's death did not differ sharply from those characteristic of many other shootings at the Wall – the bold escape attempt, its abrupt end amidst a hail of bullets, even the GDR authorities' nonchalant attitude towards a severely wounded escapee were all frequent occurrences – the confluence of the timing and the location made the case uniquely suited for politicised use by the West Germans. The shooting occurred just a few days after the first anniversary of the Wall's construction, a sombre event that had been marked by a barrage of media commentary, public commemoration, and organised protest in West Berlin and the Federal Republic. It took place at the very centre of Berlin, next to Checkpoint Charlie – a symbolically significant site at which select foreigners, but not Germans, could cross the borderline – in a relatively open area that gave West Berliners the opportunity to witness the events from the streets and the surrounding buildings. Even more importantly, the media presence was exceptionally high: by coincidence, a West German television team was filming a documentary about the Wall in the immediate vicinity, and, partly as a consequence, various other reporters also happened to be present.

As a result of these special circumstances, Peter Fechter's death became an instant *cause célèbre* in the West. In part, the reaction was one of spontaneous popular outrage, evident in the chants of 'murderers, murderers' aimed at the East German guards by a crowd of several hundred West Berliners during the incident itself, and in subsequent protest demonstrations that escalated into downright riots over the next few days.[9] But, as usual, it was the contributions of media representatives and politicians that gave broader and more enduring political significance to the tragedy. The press launched immediate broadsides against the East German rulers. One West Berlin daily viewed the latest killing as further evidence of the fact that 'refugees [had] become game park targets for Ulbricht's thugs', while another urged its readers to keep 'adding up the points in the blood-drenched guilt account of Ulbricht and his accomplices' so that they could be 'counted ... when the hour strikes'.[10] West Berlin mayor Willy Brandt expressed his 'profound indignation' at 'the horrible violation of human rights at the Wall', a sentiment echoed by many others in the West Berlin and West German governments.[11] But the pithiest crystallisation of the prevailing political sentiment came from the head of the central organisation of West German labour unions, who concluded that 'a system which needs these methods to maintain control of the people is inhumane and does not have the right to rule over a population of seventeen million.'[12]

This politicised portrayal of individual suffering quickly became institutionalised as Peter Fechter's death assumed broader significance as a Western symbol of victimisation at the Berlin Wall. The West German government kept the case in the domestic and international limelight through various means, including official statements and publications, such as a 1962 'Yellow Book' distributed by the country's Foreign Office, in which written and photographic evidence of Fechter's death served as a particularly flagrant illustration of the suffering caused by the illegitimate pseudo-regime in East Berlin.[13] A similar message reverberated in the print and broadcasting media throughout the Federal Republic and beyond, while within West Berlin the most important development was the emergence of enduring commemorative rituals. A memory site dedicated to Peter Fechter arose almost immediately. Within hours of the shooting, passers-by began bringing flowers to a spot at the Wall directly across from where the young man had bled to death, and over the next few days a wooden cross was erected at the same location.[14] The cross became an informal memorial for Fechter, which for years drew a steady stream of visitors and, on anniversaries of the Wall's erection and of Fechter's shooting, served as the venue for ceremonies to commemorate the victim and to reiterate the political implications of his suffering.[15] Even more importantly, however, Peter Fechter's brutal death remained in the limelight because of the ready availability of exceptionally striking visual evidence of it. The film cameras and photo lenses present ensured that several of the images of that fateful afternoon – particularly a picture of Fechter lying right next to the Wall, curled up and helpless in a pool of his own blood, and another of his limp, unconscious body being carried away, roughly and haphazardly, by four East German border-guards – acquired iconic status as widely propagated and instantly recognisable symbols of the senseless suffering caused by the Wall.

But West German attempts to discredit the GDR through politicised narratives of the Wall and its tragedies were not purely contemporary in character. They also drew on a predictable historical precedent: the Third Reich. Attempts to use the Wall as a way of tarring the East German regime with the brown brush of Nazi associations began as soon as the barrier had gone up on 13 August 1961. On the next day, a mass-circulation West German daily concluded that 'Ulbricht has now ... turned the Soviet Zone into a concentration camp'.[16] Other publications denounced East German soldiers stationed at the Wall as 'Ulbricht's concentration camp guards' whose 'immediate predecessors' had been the 'execution commandos of the SS and the SA that introduced the blood-soaked practice of shooting those who had "tried to escape"'.[17] Politicians and journalists also equated the Third Reich and the GDR in more sweeping ways. Shortly after the Wall's erection, an assistant mayor of West Berlin proclaimed that 'Hitler live[d] on in the [Soviet] Zone', while a subsequent newspaper editorial insisted that 'Fascism' still goose-stepped along in that polity, albeit in a 'red' rather than 'brown' incarnation.[18]

Notably, these comparisons and analogies were drawn in terms that conformed with the broader patterns of conceptualising the Nazi era established in the Federal Republic during the 1950s. The totalitarian paradigm, still in its heyday in the early 1960s, underpinned much of the rhetoric. According to a widely circulated government pamphlet about the Wall and its background, the 'Soviet Zone' was a totalitarian system, closely akin to both the Soviet Union and the Third Reich, an 'unequalled kind of tyranny' that atomised and terrorised society, leaving next to no room for protest or other types of non-conformity.[19] The regime was run by 'a small group of fanatical functionaries' largely reliant on 'terror', while the vast majority of the population suffered under this yoke, powerless and oppressed.[20]

An equation of the East German and Nazi regimes along totalitarian lines offered obvious benefits for the West German polity in its propaganda battle with the rival system across the Elbe. Such argumentation undermined the GDR's legitimacy while simultaneously excusing the absence of large-scale protest in that state as a mere sign of popular powerlessness in the face of overwhelming terror. It stressed the general superiority of the Federal Republic, whose democratic political system marked a happy departure from the darkness of totalitarianism, past and present. It sustained existing, largely exculpatory and apologetic portrayals of the Third Reich as a totally controlled society in which the vast majority of Germans had been victims, not perpetrators. And it conferred victim status upon the vast majority of Germans in the GDR and – to a more limited degree – even upon the people of West Berlin and the Federal Republic, who were also harmed by the Communist-imposed curtailment of normal human contacts. To reinforce the point about ongoing German victimisation, West German commentators even drew suggestive parallels between the suffering of the East German population and that of Jewish victims of Nazism, building on rhetorical patterns established in previous post-war discourses that had served to elide or relativise German guilt for the Third Reich's crimes. A governmental commentary likened East Germany's coercive measures against parts of its population to a 'pogrom', while a respected weekly compared the Wall in Berlin to a similar barrier constructed some two decades before: 'the Wall around the Warsaw ghetto'.[21]

This kind of suggestive rhetoric rife with Nazi allusions was primarily a feature of the 1960s, particularly the early to middle years of the decade. From the late 1960s onwards such language increasingly faded from West German public discourse. One obvious reason for that trend was the rise of détente and the accompanying emergence of more normalised relations between the two German states. But changes in West German perceptions of the Nazi period also played an important causal role. As an increasingly critical view of state–society relations during the Third Reich gained ground in the country's public debates, pushing aside earlier apologias, uncomfortable questions arose about the behaviour of ordinary Germans and about possible continuities between the Nazi era and the Federal Republic. In this atmosphere, the use of Nazi tropes as propaganda weapons against the GDR lost much of its appeal.[22]

At the same time, the overall level of public attention devoted to the victims of the Wall in West Germany also declined. To be sure, spectacular deaths – such as that of Burkhard Niering, an East German border-guard killed by a sniper at Checkpoint Charlie in January 1974 while trying to zigzag his way to the West, holding two of his colleagues hostage, or that of Chris Gueffroy, who became the Wall's last shooting victim when a bullet to the heart ended his impulsive escape attempt in February 1989 – still elicited extensive coverage and commentary from politicians and the media alike. Key anniversaries, particularly those of the Wall's construction on 13 August, continued to be commemorated with wreath-laying ceremonies, speeches and other rituals, at least in West Berlin. And publicity materials put out by the West German government drew attention to the 'murderous border' that divided the nation and proved the GDR to have been 'unable to keep up in the open competition of the systems'.[23] But the passion and intensity that had characterised the relevant discourse during the first half of the 1960s gradually diminished. Forgetting and inertia did their work, particularly in areas beyond West Berlin itself. Revealingly, by the late 1970s a small West German town that had once named a street after Peter Fechter had to turn to the West Berlin government for assistance in trying to assemble basic background information about him for a new catalogue of street names.[24]

The decline in West German public attention to the Wall and its victims was, again, partly a function of the changing political situation: an overly aggressive emphasis on blood spilled at the inter-German border seemed inappropriate in an era of increasingly extensive interaction between the two states. But the situation also resulted, in part, from the diminishing number of deaths at the borderline. As the East German authorities fine-tuned their border-control system, early detection and prevention of escapes became the norm, and fewer individuals reached the Wall itself. But the system was never perfect, as the shooting of Chris Gueffroy as late as February 1989 demonstrates. Killings continued until the very end of the GDR's existence, and so did West German interest in them. That interest may have flagged in intensity, but it never disappeared, and it was to increase again after unification.

Narratives of the Wall in East Germany

The dominant public narrative of the Berlin Wall and its victimology produced in the Federal Republic was challenged head-on by a competing, but less widely promulgated discourse emanating from the GDR. Like its western counterpart, the East German version was highly politicised and instrumentalised for Cold War purposes, and it turned much of the western narrative on its head.

The East German authorities enjoyed an advantage over their western rivals in their greater ability to control the public message they put out, thanks to the more centralised and coercive nature of their polity. But they also faced a massive disadvantage: the Wall was unpopular not only in the West but also in the GDR.[25] As a result, the first task for the East German rulers was to explain, above all to their own citizens, why its construction had been necessary. The answer, repeated time and again in governmental statements, official publications, and the news media, revolved around a particular view of victimisation. According to the official line, the building of the 'protective wall' (*Schutzwall*) had been an unavoidable move of self-defence to guard East Berlin, the GDR, and ultimately the entire community of socialist states against the 'warmongers, criminals and dangerous adventurers of all ilks' lurking in West Germany and particularly West Berlin.[26] As long as the border between East and West Berlin had remained open, 'influential circles in West Germany and West Berlin' had misused that situation for 'planning and preparing direct political and military aggression against the GDR', including 'trafficking in human beings' – a code phrase for the westward mass flight of East Germans – 'espionage and sabotage', as well as 'economic subversion' that had cost the East German state 'at least 30 billion DM'.[27] Even worse, the ultimate aim of these actions had been to provoke a major war. By foiling such nefarious schemes through the building of the Berlin Wall, the GDR – 'the first peaceful state of workers and peasants in German history' – had done nothing less than save world peace.[28]

The threat from the West had not disappeared on 13 August 1961, however. Continued vigilance – particularly through the maintenance of a sophisticated system of border fortifications – remained imperative because the enemies of peace and socialism still carried on their dirty work, especially from West Berlin. According to the East German government, the 'lives and security of [its] citizens' continued to be jeopardised by a 'full panoply of the most brutal, inhumane crimes' planned and actually committed by the West, ranging from bomb attacks and other kinds of sabotage to the infiltration of the GDR by Western agents and the kidnapping and killing of East German citizens.[29]

But who exactly were the warmongers and saboteurs in the West? To address this question, the East German narrative placed the ongoing events in a broader historical context, drawing on the Nazi past in a way that – although different from the West German equivalent in interpretative content – shared with its rival a close correspondence to a broader established discourse about the Third Reich and an ultimately exculpatory and victim-building social function. The East German narrative posited a close continuity between the Third Reich and the Federal Republic. In a representative statement, a well-known propaganda film about divided Berlin traced 'a direct road from Hitler's Third Reich to the Adenauer era' for most 'Nazi criminals'.[30] But in keeping with the ideological and historical meta-narrative prevalent in the GDR, the key point was neither continuity on the level of individuals, nor a specific link between Nazism and the Federal Republic. It was rather the generic circumstance of capitalism as the structural basis for fascism, whether in the context of the 1930s and 1940s or that of present-day West Germany. This structurally rooted fascist potential explained the threat faced by East Germany, justified the defensive *Schutzwall* in Berlin, and exposed the illegitimacy of the Federal Republic as an unreformed morass of reaction, in contrast to the peace-loving and progressive GDR.

The prevailing meta-narrative of fascism also underpinned a far-ranging East German discourse of victimisation directly linked to the Wall. All structural preconditions notwithstanding, the party line contended that in fascist or proto-fascist regimes the rulers and beneficiaries constituted just a small minority of the population. This was the official interpretation applied to the Third Reich, with obvious exculpatory implications: the system had been ruled by a narrow layer of capitalist elites and their political pawns, while the large majority of average Germans had simply suffered under this iron fist. Similar power relations also allegedly prevailed in the Federal Republic. The people in charge constituted 'the most reactionary wing' of the ruling class, drawn from 'militarist and revanchist circles', who duped members of the lumpenproletariat – 'loafers' and 'work-shy riff-raff' of different stripes – to conduct the dirty work of physical attacks, agitation and sabotage.[31] Apart from this thin layer of perpetrators, however, the majority of West Germans were oppressed and victimised by the existing system. In support of this point, the East German press argued, for example, that the demonstrations following Peter Fechter's shooting in August 1962 had actually been pro-fascist rallies, intended in large part to terrorise West Berlin's working class districts.[32]

The inhabitants of the GDR could allegedly breathe much more freely, given the just, socialist system in which they lived. But they, too, faced a constant threat of aggression from reactionary, revanchist elements in the West. The protective *Schutzwall* and the guards who patrolled it did their best to contain that threat. But the potential of suffering and victimisation in the hands of western aggressors remained, as illustrated most vividly by a number of highly publicised violent deaths at the German–German border in general and the Berlin Wall in particular. However, the deaths played up by the East German publicity machine were very different from those headlined by its West German counterpart. Escapees shot down in the border strip received barely a mention in the GDR's media, and when they did, the accompanying commentary was dismissive and abusive. Peter Fechter, for example, was described by the official Communist Party newspaper as a 'provocateur caught in the act' who had only himself to blame for his death.[33] By contrast, the Wall's true victims were East German border-guards killed in the line of duty, while defending the socialist motherland against external aggression and infiltration.

According to the official East German count, 25 GDR guards lost their lives on the German–German border. Most were shot in connection with escape attempts, often in murky circumstances. The first death occurred in August 1949 – even before the GDR had been formally founded – and the last in March 1985. Seven of the victims perished at the Berlin Wall.[34] Each case received extensive publicity in East Germany. Politicians, other public figures, and the mass media extolled the dead men as victims and heroes at once: victims of the western fascist and proto-fascist forces that had caused their deaths, directly or indirectly, and heroes who had made the ultimate sacrifice for peace and socialism. The immediate publicity barrage surrounding each death was followed by further waves of politically instrumentalised attention and commemoration: highly publicised funeral rites, frequent commentary in tailor-made publications and the general media, prominent memorials and other monuments, choreographed commemorative ceremonies on key anniversaries, and so on. As in the Federal Republic, these efforts peaked during the early years of the Wall, particularly the 1960s. But they also persisted thereafter, forfeiting much less of their urgency than their West German equivalents. The dead guards remained crucial symbols of victimisation and tools of political mobilisation through the remainder of the GDR's existence. A good example of this process at work is the public afterlife of the death that arguably generated the most sustained publicity blitz of all: the shooting of 21-year-old border-guard Sergeant Egon Schultz on 5 October 1964.

Schultz lost his life on a dark night in the inner courtyard of an East Berlin apartment building, just a stone's throw from the Wall. He and several fellow border-guards rushed to the site on the orders of secret police agents who had discovered what became known in the West as Tunnel 57: a 140-metre-long passage connecting the basement of an empty West Berlin bakery to an abandoned outdoor toilet in East Berlin. During the previous day and a half, this tunnel – prepared meticulously over the preceding six months by a group of semi-professional, West Berlin-based escape organisers (*Fluchthelfer*) – had enabled a total of 57 people to crawl their way out of the GDR. Unfortunately for Schultz, the operation was still in progress and two of the *Fluchthelfer* were hiding in the courtyard when he and the other border-guards arrived. As chaos and panic broke out, one of the escape organisers pulled out a pistol and fired it several times while he and his associate ran for the tunnel opening. Schultz, apparently hit, cried out and fell to the ground, whereupon a comrade behind him started firing his submachine gun into the unlit courtyard. When the dust had settled a few minutes later, the escape organisers had escaped, unhurt. But Egon Schultz lay on the ground, shot dead.[35]

To the GDR authorities, the young border-guard's tragic demise presented a heaven-sent propaganda opportunity for attacking the West and promoting social cohesion at home. Schultz's personal qualities made him an ideal symbolic figure. The deceased had been a handsome young man, with a serious, friendly look on his face and a schoolteacher's diploma in his pocket. Even more conveniently, he had been a convinced socialist: a child of working-class parents from Rostock, Schultz had played an active role in the ruling Socialist Unity Party (SED), its youth organ Free German Youth and the Society for German–Soviet Friendship.[36] But it was the circumstances surrounding his death that really turned the case into a GDR propagandist's dream. The young man had been killed on East German territory, in a shoot-out with shadowy western intruders uncannily like the dangerous proto-fascist agents demonised in the GDR's official rhetoric. Even more fittingly, the putative western aggressors had left behind suitably incriminating material: a search of the courtyard yielded a pistol, dropped by one of the *Fluchthelfer*, as well as two gas masks traceable to the West Berlin police.[37] The case for at least semi-official West German involvement was strengthened when details of the tunnel's funding became known: the activists had received sizeable subsidies not only from print and TV journalists but also from the West Berlin branch of the ruling CDU party.[38] On top of all this sinister evidence, the timing of the incident provided the East Germans with yet another trump card. Surely it could not be a coincidence that such aggression had occurred on 5 October 1964, merely two days before the fifteenth anniversary of the GDR's founding?

All these factors made Egon Schultz's death the perfect occasion for a massive GDR propaganda blitz, and the authorities seized the opportunity with gusto. The press immediately declared Schultz to have been 'treacherously murdered' by 'West Berlin agents'.[39] Similar rhetoric thundered on in the East German media for weeks, and its tenor intensified with the extravagant funeral ceremonies held for Schultz in both Berlin and Rostock, his hometown. Erich Honecker, the SED Politburo member who had organised the Wall's construction, pulled out all the stops in his official eulogy, hammering hard on both the black keys of accusatory victimisation and the white ones of integrative legend-building. He described the young man's death as a shocking moment that compelled the GDR to condemn 'a system that turns murder into a political weapon'. And he praised Schultz as a 'true child of our Republic' who had given 'all that you possessed: your young, glowing life' – a sacrifice that obligated other East Germans 'to hold our weapons even more firmly so that our socialist Fatherland is reliably and securely protected'.[40] In another publicity-savvy campaign, the regime pressed formal charges against Schultz's putative assassins, demanding from West Berlin full co-operation, including the extradition of the suspects. Predictably, the campaign failed. Although West Berlin prosecutors did conduct a judicial investigation, the *Fluchthelfer* only received minor fines for the illegal possession of firearms. This was in many ways the ideal outcome for the GDR authorities, who could attack the rival German state as a lawless jungle where even murderers were allowed to 'run around freely'.[41]

But the political instrumentalisation of Schultz's death in the GDR stretched far beyond the incident's immediate aftermath. The regime also made concentrated efforts to stamp its interpretation of his demise on the country's public memory. Various memorials to Schultz were unveiled, including a monument in the Rostock cemetery and several commemorative plaques in central Berlin, which pointed an accusatory finger at the 'West Berlin agents' who had 'treacherously murdered' this fine young man.[42] Such memory sites provided the venue for secular pilgrimages and elaborate commemorative ceremonies, most notably on anniversaries of the Wall's erection. Particularly on these occasions, celebrated with great fanfare from 1966 onwards, the media highlighted Schultz's life as an object lesson for all East Germans: 'Comrade Egon Schultz will always be our example. We want to imitate him and live as he did: diligently, honestly and loyally to his state.'[43] A similar message reverberated in special publications dedicated to the man and his memory, including a widely read children's book, which elevated Schultz into a Stakhanovite-like figure of sacrifice and heroism.[44] Another sign of Schultz's civic importance was the zeal with which the authorities appropriated his name. The Berlin street on which he had met his death was soon renamed Egon-Schultz-Strasse, and by the end of 1987 no fewer than 122 different GDR institutions, ranging from military units and barracks to schools, nurseries, summer camps, and even boxing centres bore his name.[45] Egon Schultz lived on in the East German pantheon of socialist victim-heroes, exhorting the people into a future that was soon to take a very unexpected turn.

Narratives of the Wall in the post-unification period

The collapse of the GDR in 1989/90 also entailed the rapid disintegration of the public narratives that had legitimated the state's existence. The facts on the ground determined the discourse: having won the inter-German duel, the West German system basked in glory while its defeated rival was buried in a pauper's grave. The result was a resurgence of interpretative paradigms familiar from earlier West German discussions: the totalitarian model reasserted itself, as the Third Reich again became the seemingly obvious point of comparison for the GDR. Even the German *Bundestag*'s official investigative commission on the GDR and its legacies placed the defunct state in this framework, deliberating extensively on the comparability of the 'SED' and 'Nazi' systems.[46] Meanwhile, the earlier East German narrative of the Federal Republic as a morass of reaction lost all credence, fading into a marginal discourse for a rapidly diminishing audience of Communist die-hards eternally stuck in the past.

This sweeping western victory was evident in unified Germany's public discourse on the Wall and its victims. Interest in the topic surged after unification, in a script lifted from the Cold War West: escapees starred as the key victims and the East German system, embodied by its top leaders, as the villain. This outlook dominated the arena that gave the Wall's victims the most publicity in the post-unification years: the trials of GDR border-guards, their commanders and leading politicians for violent acts committed on the German–German border. Most of these trials, 237 of which took place between 1991 and mid-2002, cast new light on particular cases and meted out relatively mild sentences – typically short, suspended prison terms – for most border-guards, but somewhat heavier punishment for several high-ranking political and military figures.[47] Predictably, one of the most publicised trials was that of Peter Fechter's killers, in which two guards received suspended prison terms of slightly under two years each. The trial and its coverage in the mainstream German media highlighted, again, the young man's gruesome suffering and the illegitimacy of the tyrannical system that had caused it. But in a nod to the totalitarian paradigm, the presiding judge also argued that rank-and-file guards had themselves been 'victims of the border arrangements' because of the 'indoctrination' to which they had been subjected.[48] In this perspective, Fechter's death served to perpetuate a narrative, rooted in Cold War precedent, according to which isolated, fanatical GDR functionaries had terrorised and victimised their own, alienated citizenry, which therefore had no reason to mourn the regime's demise.

This message, potentially useful for converting East Germans into citizens of united Germany, also underpinned the practical politics of commemorating the Wall's victims in unified Berlin. Whereas memory sites designed to highlight GDR-style victimology and its implied claim of an emotional bond between the regime and the people disappeared, those dedicated to escapees who had turned their backs on Communism endured. Most traces of the Egon Schultz cult, for example, vanished by the early 1990s. Egon-Schultz-Strasse reverted to its earlier name, and the various tailor-made memorials around former East Berlin were quietly dismantled. By contrast, Peter Fechter received a new monument for the thirty-eighth anniversary of the Wall's construction, which continues to provide a venue for public commemoration.[49]

This post-unification prioritisation of the West German perspective on the Wall and its victims was in many ways justified. By any civilised standard, the GDR had maintained a brutal and inhumane border regime. The prosecution of perpetrators involved in maiming and killing unarmed civilians whose only crime had been an attempt to leave a country was a legitimate, even necessary, endeavour in the transition to a unified, democratic Germany. Furthermore, the narrative constructed by the GDR to justify the Wall's existence had been too mendacious and distorted to command independent credibility. To a degree, this had been clear even during the Cold War, when one look at the elaborate border fortifications had sufficed to show that their main purpose was to prevent movement from East to West rather than vice versa. After unification, the GDR's *Schutzwall* narrative collapsed completely, not least because even many of its seemingly most appealing components – the stories of murdered border-guards – turned out to have been heavily distorted and manipulated. The most flagrant example was the legend of Egon Schultz. As declassified East German documents reveal, the authorities deliberately fabricated much of the official story for propaganda purposes. An autopsy conducted immediately after the incident confirmed that Schultz had not been killed by West German intruders. A bullet from one of the *Fluchthelfer* had wounded him in the shoulder, but not fatally. The deadly shots had come instead from the sub-machine gun of the border-guard comrade behind him who had been firing blindly in the dark. The GDR's top leaders were aware of these facts, but decided to suppress them in order to propagate an alternate story they knew to be false but politically convenient.[50]

To complicate matters, however, other post-unification investigations revealed that the Western side, too, had sometimes lied systematically in order to make propaganda with the Wall's victims. The most glaring case was the shooting of GDR border-guard Rudolf Huhn in central Berlin on 18 June 1962. Huhn had the bad luck of getting caught in the middle of an escape attempt in which Rudolf Müller – a 31-year-old former East Berliner who had fled to the West on the day the Wall was built – tried to smuggle his wife, children, and other relatives out of East Berlin through a purpose-built tunnel. Just as this group was about to enter the building where the tunnel began, Huhn ordered Müller and the others to stop. There followed an altercation and a shoot-out, at the end of which Müller and his family reached West Berlin while Huhn lost his life. The GDR always claimed that Huhn, who became a socialist icon comparable to Egon Schultz, had been killed by Müller, whereas the official Western position was that the guard had been accidentally shot by his own comrades. The East German version proved correct. As confirmed by the 1999 trial at which Müller received a one-year suspended sentence for the killing, a cabal of western politicians, journalists and intelligence agents had concocted and propagated the blame-the-guards story, in full cognizance of the fact that the guilty party had actually been

Müller.[51] Cold War convenience had got the best of Western leaders, too, suggesting that the Wall and its victims may not be suited to the construction of unambiguous moral and political lessons.

Perhaps because of this ambiguity overshadowing some of the tragedies at the Berlin Wall, German interest in these particular victim stories has declined since the 1990s. Relevant trials have ended, most debates abated and the Wall itself almost completely disappeared from the Berlin landscape, even if select memorials, such as the new Peter Fechter monument, still remain. Discussions of the Wall's victims retain much divisive potential for competing claims of suffering along an east–west axis, which makes the issue problematic for a country still struggling to heal the scars of division and to forge a shared identity. For such unity-building projects, other types of victims may seem more promising. This is perhaps why recent discussions have focused primarily on suffering rooted in the Third Reich and the Second World War, a context that is also deeply problematic but possibly more inclusive and therapeutic because it can provide interpretations with seemingly clearer dividing lines between suffering ordinary Germans and their victimisers, embodied by narrow Nazi elites and specific foreign foes.

8

The Victims of Totalitarianism and the Centrality of Nazi Genocide: Continuity and Change in German Commemorative Politics

Andrew H. Beattie

In January 2004, the Central Council of Jews in Germany suspended its participation in the Foundation for Saxon Memorial Sites, a public body in the eastern German state of Saxony charged with the administration of memorials to the victims of Nazi and Communist persecution. The Central Council's withdrawal was a reaction to what it saw as the Foundation's tendency to equate the crimes of the Nazi and Communist regimes.[1] This reaction was part of a larger controversy over a motion put by the conservative Christian Democratic Union (CDU) to the German Federal Parliament (*Bundestag*), in which the CDU objected to the allegedly insufficient attention paid to Communist tyranny and insisted on commemoration of victims of both 'totalitarian dictatorships'.[2] The contrasting positions of the Central Council and the CDU mark out the highly charged terrain of commemorative politics in Germany, where advocates of 'memory' of the crimes of one regime feel threatened or marginalised by those who call for more memory of another.

The debate in early 2004 constituted a new round in the ongoing discussion about how various regimes, crimes and sets of victims relate to one another and how they should be remembered, a discussion as old as the Federal Republic itself. Yet it also seemed like a rather anachronistic reversion to an earlier era of mutual recriminations and suspicion, and mutually exclusive understandings of the past. Fifteen years after the fall of the Berlin Wall, had Germany not moved on from the stark divisions between the Right's tendency to equate Communist and Nazi crimes on the one hand and the Left's insistence on the Holocaust's incomparability on the other? Had unified Germany not put behind it the divisive West German 'Historians' Dispute' of the mid-1980s? Worse still, was it perhaps returning to the situation of 1950s West Germany, where the notion of totalitarianism was as much a device for forgetting as remembering German guilt, and allowed Germans to see themselves as victims?

Such concerns are generally unfounded. The concept of 'totalitarianism' did undergo a renaissance after unification, and Germany arguably pursued a more thorough reckoning with Communist injustice than it had in relation to Nazi crimes. Yet it also witnessed ever-more critical discussion of complicity in, and responsibility for the latter. Fears expressed at the time of unification that Nazism would be marginalised amidst vigorous discussion of the more recent Communist past did not prove correct.[3] Instead, memory of communism was incorporated into a commemorative landscape dominated by the Third Reich and memory of the Holocaust. Nevertheless, the relationship between Nazism and communism in German commemorative politics remained fraught, precisely because of the Holocaust's centrality. This chapter argues that there was considerable continuity across the caesura of unification. The Left maintained its traditional insistence on the horrors of Nazism, whereas the Right continued its tendency to emphasise the similarities between Communist and Nazi versions of totalitarianism. These fronts were clearly drawn in the 'Historians' Dispute', and they were still evident after unification, when conservatives advocated greater memory of Communist crimes and the Left warned of the dangers of relativising Nazi criminality.[4] A key site for the contestation of such issues was a Federal Parliamentary Commission of Inquiry into the East German past. The Commission's proclamation of an 'anti-totalitarian consensus' as a foundation for unified Germany appeared to confirm the victory of the anti-totalitarian Right.

However, this was no straightforward conservative ascendancy, and even less was it a restoration of anti-communist positions of the 1950s. Significantly, all political parties except the post-Communist Party of Democratic Socialism (PDS) supported the 'anti-totalitarian consensus'. Moreover, despite a lingering proclivity among some conservatives to equate Nazism and communism, the Commission insisted that the regimes could be compared but not equated, *and* it upheld the centrality of the Holocaust. The debate thus advanced considerably beyond the entrenched fronts of the 1980s, thanks largely to the end of the Cold War and the weakening of its restrictively dichotomous thought. The collapse of communism made it possible and necessary for the Left to acknowledge the full extent of Communist crimes and the victims' entitlement to commemoration, while the disappearance of the GDR and its anti-fascist moral superiority allowed a more open approach to complicity in Nazism on the Right.

Positions had in fact been softening even before 1989. Fierce competition between East and West Germany and within the latter between Left and Right – over the correct lessons of the Nazi past, ownership of German resistance against Nazism, and the definition and acknowledgment of victims – had given way gradually to a more relaxed approach. The end of the Cold War thus accelerated a development already underway, and exclusive competition succumbed to a greater willingness to include the full range of Nazi perpetrators, resistors and victims.[5]

After 1989, such inclusiveness was extended to the victims of communism. Those who supported their memory argued that they *too* should be acknowledged. One reason for their relative success was that, unlike in the 1950s, the advocates of totalitarianism and memory of Communist crimes no longer focused on Communist barbarity to the exclusion of Nazi crimes or questioned the need for memory of the Nazis' victims, but argued that communism's victims should *share* public attention with the Nazis' victims. In the Commission of Inquiry, widespread support for the 'anti-totalitarian consensus' was only possible on the basis of the simultaneous acknowledgement of the singularity and centrality of the Holocaust. Indeed, by borrowing the vocabulary of 'coming to terms' with the (Nazi) past and applying it to the Communist past, the advocates of memory of Communist abuses drew on the very strength of Holocaust memory in order to moderate, if not assail it. Their most powerful argument was that no victim should be forgotten.

For all the advances from earlier decades, a tension remained between thinking the regimes and their victims together, and thinking them separately. Indeed, two rival notions of inclusiveness can be discerned which help explain the continuing disputes over commemoration: an encompassing and a differentiating version. Both seek to acknowledge the full range of victims, yet where the former groups them together in an inevitably rather abstract and generalised manner, the latter insists on maintaining distinctions between them and placing them in their historical contexts. The first potentially ignores fundamental differences, such as those between victims and perpetrators who may subsequently have become victims, while the second is open to complaints about its perceived selectivity and potentially hierarchical nature. The Commission of Inquiry sought to solve the problem by placing vetos on both the lumping together of various crimes and the creation of hierarchies of victims. It failed, however, to delineate more closely the relationship between the various pasts and did not resolve the tension between its anti-totalitarianism and support for the Holocaust's centrality. Nevertheless, its relative success was demonstrated precisely by the furore over the CDU motion of 2004 mentioned above, which was controversial not because it sought the commemoration of all victims, but because it failed to distinguish between the crimes they had suffered.

There are numerous parallels and connections between the post-unification discussion of Communist crimes and victims and the recently renewed debate about German suffering during and immediately after the Second World War. Indeed, the discussion of GDR history and the competitive commemorative politics associated with Germany's 'double' totalitarian past prepared the ground for the more recent debate about German suffering. Since 1989, the desire to do justice to the suffering of the victims of Communist injustice led to concentration on the fact of (Germans') suffering and the relative neglect of its causes, context and the motivation behind it. Moreover, discussion of Communist oppression in the immediate post-war period rejuvenated older tropes that cast German suffering – due to occupation, denazification, internment, national division – as the result of Communist brutality rather than the consequence of German support for Nazism and genocidal war. Similar tendencies have been evident in the more recent discussion of Germans as victims of the Second World War, as has the distinction between an encompassing and a differentiating inclusiveness. Consideration of the post-unification handling of the East German past and its continuities and discontinuities with West German debates is therefore useful for understanding the debate about remembering German suffering.

Competitive and selective memory in post-war Germany

In post-war Germany, competition and selectivity characterised memory of the German and particularly the Nazi past. East and West

Germany engaged in bitter competition over which state had learnt the appropriate lessons from history. Only one set of answers could possibly be right, because the alternative was tainted by association with Nazism. The two states developed ideologies that linked their present Cold War rival with the Third Reich, in contradistinction to which they perceived themselves. From its foundation until the late 1960s, and even thereafter in conservative circles, West Germany regarded the GDR as a 'totalitarian' dictatorship fundamentally similar to the Nazi regime. From its foundation until the collapse of Communist Party (SED) rule in late 1989, East Germany interpreted Nazism as but a highly aggressive, chauvinistic version of imperialist 'fascism' and condemned the incipient fascism of the capitalist Federal Republic. Anti-totalitarianism in the West and anti-fascism in the East served to delegitimise the other German state and legitimise one's own.[6]

For all their ostensible differences, there were numerous similarities between the two states' approaches to the past. In each doctrine, the current threat across the border was regarded as more dangerous and worthy of attention than the previous incarnation of totalitarianism or fascism. In the GDR, facing up to Germans' crimes and their victims' suffering in an honest and open fashion took second place to the regime's use of anti-fascism to legitimise itself. The official Marxist-Leninist understanding of fascism 'universalised' Nazism, removing it from its specific German context.[7] It understood fascism as a class-based phenomenon, minimising its nationalist and racial dimensions and leading to the neglect of the Holocaust and concentration on the glorious struggle of the Soviet Union and German Communists. The particular situation of Jewish survivors of the Holocaust was a matter of some discussion in eastern Germany during the occupation period and the early years of the GDR, but this debate ended abruptly with the persecution of the proponents of the Jewish cause. Subsequently, a distinction between mere passive 'victims' of fascism and more lauded 'anti-fascist resistance fighters' effectively relegated Jews (and others) to second-class victim status.[8]

To present-day observers, the Holocaust was surprisingly marginal in both East and West in the immediate post-war decade-and-a-half, a phenomenon not limited to Germany.[9] West Germany paid compensation to Israel and Jewish survivors on the territory of the FRG and throughout the Western world, a policy which stood in marked contrast to the GDR's payments only to the few surviving Jews on its territory, its derisory and belated attempts to come to an agreement with the Jewish Claims Conference from the 1970s, and its anti-Zionist hostility to Israel. But in the West, too, in the late 1940s and 1950s neither scholarly research nor public commemoration were much concerned with Jewish suffering, or sites of Jewish persecution and extermination, and compensation was by no means widely supported. There, too, Jews were seen as passive victims, and Jewish resistance was largely ignored. Widespread public and even scholarly concern with and concentration on the Holocaust developed only in the 1960s, becoming particularly strong from the late 1970s.[10]

Like eastern anti-fascism, western anti-totalitarianism played down the specifically German nature of Nazism. It also allowed Germans to stress that they, too, had suffered at the hands of a totalitarian regime, rather than focus on their complicity in supporting the regime and in war crimes and crimes against humanity. Often, their victims were mentioned only implicitly in the context of Germans' insistence on their own equivalent or similar suffering, whether during the war itself, or afterwards in the form of expulsions, occupation or denazification.[11] Not infrequently, direct parallels were drawn between German and Jewish suffering, the suggestion being that it was time the former was acknowledged and addressed just as the latter allegedly had been. Such argumentation was problematic not least because Jewish victims had not in fact received the explicit attention that, it was argued, was now due to German victims.[12]

The Cold War only reinforced a disinclination to discuss the horrendous and genocidal nature of the war particularly in Eastern Europe. Germans frequently cast German POWs and expellees as the victims of Communist oppression, rather than seeing them as suffering the consequences of the war the Germans themselves had unleashed.[13] Such tendencies were compounded by the erection of a Communist dictatorship in the Soviet Zone of Occupation and GDR. The eagerness with which West Germany embraced the commemoration of Communist abuses stood in marked contrast with its hesitance in relation to Nazi crimes. The two were compared directly, with the Communist regime often being characterised as more brutal.[14] Not atypically, in West Berlin a memorial 'to the victims of Stalinism' (1951) predated a similar memorial 'to the victims of National Socialism' (1953).[15] Similarly, the 20 July plot against Hitler received greater emphasis in the immediate wake of the popular uprising against the East German regime on 17 June 1953. West German politicians felt more comfortable drawing attention to the anti-Nazi resistance when they could connect it with more widely accepted anti-Communist resistance.[16]

Anti-fascism remained official doctrine in the GDR until the end, but in the Federal Republic German-centred memory was replaced by Holocaust memory. In the 1960s and 1970s, anti-totalitarianism was challenged by a revival of anti-fascist positions amongst the West German New Left and the generation of 'sixty-eighters' in particular.[17] They had a highly critical attitude towards the post-war handling of the Nazi past in particular and the national past more generally, which was seen as a disastrous *Sonderweg* (special path) culminating in Auschwitz. These positions were also largely supported, albeit in less anti-capitalist guise, by a generation of left-liberal historians and intellectuals known as the 'forty-fivers'.[18]

The 1980s saw fierce contestation between advocates of anti-totalitarianism and memory of German suffering and those who insisted on the uniqueness of German crimes. At a controversial ceremony at Bitburg in 1985, Christian Democrat Chancellor Helmut Kohl and US President Ronald Reagan commemorated German and American soldiers at a site that also contained the graves of SS members, provoking claims of the rehabilitation of Nazi criminals and relativisation of German guilt.[19] A critical left-liberal response to such tendencies prompted the 'Historians' Dispute'. Conservatives maintained their views about the fundamental similarities between communism and Nazism and played the one off against the other, and their opponents insisted on a critical reading of German history. While neither traditional anti-totalitarianism nor anti-fascism can be said to have won, a fragile consensus emerged about the unprecedented nature of the Holocaust and its profound ramifications for German identity and politics.[20] Even in East Germany in the 1980s, where Nazism's racial elements had been of marginal interest, the Holocaust and its Jewish victims became the focus of renewed attention (in the 1980s).[21]

A convergence of memory regimes in East and West and within the latter can also be construed in relation to German resistance against Nazism. Here, Cold War competition had been especially fierce and its exclusivity particularly salient. Both Germanys had claimed to uphold the legacy of resistance and thus to occupy the moral high ground of the 'other' Germany which was not tainted by complicity in Nazism.[22] In the 1950s and 1960s, the dominant images of resistance in the two states were diametrically opposed, and each sought to impugn the other's resistance heroes. The Communist East legitimised itself with reference to Communist resistance, which for the Federal Republic was hypocritical and meaningless, because Communists had only sought to replace one dictatorship with another. After initial reluctance, the legacy of conservative, aristocratic and military resistance and in particular the failed plot to assassinate Hitler on 20 July 1944 came to play a central role in the creation of West German political legitimacy and collective identity, but the GDR regarded it as discredited due to the protagonists' erstwhile support for the Nazis and the war effort. However, from the 1970s a more inclusive approach developed. Despite continuing disagreements, the view gained strength that all aspects of the resistance had to be documented, if not honoured and commemorated in a normative sense.[23] Competition and selectivity continued, but the alternatives were less stark.

Much the same applied to the victims. In each state, rather narrow, exclusive approaches to the various victims of Nazi persecution and wartime suffering gave way over time to greater inclusiveness. In East Germany, heroicisation had been preferred to mournful commemoration, but there was considerable focus on the suffering of the Slavic peoples of Eastern Europe, particularly the Soviet Union. While the racial nature of warfare was played down in the early decades, increasing attention was subsequently paid to Jewish persecution and suffering.[24] In West Germany, the practice of compensation for victims of political, racial and religious persecution was initially highly restrictive and selective: communists were frequently excluded and even criminalised; the Sinti and Roma were marginalised; and those persecuted on the basis of their (homo-)sexuality, physical and mental disability or 'asocial' character were ignored. From the 1970s onwards, however, these groups received increasing recognition, although they continued to struggle for attention relative to the global tendency to see Jewish victims as the ultimate victims of Nazi criminality, indeed of evil more generally.[25]

The speech by West German Federal President Richard von Weizsäcker on the occasion of the fortieth anniversary of the end of the Second World War can be seen as the culmination of these various developments in the Federal Republic and as an attempt to end the bitter competition over, and selectivity towards, the past. It encapsulated the shift of focus away from German suffering and towards German contrition, it acknowledged the diversity of resistance rather than excluding certain strands for political reasons, and emphasised the extraordinary extent of Nazi criminality and the full range of victims. While von Weizsäcker sought to recall all who had suffered, he nevertheless gave primacy to the Holocaust and its Jewish victims.[26] It was the pinnacle of an inclusive, differentiating approach to the past.

Competitive and inclusive memory in unified Germany

The end of the Cold War and German unification further promoted an inclusive understanding of the Nazis' victims and the resistance, as well as allowing more open discussion of the full range of perpetrators, including the *Wehrmacht*, and others who supported the regime.[27] Yet communism's collapse and the widespread desire to 'come to terms' with it represented challenges to what had become a Nazi- and Holocaust-centred culture of memory. For many in both East and West, revelations about the extent of Communist abuses provided confirmation that communism and Nazism were but variants of totalitarian barbarity. Questions about the comparability, similarity and equivalence of the regimes and their crimes had immediate relevance for the commemoration of their regimes' victims. How could multiple pasts be remembered and the regimes' abuses and victims commemorated? Could or should commemoration occur together, collectively, or separately? Should equal status be accorded to the different epochs, regimes, crimes and victims, or were some more significant than others?

Unification had profound consequences for the two post-war states' founding ideologies. East German anti-fascism was all but discredited, and its demise was accompanied by the reassertion of anti-totalitarianism. The victims and opponents of the East German regime initiated the discussion of the Communist past, but Western conservatives with an ideological interest in refighting the memory battles of the 1970s and 1980s were heavily involved. At times, they advocated forms of memory that were reminiscent of the 1950s in their failure to distinguish between various regimes, their crimes and groups of victims. For example, West German Minister for Inner-German Relations Dorothee Wilms (CDU) demanded in July 1990 that the Eastern anti-fascist memorial at Buchenwald concentration camp be transformed into a memorial 'for the victims of arbitrariness and persecution'.[28]

If von Weizsäcker's 1985 speech was the apotheosis of a differentiating inclusiveness in West Germany, Chancellor Kohl's establishment of the New Guardhouse (*Neue Wache*) in Berlin as a 'Central Memorial Site' in 1993 constituted the zenith of its encompassing, undifferentiated rival.[29] It also represented the victory of anti-totalitarianism in its competition with anti-fascism. The GDR memorial's anti-fascist dedication, 'To the victims of fascism and militarism', was replaced with an anti-totalitarian one: 'To the victims of war and the rule of violence'.[30] As critics objected, there was no distinction between perpetrators and victims or between various regimes. An inscription was added, listing groups of victims such as wartime civilian victims, Jews, Sinti and Roma, homosexuals, victims of political persecution and members of the resistance, but it did not mention which 'rule of violence' was at issue, made no reference to the identity of the perpetrators, and also commemorated those who had 'fallen' in the World Wars. It was most specific about 'the women and men who were persecuted and murdered because they opposed totalitarian dictatorship after 1945'.[31]

Anti-fascism's substitution with unspecific anti-totalitarianism at this memorial was by no means unique, but some memorials were more complex than others.[32] At two of the most prominent GDR 'National Sites of Admonition and Commemoration', Buchenwald and Sachsenhausen, mass graves were discovered in 1989 that added a new layer of history: they were the graves of inmates of 'Special Camps', where the Soviet occupying authorities had interned thousands of Germans after the end of the war. Former internees and their supporters called for commemoration of the victims of the Special Camps, and the memorial sites were faced not just with revising their one-sided anti-fascist exhibitions and commemorative elements, but also with the controversial issue of addressing the post-1945 history of the concentration camps. For both sites, commissions of experts established by the state governments accorded priority to the Nazi past, endorsing what Bill Niven calls a 'hierarchical system of memory'.[33] In January 1992, a Brandenburg commission called for the inclusion of documentary exhibitions on the Sachsenhausen Special Camp, but emphasis was to remain on the concentration camp, and commemoration of the Special Camp inmates was not foreshadowed.[34] A Thuringian commission acknowledged the need to commemorate as well as document Buchenwald's Special Camp history, but this was to remain 'subordinate' to (*nachgeordnet*), and spatially separate from the commemoration of the concentration camp.[35] Such recommendations failed to satisfy victims' groups on both sides. Concentration camp victims clung to an exclusive approach to the past, objecting to the inclusion at 'their' memorials of Special Camp inmates they regarded as former Nazis. Not surprisingly, the Special Camp victims favoured an unqualified inclusiveness and condemned the priority given to the Nazi past and their own apparent 'second-class' status.[36]

The state commissions prioritised Holocaust-centred memory, but federal politics soon became involved. Due to the huge tasks of reforming memorial sites and the strapped finances of the eastern state governments, the Federal Government co-funded a growing number of memorials from 1991.[37] Inevitably questions arose about which memorials should benefit, how they would be determined, whether funding should extend beyond the originally planned ten years, and whether it should be restricted to the East. It was a revealing oddity that the body charged with developing a concept for federal involvement was primarily interested in the history of Communist dictatorship: a parliamentary Commission of Inquiry 'Overcoming the Consequences of the SED Dictatorship in the Process of German Unity', which was established in 1995. The Commission saw itself, and its conservative members in particular saw themselves, as advocates of memory of Communist crimes, often in quite explicit opposition to those who insisted on the centrality of Nazism.[38] Such advocacy was understandable, but not unproblematic given the Commission's brief. Significantly, there had never been such explicit political support and high-level parliamentary consideration of appropriate and desirable efforts to remember the Nazi past. Only in the context of discussing the 'double' totalitarian past did such an institution assume responsibility for commemoration.

The Commission did not begin its deliberations with a *tabula rasa*. It was the successor to an earlier inquiry 'Working through the History and Consequences of the SED Dictatorship in Germany', established in 1992, which had undertaken a systematic examination and condemnation of the East German regime.[39] Importantly, the predecessor had addressed the GDR's relationship with Nazism in numerous areas. It examined East Germany's handling of the Nazi past and sought to destroy the GDR's lingering 'anti-fascist bonus'.[40] Conservatives in particular saw anti-fascism's role in legitimising the GDR as sufficient reason to delegitimise anti-fascism entirely. They condemned the selectivity with which East Germany had compensated the Nazis' victims and commemorated the resistance, but made no mention of similar phenomena in West Germany, of whose record on Nazism they sought to paint a more sympathetic picture.[41] Cold War competition over the Nazi past by no means came to an immediate end in 1990.

The first Commission of Inquiry also considered the crucial questions of the comparability and similarity of GDR communism and Nazism. It affirmed both the legitimacy of comparing and the dangers of equating the two regimes. Commissioners often referred to the GDR as the 'second German dictatorship' and spoke of 'two dictatorships in Germany' without reflecting on the extent to which such terminology lumped the regimes together without addressing their differences.[42] In particular, many conservatives undermined their protestations that they did not want to equate the regimes by marginalising substantial differences and emphasising partial, tenuous or superficial similarities and parallels. Not infrequently, they simply placed the Second World War and the Holocaust to one side, in order to focus on the dictatorial political systems.[43] The exceptional nature of Nazi crimes was thus regarded as far from central to the comparison. They also suggested direct parallels between Communist and Nazi inhumanity, often through reference to the crimes of 'communism' generally, rather than those of the GDR in particular, or through highly unspecific discussion of the crimes in question. Conservatives spoke broadly of the two regimes' 'systematic abuse of human and civil rights' and their common 'disregard for people'.[44] While both the GDR and the Third Reich were undoubtedly guilty of these sins, this revealed little about their quality or extent. The Christian Democrats and Liberals who comprised the majority on the Commission also sought to condemn the GDR as a *totalitarian* regime. They complained about the marginalisation of the concept in West Germany since the 1970s, gleefully welcomed its return in the 1990s, and insisted that they had been right all along about the GDR's totalitarian nature.[45]

The conservative advocates of the concept of totalitarianism did not have everything their own way. Numerous left-wing and left-liberal commissioners and experts objected to the exaggeration of similarities and the elision of historical particularities. They objected to conservatives' neglect of the motives behind various crimes and abuses and the regimes' differing ideologies.[46] The first Commission's report took left-liberal objections to conservative equationist tendencies into account to a considerable extent, upholding the 'fundamental differences' between the regimes, primarily in the area of their criminality, and asserting that 'that which makes the Nazi dictatorship an unresolved burden even for generations to come did not exist in the SED dictatorship'. Nevertheless, the Commission affirmed that the GDR was a totalitarian dictatorship and proclaimed an 'anti-totalitarian consensus' as the political bedrock of unified Germany, implying that alternative views were undemocratic and an unacceptable insult to the victims.[47]

At first glance, the Commission's firm positions on these questions suggested the return of a conservative, decidedly anti-communist position that had been dominant in West Germany in the 1950s and early 60s but was increasingly marginal thereafter, and that regarded communism as a more serious threat than Nazism.[48] However, the

Commission's insistence that one could not simply lump Communist and Nazi crimes together and the support of Social Democrats and left-liberal intellectuals for the 'anti-totalitarian consensus' indicated that this was no straightforward restoration of conservative positions of the early post-war decades.[49] Indeed, whereas in the past conservatives often had pointed to Communist crimes all-the-better to *forget* those of the Nazi dictatorship, the Left had ensured that the Commission insist on the continuing centrality of memory of Nazism for reunified Germany.

It was on the basis of such positions that the second Commission began its deliberations on commemoration. A central issue that determined the answers to questions about how to commemorate the sites with multiple pasts was the extent to which the post-war Special Camps had served denazification. Here the inquiry assumed a remarkably clear stance that failed not only to reflect the complexity of the issues and the current state of research, but even to do justice to the evidence it had gathered. Its report stated explicitly that the Special Camps 'did not serve denazification'; instead, it argued, 'the practices and methods of Stalinist repression and of the Gulag were continued' in the Special Camps.[50] The Commission did not equate the Special Camps with Nazi concentration camps, and insisted that their differences be made clear, but it saw their comparison as an avenue for promoting the totalitarian paradigm. The report paid little attention to the reasons for the inmates' presence in the camps or the causes of their deaths and suggested that all internees were there unjustly and not because of previous misdeeds.[51]

Given the discussion thus far, it is hardly surprising that the Commission endorsed a full programme of commemoration for the victims of Communist injustice and persecution, including Special Camp internees. The lack of due process and the inhumane conditions in the camps meant that, Nazis or not, the internees were victims of Communist oppression and therefore warranted commemoration. In adopting this position, the Commission ignored a number of key questions: whether some of the internees had been guilty of crimes or were compromised by their role in the Third Reich, whether their whole biographies and not just their post-1945 maltreatment should be considered, and whether all of them, or only the completely innocent members, warranted public commemoration.[52] Inevitably and with considerable justification, the PDS objected that Nazis were now to be commemorated, and conservatives' sympathetic and inclusive approach to these victims of communism stood in contrast to their lingering unwillingness to commemorate Communists who had suffered under the Nazis.[53] Lingering exclusivity on the one hand was coupled hypocritically with undifferentiated inclusiveness on the other.

How commemoration should occur was the subject of considerable debate. Some conservatives insisted that Communist oppression and its victims be accorded equal status with Nazi oppression and its victims, and argued explicitly against separate commemoration.[54] Nevertheless, the Commission was wary of equation and adopted the line developed by the Brandenburg commission of experts that 'Nazi crimes must not be relativised by the debate about the crimes of Stalinism. Stalinist crimes must not be trivialised by pointing to Nazi crimes.' Such a position suggested that both eras had to be taken seriously and treated on their own terms. At the same time, the inquiry forbade expressly the 'hierarchisation' of groups of victims and called for 'common offerings of the memorial sites for the memory of the NS dictatorship and the SED dictatorship' that could help foster the 'anti-totalitarian consensus'.[55] The Commission thus sought to appease those who were concerned about equation, while offering considerable sustenance to the advocates of encompassing totalitarianism. Sufficient ambiguity remained such that both sides could feel vindicated and could appeal to the Commissions' findings to support their case for more or less memory of competing pasts.

Continuity and change in German commemorative politics

Did the 'anti-totalitarian consensus' proclaimed in the mid-1990s constitute a genuine resolution of previous conflict, or did it merely temporarily conceal ongoing disagreements and continuing competition over the significance of various pasts? The discussion in early 2004 mentioned at the beginning of this chapter suggested that Jürgen Habermas's 1994 observation before the first Commission of Inquiry still held true ten years later: 'where those on the Right tend towards similarity, those on the Left want above all to see differences'.[56] The CDU motion that called for greater efforts to foster memory of Communist crimes and their victims employed terms such as 'both totalitarian dictatorships' and the 'double past' that stressed the commonalities between the regimes.[57] In response, Social Democrats, Greens, post-communists, Nazi victims' groups and the left-liberal press accused the Christian Democrats of relativising the Holocaust and equating the GDR and the Third Reich.[58] The old positions and fronts had not disappeared.

Significantly, however, each side claimed to uphold the Commissions' consensus and accused the other of abandoning it. In a *Bundestag* debate about a revised version of the CDU motion on 17 June 2004, its initiator, the former East German dissident Günter Nooke, insisted that he was not striving towards a 'paradigm change', but merely wanted the implementation of the Federal Government's concept for memorials which had been developed on the basis of the second Commission's report. Yet as Minister for Culture Christina Weiss observed for the Social Democrat-Green coalition, if it was merely a question of implementation, the motion's call for a new integrative concept was redundant.[59] Indeed, the parties were by no means as far apart as the heated rhetoric suggested. The specifics of the CDU position were largely consistent with government policy, because the vast majority of memorials for which funding was sought were already receiving it or were under consideration.[60]

If everyone still supported the 'anti-totalitarian consensus' and the differences in the details of policy were minor, one wonders what the commotion was about. The answer was twofold. First, the CDU motion failed to make explicit reference to the historical singularity of the Holocaust or its particular significance for contemporary Germany. This failure rendered the same language unacceptable to the other parties that the Commissions of Inquiry had used with their support.[61] The Commissions' rhetoric of 'double', 'totalitarian' pasts and the 'second German dictatorship' had only been endorsed by the liberal Left because specific prohibitions were placed on the relativisation of the Nazi past. The absence in the CDU motion of such prohibitions and of references to the Holocaust's centrality appeared to constitute a return to the equationism of old and opened the CDU to charges of relativisation. The CDU rejected such accusations and revised its motion, adding an explicit statement about the Holocaust's 'singularity' and 'special commemoration', but the damage was done and the changes appeared a belated, tokenistic gesture.[62]

The second, more fundamental reason for the furore in turn partly explains the first: the motion did not refer to the Holocaust's particular significance precisely because the CDU sought to challenge it. In his speech before the *Bundestag*, Nooke complained that while the 'national significance of the Nazi memorials for the culture of memory is uncontroversial', the 'commemoration of the SED dictatorship in contrast is insufficiently anchored in public consciousness' and is regarded as a regional, eastern issue rather than a national one.[63] He thus revealed a desire not just that public funds be allocated evenly, but that the two pasts occupy equivalent places in Germans' collective memories. Memorials were merely the pretext for more general complaints about the continuing primacy of the Nazi past.

The incident revealed that the CDU had not completely learned that the most acceptable strategy for arguing for more memory of Communist injustice lay precisely in appearing not to challenge the centrality of the Holocaust. In Germany after unification, competition over the significance of various pasts continued, and debate still revolved around the comparability and similarity of the regimes and the question of how they and their victims should be remembered. The advocates of memory of Communist crimes achieved success because they argued (not infrequently due to the resistance of the Left) that it needed to be included *alongside* Holocaust memory, rather than replace or achieve parity with the latter. For all of the vetoes the Commissions of Inquiry and others sought to place on hierarchies of memory, they could not assail the precedence and pre-eminence of Nazi crimes or the centrality of their memory. Indeed, the parallels and equivalences frequently posited by those who advocated memory of Communist crimes, while often dubious, may have helped their own cause but did little to damage the status of the Nazi past, which remained the yardstick.

Continuity and change characterised the positions of both the Left and the Right in the post-unification period. The discussion of Helmut Kohl's *Neue Wache*, of the conservatives' approach in the Commissions of Inquiry and of the 2004 CDU motion indicated considerable continuity with conservative arguments from the 1980s and indeed the 1940s and 1950s about the equivalence of various totalitarian regimes and of the suffering of their victims. Yet whereas conservatives had previously sought to focus on German suffering or Communist criminality in order to distract attention from Nazism, they now sought to commemorate various groups of victims collectively, to draw on the very strength of the memory of Nazism to support the memory of other groups. Meanwhile, the Left, which it has not been possible to discuss in much detail, displayed greater readiness to discuss the crimes and commemorate the victims of communism and accepted the latter's comparability with Nazism. However, it remained ambivalent about totalitarianism and continued to oppose the relativisation of German complicity in the Holocaust. By no means did divisions disappear, but the extent of common ground increased considerably.

Over the last 15 years, the debate about the construction of the Holocaust Memorial in Berlin – itself the product of the recognition of the singular criminality of the genocide of Europe's Jews and its centrality for contemporary German identity – produced a new dynamic in Germany's competitive memory politics.[64] Competition for entry into, and prominence in Germany's commemorative landscape entered a new phase. Commemorative exclusivity was largely consigned to the past, but new conflict emerged between encompassing and differentiating approaches to inclusive commemoration. The terms of inclusion continue to be contested between rival memory discourses that seek to either maintain or challenge the centrality of the Holocaust by highlighting or ignoring historically specific distinctions, context and causation.

The 2004 CDU motion itself was indicative of the shift caused by the decision to construct the Holocaust Memorial. In addition to insisting on more, joint commemoration of communism's victims it called tentatively for central memorials for the expellees, for civilian victims of Allied bombing raids on German cities during the war, and for the peaceful revolution in the GDR and German reunification in 1989–90.[65] Memory of German suffering or positive German historical achievements has long been deemed a necessary counterweight to memory of German guilt, and as discussed throughout this chapter, advocates of memory of German suffering or Communist crimes have often sought to commemorate all victims together. More recently, however, they have argued, as have other victims of Nazi persecution such as homosexuals or Sinti and Roma, that each group of victims or set of crimes requires its own memorial. If the debate since unification about the inclusion of Communist crimes and their victims is anything to go by, those campaigning for greater recognition of wartime and post-war German suffering only have much chance of success if they seek not to replace or even share centre stage with the Holocaust, but to be included alongside it, and if they avoid drawing all-too-simple parallels. The commemorative landscape is set to diversify even further, but an end to the competition that divides it is not in sight.

9

Representations of German Wartime Suffering in Recent Fiction

Stuart Taberner

In 1999, W. G. Sebald's *On the Natural History of Destruction* (*Luftkrieg und Literatur*, 2003) appeared as the published version of lectures delivered two years earlier in Zurich. In the lengthy essay after which the volume was named, Sebald pointed to the 'failure' of German writers to address the devastation of Germany's cities by the Allied airforces. He traced this 'omission' back to what he saw as the self-pity of a generation of authors associated with the *Gruppe 47*.[1] Writers such as Alfred Andersch and Hans-Werner Richter had been so obsessed with the ordeals of the private soldier that they had not registered the physical and psychological damage that Allied carpet bombing had inflicted upon the civilian population. In relation to this aspect of the German wartime experience at least, Sebald claimed, the literary efforts of this generation replicated the broader individual and collective amnesia of the late 1940s and 1950s regarding the Nazi past. This state of affairs, he suggested, was to continue into the present (*NHD*, 12–13).

In the ensuing debate, Sebald was either credited with daring to chip away at an enduring taboo on speaking of what 'ordinary' Germans had suffered, or criticised for overlooking a veritable deluge of post-war accounts of the horrors of the bombing raids. The sheer number of such publications, it was argued, pointed not to a silencing of German victimhood, but to an obsession with the same that had all too often undercut a more 'appropriate' focus on German perpetration. In an afterword to *On the Natural History of Destruction*, Sebald had in fact acknowledged the existence of a number of literary texts portraying Allied attacks. At the same time, he insisted that the majority of his compatriots in the present understood that the obliteration of the cities in which Germans had once lived had been provoked by Nazi crimes [*NHD*, 104].

Volker Hage's *Witnesses to Destruction: Writers and the Air War* (*Zeugen der Zerstörung. Die Literaten und der Luftkrieg*, 2003) offers a more nuanced response to a thesis which, as Hage noted, Sebald had first advanced in 1982.[2] In this text, Hage argued that the 'gap' was less one of production than of reception: a mass of poetry, fiction and reportage on the air war had been routinely overlooked.[3] This claim was substantiated with reference to Brecht, Thomas Mann and Alfred Döblin – exiles from Nazism – and writers with a more painful familiarity with the horrors endured by the civilian population. Such writers included Hans Erich Nossack, Hermann Kasack, Gerd Gaiser, Gertrud von Le Fort and Gert Ledig. (Hage had been instrumental in the re-release in 1999 of Ledig's 1955 novel *Payback* (*Die Vergeltung*)). In addition, Hage pointed to the images of ruined cities in the work of returning soldiers Hans Werner Richter and Wolfgang Borchert, and to the eerie allusions to bombers in novels set in the post-war period such as Wolfgang Koeppen's *Pigeons on the Grass* (*Tauben im Gras*, 1951). Finally, he pinpointed the echoes in fiction by those whose earliest memories relate back to the trauma of being bombarded or strafed by Allied fighters. A further volume edited by Hage, *Hamburg 1943: Literary Depictions of the Firestorm* (*Hamburg 1943. Literarische Zeugnisse zum Feuersturm*, 2003), collated a series of extracts, ranging from Brecht to Sebald, from literary accounts of the fire-bombing of the city of Hamburg in July 1943.

Hage demonstrates definitively that the devastation wreaked by Allied bombing is a theme that recurs throughout post-war German fiction. The question, then, is not whether German suffering (also taken to include expulsion, the treks and mass rapes) was ever simply taboo. Rather, it is a matter of tracing the ways in which a collective memory of victimhood has found literary expression in dialogue with the concerns shaping public debate at any given time. In this chapter, I examine the post-unification era, and in particular the period since the mid-1990s, in order to explore the social, political and cultural contexts that have shaped a recent, much remarked upon, proliferation of such depictions.

Political correctness

Notwithstanding their apparent ascendancy in the wake of unification in 1990, many conservatives felt that the key domestic battle had yet to be won. It was still necessary to defeat the left-liberal elite, which, having graduated from the student movement of the late 1960s, had established its hegemony over the cultural sphere, in the media, education and the arts. This meant slaying the 'political correctness' that plagued the country: the Left's assertion of its guardianship of German cultural memory. The discourse of 'political correctness' arrived in Germany in the early 1990s from the United States and was quickly domesticated through translated[4] and German works.[5] The main complaint, according to Sally Johnson and Stephanie Suhr, was that 'political correctness' was 'preventing Germany from shaking off the past and progressing towards a new, more positive self-identity'.[6] Thus Botho Strauß, in his 1993 *Der Spiegel* essay with the title'Anschwellender Bocksgesang' (literally 'Swelling Goat's Song') claimed that the liberal media had established the 'most effective and yet bloodless dictatorship in history'.[7] For Ulrich Schacht, co-editor of *The Self-Confident Nation* (*Die selbstbewußte Nation*, 1994), it was 'the editors and journalists from the "serious media" who get to determine who is a fascist in this country'.[8]

The charge that the cultural sphere was dominated by a left-liberal 'political correctness' with regard to the Nazi past would be heard throughout the 1990s. After the election in late 1998 of the SPD–Green coalition led by Gerhard Schröder and Joschka Fischer, for example, there appeared what Ingo Cornils terms a 'plethora of new books, essays and editorials' written to challenge the 'cultural hegemony' of the generation of '68 and its claim to an 'exclusive right to interpret the past'.[9] Similarly, discussions of the planned Holocaust Memorial in Berlin, the media outcry following the entreaties by the Austrian author Peter Handke for greater understanding for the Serbian position during the wars in ex-Yugoslavia, and the exhibition *War of Annihilation: Crimes of the Wehrmacht, 1941–1944* were all accompanied by accusations of 'political correctness'. The furore caused by Jörg Friedrich's *The Fire* (*Der Brand*, 2002), a graphic history of the Allied bombing campaign, and by the collection of photographs *Sites of Fire* (*Brandstätten*, 2003) which Friedrich published a year later, provoked comparable accusations. In each case, it was alleged that cultural memory had been usurped by an elite that had emerged from the student movement of the 1960s.

The work of Martin Walser from the early 1990s onwards illustrates the way the attack on 'political correctness' is frequently enmeshed with the theme of wartime suffering. Walser's novel of 1991 *In Defence of Childhood* (*Die Verteidigung der Kindheit*) thus not only obsessively catalogues the obliteration of Dresden's baroque heritage by the Allied airforces in February 1945 and, arguably, draws a parallel between German and Jewish suffering,[10] it also implies that the desire in the post-war era of its protagonist, Alfred Dorn, to mourn the city's destruction results in his silencing. His urge to acquire objects which refer back to Dresden as it used to be clashes with the 'politically correct' imperative to repress German suffering for the sake of the 'illusion of making amends'.[11] Here, as in the 'unification novella' *Dorle and Wolf* (*Dorle und Wolf*, 1988), Walser's protagonist refuses to accept the destruction of Germany's cities and the 'fact' of German division – the latter, according to a speech of 1988, a 'demonstration of [Allied] power, a punitive action'.[12]

Walser's 1993 *without one another* (*ohne einander*) elaborates one of the key charges levelled by conservatives: that 'political correctness' has inflicted a form of 'secondary suffering' on Germans via a vindictive emphasis on German crimes.[13] In this novel, the journalist Ellen feels compelled to write an approving report on Agnieszka Holland's film *Europa Europa* (*Hitlerjunge Salomon*, 1990). It is simply not permissible to critique the unreflected reiteration of stereotypes, as summarised by her lover Ernst: 'ALL Germans from back then were stupid and brutal, mouthing Nazi slogans, and all non-Germans were splendid, decent, magnificent people . . . . [And the Germans] deserve to be annihilated, wiped out.'[14] In common with much of the conservative critique of 'political correctness', it is insinuated that the only way it is possible to counter the 'self-righteousness and hypocrisy' of the 'producers of public opinion' (*oe,* 176) is to describe German suffering using terms normally associated with the Holocaust.

Similar arguments feature in Walser's 1998 speech in receipt of the Peace Prize of the German Book Trade. In particular, these arguments appeared to constitute a response to left-liberal philosopher Jürgen Habermas's insinuation that the burning of asylum-seeker hostels in 1992 was symptomatic of a deep-rooted and widespread German racism. 'In no other language', Walser said, 'would it be possible, at the close of the twentieth century, to speak of a people, an entire population, or society, in this way. Only of the Germans.'[15] Walser's comments to a select audience including the Federal President and the then leader of the Council of Jews, Ignatz Bubis, represented an extended assault on 'political correctness' and the 'instrumentalisation' (*EVS*, 13) of the Holocaust as a means of muting those who challenge the Left's hegemony over cultural memory.[16] At the same time, they also respond to criticisms made of Walser's *A Springing Fountain* (*Ein springender Brunnen*, 1998), specifically to the charge made by literary critic Marcel Reich-Ranicki that this novel, a semi-autobiographical tale of a young boy's absorption in the world of poetry and the imagination set between 1932 and 1945, 'failed' to mention Auschwitz.

The very premise of *A Springing Fountain* – that it is possible to tell a story set in the 1930s and 1940s and speak of things *other* than Nazism – is an attack on what Walser sees as the 'politically correct' mantra according to which subjective memory is subordinate to the brute reality of Auschwitz.[17] As if this were not sufficiently evident from the almost exclusive focus on Johann's fascination with the otherworldliness of poetry, a series of authorial intercessions reinforce the point. Contrasting with the modern-day tendency to render history 'ethically and politically "corrected", through and through',[18] the novel will make the past 'present, on its own terms' (*SB*, 9). Childhood memories will not be 'deformed' by a 'politically correct' insistence on the primacy of Auschwitz over 'German' stories.

Walser's attack on 'political correctness' continues in *Death of a Critic* (*Tod eines Kritikers*, 2002), in which the fictional murder of a Jewish critic based on Reich-Ranicki challenges sensitivities regarding anti-Semitism.[19] Just as striking is the author's defence of Jörg Friedrich. In an article of December 2002, Walser responds to the criticism that *The Fire* employs terms usually reserved for the Holocaust with a resolute rebuttal of 'politically correct' distinctions between Jewish and German victimhood. Friedrich's vivid narrative, he asserts, is a 'written memorial for the bombing war . . . to be preferred over any other attempt at a memorial'.[20] It is unclear whether this is to be taken to mean that a memorial to German suffering would be preferable to the planned Berlin Holocaust memorial, or that 'written' memorials, for German *and* Jewish victims, are preferable to concrete memorials.

A new 'inclusiveness'

In parallel to the right's attack on 'political correctness', the 1990s witnessed the rise of a more general questioning of the way Nazism had been discussed in the pre-1990 Federal Republic. This was part of a broad-based reflection that aimed not so much at destroying a 'left-liberal hegemony' over cultural memory as establishing what Bill Niven has called a new 'inclusiveness'. It was a 'process of broadening understanding' in response to the passing of time, the end of the Cold War and the proclivity to deploy the past as an ideological weapon, the changed mood after 1990, and global events, some of which are discussed later in this chapter. In practice, the need to acknowledge German perpetration had been internalised, and this meant that it was now possible to discuss German suffering and to generate a more textured picture of the past.

What Niven terms the new 'mental attitude, a willingness'[21] in the 1990s to address *all* aspects of the Nazi period was, perhaps necessarily, accompanied by an acknowledgement on the part of the generation of '68 of a need to concede ground. Peter Schneider, for example, had been an early detractor of his own generation's reluctance to reassess its previous sympathies for the GDR.[22] Later in the decade, in his Berlin novel *Eduard's Homecoming* (*Eduards Heimkehr*, 1999) depicting post-unification debates on the restitution of 'Aryanised' Jewish property, Schneider went on to critique the automatic presumption of German guilt. Finally, in response to the publication of Friedrich's *The Fire*, he argued that his generation had ignored German stories which did not fit with its favoured stereotype of German perpetration.[23]

Along with Schneider, F. C. Delius and Uwe Timm might also be adduced as examples of '68ers who have explored their generation's perhaps insufficiently flexible perspective on the Nazi past: Delius in *America-House and Dancing the Quickstep with Women* (*Amerikahaus und der Tanz um die Frauen*, 1997) and *Flutter-Tongue* (*Flatterzunge*, 1999), and Timm in *Red* (*Rot*, 2001)[24] and *In My Brother's Shadow* (*Am Beispiel meines Bruders*, 2002). With respect to Schneider, Andreas Michel insists that the author does *not* reject a critical perspective on the past *per se*, that is, his position is not to be compared with the New Right's summary dismissal of all reference to German perpetration as 'political correctness'.[25] Instead, Schneider's work promotes a differentiated perspective which takes into account motives, available choices, and human weakness without losing sight of broader moral and ethical issues. The same can be said of Delius's *Flutter-Tongue*, which critiques both a German obsession with policing the interpretation of the past *and* the persecution complex of those who feel marginalised by this. The hullabaloo which follows the protagonist's botched attempt at humour – on tour in Israel as a trombonist, he signed a bar tab with the name Adolf Hitler – is thus parodied in equal measure as his paranoia.[26]

Uwe Timm's *In My Brother's Shadow* was by no means the first attempt by an author of the generation of '68 to triangulate German perpetration with German suffering and a recognition of the '68ers' apparent indifference to this suffering. In Hans-Ulrich Treichel's *Lost* (*Der Verlorene*, 1998), for example, the protagonist's parents frame themselves as 'pure' victims – they 'lost' a son when fleeing the advancing Soviet army in 1945 – but are incapable of recognising their own complicity; at the same time, the teenage boy's refusal to acknowledge his parents' suffering is shown to derive from his resentment of the way their grief is imposed onto him.[27] What Timm's short novel depicts perhaps more vividly than most, however, is the complex mix of culpability and eventual misery that surely characterised the experience of 'ordinary' Germans under Hitler. Timm draws on the life of his older brother, Karl Heinz Timm, who was born in 1924, joined the *SS* in 1943, and died in the Ukraine in 1943; the novel explores his feelings of inadequacy, the influence of an authoritarian father, and his untimely death, within the context of his callous indifference to the suffering inflicted on non-Germans. This 'ordinary' German was both a perpetrator *and* a victim: an SS soldier who could decry the Allied fire-bombing of Hamburg but overlook the murder on the eastern front, and yet also a young man not yet 20 years old moulded by years of indoctrination.[28]

Timm's novel acknowledges suffering as part of the German wartime experience. However, it also refutes the exculpatory notion which, into the 1960s, accompanied allusions to this pain: that what Germans endured followed from a cruel twist of 'fate' (*AB*, 91), unprovoked by German crimes. Descriptions of the planning and execution of Hitler's war of annihilation are thus placed alongside extracts from the brother's diary which reveal the extent to which such atrocities were part of his everyday *normality*. The story of German suffering is told with all due empathy but the causal and temporal precedence of German perpetration remains clear.

'Ordinary' Germans

Timm's *In My Brother's Shadow* references historian Christopher R. Browning's *Ordinary Men: Reserve Police Battalion 101* (English, 1993; German: *Ganz normale Männer*, 1998; *AB*, 103), an investigation into the motives, choices and actions of a cohort of largely middle-aged, unexceptional German reservists who, with a greater or lesser degree of enthusiasm, participated in mass killings of Jews. It is evident that

Timm subscribes to Browning's proposition that involvement in murder was facilitated by an unstable brew of peer pressure, ambition, indoctrination, weakness and habituation; here, the implicit contrast is with Daniel Jonah Goldhagen's *Hitler's Willing Executioners* (1996; German: *Hitlers willige Vollstrecker*) with its monocausal insistence on an 'eliminatory anti-Semitism'. For Timm, it is just as necessary to understand the actions of his brother, and others like him, *in context* as it is to condemn his failure to dissent.

An engagement with the choices faced by 'ordinary Germans' defines post-unification discussions of the Nazi past. The imminent passing of the wartime generation has provoked an upsurge in interest in the stories never before told by a grandfather or grandmother. The publication of a rash of biographies, diaries and collections of letters has reflected and fed this fascination. In 2003, for example, *A Woman in Berlin* (*Eine Frau in Berlin*), an anonymous account of a woman's rape by Russian soldiers, became a bestseller, as did the writings of Willy Peter Reese, a soldier killed on the eastern front, *A Stranger to Myself: The Inhumanity of War: Russia, 1941–1944* (*Mir selber seltsam fremd. Die Unmenschlichkeit des Krieges. Russland 1941–44*, 2003). Almost as popular were Ulla Lachauer's *East Prussian Lives* (*Ostpreußische Lebensläufe*, 1998), which collates biographies of East Prussian expellees, and Peter Glotz's *Expulsion: Bohemia as Object-Lesson* (*Die Vertreibung. Böhmen als Lehrstück*, 2003), which includes accounts by refugees from Bohemia. Most expansive of all, Walter Kempowski's five-volume *Soundings* (*Das Echolot*, 1999–2005) juxtaposes original texts written by soldiers and civilians of all nations. Photography too has been a powerful medium. Thus Sebald's *The Emigrants* (*Die Ausgewanderten*, 1993) and *Austerlitz* (2001), Monika Maron's *Pawel's Letters* (*Pawels Briefe*, 1999), Marcel Beyer's *Spies* (*Spione*, 2000) and Ulla Hahn's *Blurred Images* (*Unscharfe Bilder*, 2003) all set photographs at the core of their explorations of the decisions made by 'real people'. Stephen Wackwitz's *An Invisible Country* (*Ein unsichtbares Land*, 2003) similarly draws on images from a family album. In the later works, the use of photography in the *Crimes of the Wehrmacht* exhibition is a key influence, often unacknowledged but occasionally directly referenced, as in Timm's novel (*AB*, 102).

In addition to the sense of urgency instilled by the impending fading of the wartime generation, it may also be the case that a contemporary cynicism with regard to ideology and master-narratives has led to a compensatory faith in the 'authentic' experiences of the individual. Consequently, literary texts such as Günter de Bruyn's *Interim Balance:*

A Youth in Berlin (*Zwischenbilanz. Eine Jugend in Berlin*, 1992), Günter Kunert's *Grown-Ups' Games: Memoirs* (*Erwachsenenspiele. Erinnerungen*, 1997) and Peter Härtling's *Learning Life* (*Leben lernen*, 2003), autobiographical novels by authors in their teens during the war, presuppose the reader's willingness to see the everyday desires, disappointments and distresses endured by their youthful protagonists as more 'valid' than any depiction of the overall political situation. Indeed, the same might be said of Härtling's *Big Sister, Little Sister* (*Große Schwester, kleine Schwester*, 1998), which relates the story of two sisters from the First World War to the present, including the transfer of their home town from Austria to Czechoslovakia in 1919, their expulsion in 1945, and their lives in West Germany. Or, we might point to non-fictional texts such as Hilke Lorenz's *Children of the War: The Fate of a Generation* (*Kriegskinder. Das Schicksal einer Generation*, 2003) and Sabine Bode's *The Forgotten Generation* (*Die vergessene Generation*, 2004), which claim to break the 'silence' on the part of those born in the midst of the bombing campaign. The trauma suffered by the *Kriegskinder* is in fact evident in works by authors such as Hans Magnus Enzensberger, Peter Handke, Christa Wolf, Wolfgang Hilbig and Wolf Biermann although Biermann, whose Jewish father was murdered in Auschwitz, recalls his mother welcoming the English bombers.[29]

A focus on the wartime reality of 'ordinary' people often emphasises suffering and may obscure the distinctions between victims. The publication in 1995 of Victor Klemperer's *Diaries 1933–45* (*Tagebücher 1933–45*), diary entries detailing Klemperer's life as a Jew in Dresden and celebrated by Walser as evidence of the 'reality' of a 'German-Jewish symbiosis' before it was 'interrupted' by the Holocaust,[30] most likely made possible the glut of accounts by non-Jews that followed. Yet texts such as Martin Doerry's *'My Wounded Heart': The Life of Lilli Jahn* (*'Mein verwundetes Herz': Das Leben der Lilli Jahn*, 2002), which collates the letters of a Jewish grandmother killed in Auschwitz, may, more recently, seem simply to complement a more central emphasis on the *German* experience of the war.

In homing in on 'ordinary' Germans, in fact, many contemporary publications adopt a 'historicising' approach, which remains distinct from the perspective promoted by Hillgruber in 1986, or neo-conservatives in the early 1990s, only to the extent that empathy for the individual's limited choices, 'poor' decisions, or human weakness is balanced against the larger picture of German perpetration. In respect of Uwe Timm, we have seen that a more 'inclusive' picture of the past need not imply a relativisation of German crimes. The same might be said of Hanns-Josef Ortheil's *Farewell to the Wartime Veterans* (*Abschied von den Kriegsteilnehmern*, 1992), in which a '68er takes unification as a spur to develop a more empathetic view of his parents' loss of four sons as a result of the war and his father's combat experiences in Poland and around Berlin. Ludwig Harig's *Woe Betide Those Who Dance out of Step* (*Weh dem, der aus der Reihe tanzt*, 1990) and Ulla Berkéwicz's *Angels Are Black and White* (*Engel sind schwarz und weiß*, 1990) achieve a similar balance in their accounts of adolescence in the Third Reich.[31] This may not be the case for other writers, however: speaking of Kempowski's *Soundings*, for example, Bill Niven notes that 'the sheer weight of emphasis it lends to German suffering' obscures German responsibility.[32] Likewise, Ulla Hahn's *Blurred Images* (2003), comparable to Timm's *In My Brother's Shadow* insofar as it tells of a daughter's struggle to confront her father's experience on the eastern front, occasionally tends towards an uncritical resignation *vis-à-vis* her father's description of his dilemma as both part of the German war machine and its victim: 'Could anyone who was not there ever really understand their father?'[33]

More generally, two issues arise. First: the accent on a protagonist's complex, often mixed responses to issues affecting his or her life directly may create the impression that the cohort, social class or geographical region of which he or she was a part displayed similar ambivalence, at the macro-level, with regard to Nazi ideology, anti-Semitism or the war of annihilation. This might apply to soldiers on the eastern front, as in *Blurred Images*, or, as we shall see, working-class communities in urban centres. Alternatively, it might apply to Walser's portrayal in *A Springing Fountain* of the intrusion of Nazism into a provincial setting intuitively hostile to it. Second: a concentration on 'ordinary' Germans may engender a sentimentalisation of their fates which excises the bigger picture of complicity.

Dieter Forte's *The Boy with the Bloody Shoes* (*Der Junge mit den blutigen Schuhen*, 1995), the second in a trilogy telling of two families, the Fontanas and the Lukacz, and of their respective migrations from Sicily and Poland to Germany, describes life in the working-class neighbourhood of Düsseldorf-Oberbilk from the rise of Hitler to the end of the war. Yet the Fontanas and the Lukacz stand in for something larger: in the union of the families in the marriage of Friedrich and Maria, Protestant and Catholic come together, as do key philosophical traditions (the Fontanas embrace rationalism, the Lukacz a melancholic fatalism), Germany's diverse immigrant legacies and working-class traditions. Thus the two families embody broader strands within German society, and their low-key but determined hostility to Hitler appears emblematic. There are certainly occasional references to denunciations, yet, on the whole, this is a story about a community which remains largely immune to Nazism and instinctively feels sympathy for Jews, forced labourers and concentration camp inmates.

Forte's novel is a masterpiece of historicisation. However, the emphasis on the reconstruction of episodes to which the narrator, a young boy at the time, only has access via half-memories or family legends, can tip over into a sentimentalised vision of a working-class solidarity, stubborn non-conformity, and unaffected humanity. A 'never-ending story-telling'[34] thus keeps alive the memory of Polka-Paul and aunt Josephine, murdered by the Nazis in a home for the mentally ill (*DJ*, 77); of the woman executed for hiding a deserter (*DJ*, 187); of Pastor Lefarth, mortally wounded by American artillery (no differentiation is made between Nazi or Allied tormentors); of Varna, whose father came from Prague and who was killed by an Allied bomb; and of Odysseus, the man originally from Hungary buried under collapsing rubble (*DJ*, 179). Their stories are inscribed on to the memory-landscape of the area: 'Varna's hole, Odysseus's wall, Quieter's grave, Lefarth's street of death, grandpa Winter's air-shaft, the park of the executed woman' (*DJ*, 195). Their lives, then, are honoured by the diverse, multi-cultural community of which they were members, in defiance of the Nazis' desire to impose their ethnic 'ideal' – and *their* names.

It seems that Forte's narrative is intended to counter the way Oberbilk's 'authentic' 'memory sites' were supplanted in the post-war period by anonymous concrete blocks. Yet the reality is that the novel embellishes and sentimentalises: a Jew called grandpa *Winter*, 'a small, white-haired and always polite and helpful man with a moustache and hesitant smile' (*DJ*, 189), and best friend of the lumbering Herkules, is 'protected' by fellow residents until he is caught by an army patrol (outsiders, of course) and executed two days before the Americans arrive. In Peter Hüttenberger's history of Düsseldorf, clearly Forte's source for the majority of the stories he relates, there is no mention of whether the Jew Moritz *Sommer*, likewise murdered two days before the coming of the Allies, was able to rely on the discretion and assistance of his neighbours. Hüttenberger, in fact, tells us only that 'some, a few, Jews were able to hide themselves away' (i.e., they were not concealed by non-Jews). In addition, Hüttenberger reports that a Jewish woman attempting to flee the third mass deportation of 11 December 1941 was denounced by the cleaning woman working in the house into which she had run, and that the relationship of the neighbourhood's inhabitants to the 'foreign workers' coerced by the Nazis was 'distanced' – not the impression communicated by Forte's text – and 'differentiated' only in so far as local people feared and disliked the different nationalities present to different extents and, in accordance with different racist stereotypes, despised the Russians and Poles most of all.[35]

Günter Grass's *Crabwalk* (*Im Krebsgang*) is an account of the torpedoing of the *Wilhelm Gustloff*, a cruise ship packed with 7000 German refugees, by a Soviet submarine in January 1945. It was the literary hit of 2002, inspiring, for example, a four-part special edition of *Der Spiegel* on 'Germans as victims'. Ostensibly a *mea culpa* on the part of the author whose generation had neglected German suffering, Grass's novella is in truth just as concerned with *how* this tale of suffering might be told in a manner which avoids sentimentalisation. In his vivid description of the passengers' final moments, the narrator thus resolves *not* to 'roll out the fates of individuals, with epic sombreness and strained empathy in order, with phrases dripping with horror, to do justice to the scale of the catastrophe'.[36] To do otherwise would be to fetishise their suffering such that the larger context of the *Gustloff*'s role in garnering support for the regime as a *Strength through Joy* ship and the enthusiasm for Nazism of many of its passengers – including the narrator's mother, Tulla – might disappear from view.

In its more popularist form, the new 'inclusiveness' identified by Niven most likely draws upon a sentimentalising version of a global 1990s' 'victim culture'. *Crabwalk*, in response, confronts the spread of this discourse via the mass media, and, more recently, the internet, with a complex, multi-layered narrative. Thus the narrator's belated recognition of German suffering, implied by his overdue acceptance of the coincidence of the demise of the ship and his own birth, makes it possible for him to give an empathetic account of the passengers' fate. This 'historicising' strand, however, is set alongside a critical analysis of both Nazi and present-day efforts to focus on Soviet atrocities and to elide German crimes.[37]

Bosnia, Rwanda and Kosovo

For Grass's narrator, the photographs of wretched German refugees in 1945 on the 'revisionist' websites hosted by his son deliberately evoke present-day atrocities, 'even if the horrors in the Balkans and in Rwanda were not mentioned by name' (*IK*, 102). Konrad, it seems, seeks to equate German suffering with the 'ethnic cleansing' of Bosnian muslims in the early 1990s or the fate of Rwandan Tutsis massacred in 1994. This, for Grass, is the risk associated with the contemporary sentimentalisation of German victimhood: that it might be subsumed into an undifferentiated 'victim culture' in which all suffering is seen as equally valid, especially if an analogy can be established with the Holocaust. In an age in which, as Niven argues, Auschwitz has become the symbol of a 'universal victimhood' within an 'increasing plurality of national, ethnic and religious discourses',[38] it would seem unjust to deny German pain its place.

There can be no doubt that media reports of events in the former Yugoslavia in particular tapped into a collective memory of what Germans had endured. Often, the parallels drawn were sentimental in the extreme. At the same time, however, German suffering was also deployed in a more thoughtful manner during the heated debates surrounding Germany's participation in multilateral interventions in these conflicts. Forte, for example, declared with regard to the 1999 Kosovo crisis that it was time to break the silence of the victims and to confront those 'who do not know war' with its reality.[39] For Christa Wolf, the NATO bombing of Serbia provoked memories of 'people in air raid shelters, sirens, explosions, fear'. Yet she also expressed solidarity with the victims of Serbian aggression: 'That too I have experienced: the treks of the expellees.'[40] The German experience, therefore, did not provide a clear-cut indication of what stance to take. Many of the pieces reprinted in *The West's Crusade: 41 Positions on the War in Kosovo* (*Der westliche Kreuzzug. 41 Positionen zum Kosovo-Krieg*, 1999), edited by Frank Schirrmacher, allude to the trauma of bombing: some support German military action, others reject it. Durs Grünbein's poetry, which similarly refers to Allied air raids, may also provoke reflection on events in Kosovo, without, however, predicting the author's stance on the more recent conflict: Grünbein supported NATO intervention.

Pervading many 1990s' recollections of German suffering in the context of events in Bosnia and Kosovo is a sense of disappointment at the turn taken by events after the Cold War – the gleeful self-exculpation that Grass fears is rare. Conflict in ex-Yugoslavia thus reminds Hans Magnus Enzensberger, 'fifty years later', of his experiences as a child, 'wrapped in a blanket in the shelter'. This does not mean that this left-thinker now subscribes to a neo-conservative fantasy of the 'absolute' victim: 'I remember, you see, how their eyes lit up whenever

Hitler spoke.'[41] Rather, he casts his gaze across the post-1990 world and edges, reluctantly, towards a 'pessimistic anthropology'[42] documenting a universal proclivity for 'chauvinism and hatred of strangers'.[43] For W. G. Sebald, on the other hand, events in Bosnia and Kosovo most likely confirmed the gloomy view of the hubris of Western modernity adumbrated in *After Nature* (*Nach der Natur*, 1989), *Vertigo* (*Schwindel-Gefühle*, 1990) and *The Rings of Saturn* (*Die Ringe des Saturn*, 1992), in which the air war is mentioned, or in *The Emigrants* and *Austerlitz*, in which Jewish and German suffering are juxtaposed, though not equated.[44] Neither author seeks to relativise cruelty as a 'given' of human nature – as Bernhard Schlink's 1995 *The Reader* (*Der Vorleser*) perhaps does –[45] or to sentimentalise German suffering as part of an 'unbroken chain' of human misery. They posit not the inalterability of the individual psyche, but the propensity of human societies to repeat past errors.

Christoph Hein's *Landgrab* (*Landnahme*, 2004) and Reinhard Jirgl's *The Incomplete* (*Die Unvollendeten*, 2003) respond, first and foremost, to the official silence in the former East Germany *vis-à-vis* the injustices suffered by ethnic Germans in Czechoslovakia and Poland and at the hands of the Soviet Army, that is, countries now allied with the Communist state.[46] Hein thus tells of Bernhard Haber, the son of a refugee from what was now Poland, his struggle for acceptance in a community hostile to 'outsiders', and of how this antagonism 'deforms' him. Similarly, Jirgl recounts the story of Johanna, mother to Hanna and Maria, and Hanna's daughter Anna, graphically depicting their expulsion from the Sudetenland, and describing the prejudice they later encounter in Germany. At the same time, these novels may have a broader ambition: to intervene in debates regarding the welcome extended to the victims of more recent conflicts in Bosnia and Kovoso. At the close of *Landgrab*, Haber scolds his son for attacking a refugee: 'Your grandfather was also an expellee', to which Paul replies: 'That's different. Grandpa was a German.'[47] On his arrival in 1945, of course, 'grandpa' had been denigrated as 'Polish'. In *The Incomplete*, the allusions to present-day refugees may be more subtle: 'for where there are refugees, there are always The Camps'; the 'REFUGEE-QUOTA', 'the fear of the *refugees* that they would be crammed inside and the barn set on fire . . . – the primal-fear of all deportees', for example.[48] In both novels, the message appears to be that Germany must not *repeat* the ill will it showed towards these 'strangers' after 1945 in respect of those currently in need of assistance.

Younger writers

In the course of its narration of the experiences of Johanna, Hanna, Maria and Anna as refugees in the GDR, *The Incomplete* introduces a digression on developments in German literature from the mid-1990s. Following an excursus on the 'myth' of 'supp-wehr-syph' ('subversive') fiction in the GDR and West Germany (*DU*, 192), there are references to the current literary scene and its fêting of the 'lads' & lassies' miracle', that is, *younger* writers focusing on lifestyle: 'their Gyrman, fashionably perfumed, hardly 1 sentence without nonsense-fragments of American words, the Joop-Gyrman of the internett –. Globalised Sensibility –' (*DU*, 194). In writing of German suffering, therefore, it may be that Jirgl also sees himself as resisting globalisation, the erasure of 'German stories', younger authors' 'pop' fixation, and what he views as the market's promotion of superficiality over substance.

In the 1990s, the theme of German suffering was largely the preserve of older writers. Certainly, in the second half of the decade, a concern with 'history' set them apart from the 'pop craze' then in full swing.[49] On those occasions on which German suffering did feature in work by younger writers, it was typically peripheral to the plot and mechanistically deployed as part of a litany of complaint regarding the dulling banality of the present or as a foil to a protagonist's current traumas. In Christian Kracht's *Frayed-Land* (*Faserland*, 1995), for instance, references to the firestorm in Hamburg or to Heidelberg as one of the few cities spared total destruction – 'Germany could still be like that, if there hadn't been a war and if the Jews hadn't been gassed' – recall neo-conservative rhetoric in the early 1990s, but most likely derive more specifically from its youthful protagonist's existential disgust with today's Germany, a country anaesthetised by prosperity.[50] In Jenny Erpenbeck's *Story of the Old Child* (*Geschichte vom alten Kind*, 1999), a mention of the devastation of Dresden is relevant only insofar as it prompts the central character to recall the abuse inflicted on her mother.[51]

The publication in 2003 of Tanja Dückers's *Heavenly Bodies* (*Himmelskörper*), which tells of a woman's efforts to induce her grandmother to recount her flight from the Russians, and Olaf Müller's *Silesian Weather* (*Schlesisches Wetter*), in which the protagonist narrates his family's expulsion from Poland, seemed to many critics, including Hage, to indicate a more profound interest in the German wartime experience on the part of younger writers in the new millennium

(Dückers was born in 1968, Müller in 1962).[52] Indeed, it is only now, thus the narrator of *Heavenly Bodies*, that her generation is ready to relate 'learnt' history to the 'real' individuals, about to fade away, who had 'themselves sat in burning houses, fled on cattle carts, been sent off to war aged 16, or, as small children, bundled into air raid shelters'.[53] For Freia, the aim is not to excuse her grandparents, Party members given preferential treatment during their escape from the Russians, but to bring the past to life. At the very least, this responds to the apathy regarding the Nazi period, a result perhaps of over-exposure to sterile debates on how to remember it – alluded to, for example, in Julia Franck's *The Love Servant* (*Der Liebediener*) or Elke Naters's *Lies* (*Lügen*, both 1999).[54] Freia's is an empathetic view of her grandparents' past, no doubt – Dückers claimed 'it is possible to look at grandparents differently than at parents'[55] – which provokes the suspicion of her '68er parents. First and foremost, however, it is the view of the 'third generation' after Nazism, attempting to define its own interest in the Third Reich between the self-exculpation of those who lived through it and the rush to condemn of those born in the shadow of its crimes. Indeed, the melancholic, and only partial, acceptance of the revelation that a neighbour was in the SS voiced by the young protagonist of Leander Scholz's short story 'SS' ('SS', 2004), might be seen as typical of this generation: 'Sometimes I wish I came from a different country . . . It's like with your parents. You'd like to imagine better parents . . . but from a certain age, you get used to them and realise they're not all that bad. Of course, this comparison doesn't quite work.'[56]

Conclusion

Novels such as *Heavenly Bodies* point, perhaps, to a 'normalisation' of German fiction: a less burdened viewpoint on the Nazi period which sees it as a rich source of 'human interest' stories, extraordinary biographies, compelling moral dilemmas and poignant family dramas rather than as a philosophical, political or ethical challenge. This is not to say that the choice of topic relates solely to aesthetic criteria. German suffering in particular, a 'weighty' matter requiring sensitivity and discernment, allows younger writers to mark their graduation from 'pop' and, with a focus on 'German' stories, to counter the charge that their fiction merely mimics Anglo-American bestsellers. Thus, in her introduction to the volume of short stories in which Scholz's 'SS' appeared, Dückers rejects labels such as the 'fun-generation'.[57] In the work of younger authors, in fact, 'German history' is more often than not integrated into a contemporary narrative featuring the 'universal' themes typical of today's globalised book market. Dückers's *Heavenly Bodies*, for example, juxtaposes the grandparents' flight from the East with her protagonist's adolescent struggle with sex, love and gender-role expectations. As the last of those directly involved in the war pass away, and their children, the '68ers, become less central to cultural and political discourse, it seems likely that this will evolve into the norm. A collective memory of Nazism, and of German suffering, will be one of a myriad of themes upon which writers draw – a dramatic, affecting subject, no doubt, but one that will be far less controversial in the future than it has been in the past.

10

Air War Legacies: From Dresden to Baghdad[1]

Andreas Huyssen

I

In the months leading up to the Anglo-American war against Saddam Hussein's regime, the legacies of the 60-year-old air war against German cities infused the German peace movement and its growing opposition to Washington's unilateralism. While all over Europe the massive opposition to the war was politically justified, the German case displays a curious mix of memory and forgetting that sets it apart. The use of treacherous and facile historical analogies was ubiquitous in Germany, and it seemed to point to a new paradigm of thinking temporality and space in our post-utopian times. Contemporary media culture generates uses of the past that tend to blur temporal and spatial boundaries in deeply problematic ways.

The fast pace of change and anticipations of the future so characteristic of an earlier modernity have radically slowed down in recent years. In a world in which visions of the future are largely discredited, the present comes to be ever-more expanded, and the past looms large, partly as a result of a wave of transnational memory politics, but also because of new media technologies of cultural recycling. We are now witnessing a kind of time–space expansion in the imaginary that stands in tension with the very real time–space compression of modernity that David Harvey has described so well.[2]

But what precisely is the nature of this time–space expansion? Are we exposed to substantive historical narratives, or are these mediated pasts only present as ciphers, quotations and fragments, image worlds offered for easy consumption and identification? What are the effects of this expansion? Which pasts are chosen to be incorporated into the present? In what form? And who does the choosing? Where is this broadening of the present culturally and politically productive, and where is it just a sign of immobility, self-indulgence and narcissism? No doubt, the parameters of our temporal imagination seem to have shifted. As various pasts take up ever-more space in our imagination, some rail against any form of nostalgia in order to safeguard modernist notions of a dynamic present, while others subject all of history to trauma theory which makes all presents and futures into mere repetitions. Both approaches fail to capture the fact that we may be witnessing the petering out of a relatively short-lived chronotope that was dominant in that earlier phase of modernity, but that is now being transformed into another constellation of space and time.

II

In this broader context, the German peace movement's selective mobilisation of the German past appears as a symptomatic case of an expanded present and its inherent contradictions and political illusions. Like everything else in Germany's widening memorial culture these days, the German opposition to the Iraq war was intensely fed by an expanded present stretching back to the Second World War, the crimes of the Third Reich, the Holocaust. Of course, this past has haunted the country for decades, but there seems to be a different quality to the haunting now by comparison with the earlier decades of silence, evasion and *Bewältigung* ('coming to terms').

While the German peace movement of 2003 was arguably much larger and more layered in its generational and social composition than its predecessors, it drew on the same arsenal of convictions and rhetoric as the anti-armament campaigns of the 1980s and the peace movement of the first Iraq war: never again war, no war for oil, the same peace songs and performers at the demonstrations, much of it a *déjà vu* to observers and a confirmation of the participants' self-righteousness. If Germany as a whole suffers from social and political immobility these days, then a cynic might say it had the peace 'movement' it deserved.

But then there also were differences that marked a significant shift in German memorial politics, though not necessarily for the better. For the first time, the peace movement bolstered its positions by referring directly to the experience of the strategic bombings of German cities in the Second World War. It seemed that the memories of Hamburg and Dresden's firestorms provided the unifying glue that brought Westerners and Easterners, old and young, Right and Left, out into the streets in larger numbers than ever before in protest against George W. Bush's war in Iraq.

In 1999, Germany had for the first time since 1945 participated in a military action 'out of area', the NATO bombing campaign against Milosevic's regime and the liberation of Kosovo. Clearly, the wars in the former Yugoslavia provide the political and historical context for the renewed debate about civilian bombings and about what in Iraq and Afghanistan is evasively referred to as collateral damage. German military participation in the Kosovo campaign was vociferously contested at the time, but in the conflict of the two German 'never agains', the 'never again Auschwitz' won out over 'never again war', as television screens showed the trains with dishevelled refugees and victims of ethnic cleansing arriving *en masse* in Albania. As in the case of the images from Bosnia in 1992 of ethnic prisoners behind barbed wire, this coverage served as a powerful memory prompt. The threat of genocide hung in the air. In 2003, sentiment reverted back to a radical no war line, but this time – and this was new – with reference to German victimhood. The youngest German protest generation, including whole elementary school classes, marched under the unlikely slogan 'We know what it's like to be bombed', carrying signs that equated Dresden with Baghdad. Here was the past as citation, as selective recall with a claim to absolute presentness – generational difference of experience eliminated, a collapsing of time zones into a broadened present.

Given that the memory of the bombings in the Second World War had not been part of public German memorial culture for several decades, how could it happen that it suddenly returned with a vengeance, occupying a central part of the discourse about the Iraq war and world peace?[3] How could the slogan 'never again war' suddenly change its underlying political motivation from Germans as perpetrators to Germans as victims? Of course, the experience and the after-effects of the Second World War bombings were never simply forgotten – neither by the generation who lived through the firestorms, nor by the first post-war generation who grew up playing cowboys and Indians in the ruins. Some may have repressed those memories because they were simply too painful and traumatic. Others may have felt inhibited to speak of their suffering because they were deeply aware of Germans' responsibility for the crimes of the Third Reich. On the other hand, and especially in the 1950s, many did speak of the bombings as crimes of the Allies in order to open up a balance sheet of war crimes, ultimately to exculpate Germany. But in the public memory debate in West Germany, the air war against German cities has never played a major role, most certainly not since the 1960s. It was 'publicly forgotten' for several decades, and the taboo existed for good reason.

In the 1950s and 1960s, speaking about the air war publicly, or privately in the family, was inescapably tied to the discourse of German victimisation: Germans as victims of the Nazis first, and then of the Allied bombers, and finally of the allied occupation. More often than not, talk of the air war was to relativise the crimes of the Holocaust. The Right spoke of Dresden and the expulsion from the East, the Left spoke of Auschwitz. Both sides displayed resistance to the other memory. Both instrumentalised memory for political purpose. Grief and mourning remained for the most part alien to this discourse. In this highly politicised memory climate, the arguments of the Left in favour of public forgetting were politically legitimate. The notion of German victimhood, tied to a long-standing nationalist discourse after the Treaty of Versailles, was fundamentally reactionary, and it had to be fought for the country to arrive at a new consensus regarding the crimes of the Third Reich. The price paid was the forgetting of the *Luftkrieg* (air war), the taboo to speak publicly of that traumatic national experience.

III

With the publication of Jörg Friedrich's hugely successful *The Fire/The Burning* (*Der Brand*) in the fall of 2002, the debate in Germany reached a new stage, pointing to an altered memoryscape.[4] Within a few months several hundred thousand copies were sold. The book was reviewed everywhere, and its publication was followed by a flood of documentary television programmes, talk-shows, special issues of *Der Spiegel*,[5] GEO[6] and other mass-circulation magazines. Friedrich, a freelance historian known for his critical work on the Nazi war machine and on post-war trials, kept appearing on television, sometimes several times a night on different channels, and at the high point of this media frenzy, it seemed like not one evening of television could go by without bombs falling on German cities, firestorms raging and survivors describing their harrowing experiences.

W. G. Sebald's 1999 book *On the Natural History of Destruction* (*Luftkrieg und Literatur*), which first broke through the public silence about the air war and clearly serves as a hidden reference for Friedrich, now appears only as a prelude to this new wave of public memorial discourse, in which the experience of an older vanishing generation of Germans is being transmitted to their children and grandchildren.[7] As with Sebald, some critics have mobilised the old taboos against Friedrich's powerful narrative of the bombings, but clearly not with much success and perhaps not even with much conviction.[8] Memory of the air war is no longer a public taboo, nor should it be. But it does raise thorny historical issues, and it remains deeply problematic in its facile projection on to current political conflicts.

Clearly, some of Friedrich's narrative strategies are susceptible to criticism. He was taken to task for his emphatic tone, his ambiguity about whether the bombings were war crimes, and the use of language usually reserved for the Holocaust (air shelters as crematoria, bomber crews as SS mobile killing squads (*Einsatzgruppen*), the bombing of libraries as a 'burning of the books' (*Bücherverbrennung*), the very title of the book approximating a German translation of 'Holocaust', etc.). Such rhetoric does suggest a subliminal link between the air war and genocide, even if the explicit argument of the book would seem to deny it. Despite such inexcusable slippages, there is wide agreement that Friedrich is not the Nolte of a second historians' debate. This is not a revisionist book about Germans *as* victims as much as it is a book about German victims whose experiences needed to be acknowledged and absorbed into the national narrative about the war and post-war years.

Even such a differentiation goes only so far. It does not fully explain the fascination the book evoked. Its resonance in Germany only makes sense in light of two facts, one external, the other internal to the book. *The Fire* appeared mid-point between New York's 9/11 and the bombing of Baghdad, a coincidence that could not have been better planned to enhance interest in Friedrich's topic. Friedrich mentions neither, and from interviews it is clear that he actually supported the Iraq war, just as he never leaves much doubt that the Allies were justified in fighting the Nazi war machine with everything they had, at least in the war's early stages. But the public reception of historical scholarship is a tricky business.

Clearly, this book would have had an impact in Germany in any case. It was timely enough even without a looming Iraq war. But the prospect of another air war provided a broader context and it intensified the reception. The book fuelled the peace movement precisely with its strategies of discussing the air war in terms of a contemporary anti-war and anti-bombing sensibility. It expanded the present backwards, offering the growing opposition to the Iraq war a decontextualised and experiential take on German history that made Baghdad look like Dresden, the firestorms of the 1940s like the 'shock and awe' campaign of the allies, and the Germans into arbiters of history.

Apart from the timing, the overwhelming reception the book received also resulted from the author's choice of style and narrative strategies. *The Fire* is a hybrid work, occupying a fault line between historiography and literature. This is not to say that Friedrich confuses fact and fiction. His facts are pretty well established, and one should not use a few mistakes inevitable in an undertaking of this scope as an excuse to dismiss the whole book. Similarly, the experiential dimension of Friedrich's account cannot be simply dismissed as 'impressionistic', as critical historians are wont to argue. It needs to be analysed and understood for what it is: a carefully deployed literary strategy of mixing factual reportage, historical documentation and point of view narration. Friedrich does not provide new facts about history. Most of what he tells is known from the work of British, American, and a few German historians and from mostly local accounts and testimonies of the bombings.[9] But rather than criticise the lack of original archival research, the literary dimension of Friedrich's book must be accounted for in more detail. He is clearly inspired and influenced by the writings about the air war by authors such as Hans Erich Nossack, Gerd Ledig and Alexander Kluge, authors whose work is included in his bibliography, yet never footnoted, and who are all treated in detail in Sebald's *On the Natural History of Destruction*. It is no coincidence that the back cover of the German edition of *The Fire* features a blurb each by Sebald and by Kluge. Sebald praises Friedrich's focus on 'the allies' strategy of destruction', and Kluge points to the 'thick language of narration', which transforms 'history into story'.[10] But the influence goes deeper. The sequence of chapters is structured on a basis of categories that Alexander Kluge deployed in his major text on the air war, *The Air Raid on Halberstadt on 8 April 1945* (*Der Luftangriff auf Halberstadt am 8. April 1945*).[11] In that text, Kluge confronted what he called the strategy from above (industrialisation and military planning, mass production of bombers, flying fortresses manned by sizeable crews of specialists, the bombs as wares to be delivered) with the experiential strategy from below (trying to find safety in air shelters, surviving the fires, not being in the wrong place at the wrong time). It is striking to see how Friedrich's narration moves from the chapters 'Weapon' and 'Strategy' (from above) via 'Land' (his longest chapter describing bombing damage city by city), to 'Protection' (bunkers, shelters, hospitals), and in ever-narrowing circles to collective experience in 'Us' and finally individual experience in 'I' (strategy from below). Except for the last chapter called 'Stone', a powerful lament about the loss of architecture, libraries, archives and art works that made up the environment of the old Germany, Friedrich clearly deploys Kluge's paradigm as an alternative to chronological narration. He may tell history as story, but it is space rather than time that organizes the material. His voice, however, lacks the ironic political punch and laconic tone so central to much of Kluge's writing. Friedrich's sensibility rather demonstrates affinities to Sebald's melancholy notion of a natural history of destruction, which – in Friedrich's case, though not in Sebald's, whose philosophical frame is much larger and more subtle – risks interpreting the bombings and the firestorms as natural disaster rather than as the result of Nazi aggression.[12]

Clearly, the book's success is rooted in the suggestive power of its narrative which distinguishes it from a more distanced and contextual historiography. The lack of emphasis on political context has indeed been one of the major criticisms. In its focus on the experience of the bombings, its mix of an emphatic reconstruction of the subjective experience of suffering with the obsessively detailed anatomical description of victims getting stuck in melting asphalt in the streets, being cooked in shelters from the waters of exploding heating ducts, or being asphyxiated and shrivelled beyond recognition in the cellars by the searing heat from the firestorms above, Friedrich takes the reader directly to the place of destruction, making Germans into voyeurs of unimaginable horrors visited on the very sites they now inhabit. The accompanying photo book *Sites of Fire* (*Brandstätten*), published in the fall of 2003, exacerbates the problem by featuring horror images, many of them hard to look at.[13]

The lack of political context in *The Fire* translates into the scarcity of commentary in *Sites of Fire*, which instead adorns its images of destruction with montages of contemporary testimony and literary quotations, including Thomas Mann and Ernst Jünger, Hans Erich Nossack, Erich Kästner and Peter Huchel. These text–image montages operate at a documentary level, but are clearly intended to generate a strong affective response. Looking at the bombing war in this way raises all the well-known questions about voyeurism and the aestheticisation of horror, which is inherent in the material and could not be avoided no matter how much commentary were to be added. As the borders between past and present become fluid, it is as if one shared the experience itself. Certainly, it becomes imaginable in ways not found in earlier historiographic work on the Allies' strategic air command and its effects on the ground. The reader of *The Fire* is caught in an imaginary in which the firestorms of Hamburg and Dresden are immediately present, ready to be linked to other sets of images soon to explode on television screens once the bombing of Baghdad began. This is where Friedrich's powerful account of the past merged with the present. The near simultaneity on German television screens of bombing runs on Hamburg or Cologne with image sequences of the fireballs from Baghdad did the rest. The experientially focused proximity of Friedrich's kind of writing of history combined with the visually generated false sense of simultaneity corresponds to the notion of an expanded present that no longer allows for sober comparison and evaluation. Instead, we get a newly mediated form of experiencing other times and spaces in which the imagined past is projected on to the screen of the present. This historiography of proximity and immediacy is not only very different from Sebald and Kluge's writings, both of whom maintain distance, though in different ways, from the historical subjects of their books. The political effect of Friedrich's book – intended or not – is to close the gap between past and present by collapsing fundamental political differences: America and England bomb and civilians suffer – a facile and fallacious historical analogy between the German past and the Iraqi present, which was eagerly taken up by the German peace movement. Even historians such as Hans Ulrich Wehler have legitimised German opposition to Bush's war with explicit references to the German experience. Of course, the simplistic equation of Dresden with Baghdad was not shared by all opponents to the war, but it came in handy as the peace movement went to great lengths to cover the nature of Saddam's brutal regime with gracious silence or with references to the fact that Saddam was the fault of the Americans in the first place. The hypocritical slogan 'no war for oil' drowned out any political argument that might question the desirability of total peace when facing one of the most murderous dictators of our times. After all, this was a German lesson completely forgotten or angrily rejected in the debate. It was as if, deep down, some Germans have still not forgiven the Americans for liberating them. And it points to another continuity with the first Iraq war, when Hans Magnus Enzensberger's provocative argument about certain structural parallels between Hussein and Hitler's regimes was vociferously rejected by all those in Germany who insisted on the uniqueness of 'our Hitler'.

I am not arguing in favour of maintaining the taboo on the bombing war against German cities and civilians. Today, in the presence of a well-established Holocaust memory discourse in Germany, there is no justification for the continued unwillingness to discuss the experience of the bombings, their legitimacy, or their military usefulness. But the facile and self-serving ways in which German suffering during the air war is amalgamated to an an otherwise legitimate political critique of the Bush government's new doctrine of pre-emptive war and 'democratisation' by force cannot be justified. The Allies' war against Nazi Germany was neither pre-emptive, nor does it have much else in common with the current conflict which rather calls up parallels in the colonial history of the Middle East. Whatever the merits of Friedrich's book, apart from the political context of its reception, the notion of Germans as victims or simply German victims will meet with vociferous resistance among the victims of the Nazis and among the nations that fought the Nazi dictatorship at great sacrifice. Seen from the outside, the bombings will still be judged by many to have been legitimate punishment of Nazi Germany. Understandable as it may be, this is a retrospective rationale, and it should not prevent questioning the strategy of bombing wars today. To do so would be to side-step the fundamental moral and political issue of such bombings and their inevitable civilian casualties. Clearly, the threshold for the acceptance of civilian bombings has been significantly raised since the Second World War. If Friedrich's dramatic account can bring attention to this issue in an international context, more power to it. But for that to happen, it must be uncoupled from German *Befindlichkeiten* (feelings) and from the discourse of German victimhood. It is one thing to raise the issue inside Germany, but quite another to raise it in an international context. Perspective does matter.

IV

The emphatic infusion of air war legacies into the German peace movement points to another, more hidden dimension: the younger generations' fear of the future. Accounts and images of urban destruction and desolation were bound to make their mark on a mentality in which the fear of ecological disaster, structural unemployment, mountains of public debt, and the looming crises of social security and health care have created a sense of paralysis. The resurgence of anti-American sentiment in the war debate, which went beyond the legitimate anger about American unilateralism, must also be seen in light of the fact that Europe feels the pressures of a globalising economy, the downsides of which are often all too quickly blamed exclusively on the United States. Peace in this situation became an easy cipher for a European identity into which German identities can safely merge.

Two significant manifestations of the desire for peace – a museum show and an intellectuals' campaign in European newspapers – saw the light of day in the early summer of 2003. The European idea of eternal peace without war was powerfully illustrated in the inaugural exhibit of I. M. Pei's impressive new addition to the German Historical Museum in Berlin, which opened only a few weeks after the end of this non-ending war. The exhibit was entitled *The Idea of Europe: Concepts for an Eternal Peace*, and subtitled, *Structures and Utopias for Europe from the 'pax romana' to the European Union.* The show consisted of innumerable repetitive and mostly boring allegories of eternal peace, but its substance was a vivid reminder of the murderous conflicts throughout European history. No doubt, European unification owes its progress to the desire for peace after two world wars. But it seems to be a self-indulgent European illusion to think that because peace may finally have come to this war-torn continent – and let's not think too much of Northern Ireland or the Balkans here – the idea of Europe at eternal peace can, or even should, be projected on to the world at large.

That, however, was the message of Jürgen Habermas and a group of Western intellectuals who, on the last Saturday of May 2003, published a series of articles in major French, Italian, Spanish, Swiss and German newspapers, calling for European unity and identity after the Iraq war. This concerted action of intellectuals was organized by Habermas in response to the letter of eight European heads of state who had earlier supported the British–American war effort. Time and again both before and during the Iraq war, Immanuel Kant's short essay of 1795 on perpetual peace had been quoted as philosophical underpinning for the European case against war. Kant and the Enlightenment were certainly on the agenda when Habermas and Derrida published their manifesto 'Our Renewal – After the War: The Rebirth of Europe' simultaneously in major French and German papers.[14] Habermas described the letter of the eight as a *Handstreich*, a *coup*, a kind of betrayal of European unity today, which for him was manifest in the Europe-wide demonstrations of 15 February, a date he prematurely and optimistically celebrated as the founding date of a new European public sphere. He then discussed five attributes he claimed all Europeans can share: the neutrality of authority, embodied in the separation of Church and State, trust in politics rather than the capitalist market, an ethos of solidarity in the fight for social justice, highest respect for international law and the rights of the individual, and support for the organisational and leading role of the state. The Kantian origin of several of these ideas is evident, but one by one they were of course primarily directed against current Washington policies. Key to Habermas's text, which was signed, though not co-written by Derrida, were two major goals: Europeans must try to 'balance' the 'hegemonic unilateralism of the US' with the help of the United Nations and other international bodies. And second: the guiding idea of the Europeans should be the creation of a Kantian 'cosmopolitan (world) order on the basis of law'. A worthy ideal, certainly, and in tune with Kant's ideas about the prerequisites for perpetual peace. But the method Habermas suggested to achieve these lofty goals did not go down well with the East Europeans, and it met with a lot of criticism at home as well. Particularly contentious was his argument that France, Germany and the Benelux countries, the original five of the Common Market, should serve as the avant-garde of European unification and play the role of locomotive in the process of further political unification of the continent. Habermas/Derrida suddenly looked like the tandem of Schröder/Chirac, endowing the rather self-serving arguments of the two political leaders with the nobility of philosophical honours. Far from advocating a desired post-nationalism, their views risked reinscribing national mechanisms of exclusion into the European project itself.

Thus it was immediately noted that no East European intellectual had contributed to the concerted effort of theorising European renewal: no Adam Michnik, no György Konrád, no István Eörsi. Of course, several, though not all, East European intellectuals supported the American intervention in Iraq, and would therefore not have seen eye to eye with Habermas and the other West European contributors. As could be expected, the reaction among the East Europeans to this French/German locomotive theory, which put the new members of the European Union into the caboose at the end of the train, was wholly negative. Thus, as a Pole suspicious of rationalist German philosophers and their biases, Adam Krzeminski pointed out that Kant had published his tract on perpetual peace in October 1795, just a month after the military suppression of the Kosciuszko revolt in Poland and the completion of the third Polish partition by Russia and Prussia, which resulted in the liquidation of a central European state by its bigger neighbours.[15] Not surprisingly, Kant failed to comment on the Poland policies of the Prussian kings. After all, he himself had painted a rather disparaging and condescending picture of Poland in his lectures on anthropology. Drawing the analogy between Kant and Habermas, Krzeminski saw Habermas's call for an avant-gardist core Europe as an exclusionary move intended to make it harder for the poor and undesirable European cousins to join: fortress Europe now within the boundaries of the continent itself. This may be unfair to Habermas's intentions, but it speaks to his tone deafness regarding Central Europe, its history and its aspirations. It seemed as if Habermas was caught in an expanded present of his own making. Thus György Konrád, the Hungarian writer, at the time president of the Academy of the Arts in Berlin, warned against the Habermasian postulation of a core Europe as a geopolitical nostalgia, with potentially divisive effects at a time when expansion rather than narrowing is on the agenda. Günter Grass, the historian Hans Ulrich Wehler and many others joined in the criticism. And, indeed, it seemed that Habermas and Derrida, rather than furthering the cause of political integration of an expanded Europe, had involuntarily given credence from inside Europe to Donald Rumsfeld's line of argument pitting the old Europe against the new, a conflict which is obviously not in the interest of any member state of the European Union, though it may be in the interest of Washington's *divide et impera* strategy.

Of course, one may ask: what does the Habermasian intervention have to do with the peace movement's use of the bombing war against German cities? The differences seem to be too salient to entertain any substantive connection. The peace movement's arguments were energised by an experientially mobilised German past while Habermas, with different rhetoric and tone, argued normatively for a political rebirth of Europe. Yet ultimately, Habermas's image of the future under the halo of international norms shared a certain narrowness of vision and loss of reality with the peace movement's image of the present seen in light of a selectively expanded past. While the peace movement was overshadowed by visions of catastrophe and destruction, Habermas's call for Franco-German leadership harkened back to the once successful politics of the Bonn Republic. That is what Konrád meant when he warned of nostalgia.

Thus Habermas's intervention and the peace movement's uses of the past are like the two sides of the same coin. Both want peace, but at some deeper level, one might suggest, the German advocates of peace and a new European self-reliance split into optimists versus pessimists significantly along generational lines. But neither the conjuring up of

German suffering nor the normative assertion of a European identity is sufficient as remedy against the deployment of raw imperial power. Both seem to have forgotten that the notion of eternal or perpetual peace, as Kant was well aware, is also deeply ironic. After all, Kant's essay begins with the description of a sign he once saw hanging outside a Dutch pub. The name of the pub, 'Zum ewigen Frieden' ('Eternal Peace') was illustrated with the image of a cemetery.

11

From the Margins to the Centre? The Discourse on Expellees and Victimhood in Germany

Karoline von Oppen and Stefan Wolff

Introduction

At the German Federal Parliament's commemoration of the sixtieth anniversary of the end of the Second World War, Federal President Horst Köhler acknowledged the victims of Nazi aggression and occupation. Yet he also reminded his audience of Germany's own victims, those who suffered at the hands of the Nazis, and those who became victims of the 'backlash' against Germany. In an otherwise uncommon 'equalisation' of victims, Köhler pointed out the suffering of German civilians, including that of the refugees and expellees from Central and Eastern Europe. Publicly drawing an analogy between the victims of German aggression and German victims, the German head of state merely reflected a trend in German public discourse in which the debate about Germans as victims had a much longer tradition.

Between 1945 and 1950, one of the largest forced migrations in European history took place: as a consequence of the Second World War almost 14 million ethnic Germans fled or were expelled from their traditional homelands in Central and Eastern Europe. Of the survivors, approximately two-thirds were resettled in the American and British Zones of occupation, and one-third in the Soviet Zone. Because of their large numbers and widespread distribution across occupied Germany, the expellees were visible victims whose sense of victimhood, however, differed in one crucial respect from that of the rest of the German population: they had lost their homeland. This loss subsequently provided an additional impetus for a collective identity to be formed among refugees and expellees from very diverse countries in Central and Eastern Europe, and it remained a potent source of mobilisation through the decades. However, the successful political and economic integration of most of the refugees and expellees by the end of the 1950s, followed by a change in the political climate in the Federal Republic of Germany in the mid-1960s meant that they were no longer seen as victims of the Second World War. Instead, their insistence on the right of return to their former homelands, on compensation from the countries from which they had been expelled and on changes to the *de facto* borders within Germany and between Germany and Poland, were considered obstacles in the 'official' reconciliation and *rapprochement* process facilitated by the new *Ostpolitik*, and they rapidly became increasingly marginal to public debate.

Against this background, this chapter examines how the refugees and expellees and their descendants, and the organisations representing them, were able to reclaim a significant presence in, and mindshare of, the discourse on Germans as victims from the late 1990s onwards that would have been unthinkable only a few years earlier. Considering the perception of the German expellees as victims, and the role and place that they have occupied in the broader discourse on the reappreciation of victimhood in Germany, we argue that a much broader reconceptualisation of the notion of Germans as victims has taken place since the late 1990s in which the reappreciation of German expellees and refugees is one among several elements. We focus on the catalytic role played by the events in the former Yugoslavia in the early 1990s, and in particular during the Kosovo crisis at the end of that decade in bringing the suffering of German refugees and expellees from Central and Eastern Europe very much (back) into the now broader German discourse on 'coming to terms with the past' (*Vergangenheitsbewältigung*). Grasped by the expellee organisations as a unique opportunity to reopen the debate on their individual suffering, the conflict in and about Kosovo proved pivotal in sensitising German public opinion to possible historical parallels. Publicised in major media and across the traditional Left–Right divide, the debate over German involvement in the NATO bombing campaign against Serbia coincided with the *rapprochement* between the political Left and the expellees that had begun prior to the Red–Green election victory in 1998, and came to its preliminary conclusion with the publication of Günter Grass's novella *Crabwalk* (*Im Krebsgang*, 2002). Yet this renewed debate has also led to controversies: the proposed Centre Against Expulsions (*Zentrum gegen Vertreibungen*) has been widely rejected in Germany and abroad, and the instrumentalisation of the expulsions in the context of the EU's eastward expansion and of the accession of the Czech Republic in particular has to some extent restored traditional Left–Right divides over how best to deal with this particular period in German and European history. This suggests that the political Left's brief flirtation with the expellees rarely went beyond mere expediency. Analysing the interplay of domestic and international events and of political agendas of various influential players in the debate, we conclude, however, that the discourse concerning the collective victimisation of German expellees and refugees over the past few years has added an important dimension to the gradual change in ordinary Germans' view of their own history.

The discourse on German victimhood

There appears to be little agreement as to when the discourse on German suffering during the Second World War began to assume a more significant role in public discourse in Germany. A number of commentators have argued that the appearance in 2002 of Grass's novella *Crabwalk*, followed quickly by the publication of Jörg Friedrich's study on the bombing of German cities, *The Fire* (*Der Brand*, 2002), brought the discussion of German suffering to the fore.[1] Literary scholars tend to underline the influence of the series of lectures given by W. G. Sebald in 1997 on literature and the air war, recognised primarily after the appearance of the two later publications. Others highlight the discursive change made visible during 1995, the fiftieth anniversary of the war.[2] Position-takings like these tend to suggest that the end of the Cold War made it easier for Germans to challenge the self-image of perpetrator nation and confront the Allies with the bombings of German cities and expulsions in the East. Those studies that focus primarily on shifts within Germany itself tend to date the change to the first *Wende*, which brought Kohl to power in the early 1980s, or to the arrival in power of the Red–Green coalition in 1998. Here it is argued that German identity politics are at the fore.[3] Thus the attempts in the 1980s by Chancellor Kohl to reconfigure German national identity, which were ultimately predicated upon a decentring of Holocaust memory that had dominated since the late 1960s, are cited in evidence. Elsewhere, the focus is on the late 1990s when the Schröder/Fischer government sought to usher in an era of so-called normalisation that entailed a reassessment of Germany's foreign policy responsibilities. Finally, those anxious to situate the shift within a broader international context highlight the effects of the eastern expansion of the EU, or indeed the war in Kosovo that saw the first out-of-area engagement of German troops.

In the following paragraphs we sketch out the key arguments of a number of analyses of the discourse of German suffering in contemporary Germany. In his analysis of changing memory regimes, Eric Langenbacher argues that what he refers to as German-centred memory was clearly placed on the political agenda in the 1980s by the Kohl government, but has never found broad resonance in the German population.[4] According to Langenbacher, Holocaust-centred memory remains hegemonic even today, despite such attempts which have intensified during the 1990s. The only recent change, according to Langenbacher, has been the attempt made by the Left to reappropriate German-centred memory as part of a more inclusive narrative of the past.

In his study on the expellee organisations themselves, Henning Süssner observes a new obsession with these in contemporary Germany, which he attributes to a rejuvenation of their leadership in the 1990s.[5] At the same time he notes the irony of the fact that most members today have no personal desire to return and take up the homeland they so passionately demand. Süssner's analysis begins with the attempts by expellee organisations to raise public awareness for their suffering in the 1950s. He argues that their success then can in part be explained by the fact that the rhetoric surrounding the homeland was also to be found amongst non-expellees, for whom '*Heimat* was a prominent element of the reconstruction of the national German community of suffering'.[6] As Süssner is concerned to point out throughout his analysis, the ethno-regional discourse of expellees did not challenge ideas of German nationhood, but could in effect reinforce a cultural vision of the nation, which enabled expellees to develop closer ties with the more conservative Bavarian Christian Social Union Party (CSU). Süssner argues that reunification and the end of communism have brought about a memory regime in Germany that has allowed expellee claims to re-enter mainstream discourse, for the reason that the two have again become more compatible. He is thus effectively suggesting that contemporary notions of German nationhood have shifted, enabling expellee claims to a German *Heimat* to achieve more resonance in the public sphere.[7]

More implicit criticism of the recent debates has come from critics who challenge the notion that the inclusion of German suffering in debates about the Second World War represents a normalisation, and thus a positive development. In his recent book Helmut Schmitz argues that the 'belated re-empathising' with German suffering is problematic in the ways that it has ignored the shift from first to third generation.[8] He also suggests tentatively that a 'decentring' of the Holocaust as the key event of the Nazi period is currently taking place. Andreas F. Kelletat, in his analysis of expellee organisations, has pointed out that suffering caused by expulsion and bombing, such as that described by Günter Grass in his controversial *Crabwalk*, was shared by all sides in the war, as well as by the inmates of concentration camps who were moved around rapidly at the end of the war, and killed by starvation or Allied bombs.[9] He thus criticises the selective and exclusionary definition of suffering that prevails in the debates:

> If only we could also commemorate these and similar deaths when discussing the refugees and expellees from the east in 1945, then maybe we could really begin talking about a 'normalisation' of memory discourse.[10]

In other words, the discourse has shifted not to debating suffering *per se*, but on to very specific suffering as the central focus of the memory politics of the period. This, Kelletat argues, is also shown by the fact that expellee associations amongst others have readopted the language of the 1950s. Overall, there is thus little agreement as to the significance of the recent shift towards the experiences of ethnic Germans during and after the Second World War. Rather than focus on the broader issues, we look specifically at how the question of the victim identity of the expellees has re-entered mainstream discourse both amongst political elites and the German media, particularly in relation to the situation in Kosovo in the 1990s.

Setting agendas: The expellee organisations post-1990

The leadership of the refugee and expellee organisations had for years emphasised the victim dimension in refugees' and expellees' identity. Now, it sought to capitalise on the opportunities offered by the transition in Central and Eastern Europe, and by the ensuing reconciliation process. Initially, victimhood continued to be framed through specific demands raised by the League of Expellees (*Bund der Vertriebenen*) and individual Homeland Societies (*Landsmannschaften*). In a time-honoured tradition, these demands were defined as the right to return (permanently) to their former homelands, the entitlement to compensation for their suffering, and to restitution of expropriated property. This particular conception of a victim identity presented the expellee organisations with unprecedented opportunities to attach their demands to the bandwagon of mainstream (institutional) politics and win some mindshare in the public discourse. The first of these opportunities presented itself in the form of the ethnic cleansing in Kosovo; the second in the form of several successful class actions in the United States, and threats thereof, aimed at compensation for forced labourers during the Second World War; and the third in the form of the European Union enlargement process. We shall briefly outline these three instances to set the stage more generally in terms of the German domestic and international environment in which the debate about expellees and refugees as specifically German victims of the Second World War re-emerged, before analysing in more detail the media debate on the subject in the context of the Kosovo conflict.

The conflict in Kosovo with its large-scale population displacements, and subsequent international intervention to reverse them, in more than one way resembled what many expellees had experienced themselves. But it also symbolised the hopes of some of them, namely for the international recognition and enforcement of the right of people not to be expelled from their homeland, or at least to return to it if an expulsion could not be prevented. Pictures from Kosovo also brought home to many others in Germany, and elsewhere, the horrors of refugee treks, sparking a broad public debate on an issue that had, for the most part, been deliberately ignored in the German media. By comparing, and linking, their own plight to that of Kosovo Albanians, expellee organisations managed to align themselves with a political strategy that was beyond moral reproach – namely the prevention, or reversal, of ethnic cleansing. By supporting the policy of Germany during the conflict, the expellee organisations sought to prepare the ground upon which they then could reopen the debate on their own suffering more than 50 years earlier. Already in 1995, the expellee organisations saw their cause elevated to higher international levels when the then UN High Commissioner on Human Rights, José Ayala Lasso, emphasised in a speech in the *Paulskirche* in Frankfurt that the right not to be expelled from one's homeland was a fundamental human right. He also noted that, while the peoples in Central and Eastern Europe had suffered terribly under German occupation during the Second World War and thus had a legitimate claim to reparations, such claims 'must not be realised through collective victimisation on the basis of general discrimination and without the thorough investigation of individual guilt'.[11] Even more relevant to the political agenda of the leadership of the expellee organisations was a report of the UN Commission on Human Rights, entitled *Human Rights and Population Transfer*, which in its Annex II, included a 'Draft Declaration on Population Transfer and the Implantation of Settlers' that emphasised the 'right to return, restoration of properties, and compensation for any property that cannot be restored'.[12]

Restitution and compensation remain very sensitive issues, particularly in German–Czech relations. In the eyes of the Sudeten German Homeland Society, the compensation of forced labourers during the Second World War, and in particular the negotiations between Germany and the representatives of survivors from Nazi labour camps, provided some of the expellees who had suffered particular hardship during the expulsion and/or in labour camps in Czechoslovakia after 1945 with an equally legitimate claim to receive a symbolic gesture of compensation from the German–Czech Future Fund. Arguing that this would be an important contribution to the reconciliation between Sudeten Germans and Czechs, the Sudeten German Homeland Society submitted a bid to the fund's executive board, where it was promptly, and with great publicity, rejected. At the same time, class action had also been considered as a possible route to realise claims for the compensation of losses resulting from collective expropriation, and where possible for the restitution of properties confiscated in this process.[13] Plans for class action in the United States, initially against insurance companies that profited from the collective expropriation of the Sudeten Germans, have been officially supported by the leadership of the Sudeten German association.

A number of opportunities on the European stage have also been exploited by expellee activists, and their success in this area has boosted the confidence of some of the political leaders of the expellee organisations. In April 1999, a resolution was passed by the European Parliament in which its members called 'on the Czech Government, in the same spirit of reconciliatory statements made by President Havel, to repeal the surviving laws and decrees from 1945 and 1946, in so far as they concern the expulsion of individual ethnic groups in the former Czechoslovakia'.[14] This is another highly sensitive issue not only in Czech–EU relations, but also in Czech–German relations and within the political processes in both countries.

The first European Parliament resolution, as well as a 1999 resolution by the Austrian National Council calling for the annulment of the Benes Decrees, were immediately seized upon by a group of members of the Federal Parliament. They proposed a motion, co-sponsored by the Christian Democratic Union/Christian Social Union (CDU/CSU) parliamentary party, in which the Federal Government was asked 'to take appropriate action in the spirit of the . . . resolutions on its own and in collaboration with the other EU member states and the institutions of the EU'.[15] A counter-motion was introduced by the parliamentary parties of the Social Democratic Party of Germany (SPD) and Alliance 90/The Greens in October 1999 in which the Federal Parliament was asked to welcome the statement by Chancellor Schröder and Czech Minister-President Zeman of March 8, 1999, that 'neither government will reintroduce property issues [into their bilateral relationship] either today or in the future'.[16] This motion received a majority vote both at committee stage and after a parliamentary debate in June 2000, while that of the CDU/CSU parliamentarians was rejected.

What is interesting in relation to these debates on restitution and compensation in general is that the old Left–Right dichotomy in the political process in Germany on issues concerning the expulsion of ethnic Germans has been restored. For a period of about three years from the mid-1990s onwards, there seemed to be a certain recognition of the fact that the expulsion had been a human tragedy, and that there had been an unjust neglect by the German Left of the suffering of the expellees and their contribution to the reconciliation process with the countries of Central and Eastern Europe.[17] This certainly contributed to the fact that issues of and related to the expulsion have recently regained considerable discursive power.

Yet there has also been a recognition of the fact that these interests could be much more effectively pursued if the expellees received a broader public recognition as victims. In order to achieve this, the leadership of the expellee organisations had to reshape the notion of victimhood of both victims of Nazi Germany, and victims of the governments established in Central and Eastern Europe at the end of the Second World War. In doing so, expellee activists have desisted from denying that groups that have long been recognised as victims have suffered and have therefore every right to claim compensation. Rather, their objective now is to achieve for their own members the same international recognition (including from countries like Poland and the Czech Republic) with all its legal consequences. From the perspective of the League of Expellees, the opportunities to do so seemed better than ever. However, it is important to realise that the notion of victimhood as a central part of expellee identity is by no means a new element, nor could it be one given the very real experience of expulsion.

The Kosovo conflict: (German) expellees as victims of war

In the next section we look at the ways in which the German media interpreted the conflict in Yugoslavia, particularly during the first out-of-area combat involvement of German military forces in the war against Serbia in 1999. A number of historical analogies were available to legitimise NATO intervention, evoke sympathy for the war's most visible victims – the refugees from Kosovo – and enlist support for participating governments. German politicians, most notoriously Rudolf Scharping, made much use of the Holocaust analogy, but the debate in Germany was highly contested, *precisely on the level of historical comparison.* Ironically, it would seem that greater consensus existed in Germany on the role of perpetrator and victim in Kosovo, than it did on the reasons for the expulsions of ethnic Germans. Historical analogies to the German past could and did serve a dual purpose. Rather than the past serving only to illuminate the Yugoslav present, the conflict in the Balkans also enabled various interest groups and political actors to intervene in a contemporary debate about their own past. This duality of purpose presented a unique opportunity for the expellee organisations to take their decade-long, fruitless struggle for public recognition of their constituents' victimhood centre stage in the public debate without being vilified for 'living in the past'.

The rehabilitation of the expellees in this period is a complex process, and was in many ways even an unintentional outcome of other key debates of the 1990s. In any case, there were several coexisting strands to the debate that need to be clearly separated. These often served conflicting purposes and, while each contributed to an overall intensification of the resonance of the comparison made between ethnic German expellees and the fate of the Kosovo Albanians, and consequently to the rehabilitation of the expellees, the different actors and discourses need to be carefully distinguished from each other. Three different discourses can be identified. First, the rhetoric of the expellee organisations themselves, which sought to profit from the dominant media image of the refugee during the Kosovo crisis. Second, the rhetoric of proponents and opponents of the NATO intervention in Kosovo when debating Germany's first out-of-area military engagement since the Second World War. Finally, both of these discourses later merged with a third and broader discussion about German suffering and the Left, which appeared to be more concerned with overturning a supposed left-liberal hegemony on the past rather than with rehabilitating the German victims of the Second World War. These three differing strands cannot be described as different phases, as they overlap and appear to coexist.

Expellee organisations

Diana Johnstone, whose book *Fools' Crusade* explores the geopolitical reasons for the war against Serbia, discusses the links between German expellee associations and Kosovo.[18] In her view, these have exerted a decisive influence on our perceptions of ethnic conflict in Yugoslavia. On the one hand, the conflict in Yugoslavia enabled them, she argues, to focus attention on expulsion and ethnic cleansing as a universal phenomenon of the twentieth century, leading to a shift in public sympathy in their favour. On the other hand, she claims that the demonisation of the Serbs as chief aggressor responsible for violent expulsions 'constituted an enormous moral victory for the post-war German expellees', for this made possible the identification of the Slavic Serbs with the Slavic Russians, adding 'an irrational but emotionally powerful element of "poetic justice"'.[19]

A closer examination of the media coverage of the conflict in the former Yugoslavia suggests that the situation is more complex than Johnstone suggests. While expellee organisations made much of the comparison in their own literature, it remained contested until after the Kosovo War in 1999. Even then it never became the dominant analogy in use in public debate in the media. Comparisons with German suffering at the hands of the Russians were also certainly not widely in evidence during the first years of conflict, although the early tensions in Yugoslavia were generally interpreted within a pre-existing Cold War framework. Thus, the demands by Croatia and Slovenia for self-determination were welcomed as part of the liberation of Europe from communism, and compared to the situation in the GDR.[20] The rhetoric of genocide, with comparisons made to the Holocaust, emerged in the mid-1990s, receiving its strongest support from left-liberal circles, particularly after the massacre of Srebrenica, which became a defining debate for the Left launched by Joschka Fischer in August 1995. During the Kosovo War itself, conservative observers rejected dominant historical analogies, particularly with the Holocaust, arguing that this was a typically German response, while left-liberal observers rushed to find parallels in German history with both the bombing of Serbia and the expulsions from Kosovo.

Left–Green debates

The use of historical analogies to comprehend and illuminate the situation in Yugoslavia may have been contested by conservative figures within Germany, but on the Left there was no shortage of attempts to (de)mystify the situation with reference to the German past. In left-liberal circles the massacre in Srebrenica in 1995 marked a turning point in the discussion. Markovits and Reich have argued that the debates about military intervention that ensued, particularly in the Green Party, articulated 'the clashes and conflicts of history, collective memory, guilt, responsibility ... – in short, the key issues of contemporary Germany' actutely and urgently.[21] What many observers failed to notice is that a leading Green Party figure had launched a second, closely interlinked, debate in the same anniversary year. In the same month that Fischer made his plea for support for military intervention in Bosnia, Antje Vollmer gave a speech in Prague in a Bertelsmann' series entitled 'Conversations with our Neighbours'. Intended as a positive reply to a speech given by Vaclav Havel in January 1995, Vollmer called for a new partnership between the two countries. Havel's January speech had made a similar point, but had received a surprisingly muted response from the German government.[22] Throughout 1995 Vollmer and others had worked towards encouraging reconciliation by calling for an end to recriminations, although this was not always welcomed by expellee associations, who refused to let Vollmer speak at one of their meetings in May 1995.[23] Even her presence at the meeting in Munich in June 1995 led to protests from participants, a meeting which also provoked controversy when a public declaration compared Havel to Karadzic 'because the [Czech Republic] had endorsed the Benes Decrees'.[24]

In October 1995, Vollmer's speech 'An End to Ambiguity – Open Answers to Open Questions in German-Czech Relations' was provocative.[25] She adopted the careful position of condemning the expulsions but pointing also to the legitimate reasons for the action. More significantly, however, Vollmer pronounced a very public *mea culpa* on behalf of the 1968 generation for having ignored the plight of the expellees, a mistake that, she felt, had led to the continued problems between Germany and the Czech Republic. She argued that while the millions of expellees had received 'considerable material support . . .', their 'personal fate' had only met with 'unsympathetic disinterest' and 'an inability to listen, show pity or sorrow'. For this she particularly blamed 'the German left and the student movement', who, she claimed, had cultivated 'an unspoken theory of collective guilt' which had led to this one-sided interpretation of victimhood. It was, she argued, time to abandon this position.[26] In this self-critique Vollmer does not make any direct reference to events unfolding either in the German Green Party or in Yugoslavia, although the parallels are evident. In the same period that Fischer asked his colleagues to rethink the foundational principle of anti-militarism, Vollmer effectively began to question the memory politics of the 1968 generation, oversimplifying the position that these had taken *vis-à-vis* the concept of collective guilt and victimhood from 1968 onwards. It was only in 1999 that the two events became linked and the expulsions from Kosovo became the supposed catalyst of a leftist reassessment of the post-war expulsions of ethnic Germans, which had clearly begun much earlier. In May 1999, *Die Welt* observed contentedly that the war against Serbia had been an important learning process for the Left. At last, the conservative broadsheet suggests, the proposed Centre against Expulsions could unite those 'for whom Auschwitz is the starting point' and those 'for whom the expulsions are the most important factor in their thinking and position-taking'.[27] In June 1999 the left-wing *tageszeitung* agreed. 'Now the hardened positions are beginning to weaken', it proclaimed, also pointing to the suffering in former Yugoslavia as a reason for this development:[28] 'the mass expulsions, first in Bosnia and then in Kosovo, have stirred up emotions and awoken a new sensitivity for the plight of the refugees in Germany and in Eastern Europe'.[29]

During the actual campaign fought against Serbia in 1999, historical analogies became the terrain on which the war was fought at home between pro- and anti-war supporters, rather than there being any agreement about the significance of the conflict. From the beginning of the military intervention the *Spiegel*, for example, adopted a vigorous anti-war, and increasingly anti-American position, reflected in its harsh criticism of the use of historical analogies by the warring parties. It was in the context of this increasing anti-Americanism that the most explicit reference was made to the German expellees. In a piece entitled 'War in the Name of Good Conscience', the magazine made its usual jibe at the moral foreign policy of the Red–Green government, and at the dominance of the Americans in the conflict: 'the unwavering US leads the way'.[30] Yet the article moved beyond its usual critical position, comparing the present situation to that of the immediate post-war period. More perniciously, it suggested that just as the United States did nothing to prevent the expulsion of Germans after the war, it was now failing to provide ground troops to prevent the expulsion of Kosovo Albanians. The *Spiegel* therefore drew a highly problematic comparison between the American position in 1945 and the present-day intervention:

> these expulsions remained unatoned for and irreversible. They almost became an established right of nations. The expulsion of the Germans from Poland, Czechoslovakia and Hungary was openly approved by the Allies at the Potsdam Conference in 1945.[31]

Unlike its usage in the rhetoric of expellees therefore, historical analogy here does not serve to criticise those who carried out the expulsions, but to remind readers of the fact that the Allied powers condoned them. The conclusion of the article, which pointed to half-hearted US attempts to prevent the present-day expulsions, appeared to show sympathy for expellees in general, but then listed only the cases of Palestinians, Kurds and Pakistanis:

> If for the first time in history the strongest military might in the world is fighting to enable an expelled minority to return to its homeland, then this basic right cannot really be denied to others. Is there a statute of limitations for expulsions?[32]

There is no suggestion that the authors of this text wish to support the claim for compensation of German expellees for past losses, for their intention appears to be mainly to attack the United States for present actions. Arguably, this had everything to do with the German foreign policy of the Red–Green government, and little to do with German suffering. Yet such rhetoric strengthened, inadvertently, the argument of the expellee organisations that they had been victims, too, of the Second World War. Almost ironically, given the *Spiegel*'s general political outlook, the magazine's condemnation of the Allied approval of the expulsion of ethnic Germans after 1945 was echoed in President Köhler's explicit acknowledgement of German victims of the Allied war effort during the commemoration ceremonies for the sixtieth anniversary of the end of the Second World War.

After the war

It was not until after the war in Kosovo that the *Spiegel* came to play a dominant role in the rehabilitation of the expellees in mainstream debate. In 2002 the magazine published a series of articles focusing on the expellees, which began with an article illustrated with an infamous picture of a Kosovar Albanian woman juxtaposed with a photograph of a German expellee.[33] Despite the use of such explicit visual comparison, the *Spiegel* hesitated in making the comparison in the accompanying text. Instead, the link construed between the two historical events was a more subtle one, and was more concerned with the coming of the 1968 generation to power than with either anti-American or anti-Serb rhetoric. The article traced the integration of the expellees in the Federal Republic and their dwindling significance, until, the magazine claimed, the conflict in former Yugoslavia provoked a political change of attitude on the Left:

> Faced with the images of the persecuted and fleeing people from Kosovo, a gradual process of rethinking took place amongst those on the Left, who had long been unwilling to reflect on this issue. Were these not the same images as seen half a century ago on the Kurische Nehrung or in the Stettiner Haff?[34]

The *Spiegel* welcomed the end of 'the dominance of those who were almost exclusively fixated on the crimes of the Nazis and their fellow travellers'.[35] At issue here again was, it seems, not so much the rehabilitation of the expellees, for the *Spiegel* was in no doubt that they were also partly responsible for their fate. The purpose was twofold. On the one hand, the *Spiegel* insisted that different narratives of the Second World War could coexist, and that the German victims of this war should be remembered as well. On the other hand, the supposed hegemony of the '68ers' narrative was rejected as an anachronism that had outlived its function. Not only had Kosovo enlightened the Left as to the suffering of expellees, but a new generation of children were now also asking about the suffering of their grandfathers. Within the context of a series focusing on the expulsions therefore, the analogy with Kosovo served to underline the gradual normalisation of a supposedly abnormal 1968 generation whose pathological fixation on Nazis had finally been overcome. The war therefore enabled Germans to 'naturalise' a political shift as a response to the wars in Yugoslavia, ignoring the fact that it had been taking place since the late 1980s, and was closely connected to the Cold War politics of commemoration and to concepts of German nationhood.

Conclusion: reckoning with the past

Identity is a complex and multi-dimensional notion. In the case of the German expellees, it has primarily manifested itself in terms of an ambiguous and contested relationship with their own status as victims of the Second World War. This has not only divided the domestic public discourse in Germany, it has also had significant implications for the Federal Republic's bilateral relations with Poland and the Czech Republic, and has impacted on the dynamics of EU enlargement.

That the expulsion of the ethnic Germans more than 50 years ago still gives rise to heated debate and has a bearing on institutional processes at the German and the European level has to do not only with the magnitude of the expulsions and the suffering endured of those affected by them. It also has to do with the fact that this particular aspect of the Second World War and its consequences has never been properly dealt with by means of a broad and open public debate in Germany, Poland or Czechoslovakia/the Czech Republic. More than 30 years after the advent of the new *Ostpolitik*, the political Left and Right continue to be divided over this issue, raising the political profile of, and stakes in a debate that should essentially be about reconciliation and forgiveness. More often than not, radicalisation and alienation inside and outside Germany have been the result. Although most of the expellees and refugees, and their descendants, have reconciled themselves with the fact that a return to their lost homelands and compensation for their suffering is unlikely, the failure and denial to recognise the injustice of collective victimisation remains a potent mobilisation source. It also enables political activists to manipulate remotely related issues and to continue to incite debates on the expulsion and their consequences, often with no positive results at all for either the expellees or their descendants on behalf of whom they claim to act.

At the same time, we must not forget that the rehabilitation of the German victims of the Second World War is undoubtedly part of a broader reassessment of the past which began in the 1980s and continues to the present day. The war in Kosovo enabled Germans to debate a number of defining questions relating to their own past including the contemporary significance of German expulsions from Central and Eastern Europe after the Second World War. As a result of such a discursive shift, there is little doubt that the expulsions attracted renewed interest in the German media, which led to an equally reinvigorated political debate in Germany about the meaning of victimhood. While the outcome of this ongoing debate is still not clear, it nevertheless indicates a profound reappreciation of German identity as a whole.

From the present perspective it would seem as if the 1990s have finally enabled the expellees to become part of national collective memory. For this, the link made between conservative parties such as the CSU and expellee organisations had to be weakened, a process that was much facilitated by the advent to power of the 1968 generation. Once the Left, motivated both by political expediency and by ideological shifts post-1989, declared expellee suffering to be of relevance to Germany's national memory, the reassessment of the theme of German suffering could begin. At the same time, expellee associations also mindful of the need to appeal to a broader constituency appropriated the language of human rights and successfully linked their experience to that of the Kosovo Albanians. However, this comparison between German and Yugoslav suffering remained contested throughout the decade in the public sphere. There is no doubt that both the expulsion of Kosovar Albanians and the experience of participating in warfare again brought debates to the fore that had remained on the margins of public debate for many years. As we have highlighted in this chapter, both national and international factors were therefore responsible for this repositioning of the discourse of German suffering from the margins to the centre. For the expellee associations this has meant broader societal recognition which may ultimately mark the beginning of the end of their role as an institution in the Federal Republic. For memory politics in Germany this repositioning may yet prove to be as far reaching. Although not in all cases, it is certainly often the case that this shift is intended as a deliberate counterbalance to the supposed dominance of Holocaust-centred memory in the Federal Republic. Whether it will be successful in actually decentring the Holocaust as the prime event of the Second World War remains to be seen.

12

On Taboos, Traumas and Other Myths: Why the Debate about German Victims of the Second World War is not a Historians' Controversy[1]

Stefan Berger

For several years now the Germans have been rediscovering themselves as victims of the Second World War. They remember one of the most gruesome bombing wars ever waged against a nation-state. Half a million civilians, mainly women and children, died in the bombardment of German cities. Innumerable cultural treasures were lost forever. Germans were also victims of ethnic cleansing. Up to 14 million fled the advancing Red Army in the final months of the war or were forcibly removed from Eastern Europe after 1945. Up to 2 million died on the long treks west. According to some estimates, one and a half million German women were victims of rape, mostly, but not exclusively, at the hands of Red Army soldiers. The facts are not in dispute. What is hotly contested is how the Germans dealt with the memories of their own victimhood in the Second World War. Have they, as W. G. Sebald, Günter Grass, Guido Knopp, Jörg Friedrich and a whole host of other writers alleged, been sidelined, repressed and forgotten?[2] Has the suffering produced had traumatic effects which prevented the victims from working through their experiences, leading to silence on the fate of millions of Germans? Have novelists and historians alike forsaken their task of making this important collective experience a topic of their writing? A tendency to psychologise rather than 'historise'[3] is strongly present in some of the writing, including historical writing. Thus, Thomas W. Neumann explains the alleged absence of a strong public discourse about the bombing war in the post-war period with reference to post-traumatic stress syndrome. According to Neumann, most people stayed alone with their experiences or privatised them in small circles of family and close friends. Their silence, he argues, was a sign of deep insecurity and real helplessness.[4]

The publications of Sebald, Grass and Friedrich, in particular, have been crucial in bringing about a debate about the status of German victims of the war in the cultural memory of the nation. It is important to emphasise that they all come from very different positions and do not see eye to eye on many issues. But their contributions together ensured that the issue of German victimhood was widely discussed in the early 2000s. Novelists whose work dealt with the impact of the bombing war are being reprinted and rediscovered.[5] As already pointed out in other contributions to the current volume, television series on the bombing war and on refugees and expellees have been flickering over several German TV channels,[6] and the pages of the newspapers have been full of articles on the new German victims' discourse. The media were crucial in propagating the idea of German victimhood as a forgotten subject and did much to remedy that alleged gap in our historical knowledge of the Second World War. *Der Spiegel* printed special issues on the German refugees and expellees in 2002 and on the bombing war in 2003. Movies such as *The Miracle of Bern* (*Das Wunder von Bern*, 2003), *Downfall* (*Der Untergang*, 2004) and *Dresden* (2006) have been taking up this theme in various forms.

Politicians have also entered the debate. Arguably the most controversial contribution came from the Christian Democratic Union (CDU) member of the Bundestag Martin Hohmann, who, in a speech commemorating the day of German unity on 3 October 2003, remarked that Germans should not collectively be seen as a people of perpetrators (*Tätervolk*), as they had been victims too. His further remarks on the responsibility of prominent Bolshevik Jews for the crimes committed by the Bolsheviks in the Soviet Union were widely regarded as anti-Semitic. He had to resign from the parliamentary party of the CDU, but arguably he had voiced an opinion about German victimhood in the war which struck a chord with many voters of the CDU. The president of the League of Expellees, Erika

Steinbach, has been running a high-profile campaign for the establishment of a centre in Berlin documenting the plight of the German expellees. Her campaign won support even among members of the Red–Green coalition government (in power from 1998 until 2005). However, faced with protests from Poland and within Germany, Gerhard Schröder, Chancellor at the time, backed away from funding such a centre and instead put his weight behind initiatives attempting to network a series of existing institutions and initiatives dealing with refugees and expellees across Europe.[7] But the new Chancellor, Angela Merkel, is known to be supportive of the idea of a Berlin-based centre.

When we look at the key protagonists in this debate on German victimhood, we find novelists, literary critics, literature specialists, publicists and journalists. Professional historians are notable mainly (although, as I will discuss below, not entirely) through their absence. They are certainly not driving the debate and are, at best, reacting to the publications and interventions of others. Given the usual prominence of the historical profession in German public debates about the past, this may come as a surprise. In the mid-1980s, the 'Historians' Dispute' (*Historikerstreit*) about the singularity of the Holocaust was started by a philosopher, Jürgen Habermas, but most of the subsequent interventions were made by historians.[8] They were also prominent in the Goldhagen debate of the mid-1990s and in the debates surrounding the *War of Annihilation: Crimes of the Wehrmacht, 1941–1944* exhibition organised by the Hamburg-based Institute for Social Research.[9] By contrast, the multifaceted debate about German victims of the Second World War is not primarily a historians' controversy despite the historical nature of the debate. Why then do professional historians at best play second fiddle in this debate? I would like to suggest that the answer to this question lies in the historiography of the topic, or rather topics, of German victimhood in the Second World War. Hence the first part of this chapter will provide a brief survey of historiographical developments between 1945 and the present day. The second part will then relate this historiographical review to the reactions of historians to the contemporary debate.

Taboo topic? The historical literature on German victimhood

In a nutshell, there is very little evidence of trauma having produced silences and resulting in the repression of memories of German suffering after 1945. A wealth of oral and written material describes in minute and often gruesome detail the fate of victims of the bombing war and of German refugees and expellees. Eyewitnesses and survivors produced floods of memory literature. As Malte Thießen has demonstrated for Hamburg, the bombing war was an integral part of Hamburg's memorial culture until well into the 1980s.[10] Much of that memory literature contributed to the many myths surrounding the bombing of German cities.[11] Soon after the war, *Wehrmacht* generals began to publish their memoirs, and the veterans' organisations dominated the cultural memory of the war in the Federal Republic (FRG) until well into the 1970s. They depicted the German soldiers as tragic victims of Hitler and the Nazis, fulfilling their duty to the fatherland whilst being misled by a demonic Führer. Germans could be proud of their military achievements and remember their own suffering.[12]

The loss of the 'German East' and the rape of German women were also prominent in the public discourses about the war in the early Federal Republic. Both were used extensively as propaganda tools in the Cold War. Continuing Goebbels's attempts to depict the Russians as subhuman Asian hordes, West German propaganda highlighted the suffering of Germans at the hands of regimes that were now Communist. In particular the killings, rape and pilfering carried out by soldiers of the Red Army were foregrounded in an attempt to warn West Germans about what to expect of the main adversary in the Cold War.[13] Russian soldiers raping German women became a prominent symbol for the rape of the German nation by the Soviet Union. The memory of women as active participants in German atrocities and crimes at the eastern front (as *Wehrmacht* auxiliaries, flak helpers, nurses' aides, and in the civilian and party administration) gave way immediately after the war to the memory of women as passive victims of violence.[14] The rapid transformation of German perpetrators into German victims also found expression in the memorialisation of the bombing war in church ruins. The *Nikolaikirche* in Hamburg, the *Kaiser-Wilhelm-Gedächtniskirche* in Berlin, the *Frauenkirche* in Dresden – they all symbolised the suffering of the German people who quickly styled themselves as victims of the Allies, the Soviets, of Hitler and of the war.

Such a victim-centred perspective was also wholeheartedly adopted by historians dealing with the themes of bombing and ethnic cleansing. The German people were portrayed as double victims: of the demon Hitler and of Allied cruelty. Initially, historians found it difficult to work on any aspect of the war, as the Allies insisted on taking charge of all archival holdings. Only from the 1950s onwards did the files find their way back into German archives, a process which has still not been entirely completed today. Major research institutes, such as the Institute of Contemporary History (in Munich) and the Research Institute for Military History (formerly based in Freiburg, now in Potsdam), were founded in the 1950s to write the history of National Socialism and war. The Central Association of Victims of Wartime Bombing (*Zentralverband der Fliegergeschädigten*) initiated a major edition of documents, published between 1958 and 1964, which, in minute detail, provided a balance sheet of damage done to German cities.[15] It had been commissioned by the Ministry of Refugees, as the West German government was preparing itself for the conference on war reparations. It was to provide the young FRG with ammunition countering Allied demands. The first volume of the edition accused Britain of unnecessarily escalating the bombing war to include non-strategic and civilian targets. In fact, the allegation of the bombing war having been a war crime originated in Goebbels's propaganda machine and continued to linger beneath the surface of many German publications on the topic after 1945. The bombing war became a way out of the moral doghouse. Germans could point to German suffering when confronted with German crimes. The bombing war and the expulsions were sometimes held up as morally equivalent to the Holocaust.[16]

Other early studies about the bombing war also readily claimed to be addressing a taboo subject, despite overwhelming evidence to the contrary.[17] One cannot help but think that by declaring the bombing war a taboo, the topic was to be boosted in its importance. If it was a taboo, it clearly needed more attention, and greater emphasis on the bombing war would further strengthen the already well-developed victim-centred discourse in the post-war Federal Republic. Some histories indeed celebrated the heroic struggle of local German officials (often active Nazis) against the Allied barbarism of the bombing war.[18]

This was, of course, not a view shared by British and American historians who produced their own histories of the bombing war in the 1960s.[19] From the 1970s onwards a wide range of local studies provided a comprehensive picture of the bombing war and its effects on German cities.[20] It is true that they were often foremost only in terms of local significance and certainly did not command the attention of Friedrich's volume, but the information was there. It was neither repressed nor hidden.

A similar story emerges when one investigates the history of historiography of the German refugees and expellees. Thus, the sinking of the *Wilhelm Gustloff*, the key topic in Grass's *Crabwalk*, commanded considerable interest well before Grass,[21] and in 1959 a popular German film about the fate of the *Gustloff*, entitled *Night over Gdynia* (*Nacht über Gotenhafen*) hit the cinema-screens in the FRG. The expellees' organisations published a steady stream of literature, often personal memoirs of the people who had gone through the ordeal of losing their home and trecking westwards. As with the bombing war, the Federal Government also had its hand in commissioning a multi-volume documentation of the expulsions of Germans from East–Central Europe. Lasting for ten years, from 1951 to 1961, and involving some of the best known West German historians, it was one of the biggest early research projects in the FRG; 5000 pages of 'scientific' evidence underlined, by and large, the message previously provided by the memory literature.[22] The weighty tomes served the purpose of strengthening the hand of the German government *vis-à-vis* the Allies by showing that millions of Germans had been victims of the war as well.

If one cannot easily speak of repression, denial and taboo of German victimhood and if, rather to the contrary, there seems to be considerable evidence that a strong victims' discourse was present in post-war West Germany, what was the situation like in the German Democratic Republic (GDR)? With some victims' groups that were central to the West German victims' discourse, the GDR had its difficulties. The expulsions of Germans from fellow Communist countries in East–Central Europe were never questioned by the GDR. And the SED also never criticised openly the rape of German women by Soviet soldiers. Any criticism of the heroic Red Army was indeed impossible. But the bombing war was a different story, and here the GDR produced its very own victims' discourse. Although it denied all responsibility for the actions of the German Reich before 1945 and therefore did not seek to protect itself against demands from the victorious Allies, the GDR sought to harness the bombing war as a tool in the ensuing Cold War. The bombing of East German cities by British and American aircraft was depicted as lacking in any strategic merit and as a devious plan to sabotage the rebuilding of a socialist Germany. Dresden, in particular, was used extensively to hammer home this message.[23] GDR citizens, like their counterparts in the FRG, were given the feeling that Germans had been primarily victims of a criminal act committed by the wartime Allies. The GDR also at times equated that suffering with the suffering of the Jewish people in the Holocaust.[24]

In the 1970s more sophisticated histories of the bombing war emerged in the GDR, thanks in particular to Olaf Groehler whose pioneering work tried to combine military history with the history of German society at war. In marked contrast to his colleagues in the GDR and some in the FRG, he left no doubt that the bombing war of the Allies was legitimate, as it helped defeat the Nazis and as it was a response to earlier bombardments of European cities by the *Luftwaffe*.[25]

Yet Dresden in particular became a symbol of Allied war crimes against the German people – not only in GDR Cold War propaganda, but also among Western extreme right-wingers. In particular David Irving's book about the Dresden bombings served the purpose of accusing the Allies of a criminal bombing campaign, confirming many of the legends and half-truths surrounding the destruction of the city on the Elbe.[26] When West German historiography, in the course of the 1960s, began to abandon many of the national conservative prejudices which had characterised it for a long time, the victims' discourse came to be regarded with suspicion and was left increasingly to the right-wing fringe or outsiders to the profession.[27] Thus, an international lawyer, Alfred M. de Zayas, earned himself some notoriety for writing extensively on the German refugees and expellees in and after 1945.[28] The expellee organisations, despite their explicit rejection of territorial revisionism,[29] increasingly operated in an environment in which a new generation of often left-of-centre historians did not look favourably on their continued propagation of a victims' discourse. The historiographical focus of attention began to change in line with the public changes of perception of the end of the Second World War. The commemorations on 8 May, for example, began to take on a different character from the 1970s onwards. Whereas in 1955 and 1965 they were still dominated by the perception of Germans as victims of war, expulsions and division, in 1975 a more self-critical perception began to make itself felt. Now it was the victims of the German war and of National Socialism who began to come into view, and the emphasis began to change from defeat to liberation, albeit a liberation which the German people were unable and unwilling to achieve on their own. The landmark speech of President Richard von Weizsäcker on 8 May 1985 anchored such a self-critical interpretation in the national and international public consciousness.[30]

But such a change of the political climate in which historians operate did not mean that the topics of the refugees, expellees and the bombing war disappeared from the historical agenda altogether. The monumental book series *Germany and the Second World War* was launched by the Research Institute for Military History in 1979.[31] Wolfgang Benz and others prominently dealt with the topic of the German expellees, emphasising that it was necessary to put the historical record straight precisely in order to counter the revisionism of the historical right.[32] The 'Working Group of Historical Peace Research' initiated a series of investigations in the second half of the 1980s, which drew attention to the strong links between German society during the war and the developments in the post-Second World War period.[33] Everyday-life history dealt with the impact of the bombing war, for example, in the LUSIR project led by Lutz Niethammer.[34] In the 1980s West German feminist authors discovered the theme of mass rape of women at the end of the Second World War. And in the 1990s a group of American historians of Germany, including, among others, Atina Grossmann, Elisabeth Heinemann and Norman Naimark, made important contributions to the attempt to historise these experiences of German victimhood.[35]

So far I have sought to demonstrate that at no point in the history of historiography on the Second World War was there anything resembling repression of the theme of German victimhood. But I have also indicated that there was indeed a major watershed in the interpretative axes of the war somewhere in the 1960s. As more critical perceptions of traditional German narratives came to the fore, the once dominant victims' discourse fell into disrepute and was left to outsiders and the far Right. Most historians now began to focus on research which dealt with victims of Germans. Germans became primarily perpetrators in these histories. University historians and many of those 'amateur' historians active in the thriving history workshop movement began to investigate ordinary Germans and their everyday support for an inhumane and criminal regime. By the 1980s the historiographical focus was firmly on German society under Nazism as a perpetrators' society.[36] Following the 'Historians' Dispute' of the mid-1980s, German historians increasingly researched aspects of the Holocaust, focusing on the institutions, mechanisms and individuals which played a crucial role in making the Holocaust happen.

Such perpetrator-centred research continued to dominate after reunification in 1990. The two *Wehrmacht* exhibitions, touring the country from 1995 to 2004, have been successful in demolishing the myth of a 'clean' *Wehrmacht* in which soldiers simply did their 'duty'. They have shown to what extent the army colluded with the SS, SD and Gestapo in mass shootings of Jews and in the Holocaust in general. An increasing amount of historical research demonstrated that wide sections of German society were deeply implicated in Nazi crimes.[37] The full acceptance of the extent of German crimes and German guilt was, in fact, the precondition for the emergence of the German victims' discourse in the second half of the 1990s. Pointing to the success of West Germany's coming-to-terms with the past, an increasing array of voices argued that it must be possible at long last to talk about German victimhood. Germany had earned the right to do so, precisely because it was so successful in working through the National Socialist past.[38] And indeed, the historical literature on ethnic cleansing of Germans and on the bombing war has been increasing.[39] But rarely was that literature apologetic or seeking to absolve Germany from its historical guilt. This made it very different from the earlier research carried out in the 1950s and 1960s. Many of the younger historians researching German victimhood in the 1990s and early 2000s were not concerned with somehow offsetting German suffering against German guilt. Rather, they were attempting to historise an era which had major repercussions on the development of both post-war German societies, while not in any way questioning the importance or dominance of the perpetrator-centred discourse so firmly established since the 1970s.

Reactions of professional historians to the new victims' discourse

Reviewing the reaction of German historians to the new victims' discourse, the importance of generational difference becomes immediately obvious.[40] The older generation, which still has personal memories of the end of the Second World War, has been far more willing to accept the merits of the debate. And this includes not just conservative-liberal historians, where one might expect this to be the case, but also left-liberals, some of whom were important in bringing about the change of focus in West German historiography during the 1960s. Thus, for example, Hans Mommsen accepted the notion of a taboo, arguing: 'the terrible consequences of the allied bombings of Germany in the Second World War had in fact been totally pushed into the background of the public consciousness of Germans for decades.' Mommsen also doubted the military value of the bombardments. Furthermore, he denied that the debate is linked to attempts to portray the Germans as victims and to provide apologies for the German people and its actions during the Second World War.[41] Hans-Ulrich Wehler found the term 'taboo' too strong, but conceded that there existed a 'deep-seated reluctance to treat the expulsions after the collapse of the Third Reich at the same level as other major questions of the time. The Germans should face their own crimes first, something that people rarely do. One does not want to relativise that . . . .' Now that Germany has gone through a phase of thoroughly confronting the demons of the past, Wehler argued, there was no danger of a revanchist discourse emerging in connection with the new victims' discourse. Rather the contrary is the case, he states: 'the debate is liberating'.[42]

By contrast, members of the younger generation tend to reject more forcefully any ideas of taboo or trauma-induced repression. In connection with the bombing war, Dietmar Süß, for example, has traced not so much the history of silence as the loud and clear construction of a 'German master narrative'.[43] Heinrich Schwendemann has pointed out that, to this very day, myths prevail about the *Wehrmacht* fighting the Red Army in the final months of the war in order to allow Germans to flee from the advancing Russians. Any proper historisation of the events, he argued, would come to the conclusion that German military commanders, in particular the admirals of the navy, completely failed to come to the help of the refugees and instead frequently supported the calls of die-hard Nazis to fight the enemy to the last.[44] Judged from the perspective of an American historian of post-war Germany, Robert G. Moeller, the notion of German victimhood was in fact one of the most powerful ideas uniting Germans well into the 1960s.[45] It was an important means by which the post-war West German state managed the integration of millions of refugees and expellees into post-war Germany.[46] Unsurprisingly Moeller has delivered powerful critiques of Grass and of the new victims' discourse more generally.[47]

It was arguably among those younger and 'foreign' historians of Germany that Friedrich's book was received most critically.[48] They pointed out that Friedrich built extensively on the existing memory literature of the bombing war. But memory, as Charles Maier observed, tends to get in the way of history: 'no history perhaps without memory, but no history that does not discipline memory'.[49] It is the historical context that is emphatically lacking in Friedrich's account of the bombing war.

The author's narrative strategy also caught the eye of many. Relating experience in a way that is normally the preserve of fiction rather than history, Friedrich produced graphic, shocking and vivid miniatures of the chaotic amorality of the bombing war. He is taken to task for relativising the Holocaust by comparing, through linguistic association, the suffering of German civilians in the bombing war with the suffering of European Jews. Thus, he refers to Bomber Command 5 as 'task force' (*Einsatzgruppe*); cellars and bomb shelters are described as 'crematoria' and the bombing victims are being 'exterminated'.

Identifying totally with the civilian victims, Friedrich draws the same sharp line between the majority of innocent German civilians and the minority of nasty German Nazis, which had already been such a strong part of the post-war German victims' discourse. By ignoring the considerable amount of research over the last decades which has concentrated on demonstrating the extensive collusion and active participation of ordinary Germans in the crimes committed in the name of National Socialism, Friedrich chose to challenge the dominance of the perpetrators' discourse in the FRG. It is not surprising therefore that some have accused him of playing into the hands of right-wing revisionists by picking up doctrinaire views on the bombing war which have their roots in National Socialist propaganda. It is precisely Friedrich's unwillingness to subscribe to the consensus that one can only discuss German victimhood within the parameters set by the perpetrator discourse which made his book unacceptable to many reviewers.

It is revealing to compare the more critical reception of Friedrich's book with the far more positive reception of Frederick Taylor's book on the bombing of Dresden. Taylor's book is archive-based rather than memory-based. It historically contextualises rather than moralises about the events described and it takes into account more than just the perspective of the civilian victims of bombing. His emphasis on the legitimacy of the bombing war as a military strategy stands in stark contrast to the moral absolutes postulated by Friedrich. Dresden was hit as an important site of armaments production and as a key transport junction for German troops passing through on their way to the eastern front. Arguably much of the more recent literature on the bombing war accepts too readily the notion of bombing as a 'war crime', thereby ignoring rather complex issues of international law. It thus gives ground to the far Right and falls back behind what was already *communis opinio* among German historians in the 1980s. Taylor does not accept the blanket denunciation of the bombing war as a 'war crime'. Yet Taylor also problematises the morality of area bombing and the book expresses a deep sorrow over the loss of the many lives and the city as it existed before 1945. In other words, Taylor stays within the parameters of the perpetrators' discourse and seeks to locate German victimhood within it rather than return to the apologetic victims' discourse of the 1950s.[50]

This is a perspective shared by other authors on the subject. The origins of the escalation of the bombing war are laid squarely at the door of Nazi Germany.[51] Bombing is perceived as one aspect of a wider history of total war.[52] Linking the history of the bombing war more firmly with the social and cultural history of war will allow historians to discuss German victims without losing sight of German perpetrators and wider German responsibilities.[53] Indeed, perpetrator and victim narratives are often closely related. Thus, for example, some of the groups most exposed and vulnerable to the Allied bombing war were groups persecuted in Nazi Germany. Concentration camp inmates, slave labourers and POWs were forced to help clear the rubble during and after air raids but often denied places in air raid shelters. How can one tell one story without keeping in mind the other? Furthermore, comparative research programmes, which look at the histories of air wars and expulsions/ refugees in different cities and among diverse populations and nations, are another useful approach preventing any one-sided return to an apologetic German victims' discourse, or to an equation of German victims with Holocaust victims.[54] Micha Brumlik has recently used the tool of comparison precisely to argue that the fate of the German refugees and expellees at the end of the Second World War should not be compared to the murder of European Jewry, but with other examples of ethnic cleansing, which left a wide trail across Europe's twentieth century.[55]

Conclusion

The new victims' discourse, as it has been initiated by Grass, Sebald and Friedrich, is not an extreme right-wing discourse. The right-wing fringe in Germany laps up the debate and functionalises it for its own purpose, as was all too apparent in the demonstrations of far right-wing groups on the anniversary of the bombing of Dresden in 2005.[56] The far Right is able to exploit the new victims' discourse in particular, if and when the participants in the debate ignore and sideline the perpetrators' discourse, which has become such an established part of West Germany's official historical culture since the 1970s.

Germany's professional historians are not going down that route. Equating the history of Germans as victims and the history of Germans as perpetrators remains unacceptable to the vast majority of them. The strong reactions against Andreas Hillgruber's *Two Kinds of Demise* (*Zweierlei Untergang*) in the 'Historians' Dispute' of the mid-1980s demonstrated how the tide had turned.[57] Hillgruber attempted to narrate the story of the destruction of European Jewry in parallel with the story of the destruction of the German East. This would have been perfectly acceptable within the dominant victims' discourse of the 1950s. But by the mid-1980s, Hillgruber's parallel story-line flew in the face of the dominant perpetrators' discourse. The current scepticism of many historians towards the 'new victims' discourse' and towards the 'outsider' Friedrich in particular, has much to do with anxieties that the dominant perpetrators' discourse is once again under attack and that one might see yet another attempt to equate the Holocaust with German suffering. Among professional historians, however, there is not much appetite for a new historians' controversy.

They seem broadly in agreement that German victimhood can only be discussed within the parameters set by the perpetrators' discourse. Indeed, the new victims' discourse has been surfacing at the same time as Germany is still coming to terms with the effects of the *Crimes of the Wehrmacht* exhibition and the opening of the Holocaust Memorial in Berlin. The task for contemporary historians of Germany is to develop the ability to think German victimhood in the context of German crimes and German guilt. They will have to weave a kaleidoscopic net of interrelated stories. Walter Kempowski's *Soundings* (*Echolot*) project is an impressive attempt to put the conflicting, differing but interrelated voices next to each other,[58] but historians will have to introduce a more conscious and foregrounded element of explanation and interpretation into their narratives of German perpetrators and German victims.

Yet while historians are attempting to find ways of narrating German victimhood within the parameters of the perpetrators' discourse, a very public debate on German victimhood is being played out in the media, in which the historical profession is not strongly involved. Hence the question arises whether the historians and their professional toolboxes are capable of acting as a counter-force to a wider cultural memory intent on raising the issue of German victimhood. Is not the latter given expression far more powerfully by the mass media, film, literature and political discourse? And why does this victims' discourse strike a chord in the German public at all? Here it might be useful to differentiate between an official reception of the theme of German victimhood and private memories. Within German families the personal memories of bombing, rape and expulsion continued to form the focus of wartime stories and were handed from one generation to the next. This family memory, as Harald Welzer has shown, often worked with the vaguest of facts and tended to fill gaps imaginatively.[59] That imagination was unable to think of members of the family as perpetrators. The family memory was characterised by strict loyalty towards family members, which meant that knowledge about history had to be brought into line with personal knowledge of family members. This specific constitution of the family memory meant that it was, first and foremost, a victim's memory, and the construction of victimhood in family memory arguably remained dominant even when, starting in the 1960s, the official historical consciousness in Germany began to be influenced by a strong perpetrators' discourse.

It is therefore the private family memory, standing up to the official historical consciousness, which finds an outlet in the new German victims' discourse. It feels even more confident to express itself in the context of the discourse of 'normality' which has brought forth a new patriotism in the reunified Germany.[60] While prominent left-of-centre participants in the new victims' discourse, such as Grass, have a point when they argue that it is dangerous to leave the private memory to be exploited publicly by the far Right, it is equally dangerous to promote a victims' discourse which does not properly take into account German guilt and responsibility for war and genocide. The private family memory of victimhood needs to be brought into line with the official historical consciousness of the FRG. But this can only be achieved by bringing discussions of German victimhood together with debates on German perpetrators.

To make matters even more complicated, contemporary debates on victims and perpetrators have moved from the national to the European stage. Just as the Holocaust discourse has been increasingly Europeanised since the end of the Cold War, so the victims' discourse no longer is the prerogative of those who fought National Socialist Germany between 1939 and 1945. The Holocaust and wartime suffering have become a crucial European memory space which is functionalised in attempts to strengthen the European people's waning commitment to Europe. Allowing the memory of German victimhood on to the stage is an attempt to integrate the German narrative more firmly with other national narratives in Europe. Chancellor Gerhard Schröder's full participation in the victory celebrations marking the sixtieth anniversary of the end of the Second World War in 2005, signalled the acceptance of a new democratic Germany into the circle of those democratic Allied nations who had defeated

Nazi Germany. As other Europeans begin to accept a share in the responsibility for the murder of European Jewry, so Germans begin to rediscover their own victimhood in the war. Such Europeanisation of Holocaust and wartime memory may well become an important driving force in strengthening the German victims' discourse. It will therefore be even more important for historians of Europe to employ their craft in order to both maintain and blur the important line between perpetrators and victims, and to insist that any such discussions move beyond the legacy of national apologia that characterised debates during the Cold War.

Chronology of Events, 1939–1950

The following chronology focuses principally on the bombing war and on the massive population transfers that were either the direct effect or the consequence of the Second World War.

1939

1 September	The German *Wehrmacht* invades Poland.
24 September	Beginning of the bombing of Warsaw by the German air force; in the course of the attack on the city, more than 20,000 civilians are killed.
28 September	Signing of the German-Soviet 'Boundary and Friendship Treaty' finalising the division of Poland between the Germans and Soviets. Both the German and Soviet occupiers proceed to expel Poles from their respective zones.
October	Following the invasion and defeat of Poland, the Nazis begin with ambitious resettlement plans in their bid to 'Germanise' parts of Eastern Europe. These plans result in the resettlement of hundreds of thousands of ethnic Germans, as well as the expulsion, resettlement and/or murder of a much higher number of Poles and Jews.
30 October	Himmler orders the deportation of 555,000 Jews from the Warthegau, which is to be 'Germanised'. In the course of 1939 and 1940, the Nazis expel 450,000 Poles from the Warthegau.

1940

February 1940–June 1941	The Soviets expel at least 330,000 Poles to Siberia and Central Asia in their bid to 'Sovietise' eastern Poland.

10 May	German planes bomb Freiburg by mistake; 57 people are killed, including children. Goebbels tries to blame the British.
14 May	At least 800 civilians die in the German bombing of Rotterdam.
September 1940–May 1941	'The Blitz', a series of aerial bombings by the German airforce against British cities, takes the lives of between 40,000 and 45,000 people and destroys over a million homes.
7 September	First of a series of bombing raids by the German airforce on London; the raids took place over 57 consecutive nights.
14 November	The bombing of Coventry by the German airforce causes the deaths of over 550 men, women and children; three-quarters of the city's factories are destroyed, along with over 4000 homes.
29–30 December	The bombing of London by the German airforce unleashes a firestorm which lays waste to the area between the Guildhall and St Paul's Cathedral.

1941

6–7 April	The German airforce bombs Belgrade, killing more than 2000 people.
22 June	Germany invades the Soviet Union.

1942

14 February	The British Air Ministry issues the 'Area Bombing Directive' to Bomber Command. This states that, in future, bombing raids 'should now be focused on the morale of the enemy civil population and, in particular, of the industrial workers'.
22 February	Arthur Harris takes over as head of RAF Bomber Command. He vigorously pursues a policy of 'area bombing', according to which entire German cities or parts of cities were targeted for destruction.

29 March	Lübeck becomes the first victim of Allied area bombing, although the expected firestorm never happens; at least 400 people are killed.
April-June	Following the bombing of Lübeck, the Germans begin with reprisal bombings against British cities. These bombings are known as 'Baedeker Raids' because they were directed against cities marked with three stars in the Baedeker tourist guide. Exeter, Bath, Canterbury, York and Norwich were bombed, causing extensive damage and killing over 1600 civilians.
31 May	The Allies launch 'Operation Millennium' against Cologne (the first 1000-bomber raid), killing about 500 people. Cologne was bombed, all in all, 262 times during the war.
August	Over 40,000 Russian civilians are killed by German aerial bombing in Stalingrad as the German 6th and 4th armies approach the city.

1943

14–24 January	The United States and Great Britain meet at Casablanca and agree on combining their air war efforts, as well as on demanding an unconditional surrender from Germany, Japan and Italy.
5–6 March	Bomber Command carries out an attack on Essen in the Ruhr, thereby starting the 'Battle of the Ruhr'. By mid-July 1943, nearly all the major cities in the Ruhr area have been heavily bombed.
16–17 May	A special RAF command destroys the water supply for the Ruhr area by attacking dams on the Möhne and Eder rivers ('Dambusters Raid'). Over 1000 people died in the subsequent floods; among these casualties are Soviet slave labourers in the town of Neheim-Husten (near the river Ruhr).

24–28 July	British and American bombers attack Hamburg ('Operation Gomorrha') in a series of devastating attacks culminating in a firestorm; between 35,000 and 40,000 people are killed.
28 November–1 December	Stalin, Roosevelt and Churchill meet at the Tehran Conference. One of the outcomes of the Conference is the agreement – at Stalin's insistence – that the boundaries of post-war Poland run along the Curzon line in the east (resulting in the loss of Polish territory to the Soviet Union), although the exact trajectory of this line remains unclear.
18 November 1943–March 1944:	British Bomber Command carries out a series of 16 aerial attacks on Berlin. As a result of this bombing campaign, sometimes known as the 'Battle of Berlin', 800,000 Berliners became homeless, and 7500 civilians were killed.

1944

22 July	A British Air Staff paper presented by Air Marshal Portal first suggests subjecting Berlin to a massive aerial bombardment ('Operation Thunderclap'). The paper envisaged '220,000 casualties, 50 per cent of these (or 110,000) may expect to be killed'. The idea, however, was initially shelved.
15 September	Roosevelt initially signals his support for the so-called 'Morgenthau Plan' which envisaged the radical de-industrialisation of Germany.
21 October	The Soviet Army commits atrocities against the German civilian population – notably mass rape and murder – in the east Prussian village of Nemmersdorf.
Winter 1944/45	The Nazis evacuate concentration camps in Eastern Europe shortly before the arrival of the Soviets. The subsequent death marches westwards result in the deaths of tens of thousands of Jews and other prisoners.

Winter 1944/45	As the Russians advance into German territory (East Prussia, then Silesia and Pomerania), millions of Germans flee westwards in fugitive treks.

1945

19 January	The Nazi Gauleiter of Breslau, Hanke, orders the evacuation of civilians from the city. One day later women and children are ordered to leave on foot – in temperatures of more than −16° centigrade. At least 18,000 of them die in the freezing temperatures. Others reach Dresden on foot, only to die in the subsequent bombing of that city.
27 January	Liberation of Auschwitz by the Soviets; only 7000 prisoners – most of them barely alive – are in the camp at liberation. Altogether some 1.5 million people were murdered in Auschwitz, some 1.1 million of them Jewish.
30 January	A Russian submarine sinks the *Wilhelm Gustloff* in the Baltic Sea; 9000 German fugitives lose their lives. A few hours later the SS murder 3000 concentration camp prisoners from Stutthof on the beach near Pillau.
4–11 February	At the Conference in Yalta, Stalin, Churchill and Roosevelt agree that the eastern boundary of Poland should be drawn to the west of Lemberg. Poland is to lose almost half of its former territory. Accordingly, agreement is also reached that Poland should be compensated with what was hitherto German territory, although exactly where the new German–Polish border should run is unclear.
13/14 February	Dresden is heavily bombed by British and then American aircraft. At least 35,000 people are killed, not least as a result of the enormous firestorm unleashed by the bombs.
23/24 February	The British bomb the town of Pforzheim, destroying or damaging 80 per cent of it;

	20,000 people die in the bombs or the subsequent firestorm.
12 March	The American airforce bombs the town of Swinemünde on the Baltic. The death toll is at least 23,000.
May	The so-called 'wild expulsions' (i.e., unsystematic and non-legalised expulsions) of Germans from the eastern territories begin. They continue until July. Thousands of Germans lose their lives during these expulsions. At the same time, the Soviets begin to set up administrative structures in those parts of former German territories they wish to see integrated into western Poland.
3 May	British planes sink the *Cap Arcona*, the *Thielbek*, the *Athen* and the *Deutschland* in Lübeck Bay; 7500 concentration camp prisoners evacuated by the Nazis on to these ships are killed.
7–9 May	Germany capitulates.
31 May	25,000 ethnic Germans – many of them women and children – are forced by Czech militia to abandon their homes in Brno and embark on a trek to Austria. Some 2000 die on the long march or are killed by guards.
9–12 June	Some 8000 male Germans are expelled from the Czech town of Komotau on a march westwards. At least 70 of them die on the march; before this, a number of ethnic Germans are murdered in Komotau by Czechs.
17 July–2 August	At the Potsdam Conference, the Allies stipulate that the transfer of Germans from Poland, Hungary and Czechoslovakia should continue, but that this transfer should proceed in an orderly and humane fashion. This marks the beginning of the period of 'legalised' expulsions. The Allies *de facto* recognise the Oder-Neiße line (along the Görlitzer Neiße) as the new western border of Poland, although a final decision is postponed until a peace treaty with Germany is drawn up.

28 October — Edvard Benes, the Czech president in exile, issues the last of the so-called 'Benes Decrees' (143 in all). According to the most controversial of these, Germans and Hungarians who had been living in Czechoslovakia are deprived of both their citizenship and rights to their property. An 'amnesty law' legalises acts of violence against Germans committed during the expulsions.

1948

By this time, some 11.7 million ethnic Germans expelled from Eastern Europe have settled either in the Western or Eastern Zone of Germany. By 1950, 16.5 per cent of the population in West Germany is made up of expellees; in East Germany, the figure is even higher (24.2 per cent).

1950

Dissolution of the last of the 'Special Camps' at Bautzen, Buchenwald and Sachsenhausen. As of 1945, the Soviets incarcerated over 250,000 Germans in 10 so-called Special Camps throughout eastern Germany. While such practice was loosely in line with Allied denazification statutes, a considerable number of Germans innocent of responsibility for Nazism – including women and children arrested 'to make up numbers', or, increasingly, political opponents of communism – were amongst those held at these camps. About 45,000 Germans died in the Special Camps as a result of hunger, malnutrition and disease; many were buried in shallow mass graves.

Notes

Introduction: German Victimhood at the Turn of the Millennium

1 See Bundesarchiv Koblenz, B102/144137: Prüfung von Filmen durch den interministeriellen Ausschuss für Ost/West-Filmfragen. Band 1: Mai 1961–April 1962.

2 For a good account of the integration of expellees in East Germany, see Philipp Ther, *Deutsche und polnische Vertriebene: Gesellschaft und Vertriebenenpolitik in der SBZ/DDR und in Polen 1945–1956* (Göttingen 1998).

3 Pertti Ahonen, *After the Expulsion: West Germany and Eastern Europe, 1945–1990* (Oxford 2003).

4 Gerhard Schröder, speech on 'Nation, Patriotismus, Demokratische Kultur', 8 May 2002. See http://www.berlin.spd.de/servlet/PB/menu/1534815/1016827.html

5 Gerhard Schröder, 'Wir stehen erst jetzt am Ende einer langen Nachkriegszeit', *Süddeutsche Zeitung*, 7/8 May 2005, 7.

6 See Jörg Quoos, '"Aus Feinden wurden Freunde": Interview with Tony Blair', *BILD*, 8 May 2005.

7 Schröder, 'Nation, Patriotismus, Demokratische Kultur'.

8 Hans Jörg Hennecke, *Die Dritte Republik: Aufbruch und Ernüchterung* (Munich 2003), p. 146.

9 Richard Meng, *Der Medienkanzler: Was bleibt vom System Schröder?* (Frankfurt am Main 2002), pp. 41–2.

10 The remark was made on the German television programme SAT1 on 1 November 1998. I am grateful to Alan Johnson for helping me to identify the source, and to Cornelia Berens for drawing my attention to a full citing of Schröder's comments in Claus Leggewie und Erik Meyer, *'Ein Ort, an den man gerne geht': Das Holocaust-Mahnmal und die deutsche Geschichtspolitik nach 1989* (Munich 2005), pp. 179f.

11 Quoted in 'Regierung verdrängt NS-Geschichte', *Süddeutsche Zeitung*, 16 September 1999, p. 17.

12 Reinhard Mohr, 'Total Normal?', *Der Spiegel*, 49 (1998), 40–8, here 41.

13 See Frank Schirrmacher (ed.), *Die Walser-Bubis Debatte: Eine Dokumentation* (Frankfurt am Main 1999); and Johannes Klotz and Gerd Wiegel (eds), *Geistige Brandstiftung? Die Walser-Bubis-Debatte* (Cologne 1999). See also Bill Niven, *Facing the Nazi Past* (London and New York 2002), pp. 175–93.

14 See, for instance, Armin Mohler, *Der Nasenring: Die Vergangenheitsbewältigung vor und nach der Mauer* (Munich 1991, new edn 1996).

15 Martin Walser, *Tod eines Kritikers* (Frankfurt am Main 2002).

16 See Klaus Rainer Röll, *Verbotene Trauer: Ende der deutschen Tabus* (Munich 2002), particularly pp. 62–71.
17 For the sources of these quotations, see Niven, *Facing the Nazi Past*, p. 218.
18 See, for instance, Dominik Cziesche et. al., 'Der ganz rechte Weg', *Der Spiegel*, 45 (2003), 3 November 2003, 40–2.
19 See 'Provozierende Frage: Auszüge aus der Rede Hohmanns zum 3. Oktober', *Süddeutsche Zeitung*, 12 November 2003, 8.
20 See 'Null Prozent für Möllemann', *Süddeutsche Zeitung*, 21 May 2002, 6.
21 See 'Gerhardt: Möllemann schädigt Ansehen der Liberalen', *Süddeutsche Zeitung*, 22 May 2002, 6.
22 There are many other examples. Thus Christoph Dieckmann, in a 2001 newspaper article for the national weekly *Die Zeit*, suggested that National Socialism might have been inspired by the 'Jewish creed of the chosen people', which Dieckmann also makes responsible for the Jewish–Palestinian conflict (9 November 2001).
23 See, for instance: Thomas Siemon and Werner Dettmar, *Der Horizont in hellen Flammen. Die Bombardierung Kassels am 22. Oktober 1943* (Gudensberg-Gleichen 2003); Volker Keller, *Mannheim im Bombenkrieg 1940–1945* (Gudensberg-Gleichen 2003); and Birgit Horn, *Die Nacht, als der Feuertod vom Himmel stürzte. Leipzig, 4. Dezember 1943* (Gudensberg-Gleichen 2003).
24 See Jörg Arnold's review article on books about the bombing of German cities at H-Sozkult (http://hsozkult.geschichte.hu-berlin.de/rezensionen/type=rezbuecher&id=2861).
25 Walter Kempowski, *Das Echolot. Ein kollektives Tagebuch. Januar und Februar 1943* (Munich 1993), and *Das Echolot. Fuga furiosa. Ein kollektives Tagebuch. Winter 1945* (Munich 1999).
26 See Walter Kempowski, *Der rote Hahn: Dresden im Februar 1945* (Munich 2001).
27 Dieter Forte, *Der Junge mit den blutigen Schuhen* (Frankfurt am Main 1995).
28 See Jörg Friedrich, *Der Brand: Deutschland im Bombenkrieg 1940–1945* (Munich 2002), p. 11 and p. 296.
29 Ibid., p. 77.
30 Ibid., p. 321.
31 Ibid., p. 64.
32 Hubertus Knabe, *Tag der Befreiung: Das Kriegsende in Ostdeutschland* (Berlin 2005), p. 10.
33 Ibid., pp. 24–5.
34 See http://www.z-g-v.de/english/aktuelles/?id=49
35 See http://www.z-g-v.de/english/aktuelles/?id=51
36 'Menschen bei Maischberger', *ARD*, 10 May 2005 (23.00 German time).
37 For a scathing review, see David Cesarani and Peter Longerich, 'The Massaging of History', The *Guardian*, 7 April 2005, 23.
38 See Erich Später, 'Siebzig Jahre Völkischer Nationalismus: Von der "Sudetendeutschen Volksgemeinschaft" zur "Volksgruppe im Exil" ',

in Michael Klundt (ed.), *Heldenmythos und Opfertaumel: Der Zweite Weltkrieg und seine Folgen im deutschen Geschichtsdiskurs* (Cologne 2004), pp. 104–33, here p. 107.

39 Günter Grass, *Im Krebsgang* (Göttingen 2002).

40 Martin Heinzelmann, *Göttingen im Luftkrieg 1935–1945* (Göttingen 2003), p. 7.

41 Thomas Urban, *Der Verlust: Die Vertreibung der Deutschen und Polen im 20. Jahrhundert* (Munich 2004).

42 Gregor Thum, *Die fremde Stadt: Breslau 1945* (Munich 2003).

43 Ther, *Deutsche und polnische Vertriebene.*

44 See Norbert Frei, *1945 und Wir: Das Dritte Reich im Bewußtsein der Deutschen* (Munich 2005); and Micha Brumlik, *Wer Sturm sät: Die Vertreibung der Deutschen* (Berlin 2005).

45 For a sympathetic account of the fate of German children during the bombing war, see Nicholas Stargardt, *Witnesses of War: Children's Lives under the Nazis* (London 2005), pp. 231ff.

46 See 'Denkmal für Opfer der Vertreibung in Tschechien', *Süddeutsche Zeitung*, 16 September 2002, 6.

47 See Thomas Urban, 'Ungeteilte Aufmerksamkeit', *Süddeutsche Zeitung*, 18 September 2002, 9.

48 See Klaus Brill, 'Wo die Vergangenheit im Fluss ist', *Süddeutsche Zeitung*, 2 August 2005, 3.

49 Thus some in the CDU continue to call for the Czech Republic to repeal the Benes Decrees (which formed the basis for the expulsion of the ethnic Germans), and some Czech politicians have been dismissive of the right of Sudeten Germans to sympathy.

50 See Anthony Clayton and Alan Russell, *Dresden: A City Reborn* (Oxford and New York 2001).

51 Harald Welzer, Sabine Moller and Karoline Tschuggnall, *'Opa war kein Nazi': Nationalsozialismus und Holocaust im Familiengedächtnis* (Frankfurt am Main 2002).

52 Mona Sue Weissmark, *Justice Matters: Legacies of the Holocaust and World War II* (Oxford and New York 2004).

53 *Der Spiegel*, 51 (2003), 15 December 2003, 77.

54 Lothar Kettenacker's edited volume *Ein Volk von Opfern? Die neue Debatte um den Bombenkrieg 1940–1945* (Berlin 2003) focuses exclusively on the bombing-war.

Chapter 1: The Politics of the Past in the 1950s: Rhetorics of Victimisation in East and West Germany

1 This chapter is a much shortened version of a piece that initially appeared as 'Germans as Victims? Thoughts on a Post-Cold War

History of World War II's Legacies', *History & Memory*, 17:1/2 (2005), 147–94. It appears here with the kind permission of the publisher.

2 Norbert Frei, *Adenauer's Germany and the Nazi Past: The Politics of Amnesty and Integration,* trans. Joel Golb (New York 2002). The original title of Frei's book is *Vergangenheitspolitik* or the 'Politics of the Past'.

3 'Remarks of President Ronald Reagan to Regional Editors, White House, April 18, 1985', in Geoffrey H. Hartman (ed.), *Bitburg in Moral and Political Perspective* (Bloomington 1986), p. 240.

4 Charles S. Maier, *The Unmasterable Past: History, Holocaust, and German National Identity* (Cambridge, MA, 1988).

5 Alice Förster and Birgit Beck, 'Post-Traumatic Stress Disorder and World War II: Can a Psychiatric Concept Help Us Understand Postwar Society?', in Richard Bessel and Dirk Schumann (eds), *Life after Death: Approaches to a Cultural and Social History of Europe during the 1940s and 1950s* (Cambridge 2003), p. 28; Rüdiger Overmanns, *Deutsche militärische Verluste im Zweiten Weltkrieg* (Munich 1999), pp. 283 and 299; Elizabeth Heineman, *What Difference Does a Husband Make? Women and Marital Status in Nazi and Postwar Germany* (Chapel Hill 1999), pp. 21–2 and 79; and Robert G. Moeller, *War Stories: The Search for a Usable Past in the Federal Republic of Germany* (Berkeley 2001), p. 3, and *Protecting Motherhood: Women and the Family in the Politics of Postwar West Germany* (Berkeley 1993), p. 27.

6 See also in particular, Klaus Naumann (ed.), *Nachkrieg in Deutschland* (Hamburg 2001); Bessel and Schumann, *Life after Death*; James M. Diehl, *The Thanks of the Fatherland: German Veterans after the Second World War* (Chapel Hill, NC, 1993); and Michael L. Hughes, *Shouldering the Burdens of Defeat: West Germany and the Reconstruction of Social Justice* (Chapel Hill 1999).

7 See Heike Amos, *Auferstanden aus Ruinen . . . . Die Nationalhymne der DDR 1949 bis 1990* (Berlin 1997).

8 Quoted in Frank Biess, ' "Pioneers of a New Germany": Returning POWs from the Soviet Union and the Making of East German Citizens, 1945–1950', *Central European History*, 32:2 (1999), 147.

9 See, e.g., Jürgen Danyel (ed.), *Die geteilte Vergangenheit: Zum Umgang mit Nationalsozialismus und Widerstand in beiden deutschen Staaten* (Berlin 1995); and Jeffrey Herf, *Divided Memory: The Nazi Past in the Two Germanys* (Cambridge, MA, 1997).

10 Max Seydewitz, *Die unbesiegbare Stadt: Zerstörung und Wiederaufbau von Dresden* (Berlin 1956), p. 7.

11 Gilad Margalit, 'Der Luftangriff auf Dresden: Seine Bedeutung für die Erinnerungspolitik der DDR und für die Herauskristallisierung einer historischen Kriegserinnerung im Westen', in Susanne Düwell and Matthias Schmidt (eds), *Narrative der Shoah: Repräsentationen der Vergangenheit in Historiographie, Kunst und Politik* (Paderborn 2002),

pp. 189–208; also Thomas W. Neumann, 'Der Bombenkrieg: Zur ungeschriebenen Geschichte einer kollektiven Verletzung', in Naumann (ed.), *Nachkrieg in Deutschland,* pp. 319–42. See also Niven's chapter in the present volume.

12 Jörg Echternkamp, 'Von Opfern, Helden und Verbrechern: Anmerkungen zur Bedeutung des Zweiten Weltkriegs in den Erinnerungskulturen der Deutschen 1945–1955', in Jörg Hillmann and John Zimmermann (eds), *Kriegsende 1945 in Deutschland* (Munich 2002), pp. 308–9.

13 Biess, ' "Pioneers of a New Germany" '.

14 Karin Hartewig, 'Militarismus und Antifaschismus: Die Wehrmacht im kollektiven Gedächtnis der DDR', in Michael T. Greven and Oliver von Wrochem (eds), *Der Krieg in der Nachkriegszeit: Der Zweite Weltkrieg in Politik und Gesellschaft der Bundesrepublik* (Opladen 2000), pp. 236–54.

15 Dorothee Wierling, 'Erzieher und Erzogene: Zu Generationenprofilen in der DDR der 60er Jahre', in Axel Schildt, Detlef Siegfried and Karl Christian Lammers (eds), *Dynamische Zeiten: Die 60er Jahre in den beiden deutschen Gesellschaften* (Hamburg, 2000), p. 629, and *Geboren im Jahr Eins: Der Jahrgang 1949 in der DDR. Versuch einer Kollektivbiographie* (Berlin 2002), pp. 107–9.

16 Detlef Kannapin, *Antifaschismus im Film der DDR: DEFA-Spielfime 1945–1955/56* (Cologne 1997).

17 Wierling, 'Erzieher und Erzogene', pp. 624–41.

18 Alf Lüdtke, 'Histories of Mourning: Flowers and Stones for the War Dead, Confusion for the Living – Vignettes from East and West Germany', in Gerald Sider and Gavin Smith (eds), *Between History and Histories: The Making of Silences and Commemorations* (Toronto 1997), pp. 152–3.

19 Quoted in Moeller, *War Stories,* p. 21.

20 Rolf Vogel (ed.), *Deutschlands Weg nach Israel: Eine Dokumentation mit einem Geleitwort von Konrad Adenauer* (Stuttgart 1967), p. 36.

21 Hughes, *Shouldering the Burdens of Defeat.*

22 Frank Biess, 'Men of Reconstruction – The Reconstruction of Men: Returning POWs in East and West Germany, 1945–1955', in Karen Hagemann and Stefanie Schüler-Springorum (eds), *Home/Front: The Military, War and Gender in Twentieth-Century Germany* (Oxford 2002), pp. 335–58.

23 Jay Lockenour, *Soldiers as Citizens: Former Wehrmacht Officers in the Federal Republic of Germany, 1945–1955* (Lincoln, NB, 2001).

24 Franka Schneider, ' "Einigkeit im Unglück"? Berliner Eheberatungsstellen zwischen Ehekrise und Wiederaufbau', in Naumann (ed.), *Nachkrieg in Deutschland,* p. 208.

25 Moeller, *Protecting Motherhood,* p. 3.

26 Merith Niehuss, *Familie, Frau und Gesellschaft: Studien zur Strukturgeschichte der Familie in Westdeutschland 1945–1960* (Göttingen 2001),

esp. pp. 34–40, 106, 112 and 139; and Uta G. Poiger, *Jazz, Rock and Rebels: Cold War Politics and American Culture in a Divided Germany* (Berkeley 2000).

27 Eva Hahn and Hans Henning Hahn, 'Flucht und Vertreibung', in Etienne François and Hagen Schulze (eds), *Deutsche Erinnerungsorte,* vol. 1 (Munich 2001), pp. 335–51; and in general, Pertti Ahonen, *After the Expulsion: West Germany and Eastern Europe, 1945–1990* (Oxford 2003), pp. 1–115.

28 Ralph Bollman, 'Im Dickicht der Aufrechnung', in Lothar Kettenacker (ed.), *Ein Volk von Opfern? Die neue Debatte um den Bombenkrieg 1940–45* (Berlin 2003), pp. 137–8.

29 'Ansprache des Bundestagspräsidenten Dr. Ehlers anlässlich der Enthüllung des Ehrenmals für die Hamburger Luftgefallenen am 15. August 1952 auf dem Ohlsdorfer Friedhof', in Bundesminister für Vertriebene, Flüchtlinge und Kriegsgeschädigte (ed.), *Dokumente Deutscher Kriegsschäden: Evakuierte, Kriegssachgeschädigte, Währungsgeschädigte,* vol. 1 (Düsseldorf 1958), p. 63.

30 Margalit, 'Der Luftangriff auf Dresden', p. 205.

31 Quoted in Karin Hausen, 'The "Day of National Mourning" in Germany', in Sider and Smith (eds), *Between History and Histories,* p. 141.

32 Sabine Behrenbeck, 'Heldenkult oder Friedensmahnung? Kriegerdenkmale nach beiden Weltkriegen', in Gottfried Niedhart and Dieter Riesenberger (eds), *Lernen aus dem Krieg? Deutsche Nachkriegszeiten 1918 und 1945* (Munich 1992), p. 359.

33 Robert R. Shandley, *Rubble Films: German Cinema in the Shadow of the Third Reich* (Philadelphia 2001). And in general, Heide Fehrenbach, *Cinema in Democratizing Germany: Reconstructing National Identity after Hitler* (Chapel Hill 1995).

34 For a discussion of the projects that detailed the POW and expellee experience, see Moeller, *War Stories,* pp. 51–87, 177–80.

35 Karl Jaspers, *The Question of German Guilt,* trans. E. B. Ashton (New York 1961), pp. 21 and 114.

36 Frank Stern, *The Whitewashing of the Yellow Badge: Antisemitism and Philosemitism in Postwar Germany,* trans. William Templer (Oxford 1992); and Patrick Major, *The Death of the KPD: Communism and Anti-Communism in West Germany, 1945–1956* (Oxford 1997).

37 Birgit Dahlke, '"Frau komm!" Vergewaltigungen 1945: Zur Geschichte eines Diskurses', in Dahlke, Martina Langermann and Thomas Taterka (eds), *LiteraturGesellschaft DDR: Kanonkämpfe und ihre Geschichte(n)* (Stuttgart 2000), pp. 275–311.

38 Elke Mehnert, 'Vertriebene versus Umsiedler – der ostdeutsche Blick auf ein Kapitel Nachkriegsgeschichte,' in Mehnert (ed.), *Landschaften der Erinnerung: Flucht und Vertreibung aus deutscher, polnischer und tschechischer Sicht* (Frankfurt am Main 2001), pp. 133–57.

39 Heineman, *What Difference Does a Husband Make?*

40 Kurt Zentner, *Aufstieg aus dem Nichts: Deutschland von 1945 bis 1953. Eine Soziographie in zwei Bänden,* 2 vols (Cologne 1954).
41 Constantin Goschler, *Wiedergutmachung: Westdeutschland und die Verfolgten des Nationalsozialismus (1950–1954)* (Munich 1992).
42 Rudy Koshar, *From Monuments to Traces: Artifacts of German Memory, 1870–1990* (Berkeley 2000), p. 162.
43 OMGUS, Daily Intelligence Digest no. 158, 2 May 1946, 'Reactions to KZ Film', National Archive, OMGUS, Information Control Division, Opinion Surveys Branch, box 146, file 20, 'Daily Intelligence Digest, 1 April–20 June 1946'.
44 Quoted in Diehl, *Thanks of the Fatherland,* p. 63; and *Der Teufel spielte Balalaika,* discussed in Moeller, *War Stories,* p. 162.
45 Moeller, *War Stories,* pp. 74–82.
46 'Gebt die Kriegsgefangenen frei!' *Stuttgarter Zeitung,* 11 November 1949.
47 Quoted in Moeller, *War Stories*, p. 44.
48 Vera Neumann, *Nicht die Rede wert: Die Privatisierung der Kriegsfolgen in der frühen Bundesrepublik* (Münster 1999); Svenja Goltermann, 'Im Wahn der Gewalt: Massentod, Opferdiskurs und Psychiatrie 1945–1956', in Naumann, *Nachkrieg in Deutschland,* pp. 343–63; Michael Schwartz, '"Zwangsheimat Deutschland": Vertriebene und Kernbevölkerung zwischen Gesellschaftskonflikt und Integrationspolitik', in Naumann (ed.), *Nachkrieg in Deutschland,* pp. 114–48.
49 Hermann Lübbe, 'Der Nationalsozialismus im politischen Bewusstsein der Gegenwart', in Martin Broszat (ed.), *Deutschlands Weg in die Diktatur: Internationale Konferenz zur nationalsozialistischen Machtübernahme im Reichstagsgebäude zu Berlin* (Berlin 1983), pp. 329–49, esp. 334–5.
50 W. G. Sebald, *On the Natural History of Destruction,* trans. Anthea Bell (New York 2003), p. 13.
51 Richard Bessel, *Germany after the First World War* (Oxford 1993).
52 James M. Diehl, 'Germany in Defeat, 1918 and 1945: Some Comparisons and Contrasts', *The History Teacher* 22:4 (1989), 397–409; and Michael L. Hughes, 'Restitution and Democracy in Germany after Two World Wars', *Contemporary European History*, 4:1 (1994), 1–18.
53 'Regierungserkärung vom 10. November 1965, Bundeskanzler Dr. Erhard', in Peter Pulte (ed.), *Regierungserklärungen 1949–1973* (Berlin 1973), p. 161; *Protokoll der Verhandlungen des VI. Parteitages der Sozialistischen Einheitspartei Deutschlands 15. bis 21. Januar 1963* (Berlin 1963), p. 28.
54 For an excellent summary, see Harold Marcuse, *Legacies of Dachau: The Uses and Abuses of a Concentration Camp, 1933–2001* (Cambridge 2001).
55 Quoted in Helmut Dubiel, *Niemand ist frei von der Geschichte: Die nationalsozialistische Herrschaft in den Debatten des Deutschen Bundestags* (Munich 1999), p. 133.
56 Edgar Wolfrum, *Geschichtspolitik in der Bundesrepublik Deutschland: Der Weg zur bundesrepublikanischen Erinnerung 1948–1990* (Darmstadt 1999), pp. 232 and 352.

57 Michael Berenbaum (ed.), *A Mosaic of Victims: Non-Jews Persecuted and Murdered by the Nazis* (New York 1990).
58 Marcuse, *Legacies of Dachau,* p. 346.
59 'Speech by Richard von Weizsäcker, President of the Federal Republic of Germany, in the Bundestag during the Ceremony Commemorating the 40th Anniversary of the End of the War in Europe and of National Socialist Tyranny, May 8, 1985', in Hartman (ed.), *Bitburg,* p. 263.
60 Neumann, 'Der Bombenkrieg', p. 334; and in general, Herf, *Divided Memory.*

Chapter 2: Victims in Uniform: West German Combat Movies from the 1950s

1 Jay Lockenour, *Soldiers as Citizens: Former Wehrmacht Officers in the Federal Republic of Germany, 1945–1955* (Lincoln 2002), p. 7.
2 Jörg Echternkamp, 'Arbeit am Mythos: Soldatengenerationen der Wehrmacht im Urteil der west- und ostdeutschen Nachkriegsgesellschaft', in Klaus Naumann (ed.), *Nachkrieg in Deutschland* (Hamburg 2001), pp. 421–43; and Norbert Frei, *Adenauer's Germany and the Nazi Past: The Politics of Amnesty and Integration,* trans. Joel Golb (New York 2002).
3 Donald Abenheim, *Reforging the Iron Cross: The Search for Tradition in the West German Armed Forces* (Princeton 1988), p. 70; also David Clay Large, *Germans to the Front: West German Rearmament in the Adenauer Era* (Chapel Hill 1996); and James M. Diehl, *The Thanks of the Fatherland: German Veterans after the Second World War* (Chapel Hill 1993).
4 Knut Hickethier, 'Kriegserlebnis und Kriegsdeutung im bundesdeutschen Fernsehen der fünfziger Jahre', *Amsterdamer Beiträge zur neueren Germanistik,* 50:2 (2001), 759–76; and in general, Wolfgang Wegmann, *Der westdeutsche Kriegsfilm der fünfziger Jahre* (Dissertation, University of Cologne, 1980); Gerhard Paul, 'Krieg und Film im 20. Jahrhundert: Historische Skizze und methodologische Überlegungen', in Bernard Chiari, Matthias Rogg and Wolfgang Schmidt (eds), *Krieg und Militär im Film des 20. Jahrhunderts* (Munich 2003), pp. 3–76; and Peter Reichel, *Erfundene Erinnerung: Weltkrieg und Judenmord in Film und Theater* (Munich 2004). Reichel writes about *Hunde, wollt ihr ewig leben?* and *Die Brücke.*
5 Friedrich A. Wagner, 'Null-acht-fuffzehn im russischen Winter: Der zweite Teil des Films nach dem Roman von Kirst', *Frankfurter Allgemeine Zeitung,* 20 August 1955. All reviews come from the superb collection of the German Film Institute in Frankfurt am Main.
6 Knut Hickethier, 'Der Zweite Weltkrieg und der Holocaust im Fernsehen der Bundesrepublik der fünfziger und frühen sechziger Jahre', in Michael T. Greven and Oliver von Wrochem (eds), *Der Krieg in der Nachkriegszeit: Der Zweite Weltkrieg in Politik und Gesellschaft*

der Bundesrepublik (Opladen 2000), pp. 93–112; Reichel, *Erfundene Erinnerung,* pp. 51–82 and 87–91; Robert G. Moeller, *War Stories: The Search for a Usable Past in the Federal Republic of Germany* (Berkeley 2001), pp. 148–65, and 'What Did You Do in the War, Mutti? Courageous Women, Compassionate Commanders, and Stories of the Second World War', *German History*, 22 (2004), 563–94.

7 Ludwig Gatter, 'Appassionata in Panje-Moll', *Kölnische Rundschau,* 27 August 1955.

8 ' "Gegen das Übel der Macht in unrechten Händen": Paul Mays Verfilmung von Hans Hellmuth Kirsts Roman "08/15" ', *Süddeutsche Zeitung,* 7 April 1992; ' "08/15": Ein unerfreulicher Film', *Neue Presse,* 6 November 1954.

9 Heinz Ohff, 'Wie macht man aus Menschen Soldaten? Paul May's langerwarteter Film lief gestern in vielen deutschen Städten gleichzeitig an', *Heidelberger Tageblatt*, 2 October 1954.

10 'Germans Laugh at Wehrmacht Film', *Dundee Evening Telegraph,* 21 October 1954.

11 'Ein Buch und eine Neurose', comments of Konrad Kraske, a former press secretary for Blank's office who was the head of the 'Circle of Christian-Democratic Students', in 'Des Teufels Hauptwachtmeister: Eine Debatte rund um "Null-acht Fünfzehn"', *Der Monat*, 6:69 (1954), 258.

12 Walter Bittermann, 'Salomonischer Kirst', *Rheinischer Merkur*, 22 October 1954.

13 Georg Michael Kahn-Ackermann, 'Der deutsche Film ist "Zeitgerecht" ', *Die neue Gesellschaft*, 3:31 (1956), 190–3; and 'Haben sich die Menschen in Uniform geändert?', *Südkurier*, 11 February 1956.

14 Karl Korn, 'Ordnung? Gehorchen? Ein Nachwort zu 08/15', *Frankfurter Allgemeine Zeitung*, 3 November 1954.

15 Herbert Hohenemser, '... übrig bleibt brüllendes Vergnügen', *Münchner Merkur,* 28 May 1955; and Fred Hepp, 'Das dicke Ende kommt nicht nach', *Süddeutsche Zeitung*, 8 March 1956.

16 'Die Helden grüssen: "Der Stern von Afrika" – ein Fliegerfilm', *Frankfurter Allgemeine Zeitung*, 2 September 1957.

17 Rolf Seubert, 'Junge Adler: Retrospektive auf einen nationalsozialistischen Jugendfilm', *Medium*, 18 (1988), 31–43.

18 'Glücklicher Dämmerzustand: Herbert Reinecker über "Junge Adler" und seine Vergangenheit im Nationalsozialismus im Gespräch mit Hort Pöttker und Rolf Seubert', *Medium* 18 (1988), 37–43.

19 For example, the review in the *Rheinische Post*, 15 August 1957; and Margret Schmidt-Paetzold, 'Hans Joachim Marseille: Sinnbild einer Generation', *Westdeutsche Zeitung,* 18 August 1957.

20 Review in *Süddeutsche Zeitung*, 9 September 1957.

21 H. G. Sellenthin, 'Sind Heldenflieger Filmhelden? Zum einem neuen Film im UFA-Stil', *Vorwärts*, 13 September 1957.

22 Karena Niehoff, 'Gefährliche Neutralität', *Der Tagesspiegel*, 17 August 1957.
23 'Am Leinwandhimmel unbesiegt', *Die andere Zeitung*, 29 August 1957. See also Guido Limburg, 'Fliegen und Abschiessen – Ja, was soll ich da anderes denken? *Der Stern von Afrika* und der bundesdeutsche Nachkriegs-Kriegsfilm', in Hans-Arthur Mariske (ed.), *Zeitmaschine Kino: Darstellungen von Geschichte im Film* (Marburg 1992), pp. 116–25.
24 'Tragödie eines jungen Idealisten', *Westdeutsches Tageblatt*, 2 March 1957.
25 See Heide Fehrenbach, *Race after Hitler: Black Occupation Children in Postwar Germany and America* (Princeton 2005); also Limburg, 'Fliegen und Abschiessen'.
26 Dagmar Herzog, *Sex after Fascism: Memory and Morality in Twentieth-Century Germany* (Princeton 2005), pp. 28–30.
27 Manes Kadow, 'Filmisches Heldendenkmal', *Frankfurter Neue Presse*, 3 August 1957.
28 Walter Görlitz, 'Müssen Filme über den Krieg so sein?', *Die Welt*, 15 August 1957. I draw on arguments in Robert G. Moeller, '"In a Thousand Years, Every German Will Speak of This Battle": Celluloid Memories of Stalingrad', in Omer Bartov, Atina Grossmann and Mary Nolan (eds), *Crimes of War: Guilt and Denial in the Twentieth Century* (New York 2003), pp. 161–90.
29 Norbert Frei, ' "Stalingrad" im Gedächtnis der (West-) Deutschen', in Peter Jahn (ed.), *Stalingrad Erinnern: Stalingrad im deutschen und im russischen Gedächtnis* (Berlin 2003), pp. 16–23.
30 Peter Miska. 'Frank Wisbars Stalingrad-Film "Hunde, wollt ihr ewig leben?" ', *Frankfurter Rundschau*, 4 April 1959.
31 'Frank Wisbar hasst den Krieg', *Stuttgarter Zeitung*, 30 January 1959.
32 Frank Wisbar, 'Filme sind Leitartikel', *Die Kultur*, 1 November 1958.
33 'Frei nach Schiller', *Der Spiegel*, 15 April 1959.
34 *Verhandlungen des deutschen Bundestags*, 3. Wahlperiode, 70. Sitzung, 3 June 1959.
35 ' "Goldene Schale" und 150000 DM für "Helden" ', *General-Anzeiger*, 29 June 1959.
36 'So hart wie der Titel?', *Telegraf*, 1 February 1959; Hans Hellmut Kirst, 'Filmunternehmen Stalingrad', *Münchner Merkur*, 14 May 1959.
37 'So ging die 6. Armee zugrunde', *Hamburger Abendblatt*, 18 April 1959.
38 Friedrich A. Wagner, 'Die Wolga war ihr Schicksal', *Frankfurter Allgemeine Zeitung*, 13 April 1959.
39 Wolfgang Bartsch, 'Die "verheitzte" Armee', *Frankfurter Rundschau*, 23 April 1959.
40 Clemens Riemenschneider in *Die Tat*, 2 May 1959.
41 'Ewig lebt am längsten', *Vorwärts*, 17 April 1959.
42 Hans-Dieter Roos in *Süddeutsche Zeitung*, 15 May 1959.
43 'Schicksal an der Volga', *Telegraf*, 7 May 1959.
44 'Frei nach Schiller'.

45 Hannes Schmidt in *Neue Rhein Zeitung*, 9 April 1959.
46 Horst Oberstrass, 'Fettschicht', *Velberter Zeitung*, 11 April 1959.
47 Alexander Mitscherlich, 'Der unsichtbare Vater: Ein Problem für Psychoanalyse und Soziologie', *Kölner Zeitschrift für Soziologie und Sozialpsychologie*, 7 (1955), 188–201.
48 Gert Koegel, 'Kerls, wollt ihr niemals lernen?', *Vorwärts*, 8 May 1959.
49 'So ging die 6. Armee zugrunde', *Hamburger Abendblatt*, 18 April 1959.
50 'Stalingrad auf Leinwand', *Christ und Welt*, 16 April 1959.
51 Enno Patalas, 'Die Brücke', *Filmkritik*, 3 (1959), 315–17.
52 Andreas Burger, 'Die Brücke', *Hessische Jugend*, 12:1 [n.d., 1959?]; and Karl-Heinz Krüger, 'Die Brücke', *Der Abend*, 14 November 1959.
53 Klaus Arnsperger, 'Sowjetische Stimmen über deutschen Anti-Kriegsfilm', *Süddeutsche Zeitung*, 20 February 1963; Harri Czepuck, '"Die Brücke" in den sinnlosen Tod: Zu dem Antikriegsfilm "Die Brücke" von Bernhard Wicki', *Neues Deutschland*, 30 November 1959.
54 'Aufrüttelnder Antikriegsfilm: "Die Brücke" von Bernhard Wicki und ein weiterer Film', *Frankfurter Rundschau*, 26 October 1979.
55 Günter Seuren, 'Geht nach Hause, statt zu sterben', *Deutsche Zeitung*, 1 September 1959.
56 Paul, 'Krieg und Film', 7.
57 Hans-Dieter Roos, 'Bernhard Wickis Film von der "Brücke"', *Süddeutsche Zeitung*, 25 October 1959. See also the discussion in Klaus Kanzog, '"Warten auf das entscheidende Wort": Pubertät und Heldenwahn in Bernhard Wickis *Die Brücke* (1959)', in Kanzog (ed.), *Der erotische Diskurs: Filmische Zeichen und Argumente* (Munich 1989), pp. 127–55.
58 'Schuld und kein Täter', *Darmstädter Echo*, 11 December 1959.
59 Walter Hurck, 'Ein Stalingrad der Kinder', *Ruhr-Nachrichten*, 7 November 1959.
60 Gerhard Schüler, 'Die Brücke', *Göttinger Tageblatt*, 21 November 1959.
61 'Wicki: Die Brücke', *Rheinische Post*, 26 October 1979.
62 Theodor W. Adorno, 'What Does Coming to Terms with the Past Mean?', in Geoffrey Hartmann (ed.), *Bitburg in Moral and Political Perspective* (Bloomington 1986), pp. 114–26.
63 Ibid., p. 124.
64 Burger, 'Die Brücke'.
65 Wilfried von Bredow, 'Filmpropaganda für Wehrbereitschaft: Kriegsfilme in der Bundesrepublik', in Wilfried von Bredow and Rolf Zurek (eds), *Film und Gesellschaft in Deutschland: Dokumente und Materialien* (Hamburg 1975), pp. 316–26; also Erich Kuby, *Mein ärgerliches Vaterland* (Munich 1989), p. 210.
66 Kuby, *Mein ärgerliches Vaterland*, p. 210; see also Irmgard Wilharm, 'Krieg in den deutschen Nachkriegsspielfilmen', in Gottfried Niedhart and Dieter Riesenberger (eds), *Lernen aus dem Krieg? Deutsche Nachkriegszeiten 1918 und 1945* (Munich 1992), pp. 281–99; and Bredow, 'Filmpropaganda für Wehrbereitschaft'.

67 Paul, 'Krieg und Film'; and Wegmann, *Der westdeutsche Kriegsfilm*.
68 Wegmann, *Der westdeutsche Kriegsfilm*, p. 227.
69 See Hamburger Institut für Sozialforschung (ed.), *Verbrechen der Wehrmacht: Dimensionen des Vernichtungskrieges 1941–1944* (Hamburg 2002).

Chapter 3: Taboo or Tradition? The 'Germans as Victims' Theme in the Federal Republic until the mid-1990s

1 I would like to thank The British Academy for their financial support which enabled me to go on research visits to Munich. I would also very much like to thank my friend Steffi Boothroyd for her comments on an earlier draft of this chapter.
2 Maurice Halbwachs, *On Collective Memory*, edited, translated, and with an introduction by Lewis A. Coser (Chicago 1992), pp. 39–40.
3 Ibid., p. 34.
4 See, for example, Aleida Assmann, 'Erinnerung als Erregung. Wendepunkte der deutschen Erinnerungsgeschichte', *Wissenschaftskolleg Jahrbuch 1998/99* (2000), 200–20, here 218; and Helmut König, *Die Zukunft der Vergangenheit: Der Nationalsozialismus im politischen Bewußtsein der Bundesrepublik* (Frankfurt am Main 2003), p. 17
5 Robert G. Moeller, *War Stories: The Search for a Usable Past in the Federal Republic of Germany* (Berkeley 2001), p. 3
6 Assmann, 'Erinnerung als Erregung', 216.
7 Lars Rensmann as quoted in Ilko-Sascha Kowalczuk, 'Literaturbericht: "Vergangenheitsbewältigung", Erinnerung und Geschichtspolitik in Deutschland', in Uwe Backes and Eckhard Jesse (eds), *Extremismus und Demokratie* (Baden-Baden 2000), pp. 325–49, here 345.
8 For an in-depth discussion of this debate, see Bill Niven, *Facing the Nazi Past* (London and New York 2002), p. 175ff. See also the chapter by Helmut Schmitz in the current volume.
9 Julia Kölsch, 'Politik und Gedächtnis: Die Gegenwart der NS-Vergangenheit als politisches Sinnstiftungspotential', in Wolfgang Bergem (ed.), *Die NS-Diktatur im deutschen Erinnerungsdiskurs* (Opladen 2003), pp. 137–50, here 147.
10 Ole Frahm, ' "Ein deutsches Trauma?": Zur Schamlosigkeit Deutscher Opferidentifikation', *German Life and Letters*, 57:4 (2004), 372–90.
11 Alfred Theisen, 'Die Vertreibung der Deutschen – Ein unbewältigtes Kapitel europäischer Zeitgeschichte', *Aus Politik und Zeitgeschichte. Beilage zur Wochenzeitung Das Parlament*, B7–8 (10 February 1995), 20–33.
12 Michael Schwartz, 'Vertreibung und Vergangenheitspolitik: Ein Versuch über geteilte deutsche Nachkriegsidentitäten', *Deutschland Archiv*, 30 (1997), 177–95, here 182.
13 König, *Die Zukunft der Vergangenheit*, p. 17.
14 See, for example, Moeller, *War Stories*, and Jörg Echternkamp, 'Von Opfern, Helden und Verbrechern – Anmerkungen zur Bedeutung des

Zweiten Weltkriegs in den Erinnerungskulturen der Deutschen 1945–1955', in Jörg Hillmann and John Zimmermann (eds), *Kriegsende 1945 in Deutschland* (Munich 2002), pp. 301–16.

15 König, *Die Zukunft der Vergangenheit*, p. 26.

16 Echternkamp, 'Von Opfern, Helden und Verbrechern', p. 305. See also Moeller's first chapter in the present volume.

17 Echternkamp, 'Von Opfern, Helden und Verbrechern', p. 305.

18 Moeller, *War Stories*, p. 3.

19 Moeller, *War Stories*, p. 7.

20 Assmann, 'Erinnerung als Erregung', 206.

21 Wilfried Mausbach, '"Man muß die ganze Wut diesen Herrenrassenbanditen ins Gesicht schreien": Die 68er und die nationalsozialistische Vergangenheit', *Deutschland Archiv*, 38:2 (2005), 273–80, here 275.

22 Matthias Frese and Julia Paulus, 'Geschwindigkeiten und Faktoren des Wandels – die 1960er Jahre in der Bundesrepublik', in Matthias Frese, Julia Paulus and Karl Teppe (eds), *Demokratisierung und gesellschaftlicher Aufbruch: die sechziger Jahre als Wendezeit der Bundesrepublik* (Paderborn 2003), pp. 1–23, here 21.

23 Edgar Wolfrum, 'Das westdeutsche "Geschichtsbild" entsteht. Auseinandersetzung mit dem Nationalsozialismus und neues bundesrepublikanisches Staatsbewußtsein', in Frese, Paulus and Teppe, *Demokratisierung und gesellschaftlicher Aufbruch*, p. 242.

24 Axel Schildt, 'Materieller Wohlstand – pragmatische Politik – kulturelle Umbrüche. Die 60er Jahre in der Bundesrepublik', in Axel Schildt, Detlef Siegfried and Karl Christian Lammers (eds), *Dynamische Zeiten: Die 60er Jahre in den beiden Gesellschaften* (Hamburg 2000), pp. 21–53, here 48.

25 Axel Schildt, 'Aufarbeitung und Aufbruch: Die NS-Vergangenheit in der bundesdeutschen Öffentlichkeit der 1960er Jahre', *Vorgänge*, 41:1 (2002), 122–33, here 122.

26 Schildt, 'Aufarbeitung und Aufbruch', 124.

27 Wolfrum, 'Das westdeutsche "Geschichtsbild" entsteht', pp. 231–2.

28 Schildt, 'Aufarbeitung und Aufbruch', 125.

29 Moeller, *War Stories*, p. 86.

30 Dubiel quoted in Schildt, 'Aufarbeitung und Aufbruch', 127–8.

31 Kölsch, 'Politik und Gedächtnis', p. 145.

32 Moeller, *War Stories*, p. 180.

33 See, for example, Ingo Cornils, 'The German Student Movement: Legend and Legacy', *Debatte*, 4:2, 36–62; and Franz-Werner Kersting, '"Unruhediskurs". Zeitgenössische Deutungen der 68er-Bewegung', in Frese, Paulus and Teppe, *Demokratisierung und gesellschaftlicher Aufbruch*, pp. 715–40.

34 Detlef Siegfried, 'Zwischen Aufarbeitung und Schlußstrich. Der Umgang mit der NS-Vergangenheit in den beiden deutschen Staaten

1958 bis 1969', in Schildt, Siegfried and Lammers, *Dynamische Zeiten*, pp. 77–113, here 104.

35 Martina Althoff, 'Kiesinger, die APO und der Nationalsozialismus: Zur Dynamik eines NS-Konfliktes', in Wolfgang Benz (ed.), *Jahrbuch der Antisemitismusforschung 5* (Frankfurt 1996), pp. 211–32, here 211.

36 Schildt, 'Aufarbeitung und Aufbruch', 129–30.

37 Ibid., 130.

38 Gerd Koenen, *Das rote Jahrzehnt* (Cologne 2001), p. 96.

39 Ibid., p. 95.

40 Detlef Siegfried, ' "Trau keinem über 30"? Konsens und Konflikt der Generationen in der Bundesrepublik der langen sechziger Jahre', *Aus Politik und Zeitgeschichte. Beilage zur Wochenzeitung Das Parlament*, B45 (3 November 2003), 25–32, here 31–2.

41 *Der Spiegel*, 35 (2001), 156–61, here 159.

42 Koenen, *Das rote Jahrzehnt*, p. 97.

43 Alain Finkielkraut, *The Imaginary Jew*, trans. by Kevin O'Neill and David Suchoff (Lincoln 1994), p. 17.

44 Karl Wilds, 'Identity Creation and the Culture of Contrition: Recasting "Normality" in the Berlin Republic', *German Politics*, 9:1 (2000), 83–102, here 98.

45 Ibid., 98.

46 Gerhard Reichling as quoted in Pertti Ahonen, *After the Expulsion: West Germany and Eastern Europe, 1945–1990* (Oxford 2003), pp. 1–2.

47 http://www.bundestag.de/parlament/geschichte/parlhist/dok26 (17 April 2004).

48 For more details on the project, see Theodor Schieder, 'Die Vertreibung der Deutschen aus dem Osten als wissenschaftliches Problem', *Vierteljahrshefte für Zeitgeschichte*, 8:1 (1960), 1–16; and Matthias Beer, 'Die Dokumentation der Vertreibung der Deutschen aus Ost-Mitteleuropa', *Geschichte in Wissenschaft und Unterricht*, 50:1 (1999), 99–117.

49 Ahonen, *After the Expulsion*, p. 243.

50 Ibid., p. 243.

51 Hermann Weiß, 'Die Organisationen der Vertriebenen und ihre Presse', in Wolfgang Benz (ed.), *Die Vertreibung der Deutschen aus dem Osten: Ursachen, Ereignisse, Folgen* (Frankfurt am Main 1995), pp. 244–64, here 258–9.

52 Ahonen, *After the Expulsion*, p. 267.

53 Ibid., p. 268.

54 Benz, *Die Vertreibung der Deutschen aus dem Osten*, p. 11.

55 Schwartz, 'Vertreibung und Vergangenheitspolitik', 190.

56 Ahonen, *After the Expulsion*, p. 266.

57 The *Dokumentation der Vertreibung der Deutschen aus Ost-Mitteleuropa* was first published between 1954 and 1963. It was reprinted in 1984 and published as a paperback in 2004. In addition to this, *Die Deutschen*

Vertreibungsverluste published by the Statistisches Bundesamt Wiesbaden in 1958 supplied detailed statistics, and in 1969 the Bundesarchiv in Koblenz compiled the *Dokumentation von Vertreibungsverbrechen* which – due to political sensitivities – was not published after it had been completed in 1974, but only in 1984.

58 Hellmuth Auerbach, 'Literatur zum Thema. Ein kritischer Überblick', in Benz, *Die Vertreibung der Deutschen aus dem Osten*, pp. 77–294.

59 Here is a small selection of publications on the theme from the 1980s (some of them were updated and/or reprinted in the 1990s): Günter Böddeker, *Die Flüchtlinge. Die Vertreibung der Deutschen im Osten* (Munich and Berlin 1980); Wilfried Ahrens, *Verbrechen an Deutschen. Dokumente der Vertreibung* (Rosenheim 1983); Heinz Nawratil, *Vertreibungsverbrechen an Deutschen. Tatbestand, Motive, Bewältigung* (Munich 1984); Wolfgang Benz (ed.), *Die Vertreibung der Deutschen aus dem Osten. Ursachen, Ereignisse, Folgen* (Frankfurt am Main 1985, new updated edn in 1995); Alfred M. de Zayas, *Anmerkungen zur Vertreibung der Deutschen aus dem Osten* (Stuttgart 1986).

60 Edgar Wolfrum, 'Zwischen Geschichtsschreibung und Geschichtspolitik. Forschungen zu Flucht und Vertreibung nach dem Zweiten Weltkrieg', *Archiv für Sozialgeschichte*, 36 (1996), 500–22, here 502.

61 See, for example, Sascha Feuchert (ed.), *Flucht und Vertreibung in der deutschen Literatur* (Frankfurt am Main 2001); Louis Ferdinand Helbig, *Der ungeheure Verlust. Flucht und Vertreibung in der deutschsprachigen Belletristik*, 3rd edn (Wiesbaden 1996); Louis Ferdinand Helbig, 'Fünfunddreissig Jahre Literatur der Vertreibung. Versuch einer Bilanz 1945–1980', *Deutsche Studien*, 18 (1980), 234–50.

62 Ute Flögel, 'Die Geschichte ist kein Eisberg', *Kulturpolitische Korrespondenz*, 1167 (10 May 2003), http://www.mitteleuropa.de/literatur01.htm (22 April 2004).

63 Jutta Faehndrich, 'Erinnerungskultur und Umgang mit Vertreibung in Heimatbüchern deutschsprachiger Vertriebener', *Zeitschrift für Ostmitteleuropa-Forschung*, 52:2 (2003), 191–228, here 192–3.

64 Moeller, *War Stories*, p. 180.

65 Theisen, 'Die Vertreibung der Deutschen', 21.

66 Harald Welzer, Sabine Moller and Karoline Tschnuggnall, '*Opa war kein Nazi*'*: Nationalsozialismus und Holocaust im Familiengedächtnis* (Frankfurt am Main 2002).

67 Ibid., p. 82.

68 Ibid., p. 14.

69 Ibid., p. 247.

70 Ibid., p. 248.

71 Ibid., p. 10.

72 Ibid., p. 10.

73 A campaign in the media which called for 8 May to be remembered as the beginning of a new oppression in Eastern Europe.

74 Germany's Nazi past still features strongly in British perceptions of Germany and the Germans, for example. For a discussion of this, see Ruth Wittlinger, 'Perceptions of Germany and the Germans in Post-War Britain', *Journal of Multilingual and Multicultural Development*, 25:5/6 (2004), 453–65.

Chapter 4: The Continually Suffering Nation? Cinematic Representations of German Victimhood

1 For further discussion of the film, including how it can in fact be seen as a product of a specifically German tradition, see Owen Evans, 'Tom Tykwer's *Run Lola Run*: Postmodern, Posthuman or "Post-theory"?', *SEC*, 1 (2004), 105–15.

2 Other notable recent examples of this trend include Max Färberböck, *Aimée & Jaguar* (1999); Margarethe von Trotta, *Rosenstrasse* (2003); Marc Rothemund, *Sophie Scholl – Die Letzten Tage* (*Sophie Scholl – The Last Days*, 2005); and Volker Schlöndorff, *Der neunte Tag* (*The Ninth Day*, 2004).

3 Allan Hall, 'Is Germany Finally Forgiving Hitler?', *Daily Mail*, 25 August 2004.

4 Robert G. Moeller, 'Remembering the War in a Nation of Victims: West German Pasts in the 1950s', in Hanna Schissler (ed.), *The Miracle Years: A Cultural History of West Germany, 1949–1968* (Princeton 2001), pp. 83–109, here 85.

5 Stefan Aust, *Der Baader Meinhof Komplex* (Munich 1990), p. 60.

6 For further discussion of DEFA, see Sean Allan and John Sandford (eds), *DEFA: East German Cinema, 1946–1992* (New York 1999).

7 Quoted in Fritz Göttler, 'Westdeutscher Nachkriegsfilm', in Wolfgang Jacobsen, Anton Kaes and Hans Helmut Prinzler (eds), *Geschichte des Deutschen Films* (Stuttgart 1993), pp. 171–210, here 174. See also Robert G. Moeller's chapter on West German film (Chapter 2) in this volume.

8 For an excellent discussion of the historical trajectory of the term *Heimat* within German culture and in particular with regard to film, see Elizabeth Boa and Rachel Palfreyman, *Heimat – a German Dream: Regional Loyalties and National Identity in German Culture, 1890–1990* (Oxford 2000).

9 Boa and Palfreyman, *Heimat*, p. 91.

10 For further discussion of this aspect of the genre, see Johannes von Moltke, 'Evergreens: The *Heimat* Genre', in Tim Bergfelder, Erica Carter and Deniz Göktürk (eds), *The German Cinema Book* (London 2002), pp. 18–28.

11 Boa and Palfreyman, *Heimat*, p. 91.

12 For a detailed discussion of this cinema, see Thomas Elsaesser, *New German Cinema: A History* (New Brunswick 1989).

13 Anton Kaes, *From Hitler to Heimat: The Return of History as Film* (Cambridge 1989), p. 10.
14 For further discussion see Wolfgang Kraushaar (ed.), *Frankfurter Schule und Studentenbewegung: Von der Flaschenpost zum Molotowcocktail 1946–1995*, Vol. 1 (Frankfurt am Main 1998), pp. 244–8.
15 Eric L. Santner, *Stranded Objects: Mourning, Memory and Film in Postwar Germany* (Ithaca 1990), p. 41.
16 John E. Davidson, *Deterritorializing the New German Cinema* (Minneapolis 1999), pp. 18–9.
17 Marc Silbermann, *German Cinema: Texts in Context* (Detroit 1995), p. 203.
18 See Gerd Koenen, *Das rote Jahrzehnt: Unsere kleine deutsche Kulturrevolution 1967–1977* (Cologne 2001).
19 See, for example, Dietrich Kuhlbrodt, 'Papa ist der Größte', *taz*, 15 October 2003.
20 Stuart Taberner, 'Philo-Semitism in Recent German Film: *Aimée und Jaguar, Rosenstrasse* and *Das Wunder von Bern*', *German Life and Letters*, 58:3 (July 2005), 357–72.
21 Eric Rentschler, 'From New German Cinema to the Post-Wall Cinema of Consensus', in Mette Hjort and Scott Mackenzie (eds), *Cinema and Nation* (London 2000), pp. 260–77.

Chapter 5: The Birth of the Collective from the Spirit of Empathy: From the 'Historians' Dispute' to German Suffering

Unless otherwise indicated, all translations from German are my own.

1 See Ernestine Schlant, *The Language of Silence. West German Literature and the Holocaust* (London and New York 1999), p. 3; and Bill Niven, *Facing the Nazi Past* (London and New York 2001), p. 2.
2 This alleged 'taboo' is an essential prerequisite for the legitimacy of representations of German suffering. On the reception of Sebald's lectures, see Stefan Braese, 'Bombenkrieg und literarische Gegenwart', *Mittelweg*, 36:1 (2002), 2–24. On Grass's *Crabwalk*, see the relevant chapter in my *On Their Own Terms: The Legacy of National Socialism in Post-1990 German Literature* (Birmingham 2004), pp. 263–86.
3 The five episodes were broadcast between 20 November 2001 and 18 December 2001.
4 Avishai Margalit and Gabriel Motzkin, 'Der Holocaust. Zur Einzigartigkeit eines historischen Geschehens', *lettre international*, 35:4 (1996), 23–7, here 27.
5 Horkheimer and Adorno argue that the rational and administrative organisation of the Holocaust in 'death factories' and the totalitarian creation of homogeneous collectives (the German *Volk* and the Jewish 'race') are an outcome of Enlightenment thinking that is obsessed with

the domination of nature through instrumental reason, technology and scientific classification. For both the French philosopher Jean François Lyotard and the social theorist Zygmunt Baumann, the Holocaust necessitates a revision of their respective discipline's methodology. See Lyotard, *The Differend: Phrases in Dispute* (Manchester 1988); and Baumann, *Modernity and the Holocaust* (Cambridge 1989).

6 Dan Diner, 'Between Aporia and Apologia: On the Limits of Historicising National Socialism', in Peter Baldwin (ed.), *Reworking the Past: Hitler, the Holocaust and the Historians' Debate* (Boston, MA, 1990), pp. 135–45, here 143.

7 See Saul Friedlander, 'Trauma, Memory and Transference', in Geoffrey Hartman (ed.), *Holocaust Remembrance: The Shapes of Memory* (Cambridge, MA, 1994), pp. 252–63, here 257. The issue of the different traumatisation of Germans and Nazi victims has also been discussed recently by Dominick LaCapra in *Writing History, Writing Trauma* (Baltimore 2001), p. 44.

8 The essay is reprinted in James Knowlton and Truett Cates (trans.), *Forever in the Shadow of Hitler? Original Documents on the Historikerstreit concerning the Singularity of the Holocaust* (Atlantic Highlands 1993), pp. 1–15, here 13–14.

9 Ibid., p. 8.

10 Ernst Nolte, 'The Past that will not Pass: A speech that could be written but not be given', ibid., pp. 18–23, here 19.

11 Andreas Hillgruber, *Zweierlei Untergang. Die Zerschlagung des deutschen Reiches und das Ende des europäischen Judentums* (Berlin 1986), p. 24.

12 Hillgruber places the expulsion of the Germans in the context of the European history of forced mass resettlements in the early twentieth century, from the Armenian genocide to Stalin's resettlement and extermination policies (ibid., p. 67).

13 See Charles Maier, *The Unmasterable Past: History, Holocaust, and German National Identity* (Cambridge, MA, 1988), p. 22.

14 Quoted from an interview with Hillgruber in *Rheinischer Merkur* (31 October 1986). See Hans-Ulrich Wehler, *Entsorgung der deutschen Vergangenheit? Ein polemischer Essay zum 'Historikerstreit'* (Munich 1988), pp. 207–8.

15 Diner, 'Between Aporia and Apologia', p. 141.

16 Martin Broszat, 'A Plea for the Historisation of National Socialism', reprinted in Baldwin (ed.), *Reworking the Past.*, pp. 77–87, here 87 and 78.

17 Broszat in his first letter to Saul Friedlander, reprinted as 'A Controversy about the Historicisation of National Socialism', in Baldwin (ed.), *Reworking the Past*, pp. 103–34, here 104. While the German original does not contain the word 'empathetic', Broszat's use of *Nachvollzug* implies an approach based on historicist empathy.

18 Ibid., p. 108.

19 Walser, 'Erfahrungen beim Verfassen einer Sonntagsrede', *Frankfurter Allgemeine Zeitung*, 12 October 1998, reprinted in Frank Schirrmacher (ed.), *Die Walser-Bubis-Debatte* (Frankfurt am Main 1999), pp. 7–17. For a concise introduction to the debate, see the relevant chapter in Niven, *Facing the Nazi Past*.

20 All quotes from Ignatz Bubis/Salomon Korn/Frank Schirrmacher/ Martin Walser, 'Wir brauchen eine neue Sprache für die Erinnerung', *FAZ*, 14 December 1998, pp. 39–41, reprinted in Schirrmacher (ed.), *Die Walser-Bubis-Debatte*, pp. 438–65.

21 See Walser's riposte to Bubis: 'I want my soul's peace. . . . And I won't suffer any interference, from nobody, not even you', ibid., p. 460.

22 See Harald Welzer, Sabine Moller and Karoline Tschuggnall, *'Opa war kein Nazi'. Nationalsozialismus und Holocaust im Familiengedächtnis* (Frankfurt am Main 2002), pp. 10ff. Welzer, Moller and Tschuggnall note a disparity between public memory of National Socialism in Germany that focuses on German crimes, and family memory in which family members figure largely (and almost exclusively) as victims.

23 A number of recent German works, including Walser's novel *In Defence of Childhood* (*Die Verteidigung der Kindheit*, 1991); Max Färberböck's film *Aimée und Jaguar* (1989); Caroline Link's film *Nowhere in Africa* (*Nirgendwo in Afrika*, 2001); and Margarethe von Trotta's film *Rosenstrasse* (2003) attempt to circumvent the post-Holocaust division into victims and perpetrators by reimagining a German–Jewish symbiosis, reinscribing the excluded Jews back into the German collective. See Stuart Taberner, 'Philo-Semitism in Recent German Film: *Aimée und Jaguar, Rosenstrasse* and *Das Wunder von Bern*', *German Life and Letters*, 58:3 (July 2005), 357–72.

24 For a detailed discussion of this novel, see Chapter 9 in this volume.

25 See the official website of the Centre against Expulsions: http://www.zentrum-gegen-vertreibungen.de/aktuelles/?id=49

26 Quoted in Michael Klundt, '"Normalisierung" und "historische Anthropologie". Geschichtspolitische Kontroversen um die alte und neue Wehrmachtsausstellung', in Michael Klundt, Samuel Salzborn, Marc Schwietring and Gerd Wiegel, *Erinnern Verdrängen Vergessen. Geschichtspolitische Wege im 21. Jahrhundert* (Gießen 2003), pp. 77–102, here 81 and 79. Bill Niven also makes the point that the exhibition engendered a reconciliatory dialogue between the generations. See Niven, *Facing the Nazi Past*, pp. 143ff.

27 'Die Deutschen als Opfer', *Der Spiegel*, 13 (2002).

28 'Als Feuer vom Himmel fiel', *Der Spiegel*, 2 (2003).

29 See Heinz-Peter Preußer, 'Betrachten und Vorstellen. Inszenierte Unmittelbarkeit des Bombenkrieges in Fotografie, Roman und Geschichtsschreibung', in *Neue Deutsche Literatur*, August (2004), 32–42, here 34. The photograph in *Brandstätten* bears a caption taken from a citizen's diary of 10 March 1945: 'Russian commandos are still busy

incinerating the charred corpses on large pyres, in the middle of the city', *Brandstätten* (Munich 2003), p. 134. In fact, the Red Army did not reach the city until May 8, the day of capitulation. The 'Russian commandos' are most likely POWs. In all likelihood they were working under instructions from the SS, who had practice in burning large amounts of corpses. Sebald notes that in February 1945, an SS commando 'with experience from Treblinka' incinerated 6865 corpses. Sebald, 'Air War and Literature', in Sebald, *On the Natural History of Destruction* (London 2003), p. 98.

30 See Jörg Friedrich, *Der Brand: Deutschland im Bombenkrieg 1940–1945* (Berlin 2002), pp. 176, 187 and 234 ('Massaker') and p. 194 ('Vernichtung'). Friedrich also refers to the cellars where people in the burning cities were trapped as 'crematoria' (p. 195).

31 Ibid., p. 378.

32 Ibid., p. 326.

33 See, for example, Bernhard Schlink's *The Reader* (*Der Vorleser*, 1995); Dieter Wellershoff's recollections of his experiences as a soldier on the eastern front, *For Real* (*Der Ernstfall*, 1997); Günter Grass's *Crabwalk* (*Im Krebsgang*, 2002); and Ulla Hahn's recent novel *Blurred Images* (*Unscharfe Bilder*, 2003).

34 See Hannes Heer, 'Warum Soldaten Mörder wurden. Dankrede zur Verleihung der Carl-von-Ossietzky-Medaille', *Neue Deutsche Literatur*, 3 (1998), 25–40.

35 See Peter Schneider, 'Deutsche als Opfer. Über ein Tabu der Nachkriegsgeneration', in Lothar Kettenacker (ed.), *Ein Volk von Opfern? Die neue Debatte um den Bombenkrieg 1940–45* (Berlin 2003), pp. 158–65, here 162–3.

36 Günter Franzen, 'Links, wo kein Herz ist', *Der Spiegel*, 44 (2003), 216–18, here 216 and 218.

37 See W. G. Sebald, 'Air War and Literature', in Sebald, *On the Natural History of Destruction* (London 2004), pp. 1–105, here 99. It is one characteristic of Sebald's literary ethics that his assessment of the bombing war gives an impression of the dimensions of its horrors *without* a national subtext.

38 It is signficant that the story told by Friedrich's arrangement of photographs takes no account of the urban planning disasters of the 1950s and 1960s, which affected European cities irrespective of war damage.

39 In her analysis of expellee periodicals and observation towers at West Germany's eastern border, Yuliya Komska demonstrates that they constitute a melancholic gaze on to the lost country, which freezes it in time and does not acknowledge change. See Yuliya Komska, 'Border Looking: The Cold War Visuality of the Sudeten German Expellees and its Afterlife', *German Life and Letters*, 57:4 (2004), 401–26.

40 Benedict Anderson, *Imagined Communities* (London 1983), pp. 11 and 206.

Chapter 6: The GDR and Memory of the Bombing of Dresden

1 Bernardo Bellotto, *Die Trümmer der ehemaligen Kreuzkirche in Dresden* (1765). For a colour plate photograph of the painting, see Staatliche Kunstsammlungen Dresden (ed.), *Dresden: Bekenntnis und Verpflichtung* (Dresden 1985), p. 62.
2 See, for instance, Gert Claußnitzer, 'Dresden – Schicksal einer Stadt in der bildenden Kunst', in *Dresden: Bekenntnis und Verpflichtung*, pp. 34–49, here 38.
3 Quoted in Frederick Taylor, *Dresden: Tuesday 13 February 1945* (London 2004), p. 181.
4 Ibid., pp. 185–6.
5 Mark Connelly, *Reaching for the Stars: A New History of Bomber Command in World War II* (London and New York 2001), p. 133.
6 Taylor, *Dresden*, p. 185.
7 Ibid., p. 191. According to the British Official History of the bombing war, Soviet General Antonov also explicitly requested 'paralysing the centres' of Berlin and Leipzig. See Charles Webster and Noble Frankland, *The Strategic Air Offensive against Germany 1939–1945, Volume III: Victory, Part 5* (London 1961), p. 105.
8 See Götz Bergander, *Dresden im Luftkrieg: Vorgeschichte – Zerstörung – Folgen* (Würzburg 1998), p. 300.
9 Harris suggested to Norman Bottomley supplementing the attack on Berlin with one on these other three cities. See Frankland and Noble, *The Strategic Air Offensive*, p. 100.
10 Bergander, *Dresden im Luftkrieg*, pp. 332–3.
11 See Jörg Friedrich, *Der Brand: Deutschland im Bombenkrieg 1940–1945* (Munich 2002), p. 85.
12 David Irving, *The Destruction of Dresden* (London 1985), p. 158.
13 See Richard Evans, *Lying about Hitler: History, Holocaust and the David Irving Trial* (London 2002), p. 157.
14 Taylor, *Dresden*, p. 284.
15 For a selection of descriptions of, and reactions to, the bombing, see Walter Kempowski, *Der rote Hahn: Dresden im Februar 1945* (Munich 2001).
16 Taylor, *Dresden*, p. 416.
17 See, for instance, Walter Lehwess-Litzmann, 'Warum Dresden sterben sollte', in Deutsches Friedenskomitee Berlin (ed.), *Dresden, Unsterbliche Stadt* (Berlin 1952), pp. 6–15.
18 Walter Weidauer, *Inferno Dresden: Über Lügen und Legenden um die Aktion 'Donnerschlag'* (Berlin 1966).
19 See Gilad Margalit, 'Der Luftangriff auf Dresden. Seine Bedeutung für die Erinnerungspolitik der DDR und für die Herauskristallisierung einer historischen Kriegserinnerung im Westen', in Susanne Düwell and Mathias Schmidt (eds), *Narrative der Shoah. Repräsentationen der*

Vergangenheit in Historiographie, Kunst und Politik (Paderborn 2002), pp. 189–207, here 194.

20 Ibid., p. 190.

21 For an account of the Soviet occupation of the Dresden area immediately after the war, see Thomas Widera, *Dresden 1945–1948: Politik und Gesellschaft unter sowjetischer Besatzungsherrschaft* (Göttingen 2005).

22 See, for instance, Museum für Geschichte der Dresdner Arbeiterbewegung (ed.), *Beginn eines neuen Lebens* (Dresden 1960).

23 See Staatliche Kunstsammlungen (ed.), *Schätze der Weltkultur – vom Altertum bis zur Gegenwart – von der Sowjetunion vor Kriegsschäden bewahrt, vor Verderb und Zerstörung gerettet, und der Deutschen Demokratischen Republik übergeben* (Dresden 1959).

24 For a particularly effusive panegyric to the Soviet return of the *Sistine Madonna*, see Ruth Seydewitz, *Wenn die Madonna reden könnte* (Leipzig 1962).

25 See Kurt Pätzold, 'Auch die Geschichte kennt ihre Zahltage: Die Debatte über den Bombenkrieg', in Michael Klundt (ed.), *Heldenmythos und Opfertaumel: Der Zweite Weltkrieg und seine Folgen im deutschen Geschichtsdiskurs* (Cologne 2004), pp. 15–40, esp. pp. 16–17.

26 Stiftung Archiv der Parteien und Massenorganisationen der DDR im Bundesarchiv (SAPMO-BArch) DZ9/1751: Deutsches Friedenskomitee, 'Plan zur Wiederkehr des 13. Februar, des Tages der Zerstörung Dresdens', 4 January 1952.

27 See, for instance, Richard Peter's book of photographs, *Dresden – Eine Kamera klagt an* (Dresden 1949); and Max Seydewitz, *Dresden: Musen und Menschen* (Berlin 1973).

28 SAPMO-BArch DZ9/1751: Deutsches Friedenskomitee, 'Plan zur Wiederkehr des 13. Februar, des Tages der Zerstörung Dresdens', 4 January 1952.

29 For an excellent account of the 1980s commemoration (official and unofficial), see Matthias Neutzner, 'Vom Anklagen zum Erinnern: Die Erzählung vom 13. Februar', in Oliver Reinhard, Matthias Neutzner and Wolfgang Hesse, *Das Rote Leuchten: Dresden und der Bombenkrieg* (Dresden 2005), pp. 128–63, here 157ff.

30 SAPMO-BArch DY30/2182: 'Information der Bezirksleitung Dresden über die Veranstaltung anläßlich des 44. Jahrestages der Zerstörung Dresdens am 13. Februar 1945'.

31 For a selection of these drawings, see Wilhelm Rudolph, *Das zerstörte Dresden* (Leipzig 1988).

32 Griebel himself gave a moving account of the burning of Dresden and of the struggle of his family for survival, see Otto Griebel, *Ich war ein Mann der Straße* (Halle and Leizpig 1986), particularly pp. 425–64.

33 Staatliche Kunstsammlungen Dresden (ed.), *Dresden: Bekenntnis und Verpflichtung*, p. 210.

34 The German original is: 'Wer das Weinen verlernt hat, der lernt es wieder beim Untergang Dresdens'. Quoted, for instance, as 'Die Untat von Dresden', in Deutsches Friedenskomitee Berlin (ed.), *Dresden: Unsterbliche Stadt*, p. 29.

35 See the poem 'Schnee über Dresdens Trümmern' ('Snow above Dresden's Ruins'), in Max Zimmering, *Im Antlitz der Zeit: Ausgewählte Gedichte 1930–1946* (Berlin 1948), pp. 141–2, here 142.

36 Max Zimmering, *Phosphor und Flieder: Vom Untergang und Wiederaufstieg der Stadt Dresden* (Berlin 1954), pp. 57–61. Henceforth *PL*.

37 Such a socialist reappropriation of Dresden's aristocratic history also characterised the highly successful historical novels of Kurt Arnold Findeisen, such as *The Golden Horseman and His Fate* (*Der Goldene Reiter und sein Verhängnis*, 1954), in which Balthasar Permoser, sculptor at the court of Augustus II of Saxony, develops an anti-feudalist position. See also the more ironic take on Dresden's revolutionary tradition in Joachim Kupsch's Richard Wagner novel *An End in Dresden* (*Ein Ende in Dresden*, 1983).

38 The considerable amount of East German literature in which the theme of the flight and expulsion of Germans from the eastern territories and/or their subsequent integration is depicted still needs to be examined by literary historians. The most famous example is, of course, Christa Wolf's *Patterns of Childhood* (*Kindheitsmuster*, 1976). Other, less well known novels include: Annemarie Reinhard, *Flotsam* (*Treibgut*, 1958); Fritz Selbmann, *The Homecoming of Joachim Ott* (*Die Heimkehr des Joachim Ott*, 1963); and Benno Voelkner, *The People of Karvenbruch* (*Die Leute von Karvenbruch*, 1959). Plays on the subject include Helmut Baierl, *Frau Flinz* (1961) and – much better known – Heiner Müller, *The Resettler Woman or Life in the Country* (*Die Umsiedlerin oder das Leben auf dem Lande*, 1961).

39 Thus in Rauchfuß's novel, Karla is anything but emancipated: she is shown as needing the guiding hand of Manfred.

40 Karl Otto, *Leuchtendes Erbe* (Lengefeld 1956), p. 15.

41 Ibid., p. 13.

42 Eberhard Panitz, *Meines Vaters Straßenbahn* (Halle/Leizpig 1979), pp. 114–15.

43 Ibid., p. 82.

44 Heinz Czechowski, *Auf eine im Feuer versunkene Stadt* (Halle/Leipzig 1990), p. 8.

45 Ibid., p. 13.

46 See, for instance, the poem 'Liberty', ibid., p. 114.

47 Ibid., pp. 110–11, here 111.

48 'Liberty', ibid., p. 114.

49 'Stadtgang' ('Walk through the City'), ibid., pp. 41–3, here 41.

50 For a selection of literary texts relating to the bombing of Dresden, and an overview of representations in art, see Walter Schmitz (ed.), *Die Zerstörung Dresdens: Antworten der Künste* (Dresden 2005).

51 See Matthias Neutzner, 'Vom Anklagen zum Erinnern', p. 156.
52 Peter von Zahn, 'Erinnerung an Dresden', in Bundeslandmannschaft Dresden (ed.), *Erinnerung an Dresden* (Bonn 1965). For a more detailed discussion of the reception of the bombing of Dresden in West Germany, see Margalit, 'Der Luftangriff auf Dresden', pp. 202–6.
53 For a discussion of Friedrich's book, see the chapters by Huyssen and Schmitz in this volume.
54 See Max Seydewitz, *Zerstörung und Wiederaufbau von Dresden* (Berlin 1955), esp. pp. 66–155.
55 See Friedrich, *Der Brand*, p. 358ff.
56 It will suffice here to point to the series of books on the bombing of German cities published by the Wartberg publishing house in recent years (the cities include Osnabrück, Bonn, Mannheim, Ludwigshafen, Hannover, Leipzig, Dresden and Magdeburg).

Chapter 7: Victims of the Berlin Wall

1 '13. August 1961', *Welt der Arbeit*, 10 August 1962.
2 'Deutschlandspiegel', 89 (August 1962), Bundesarchiv – Filmarchiv (BA/FA), Berlin: Städte und Orte: Berlin ab 1945.
3 'Fox tönende Wochenschau; Ein Jahr danach', 45:77 (10 August 1962), BA/FA: Fox tönende Wochenschau 1950–63.
4 *Zur Situation in der Sowjetzone nach dem 13. August 1961* (Bonn 1961), p. 7.
5 Ernst Lemmer in *Der Bau der Mauer durch Berlin* (Bonn 1986, reprinted from 1961), p. 5.
6 'Der einzige Fluchtweg führte in den Tod', *Telegraf* (Berlin), 23 August 1961; 'Der Mord im Kanal', *Hamburger Abendblatt*, 26 August 1961.
7 *Zur Situation*, p. 12.
8 Roman Grafe, '"Ein Akt barbarischer Unmenschlichkeit". Der Tod des Mauerflüchtlings Peter Fechter vor 40 Jahren', *Deutschland Archiv*, 5 (2002), 793–8; Klaus Marxen and Gerhard Werle (eds), *Strafjustiz und DDR-Unrecht. Dokumentation. Band 2/1: Gewalttaten an der deutsch-deutschen Grenze* (Berlin 2002), pp. 241–8.
9 West Berlin Senate's reports ('*Ereignismeldungen*') to the Dienststelle Berlin in Bonn, 18–22 August 1962, Politisches Archiv des Auswärtigen Amtes (PA/AA), B 12, 189.
10 'Unsere Meinung: Grenze des Erträglichen', *Tagesspiegel*, 18 August 1962; 'Mord an der Mauer', *Kurier*, 18 August 1962.
11 'Appell des Regierenden Bürgermeisters Willy Brandt', 20 August 1962, Landesarchiv Berlin (LAB): B Rep. 002, Nr. 13330, p. 11.
12 Deutscher Gewerkschaftsbund (DGB) Chairman Richter, cited in 'Bonn verurteilt den Mord an der Mauer', *Deutsche Zeitung*, 21 August 1962.
13 'Verletzungen der Menschenrechte, Unrechtshandlungen und Zwischenfälle an der Berliner Sektorengrenze seit Errichtung der Mauer', PA/AA: B 38 – IIA1, 158, pp. 388–432.

14 'Mordschüsse – Ulbrichts einzige Argumente', *Berlin-Kurier*, 18 August 1962; 'Jugend ruft zum Aufstand gegen die Barbarei', *Berliner Anzeiger*, 19 August 1962.
15 'Gedenkstunde für Peter Fechter', *Süddeutsche Zeitung*, 18 August 1964; 'Kranzniederlegung zum Gedenken an Peter Fechter', *Die Welt*, 18 August 1966.
16 'Endgültig zum KZ gemacht', *Deutsche Zeitung*, 14 August 1961.
17 'Von "Volkspolizei" verschleppt. KZ-Wächter jagen Westberliner', *Berliner Morgenpost*, 10 October 1961; 'Mord an der Mauer', *Der Kurier*, 18 August 1962.
18 Franz Amrehn, 18 August 1961, cited in *Es begann am 13. August* (Berlin 1961), p. 4; 'Mord an der Mauer', *Der Kurier*, 18 August 1962.
19 *Bau der Mauer*, esp. p. 19.
20 Lemmer, *Der Bau der Mauer durch Berlin*, p. 5.
21 *Zur Situation*, p. 16; 'Die Mauer: Rote Nazis', *Die Zeit*, 31 August 1962.
22 Axel Schildt, Detlef Siegfried and Karl Christian Lammers (eds), *Dynamische Zeiten: Die 60er Jahre in den beiden deutschen Gesellschaften* (Hamburg 2000), pp. 77–165 .
23 *Die innerdeutsche Grenze* (Bonn 1987), pp. 36, 19.
24 Fritz Kopp from Sulzbach-Rosenberg to Stadtverwaltung Berlin, 26 January 1979, LAB: B. Rep. 002, 13330.
25 Patrick Major, 'Vor und nach dem 13. August 1961: Reaktionen der DDR-Bevölkerung auf den Bau der Berliner Mauer', *Archiv für Sozialgeschichte*, 39 (1999), 325–54.
26 GDR pamphlet 'Tatsachen über Westberlin', p. 13, PA/AA: B38-IIA1, 26.
27 GDR pamphlet 'Beweise für die aggressiven, verbrecherischen Anschläge auf die Staatsgrenze der DDR zu Westberlin und das Leben sowie die Sicherheit ihrer Bürger in der Zeit vom 13. August 1961 bis zum 13. August 1963', p. 3, PA/AA: MfAA, C 881/74.
28 'Tatsachen', p. 12.
29 'Beweise', esp. p. 4.
30 1962 DEFA documentary 'Schaut auf diese Stadt', BA/FA: Dokumentarfilme ab 1945, G-Z.
31 'Beweise', p. 4; 'Tatsachen', p. 14; 'Frontstadt-Mob terrorisiert Westberliner Bevölkerung', *Neues Deutschland*, 21 August 1962.
32 'OAS-Terror in Westberlin', *Der Morgen*, 21 August 1962; 'Das Chaos', *Neues Deutschland*, 21 August 1962.
33 'Wir warnen Provokateure', *Neues Deutschland*, 19 August 1962.
34 Horst Liebig, 'Sie fielen im Kalten Krieg', in Klaus-Dieter Baumgarten and Peter Freitag (eds), *Die Grenzen der DDR* (Berlin 2004), pp. 296–308.
35 Bodo Müller, *Faszination Freiheit* (Berlin 2000), pp. 80–108; Stasi Hauptabteilung IX/7, 'Bericht über die Ermordung des Angehörigen der NVA-Grenze, Genossen Unteroffizier Schultz, Egon, am 5.10.1964 in

Berlin-Mitte, Strelitzer Str 55', 19 October 1964, Bundesbeauftragte für die Unterlagen des Staatssicherheitsdienstes der ehemaligen DDR (BStU), Berlin: MfS, AU 8795/65.
36 Pamphlet 'Egon Schultz – ein Beispiel für die treue Pflichterfüllung gegenüber dem Arbeiter-und-Bauern-Staat', Mauerarchiv, Berlin: file Egon Schultz.
37 'Bericht über die Ermordung . . .', esp. p. 6.
38 'Das tragische Ende der Tunnelflucht', *Stuttgarter Nachrichten*, 8 October 1964.
39 'Unteroffizier Egon Schultz von Westberliner Agenten meuchlings ermordet', *Neues Deutschland*, 6 October 1964.
40 'Dein Vermächtnis wird uns unvergessen bleiben', *Neues Deutschland*, 10 October 1964.
41 'Freches Geständnis des Mörders', *Neues Deutschland*, 21 October 1964.
42 Hans Maur, *Mahn-, Gedenk- und Erinnerungsstätten der Arbeiterbewegung in Berlin-Mitte* (Berlin 1974), pp. 6, 33, 54–5, 79; Anna Dora Miethe, *Gedenkstätten* (Leipzig 1974), pp. 73–4.
43 'Zwei wahre Helden unserer Nation', *Berliner Zeitung*, 12 August 1966.
44 Herbert Mühlstadt, *172 Tage aus dem Leben des Lehrers Egon Schultz* (Berlin 1973).
45 'Namenskollektive "Unteroffizier Egon Schultz"', Mauerarchiv: file Egon Schultz.
46 *Materialien der Enquete-Kommission. Aufarbeitung von Geschichte und Folgen der SED-Diktatur in Deutschland*, esp. vol. IX (Baden-Baden 1995).
47 Roman Grafe, *Deutsche Gerechtigkeit* (Munich 2004).
48 'Schüsse auf Fechter geahndet', *Berliner Zeitung*, 6 March 1997.
49 'Neues Mahnmal erinnert an Maueropfer Peter Fechter', *Bild*, 14 August 1999.
50 Autopsy records, 5 October 1964, BStU: MfS: AU 8795/65, esp. 162–5; Müller, *Faszination*, pp. 104–8.
51 Sentence of the Landgericht Berlin, 22 April 1999, Staatsanwaltschaft Berlin Archive: Alz. 540–3/97.

Chapter 8: The Victims of Totalitarianism and the Centrality of Nazi Genocide: Continuity and Change in German Commemorative Politics

1 B. Honnigfort, 'Streit um Erinnerungskultur', *Frankfurter Rundschau*, 28 January 2004.
2 Deutscher Bundestag, 15. Wahlperiode, 'Förderung von Gedenkstätten zur Diktaturgeschichte in Deutschland – Gesamtkonzept für ein würdiges Gedenken aller Opfer der beiden deutschen Diktaturen', *Drucksache* 15/1874 (4 November 2003), p. 1.
3 See Ian Kershaw, *Germany's Present, Germany's Past* (London 1992), p. 12.

4 See Charles S. Maier, *The Unmasterable Past: History, Holocaust and German National Identity* (Cambridge, MA, 1988).

5 Cf. Bill Niven, *Facing the Nazi Past: United Germany and the Legacy of the Third Reich* (London 2002), pp. 2–3.

6 Antonia Grunenberg, 'Antitotalitarianism versus Antifascism – Two Legacies of the Past in Germany', *German Politics and Society*, 15:2 (1997), 76–90, here 77.

7 M. Rainer Lepsius, 'Das Erbe des Nationalsozialismus und die politische Kultur der Nachfolgestaaten des "Großdeutschen Reiches"', in *Demokratie in Deutschland: Soziologisch-historische Konstellationsanalysen* (Göttingen 1993), pp. 229–45.

8 See Jeffrey Herf, *Divided Memory: The Nazi Past in the Two Germanys* (Cambridge, MA, 1997), pp. 80–107, 135; Mary Fulbrook, *German National Identity after the Holocaust* (Cambridge 1999), pp. 57–9.

9 Moshe Zimmermann, 'Die Erinnerung an Nationalsozialismus und Widerstand im Spannungsfeld deutscher Zweistaatlichkeit', in Jürgen Danyel (ed.), *Die geteilte Vergangenheit: Zum Umgang mit Nationalsozialismus und Widerstand in beiden deutschen Staaten* (Berlin 1995), pp. 133–8, esp. p. 134; Edgar Wolfrum, 'Die beiden Deutschland', in Volkhard Knigge and Norbert Frei (eds), *Verbrechen erinnern: Die Auseinandersetzung mit Holocaust und Völkermord* (Munich 2002), pp. 133–49, here 136. See also Pieter Lagrou, 'The Nationalization of Victimhood: Selective Violence and National Grief in Western Europe, 1940–1960', in Richard Bessel and Dirk Schumann (eds), *Life after Death: Approaches to a Cultural and Social History of Europe during the 1940s and 1950s* (Cambridge 2003), pp. 243–57.

10 Herf, *Divided Memory*, pp. 317–21; Dirk van Laak, 'Der Platz des Holocaust im deutschen Geschichtsbild'; in Konrad H. Jarausch and Martin Sabrow (eds), *Die historische Meistererzählung: Deutungslinien der deutschen Nationalgeschichte nach 1945* (Göttingen 2002), pp. 163–93.

11 Josef Foschepoth, 'German Reaction to Defeat and Occupation', in Robert G. Moeller (ed.), *West Germany under Construction: Politics, Society, and Culture in the Adenauer Era* (Ann Arbor 1997), pp. 73–89. Cf. Fulbrook, *German National Identity*, p. 113.

12 Robert G. Moeller, 'Deutsche Opfer, Opfer der Deutschen: Kriegsgefangene, Vertriebene, NS-Verfolgte: Opferausgleich als Identitätspolitik', in Klaus Naumann (ed.), *Nachkrieg in Deutschland* (Hamburg 2001), pp. 29–58; Moeller, *War Stories: The Search for a Usable Past in the Federal Republic of Germany* (Berkeley 2001), pp. 51–87.

13 Donald Bloxham, 'The Genocidal Past in Western Germany and the Experience of Occupation, 1945–6', *European History Quarterly*, 34 (2004), 305–35; Tom Lawson, 'Constructing a Christian History of Nazism: Anglicanism and the Memory of the Holocaust, 1945–49', *History and Memory*, 16:1 (2004), 146–76. See Moeller, 'Deutsche Opfer, Opfer der Deutschen', p. 46.

14 Norbert Frei et al., 'Kalter Krieg, Antikommunismus und die Vergangenheit', in idem, *Karrieren im Zwielicht: Hitlers Eliten nach 1945* (Frankfurt am Main 2001), pp. 238–9, here 239.
15 Annette Kaminsky (ed.), *Orte des Erinnerns: Gedenkzeichen, Gedenkstätten und Museen zur Diktatur in SBZ und DDR* (Leipzig 2004), p. 52.
16 Edgar Wolfrum, *Geschichtspolitik in der Bundesrepublik Deutschland: Der Weg zur bundesrepublikanischen Erinnerung 1948–1990* (Darmstadt 1999), pp. 77–9.
17 Eric Langenbacher, 'Changing Memory Regimes in Contemporary Germany?', *German Politics and Society*, 21:2 (2003), 46–68.
18 A. Dirk Moses, 'The Forty-Fivers: A Generation between Fascism and Democracy', *German Politics and Society*, 17:1 (1999), 94–126.
19 See Geoffrey H. Hartmann (ed.), *Bitburg in Moral and Political Perspective* (Bloomington 1986).
20 For the debate, see *Historikerstreit: Die Dokumentation der Kontroverse um die Einzigartigkeit der nationalsozialistischen Judenvernichtung* (Munich 1987). Cf. Maier, *The Unmasterable Past*, p. 169; Bernhard Giesen, *Intellectuals and the Nation: Collective Identity in a German Axial Age* (Cambridge 1998).
21 See Thomas C. Fox, *Stated Memory: East Germany and the Holocaust* (Rochester 1999); and Joachim Käppner, *Erstarrte Geschichte: Faschismus und Holocaust im Spiegel der Geschichtswissenschaft und Geschichtspropaganda der DDR* (Hamburg 1999).
22 Cf. Bernd Faulenbach, 'Die doppelte "Vergangenheitsbewältigung": Nationalsozialismus und Stalinismus als Herausforderungen zeithistorischer Forschung und politischer Kultur', in Danyel (ed.), *Die geteilte Vergangenheit*, pp. 107–24, here 112.
23 See David Clay Large, '"A Beacon in the German Darkness": The Anti-Nazi Resistance Legacy in West German Politics', *Journal of Modern History*, 64 (suppl.) (1993), 173–86; Ines Reich, 'Geteilter Widerstand: Die Tradierung des deutschen Widerstands in der Bundesrepublik und der DDR', *Zeitschrift für Geschichtswissenschaft*, 42 (1994), 635–43.
24 Alexander von Plato, 'Eine zweite "Entnazifizierung"? Zur Verarbeitung politischer Umwälzungen in Deutschland 1945 und 1989', *Gewerkschaftliche Monatshefte*, 42 (1991), 415–28, here 417.
25 See Hans Günter Hockerts, 'Wiedergutmachung in Deutschland: Eine historische Bilanz', *Vierteljahreshefte für Zeitgeschichte*, 49 (2001), 167–214. On the globalisation of Holocaust discourse, see Jeffrey C. Alexander, 'On the Social Construction of Moral Universals: The "Holocaust" from War Crime to Trauma Drama', *European Journal of Social Theory*, 5:1 (2002), 5–85.
26 See http://www.bundestag.de/parlament/geschichte/parlhist/dok26.html (accessed 15 April 2005).
27 Cf. Niven, *Facing the Nazi Past*, pp. 2–3.

28 Hasko Zimmer, *Der Buchenwald-Konflikt: Zum Streit um Geschichte und Erinnerung im Kontext der deutschen Vereinigung* (Münster 1999), p. 14.
29 See the introduction to this volume for more on the *Neue Wache*.
30 See Siobhan Kattago, *Ambiguous Memory: The Nazi Past and German National Identity* (Westport 2001), pp. 129–41.
31 Peter Reichel, *Politik mit der Erinnerung: Gedächtnisorte im Streit um die nationalsozialistische Vergangenheit*, revised ed. (Frankfurt am Main 1999), p. 208.
32 See Kaminsky (ed.), *Orte des Erinnerns*, pp. 14, 471–84.
33 Niven, *Facing the Nazi Past*, p. 46.
34 See Ministerium für Wissenschaft, Forschung und Kultur des Landes Brandenburg (ed.), *Brandenburgische Gedenkstätten fur die Verfolgten des NS-Regimes: Perspektiven, Kontroversen und internationale Vergleiche* (Berlin 1992), pp. 230, 237, 256, 263.
35 Stiftung Gedenkstätten Buchenwald und Mittelbau-Dora (ed.), *Die Neukonzeption der Gedenkstätte Buchenwald* (Weimar 2001), p. 8.
36 Cf. Bernd Pampel, 'Bagatellisierung durch Gedenken? Gedenkstättenarbeit an Orten aufeinanderfolgenden nationalsozialistischen und kommunistischen Unrechts', *Deutschland Archiv*, 31:3 (1998), 438–53, here 445.
37 See Deutscher Bundestag, 13. Wahlperiode, 'Bericht der Bundesregierung über die Beteiligung des Bundes und Gedenkstätten in der Bundesrepublik Deutschland', *Drucksache* 13/8486 (5 September 1997).
38 See, for example, the comments by Karl Wilhelm Fricke, Deutscher Bundestag (ed.), *Materialien der Enquete-Kommission 'Überwindung der Folgen der SED-Diktatur im Prozess der deutschen Einheit' (13. Wahlperiode des Deutschen Bundestages)* VI (Frankfurt am Main 1999), p. 50. Further references to the published materials of this Commission are provided in italics as follows: *roman numeral volume number: page number*, e.g. here *VI: 50.*
39 See Deutscher Bundestag (ed), *Materialien der Enquete-Kommission 'Aufarbeitung von Geschichte und Folgen der SED-Diktatur in Deutschland' (12. Wahlperiode des Deutschen Bundestages)* I (Frankfurt am Main 1995). References to the first Commission's published materials are given as follows: Roman numeral volume number: page number.
40 Lothar Probst, 'Germany's Past, Germany's Future: Intellectual Controversies since Reunification', *German Politics and Society*, 30 (1993), 21–33, here 27.
41 See the protocol of a public hearing, III: 95–201; and the Commission's report, I: 263, 278–83. See also the second Commission's discussion, *I: 589–92, 600, 628*.
42 The Commission's report explicitly stated that comparison of the two dictatorships was 'admissible' and that 'comparison does not mean equation' (I: 744). See I: v, viii, 67, 160, 161, 340, 485, 708, 738, 739, 743, 746 twice, 805.

43 III: 1531, 1543; IX: 575, 577, 580.
44 III: 1543; IX: 575. See also IX: 579, 582, 586, 623.
45 For explicit calls to adopt the notion of totalitarianism, see I: 129, 150–1. For examples of its application, see I: 57–67, 75, 89, 110, 123; IX: 678. For comments on the paradigm's historical treatment, see I: 129, 489–90; II: 157–8; III: 1531; IX: 577, 602–3, 605–6, 607, 629, 647.
46 IX: 588, 593, 611–12, 619, 620, 625. For differing views on ideology's significance, see IX: 582, 600–1, 608.
47 I: 744–5. See IX: 592.
48 Cf. Sigrid Meuschel, 'Legitimationsstrategien in der DDR und in der Bundesrepublik', in Christoph Kleßmann, Hans Misselwitz and Günther Wichert (eds), *Deutsche Vergangenheiten – eine gemeinsame Herausforderung: Der schwierige Umgang mit der doppelten Nachkriegsgeschichte* (Berlin 1999), pp. 115–27; Stefan Berger, *The Search for Normality: National Identity and Historical Consciousness in Germany since 1800* (Providence 1997), pp. 254–5.
49 I: 280. Importantly, Jürgen Habermas endorsed an anti-totalitarian consensus 'that deserves its name because it is not selective' (IX: 690).
50 *I: 606–7.*
51 *I: 614, 602–3.*
52 IX: 262, 338, 354, 361; *VI: 9–10, 31–32. I: 633.*
53 For the PDS objection, see *I: 628*. On the latter point, see *I: 598, 601–2.*
54 IX: 319; *VI: 14.*
55 *I: 614, 617, 623.*
56 IX: 689.
57 Deutscher Bundestag, 'Förderung', p. 1.
58 Deutscher Bundestag, 15. Wahlperiode, *Plenarprotokoll*, 114. Sitzung (17 June 2004), pp. 10456, 10458–9, 10461–4; Tom Strohschneider, 'Erinnerungskatalog für den antitotalitären Grundkonsens', *Neues Deutschland*, 2 February 2004; Jörg Lau, 'Fatales Abwägen', *Die Zeit*, 5 February 2004; 'Gedenkstättenkonzept: Jüdische Organisationen werfen Union Verharmlosung von NS-Verbrechen vor', *Der Spiegel*, 17 June 2004; Christian Semler, 'Verharmlosung des Massenmordes', *Die Tageszeitung*, 18 June 2004.
59 Deutscher Bundestag, *Plenarprotokoll*, p. 10456.
60 Compare Deutscher Bundestag, 'Förderung', pp. 2–3, with Deutscher Bundestag, 'Bericht der Bundesregierung'.
61 Nooke rightly rejected the claim by Claudia Roth (The Greens) that merely referring to the 'double past' amounted to abandoning the consensus, Deutscher Bundestag, *Plenarprotokoll*, p. 10461.
62 See the revised motion, Deutscher Bundestag, 15. Wahlperiode, 'Förderung von Gedenkstätten zur Diktaturgeschichte in Deutschland – Gesamtkonzept für ein würdiges Gedenken aller Opfer der beiden deutschen Diktaturen', *Drucksache* 15/3048 (4 May 2004), p. 1.
63 Deutscher Bundestag, *Plenarprotokoll*, p. 10456.

64 See Jan-Holger Kirsch, *Nationaler Mythos oder historische Trauer? Der Streit um ein zentrales 'Holocaust Mahnmal' für die Berliner Republik* (Cologne 2003).
65 Deutscher Bundestag, 'Förderung', p. 6.

Chapter 9: Representations of German Wartime Suffering in Recent Fiction

1 W. G. Sebald, *Luftkrieg und Literatur* (Munich 1999). Hereafter *NHD* (Sebald's book was translated into English as *On the Natural History of Destruction* (London 2003); page-numbers refer to the English edition).
2 W. G. Sebald, 'Zwischen Geschichte und Naturgeschichte: Versuch über die literarische Beschreibung totaler Zerstörung mit Anmerkungen zu Kasack, Nossack und Kluge', *Orbis Litterarum*, 37 (1982), 345–66.
3 Volker Hage, *Zeugen der Zerstörung. Die Literaten und der Luftkrieg* (Frankfurt am Main 2003), pp. 119–20.
4 Michael Bonder, *'Political Correctness': Ein Gespenst geht um die Welt* (Frankfurt am Main 1995).
5 See Michael Behrens and Robert von Rimscha, *Politische Korrektheit in Deutschland: Eine Gefahr für die Demokratie* (Bonn 1995).
6 Sally Johnson and Stephanie Suhr, 'From "Political Correctness" to "*Politische Korrektheit*": Discourses of "PC" in the German Newspaper *Die Welt*', *Discourse and Society*, 14:1 (2002), 49–68, here 52.
7 Botho Strauß, 'Anschwellender Bocksgesang', in Botho Strauß, *Der Aufstand gegen die sekundäre Welt* (Munich 1999), pp. 55–79, here 68.
8 Ulrich Schacht, 'Stigma und Sorge. Über deutsche Identität nach Auschwitz', in Heimo Schwilk and Ulrich Schacht (eds), *Die selbstbewußte Nation* (Frankfurt am Main 1994), pp. 57–68, here 59.
9 Ingo Cornils, 'Successful Failure? The Impact of the German Student Movement on the Federal Republic of Germany', in Stuart Taberner and Frank Finlay (eds), *Recasting German Identity* (Rochester 2002), pp. 109–26, here 109.
10 See my '"Wie schön wäre Deutschland, wenn man sich noch als Deutscher fühlen und mit Stolz als Deutscher fühlen könnte": Martin Walser's Reception of Victor Klemperer's *Tagebücher 1933–1945* in *Das Prinzip Genauigkeit* and *Die Verteidigung der Kindheit*', *Deutsche Vierteljahrsschrift*, 73 (1999), 710–32.
11 Martin Walser, *Die Verteidigung der Kindheit* (Frankfurt am Main 1991), p. 315.
12 Martin Walser, 'Über Deutschland reden. Ein Bericht', in Martin Walser, *Deutsche Sorgen* (Frankfurt am Main 1997), pp. 406–27, here 411–12.
13 See my 'The Final Taboo?: Philosemitism, the *Meinungsindustrie*, and the New Right in Martin Walser's *ohne einander*', *Seminar*, 37:2 (2001), 154–66.

14 Martin Walser, *ohne einander* (Frankfurt am Main 1993), p. 65. Hereafter *oe*.
15 Martin Walser, 'Erfahrungen beim Verfassen einer Sonntagsrede', in Frank Schirrmacher (ed.), *Die Walser-Bubis-Debatte* (Frankfurt am Main 1999), pp. 7–17, here 11. Hereafter *EVS*.
16 See Kathrin Schödel, 'Normalising Cultural Memory? The "Walser-Bubis-Debate" and Martin Walser's novel *Ein Springender Brunnen*', in Taberner and Finlay (eds), *Recasting German Identity*, pp. 69–87.
17 See my 'A Manifesto for Germany's 'New Right'? – Martin Walser, The Past, Transcendence, Aesthetics, and *Ein Springender Brunnen*', *German Life and Letters*, 53:1 (2000), 126–41.
18 Martin Walser, *Ein Springender Brunnen* (Frankfurt am Main 1998), p. 282. Hereafter *SB*.
19 See Bill Niven, 'Martin Walser's *Tod eines Kritikers* and the Issue of Anti-Semitism', *German Life and Letters*, 56:3 (2003), 299–311.
20 Martin Walser, 'Bombenkrieg als Epos', in Kettenacker (ed.), *Ein Volk von Opfern?*, pp. 127–30, here 130 and 129.
21 Niven, *Facing the Nazi Past* (London and New York 2002), p. 5.
22 Peter Schneider, 'Man kann sogar ein Erdbeben verpassen', in Peter Schneider, *Extreme Mittellage: Eine Reise durch das deutsche Nationalgefühl* (Reinbek 1990), pp. 54–78, here 64.
23 Peter Schneider, 'Deutsche als Opfer?', in Kettenacker (ed.), *Ein Volk von Opfern?*, pp. 158–65, here 163.
24 See Ingo Cornils, 'Long Memories: The German Student Movement in Recent Fiction', *German Life and Letters*, 56:1 (2003), 89–101.
25 Andreas Michel, 'Convergences? Peter Schneider's Critique of the Left-Liberal Consensus and the Emergence of the German New Right', *Colloquia Germanica*, 31:3 (1998), 237–58, here 255.
26 See my *German Literature of the 1990s and Beyond* (Rochester 2005), pp. 114–19.
27 See my 'Hans-Ulrich Treichel's *Der Verlorene* and The "Problem" of German Wartime Suffering', *The Modern Language Review*, 97 (2002), 123–34.
28 Uwe Timm, *Am Beispiel meines Bruders* (Köln 2003), p. 93. Hereafter *AB*.
29 Cited in Volker Hage, *Hamburg 1943* (Frankfurt am Main 2003), p. 301.
30 Martin Walser, *Das Prinzip Genauigkeit* (Frankfurt am Main 1995).
31 See Helmut Schmitz, *On Their Own Terms: German Literature and the Legacy of National Socialism after Unification* (Birmingham 2004).
32 Bill Niven, 'The Globalisation of Memory and the Rediscovery of Suffering', in Stuart Taberner (ed.), *German Literature in the Age of Globalisation* (Birmingham 2004), pp. 230–46, here 240.
33 Ulla Hahn, *Unscharfe Bilder* (Munich 2003), p. 174.
34 Dieter Forte, *Der Junge mit den blutigen Schuhen* (Frankfurt am Main 2003 [1995]), p. 109. Hereafter *DJ*.

35 Peter Hüttenberger, *Düsseldorf. Geschichte von den Anfängen bis ins 20. Jahrhundert. Die Industrie- und Verwaltungsstadt* (Düsseldorf 1989), pp. 631 and 640–2. Forte draws on Hüttenberger's description of the air war, the fates of individual residents and the fall of Düsseldorf on pages 631–48.

36 Günter Grass, *Im Krebsgang* (Göttingen 2002), p. 136. Hereafter *IK*.

37 See my '"Normalization" and the New Consensus on the Nazi Past: Günter Grass's *Im Krebsgang* and the Problem of German Wartime Suffering', *Oxford German Studies*, 31 (2002), 161–86.

38 Niven, 'The Globalisation of Memory and the Rediscovery of Suffering', p. 233.

39 Dieter Forte, 'Schweigen oder sprechen', in Dieter Forte, *Schweigen oder sprechen* (Frankfurt am Main 2002), pp. 69–80, here 71 and 69. Hans Mommsen claimed, similarly, that Friedrich's *The Fire* was understood by its readers less as an attempt at exculpation than as a warning against the horrors that would follow from the British and American attack on Iraq in 2003 ('Moralisch, strategisch, zerstörerisch', in Kettenacker (ed.), *Ein Volk von Opfern*, pp. 145–51, here 150–1).

40 Cited in Hage, *Zeugen der Zerstörung*, p. 107.

41 Hans Magnus Enzensberger, *Aussichten auf den Bürgerkrieg* (Frankfurt am Main 1993), pp. 63 and 64.

42 David Roberts, 'Introduction: Debating Enzensberger', in Gerhard Fischer (ed.), *Debating Enzensberger* (Tübingen 1996), pp. ix–xvi, here xi.

43 Hans Magnus Enzensberger, *Die große Wanderung* (Frankfurt am Main 1992), p. 13.

44 See my 'German Nostalgia? Remembering German-Jewish Life in W. G. Sebald's *Die Ausgewanderten* and *Austerlitz*', *The Germanic Review*, 79:3 (2004), 181–202.

45 See William Collins Donahue, 'Illusions of Subtlety: Bernhard Schlink's *Der Vorleser* and the Moral Limits of Holocaust Fiction', *German Life and Letters*, 54:1 (2001), 60–81.

46 Jirgl's 1990 *Mutter Vater Roman* had already spoken of indifference to the fate of returning POWs in East Germany. The mass rapes of German women by Soviet soldiers, equally taboo in the GDR, is also thematised, as it is in Christoph Hein's 1989 short story 'Die Vergewaltigung' ('The Rape', 1989).

47 Christoph Hein, *Landnahme* (Frankfurt am Main 2004), p. 353.

48 Reinhard Jirgl, *Die Unvollendeten* (Munich 2003), pp. 6 and 29. My translations reproduce Jirgl's highly original orthography. Hereafter *DU*.

49 Marcel Beyer's *Flughunde* (Frankfurt am Main 1995) is a notable exception (Beyer was born in 1965).

50 Christian Kracht, *Faserland* (Munich 2002 [1995]), pp. 47 and 85.

51 Jenny Erpenbeck, *Geschichte vom alten Kind* (Berlin 1999), p. 85.

52 Volker Hage, 'Die Enkel wollen es wissen', *Der Spiegel*, 12 (17 March 2003), 170–3.

53 Tanja Dückers, *Himmelskörper* (Berlin 2003), p. 94.
54 Julia Franck, *Der Liebediener* (Cologne 1999), p. 181; and Elke Naters, *Lügen* (Cologne 1999), p. 78.
55 'Das Flüchtige und das Doppelbödige. Gespräch mit Tanja Dückers', *neue deutsche literatur*, 51:2 (2003), 54–62, 55.
56 Leander Scholz, 'SS', in Tanja Dückers and Verena Carl (eds), *stadt land krieg. Autoren der Gegenwart erzählen von der deutschen Vergangenheit* (Berlin 2004), pp. 123–34, here 134.
57 'Vorwort', in Dückers and Carl (eds), *stadt land krieg*, pp. 7–13, here 8.

Chapter 10: Air War Legacies: From Dresden to Baghdad

1 This chapter first appeared as 'Air War Legacies: From Dresden to Baghdad', *New German Critique*, 90 (Fall 2003), 163–76. It appears here with the kind permission of the publishers.
2 David Harvey, *The Condition of Postmodernity* (Oxford 1989), pp. 260–307.
3 Of course, the bombing of Dresden has always been part of official GDR propaganda against British–American terror bombing (see the chapter by Niven in this volume). The public taboo or inhibition to speak of the bombing of German cities pertained to West Germany alone.
4 Jörg Friedrich, *Der Brand: Deutschland im Bombenkrieg 1940–1945* (Berlin 2002).
5 See 'Als das Feuer vom Himmel fiel', *Der Spiegel* (special edition), 2 (2003).
6 See 'Verbrechen gegen die Deutschen', *GEO*, 2 (2003).
7 W. G. Sebald, *Luftkrieg und Literatur* (Munich 1999). Translated into English as *On the Natural History of Destruction* (London 2003). For more on Sebald and the literature of the air war, see Volker Hage, *Zeugen der Zerstörung: Die Literaten und der Luftkrieg* (Frankfurt am Main 2003). The book includes telling interviews with Sebald, Kluge and other German writers.
8 For a collection of some of the major responses to Friedrich in Germany and England, see Lothar Kettenacker (ed.), *Ein Volk von Opfern? Die neue Debatte um den Bombenkrieg 1940–45* (Berlin 2003).
9 For an excellent discussion of the military and the moral aspects of the bombings, see the two reviews by Douglas Pfeifer and Jörg Arnold on H-Net. Pertinent historical literature is listed there in some detail.
10 Sebald's blurb was taken from *On the Natural History of Destruction*, trans. Anthea Bell (New York 2003). He obviously knew of Friedrich's work, but it is doubtful whether he read all or any of *The Fire* in manuscript form before his death in late 2001. The book was published the following year.
11 Alexander Kluge, *Neue Geschichten: Hefte 1–18 ⟨Unheimlichkeit der Zeit⟩* (Frankfurt am Main 1978), pp. 33–110.

12 This is not to deny that there are also problems with Sebald in this regard. See my essay 'Rewritings and New Beginnings: W. G. Sebald and the Literature on the Air War', in Andreas Huyssen, *Present Pasts: Urban Palimpsests and the Politics of Memory* (Stanford, CA, 2003), 138–57.

13 Jörg Friedrich, *Brandstätten: Der Anblick des Bombenkrieges* (Munich 2003).

14 Jacques Derrida and Jürgen Habermas, 'Unsere Erneuerung. Nach dem Krieg: Die Wiedergeburt Europas', *Frankfurter Allgemeine Zeitung*, 31 May 2003, 33.

15 Adam Krzeminski, 'Wie einst Kant, so heute Habermas', *Neue Zürcher Zeitung* (11 July 2003). For a polemic against Krzeminski and others in Eastern Europe who supported US policies, see István Eörsi, 'Tief verwurzelte Vasalleninstinkte', *Frankfurter Rundschau*, 11 August 2003.

Chaper 11: From the Margins to the Centre? The Discourse on Expellees and Victimhood in Germany

1 For a discussion of these two texts, see Eric Langenbacher, 'The Return of Memory: New Discussions about German Suffering in World War II', *German Politics and Society*, 3 (2003), 74–88.

2 Helmut Peitsch, 'Introduction: Studying European Literary Memories', in Helmut Peitsch, Charles Burdett and Claire Gorrara, *European Memories of the Second World War* (Oxford and New York, 1999), pp. xiii–xxxi, here xv.

3 See, for example, Graham Jackman's introduction to the special number of *German Life and Letters*, 'The End of a Taboo: The Experience of Bombing and Expulsion in Contemporary German "Gedächtniskultur" ', 4 (2004), 343–55, here 345.

4 Eric Langenbacher, 'Changing Memory Regimes in Contemporary Germany?' *German Politics and Society*, 2 (2003), 46–68.

5 Henning Süssner, 'Still Yearning for the Lost Heimat?: Ethnic German Expellees and the Politics of Belonging', *German Politics and Society*, 2 (2004), 1–26, here 2.

6 Ibid., 8.

7 Ibid., 16.

8 Helmut Schmitz, *On Their Own Terms: The Legacy of National Socialism in Post-1990 German Fiction* (Birmingham 2004), p. 15.

9 Andreas F. Kelletat, 'Von der Täter- zur Opfernation: Die Rückkehr des Themas "Flucht und Vertreibung" in dem deutschen Vergangenheitsdiskurs bei Grass und anderen', in anon., *Germanistentreffen Deutschland – Großbritannien, Irland 30.9–3.10.2004: Dokumentation der Tagungsbeiträge* (DAAD 2005), pp. 167–80.

10 Ibid., p. 179.

11 José Ayala Lasso, 'Address to the German Expellees', 28 May 1995.
12 UN Commission on Human Rights, 'Human Rights and Population Transfer: Final Report of the Special Rapporteur, Mr. Al-Khasawneh', (E/CN.4/Sub.2/1997/23).
13 Sudetendeutsche Landsmannschaft, 'SL für Ausschöpfung weiterer Rechtswege', Press Release, 7 July 1999.
14 European Parliament, 'Resolution on the Regular Report from the Commission on the Czech Republic's Progress towards Accession', (COM[98]0708 – C4–0111/99).
15 Deutscher Bundestag, 'Antrag der Abgeordneten Hartmut Koschyk, Christian Schmidt (Fürth), Karl Lamers, Peter Hintze und der Fraktion der CDU/CSU: Versöhnung durch Ächtung von Vertreibung', Bundestagsdrucksache 14/1311, 29 June 1999.
16 Deutscher Bundestag, 'Antrag der Fraktionen SPD und Bündnis 90/Die Grünen: Weiterentwicklung der deutsch-tschechischen Beziehungen', Bundestagsdrucksache 14/1873, 26 October 1999.
17 In a speech at the commemoration ceremony of the fiftieth anniversary of the League of Expellees in May 1999, the German Minister of the Interior noted that '[c]ontrary to frequent prejudice, the ethnic German expellees have, in their overwhelming majority, actively participated in the process of reconciliation between the European nations, and they continue to do so today' (Otto Schily, 'Die Erinnerung und das Gedenken findet ihren Sinn in dem Willen für eine bessere Zukunft', 29 May 1999). In her address on the occasion of the twenty-fifth anniversary of the Cultural Foundation of the German Expellees, the chairperson of the Culture and Media Committee of the Bundestag, Elke Leonhard of the SPD, emphasised that nobody had the right to 'discredit as revanchism the legitimate interests of the expellees in the preservation of their culture and the public acknowledgement of their fate . . .' (Elke Leonhard, 'Die Verantwortung der Politik für die gesamtdeutsche Kultur', 14 June 1999). Ironically, a dispute with the Secretary of State for Culture, Michael Naumann, over the (under)-funding of cultural institutions of the expellees prompted Leonhard to resign her post on 30 June 2000.
18 Diana Johnstone, *Fools' Crusade: Yugoslavia, NATO and Western Delusions* (London 2002).
19 Ibid., p. 176.
20 See Andrei S. Markovits and Simon Reich, *The German Predicament: Memory and Power in the New Europe* (Ithaca 1997).
21 Ibid., p. 145.
22 Vollmer's response in March 1995 in which she interprets the silence as opportunistic electioneering is revealing for its silence on the expellees themselves. She points out that Havel is willing to use the term 'expulsions', but focuses on the need to complete the policy of *Ostpolitik* by

overcoming old patterns of accusation and suspicion: 'Appell zum Aufbruch aus der Vergangenheit', *Focus Magazin*, 13 March 1995.

23 Anon., 'Vertriebene vertreiben Antje Vollmer', *die tageszeitung*, 29 May 1995.

24 Anon., 'Havel mit Karadzic-Regime verglichen', *die tageszeitung*, 6 June 1995.

25 Her speech was not published but widely cited. See, for example, anon., 'Frau Vollmer ruft Tschechen und Deutsche zu einem mutigen Neuanfang auf', *Frankfurter Allgemeine Zeitung*, 6 October 1995.

26 Ibid..

27 Thomas Schmid, 'Linke Selbstkritik', *Die Welt*, 31 May 1999.

28 Christian Semler, 'Kalte Herzen, kalte Heimat', *die tageszeitung*, 19 June 1999.

29 Ibid..

30 Anon., 'Krieg für das gute Gewissen', *Der Spiegel*, 17 (1999), 36.

31 Ibid., 37.

32 Ibid., 38.

33 Anon., 'Die Deutschen als Opfer', *Spiegel*, 13 (2002), 36–64, here 37. All the following citations are taken from the first article. The other parts of the series were entitled as follows: anon., 'Schrecken der wilden Vertreibung', 14 (2002), 65–73; anon., 'Eine teuflische Lösung', 15 (2002), 56–74.

34 Ibid., 39.

35 Ibid., 37.

Chapter 12: On Taboos, Traumas and Other Myths: Why the Debate about German Victims of the Second World War is not a Historians' Controversy

1 I am grateful to Jörg Echternkamp and Dietmar Süß for discussing 'the new victims' discourse' in Germany with me. Their suggestions have improved this article, whilst any shortcomings and errors remain, as always, my own.

2 W. G. Sebald, *On the Natural History of Destruction* (New York 1999); Günter Grass, *Im Krebsgang* (Munich 2002), translated as *Crabwalk* (New York 2003); Guido Knopp's TV series on the German refugees and expellees, entitled 'Die grosse Flucht. Das Schicksal der Vertriebenen', was broadcast in five parts between November 2001 and December 2002; Jörg Friedrich, *Der Brand. Deutschland im Bombenkrieg 1940–1945* (Munich 2002) and *Brandstätten: Der Anblick des Bombenkriegs* (Munich 2003). The idea of a taboo has been reinforced by Peter Schneider, 'The Germans are Breaking an Old Taboo', *New York Times*, 18 January 2003. One of the most recent examples is Dagmar Barnouw's *The War in the Empty Air: Victims, Perpetrators, and Postwar Germans*

(Bloomington 2005); Barnouw claims that German suffering was totally excluded from historical memory as a result of Allied re-education and the centrality of the Holocaust to post-Second World War memory.

3 I deliberately use the term 'historism' rather than 'historicism' in this chapter. Whereas 'historism' (in German, *Historismus*), as defined by Leopold von Ranke, can be seen as an evolutionary, reformist concept which understands all political order as historically developed and grown, 'historicism' (*Historizismus*), as defined and rejected by Karl Popper, is based on the notion that history develops according to predetermined laws towards a particular end.

4 Thomas W. Neumann, 'Der Bombenkrieg. Zur ungeschriebenen Geschichte einer kollektiven Verletzung', in Klaus Naumann (ed.), *Nachkrieg in Deutschland* (Hamburg 2001), p. 319.

5 For example, Hans-Erich Nossack, *Der Untergang. Hamburg 1943* (Frankfurt am Main 1948), translated as *The End: Hamburg, 1943* (Chicago 2004); Gerd Ledig, *Vergeltung* (Frankfurt am Main 1956), translated as *Payback* (London 2003).

6 For example, 'Der Bombenkrieg', shown on ZDF in February 2003; and an ARD series on the expellees which came complete with accompanying book: K. Erik Franzen, *Die Vertriebenen. Hitlers letzte Opfer* (Munich 2002).

7 On this idea of a European network, see Anja Kruke (ed.), *Zwangsmigration und Vertreibung. Europa im 20. Jahrhundert* (Bonn 2005).

8 See Chapter 5 by Helmut Schmitz in this volume.

9 For a good survey of major historical debates in the FRG, see Martin Sabrow, Ralph Jessen and Klaus Große Kracht (eds), *Zeitgeschichte als Streitgeschichte. Grosse Kontroversen seit 1945* (Munich 2003).

10 Malte Thießen, 'Gedenken an "Operation Gomorrha": Zur Erinnerungskultur des Bombenkrieges von 1945 bis heute', *Zeitschrift für Geschichtswissenschaft*, 53 (2005), 46–61; a shorter version is also available online as Malte Thießen, 'Gedenken an Hamburgs "schrecklichste Stunden": Zur Erinnerungskultur des Bombenkrieges von 1945 bis heute', *historicumnet* [9.3.2005], URL: http://www.bombenkrieg.historicum.net/themen/hamburg.pdf.

11 Götz Bergander, 'Vom Gerücht zur Legende. Der Luftkrieg über Deutschland im Spiegel von Tatsachen, erlebter Geschichte, Erinnerung, Erinnerungsverzerrung', in Thomas Stamm-Kuhlmann, Jürgen Elvert, Birgit Aschmann and Jens Hohensee (eds), *Geschichtsbilder. Festschrift für Michael Salewski* (Stuttgart 2003), pp. 591–616.

12 Thomas Kühne, 'Zwischen Vernichtungskrieg und Freizeitgesellschaft. Die Veteranenkultur der Bundesrepublik (1945–1995)', in Naumann (ed.), *Nachkrieg*, p. 90 ff. See also Jörg Echternkamp, 'Mit dem Krieg seinen Frieden schliessen – Wehrmacht und Weltkrieg in der Veteranenkultur (1945–1960)', in Thomas Kuehne (ed.), *Von der Kriegskultur*

zur Friedenskultur? Zum Wandel der politischen Mentalität in Deutschland nach 1945 (Münster 2000), pp. 78–93.

13 On the discourses surrounding the issue of rape, see Regina Mühlhauser, 'Vergewaltigungen in Deutschland 1945. Nationaler Opferdiskurs und individuelles Erinnern betroffener Frauen', in Naumann (ed.), *Nachkrieg*, p. 384 ff.

14 Gudrun Schwarz, '"During Total War We Girls Want to Be Where We Can Really Accomplish Something": What Women Do in Wartime', in Omer Bartov, Atina Grossmann and Mary Nolan (eds), *Crimes of War: Guilt and Denial in the Twentieth Century* (New York 2002), pp. 121–37.

15 Bundesministerium für Vertriebene, Flüchtlinge und Kriegssachgeschädigte (ed.) *Dokumente deutscher Kriegsschäden. Evakuierte, Kriegssachgeschädigte, Währungsgeschädigte. Die geschichtliche und rechtliche Entwicklung*, 5 vols (Bonn 1958–64).

16 Sabine Behrenbeck, 'Remembering the Victims of Violence in Germany', in Richard Bessel and Dirk Schumann (eds), *Life after Death: Approaches to a Cultural and Social History of Europe during the 1940s and 1950s* (Cambridge 2003), pp. 37–64.

17 See, in particular, Hans Rumpf, *Das war der Bombenkrieg. Deutsche Städte im Feuersturm* (Oldenburg 1961), English translation as *The Bombing of Germany* (London 1963). Other early accounts include Hans Rumpf, *Der hochrote Hahn* (Darmstadt 1952); Max Domarus, *Der Untergang des alten Würzburg und seine Vorgeschichte* (Gerolzhofen 1950); and Georg W. Feuchter, *Der Luftkrieg* (Frankfurt/Main 1964).

18 See, for example, Erich Hampe, *Der zivile Luftschutz im Zweiten Weltkrieg. Dokumentation und Erfahrungsberichte über Aufbau und Einsatz* (Frankfurt am Main 1963).

19 The official history is Charles Webster and Noble Frankland, *The Strategic Air Offensive against Germany, 1939–1945*, 4 vols (London 1961). See also Noble Frankland, *The Bombing Offensive against Germany: Outlines and Perspectives* (London 1965). More recently the subject has been dealt with by Mark Connelly, *Reaching for the Stars: A New History of Bomber Command in World War II* (London 2001); and Robin Neillands, *The Bomber War: Arthur Harris and the Allied Bomber Offensive, 1939–1945* (London 2001).

20 Some good examples include: Götz Bergander, *Dresden im Luftkrieg*, 2nd edn (Würzburg 1998, first published 1977); Hans Brunswig, *Feuersturm über Hamburg* (Stuttgart 1978); Friedhelm Golücke, *Schweinfurt und der strategische Luftkrieg 1943. Der Angriff der US Air Force vom 14. Oktober 1943 gegen die Schweinfurter Kugellagerindustrie* (Paderborn 1980); Helmut Schnatz, *Der Luftkrieg im Raum Koblenz 1944/5* (Boppard 1981); Georg Wolfgang Schramm, *Bomben auf Nürnberg. Luftangriffe 1940–45* (Munich 1988); Gerd E. Überschär, *Freiburg im Luftkrieg*

1939–1945 (Freiburg 1990); Wilfried Beer, *Kriegsalltag zur Abwehr- und Schadensbegrenzung, dargestellt für den Raum Münster* (Bremen 1990); Ursula Moessner-Heckner, *Pforzheim-Code Yellowfin. Eine Analyse der Luftangriffe 1944–1945* (Sigmaringen 1991); Martin Rüther, *Köln, 31. Mai 1942. Der 1000-Bomber-Angriff* (Cologne 1992); Herbert Pogt (ed.), *Vor fünfzig Jahren. Bomben auf Wuppertal* (Wuppertal 1993); Fritz Bauer, *Würzburg im Feuerofen. Tagebuchaufzeichnungen und Erinnerungen an die Zerstörung Würzburgs* (Würzburg 1995); Gerhard E. Sollbach, *Dortmund. Bombenkrieg und Nachkriegsalltag 1939–1945* (Hagen 1996); Irmtraud Permooser, *Der Luftkrieg über München 1942–1945. Bomben auf die Hauptstadt der Bewegung* (Oberhaching 1997); Christian Hanke, Joachim Paschen and Bernhard Jungwirth, *Hamburg im Bombenkrieg 1940–1945. Das Schicksal einer Stadt* (Hamburg 2001).

21 Heinz Schön, *Die 'Gustloff' – Katastrophe: Bericht eines Überlebenden über die größte Schiffskatastrophe im zweiten Weltkrieg* (Stuttgart 1984). See also Christopher Dobson, *The Cruellest Night* (Boston 1979); and Arthur V. Sellwood, *The Damned Don't Drown: The Sinking of the Wilhelm Gustloff* (Annapolis 1973).

22 *Dokumentation der Vertreibung der Deutschen aus Ost-Mitteleuropa*, 8 vols (Bonn 1953–62). See also the analysis by Matthias Beer, 'Im Spannungsfeld von Politik und Zeitgeschichte. Das Großforschungsprojekt "Dokumentation der Vertreibung der Deutschen aus Ost-Mitteleuropa" ', *Vierteljahreshefte für Zeitgeschichte*, 46 (1998), 345–89.

23 For discussions on Dresden and the extensive literature on it, see Bill Niven's chapter in this volume.

24 Gilad Margalit, 'Dresden und die Erinnerungspolitik der DDR', *historicum.net*, URL: http://www.bombenkrieg.historicum.net/themen/ddr.html.

25 Olaf Groehler, *Geschichte des Luftkriegs* (Berlin 1975), and *Bombenkrieg gegen Deutschland* (Berlin 1990).

26 David Irving, *The Destruction of Dresden* (London 1963); German translation as *Der Untergang Dresdens* (Gütersloh 1964).

27 See, for example, Frank Kurowski, *Der Luftkrieg über Deutschland* (Düsseldorf 1977); Heinz Schön, *Im Heimatland in Feindeshand* (Kiel 1998), and *Tragödie Ostpreußen* (Kiel 1999).

28 Alfred M. de Zayas, *Die Anglo-Amerikaner und die Vertreibung der Deutschen* (Munich 1977). By 2000 the book had gone through 14 editions. The English edition is called *Nemesis at Potsdam* (London 1977). See also Alfred M. de Zayas, *Anmerkungen zur Vertreibung* (Stuttgart 1986), *The German Expellees: Victims in War and Peace* (London 1993), *A Terrible Revenge. The Ethnic Cleansing of the East European Germans, 1944–1950* (New York 1994), and *Heimatrecht ist Menschenrecht* (Munich 2001).

29 See, for example, Hans-Walter Krumwiede (ed.), *Versöhnung in Europa: 30 Jahre Charta der deutschen Heimatvertriebenen* (Göttingen 1980).

30 Gerd Wiegel, 'Niederlage, Befreiung oder Sieg. Der 8. Mai im Spiegel seiner Jubiläen', *Blätter für deutsche und internationale Politik*, 5 (2005), 564–70.

31 Specifically on the bombing war, see: Horst Boog, 'Der anglo-amerikanische Luftkrieg über Europa und die deutsche Luftverteidigung', in *Das Deutsche Reich und der Zweite Weltkrieg, Bd. 6: Der globale Krieg* (Stuttgart 1990), pp. 429–560 (English edition: *Germany and the Second World War*, vol. 6: *The Global War* (Oxford 2001)); Horst Boog, 'Strategischer Luftkrieg in Europa und Reichsverteidigung 1943–1945', in Horst Boog, Gerhard Krebs and Detlef Vogel (eds), *Das deutsche Reich und der Zweite Weltkrieg, Bd. 7: Das Deutsche Reich in der Defensive: Strategischer Luftkrieg in Europa, Krieg im Westen und in Ostasien, 1943–1944/45* (Stuttgart 2001), pp. 3–415 (English edition: *Germany and the Second World War*, vol. 7: *The Strategic Air War in Europe and the War in the West and East Asia, 1943–1944/5* (Oxford 2005)). See also: Willi Mues, *Der grosse Kessel. Eine Dokumentation über das Ende des zweiten Weltkrieges zwischen Lippe und Ruhr/Sieg und Lenne* (Erwitte 1984); and Klaus-Dietmar Henke, *Die amerikanische Besatzung Deutschlands* (Munich 1995).

32 Wolfgang Benz, *Die Vertreibung der Deutschen aus dem Osten. Ursachen, Ereignisse, Folgen* (Frankfurt am Main 1985); see also from the same year, Siegfried Kogelfranz (ed.), *Die Vertriebenen* (Reinbek 1985). And, as interesting case studies, see Bertram Gresh Lattimore, *The Assimilation of German Expellees into the West German Polity and Society since 1945: A Case Study of Eurin, Schleswig-Holstein* (The Hague 1974); Franz J. Bauer, *Flüchtlinge und Flüchtlingspolitik in Bayern 1945–1950* (Stuttgart 1982).

33 Gottfried Niedhart, 'Deutsche Nachkriegszeiten im Vergleich: Verarbeitung und Auswirkungen der Weltkriege. Ein Tagungsbericht', *Tel Aviver Jahrbuch für deutsche Geschichte*, 19 (1990), 451–9; also see Gottfried Niedhart and Dieter Riesenberger (eds), *Lernen aus dem Krieg? Deutsche Nachkriegszeiten 1918 und 1945* (Munich 1992).

34 Ulrich Herbert, 'Zur Entwicklung der Ruhrbergarbeiterschaft 1930–1960 aus erfahrungsgeschichtlicher Perspektive', in Lutz Niethammer and Alexander von Plato (eds), *Lebensgeschichte und Sozialkultur im Ruhrgebiet 1930–1960*, vol. 3: *'Wir kriegen jetzt andere Zeiten'. Auf der Suche nach der Erfahrung des Volkes in nachfaschistischen Ländern* (Berlin 1985), pp. 19–52.

35 Atina Grossmann, *Reforming Sex. The German Movement for Birth Control and Abortion Reform, 1920–1950* (Oxford 1995); Elisabeth Heinemann, 'The Hour of the Women. Memories of Germany's "Crisis Years" and West German National Identity', *American Historical Review*, 2 (1996), 354–9; Norman Naimark, *The Russians in Germany* (Cambridge, MA, 1995).

36 For the move from a German-centred to a Holocaust-centred 'memory regime' in Germany, compare Eric Langenbacher, 'Changing

Memory Regimes in Contemporary Germany?', *German Politics and Society*, 21:1 (2003), 46–69.

37 See, for example, Hannes Heer and Klaus Naumann (eds), *Vernichtungskrieg. Verbrechen der Wehrmacht 1941–1944* (Hamburg 1995); Christian Gerlach, *Kalkulierte Morde: Die deutsche Wirtschafts- und Vernichtungspolitik in Weissrussland 1941–1944* (Hamburg 1999); Omer Bartov, *The Eastern Front, 1941–1945: German Troops and the Barbarisation of Warfare*, 2nd edn (Basingstoke 2001).

38 The success story of Germans in coming to terms with their Nazi past is told by Bill Niven, *Facing the Nazi Past: United Germany and the Legacy of the Third Reich* (London 2002).

39 See, for example, Philip Ther, *Deutsche und polnische Vertriebene* (Göttingen 1998); Bernadetta Nitschke, *Vertreibung und Aussiedlung der deutschen Bevölkerung aus Polen 1945–1949* (Munich 2003); Niels von Redecker, *Die polnischen Vertreibungsdekrete und die offenen Vermögensfragen zwischen Deutschland und Polen* (Frankfurt am Main 2003); Angelika Fox, *Flüchtlinge und Vertriebene im Landkreis Fürstenfeldbruck. Aspekte ihrer Eingliederung seit 1945* (Fürstenfeldbruck 1998); the term 'expulsion' (*Vertreibung*) has also been incorporated into the three-volume *Deutsche Erinnerungsorte*, ed. Hagen Schulze and Etienne François (Munich 2001). For a bibliography on the wealth of new publications concerning the bombing war, see the special website of *historicum.net* which deals with the bombing war and is edited and managed by Ralf Koch, at www.bombenkrieg.historicum.net.

40 That generational aspect of the debate is also discussed in Dietmar Süß, '"Heimatfront" und "People's War": Neue Literatur zur Geschichte des Luftkrieges', *sehepunkte*, 4:7/8 (2004), [15.07.2004], URL: http://www.sehepunkte.historicum.net/2004/07/6714.html.

41 Hans Mommsen, 'Moralisch, strategisch, zerstörerisch', in Lothar Kettenacker (ed.), *Ein Volk von Opfern? Die neue Debatte um den Bombenkrieg 1940–1945* (Berlin 2003), pp. 145–51.42

42 Hans Ulrich Wehler, 'Die Debatte wirkt befreiend', *Der Spiegel Spezial*, 2 (2002): *Die Flucht der Deutschen*.

43 Dietmar Süß, 'Erinnerungen an den Luftkrieg', *Aus Politik und Zeitgeschichte*, 18/19 (2005), 19–26.

44 Heinrich Schwendemann, '"Schickt Schiffe!"', *Die Zeit*, 13 January 2005.

45 See Moeller's opening chapters, 1 and 2, in the current volume.

46 Robert G. Moeller, *War Stories: The Search for a Usable Past in the Federal Republic of Germany* (Berkeley 2001). For the importance of the memory of war for all post-war developments, see also Klaus Naumann, *Der Krieg als Text. Das Jahr 1945 im kulturellen Gedächtnis der Presse* (Hamburg 1998).

47 Robert G. Moeller, 'Sinking Ships, the Lost *Heimat* and Broken Taboos: Günter Grass and the Politics of Memory in Contemporary

Germany', *Contemporary European History*, 12 (2003), 147–81, and 'Germans as Victims? Thoughts on a Post-Cold War History of World War II's Legacies', *History and Memory*, 17:1/2 (2005), 147–94.

48 See Dietmar Süß, '"Massaker und Mongolensturm". Anmerkungen zu Jörg Friedrichs umstrittenem Buch "Der Brand. Deutschland im Bombenkrieg 1940–1945"', *Historisches Jahrbuch*, 124 (2004), 521–43; and Ralf Blank, review of Friedrich in *sehepunkte*, 2:12 (15 December 2002), http://www.sehepunkte.historicum.net/2002/12/3549071655.html. Jörg Arnold's perceptive review of Friedrich's book can be found on www.h-net-org/h~german. See also Nick Stargardt, 'Opfer der Bomben und der Vergeltung', and Richard Overy, 'Barbarisch, aber sinnvoll', both in Kettenacker (ed.), *Ein Volk von Opfern?*, pp. 56–71, and 183–87; and Julius Schoeps, 'Holocaust und Bombenkrieg sind nicht vergleichbar', *Die Welt*, 24 October 2003.

49 Charles Maier's contribution to H-German's forum on the bombing war. See: www.h-net-org/h-german.

50 Frederick Taylor, *Dresden: February 13, 1945* (New York 2004); German translation: *Dresden, Dienstag, 13. Februar 1945* (Munich 2004); in reviews of the German translation Taylor was often praised as a good antidote to Friedrich. See, for example, Volker Ullrich, 'Bomben auf Dresden', *Die Zeit*, 10 February 2005. The importance of the bombing war for military reasons has also been emphasised by Thomas Childers, '"Facilis descensus averni est": The Allied Bombing of Germany and the Issue of German Suffering', *Central European History*, 38 (2005), 75–105, and by Richard Overy, 'Die alliierte Bombenstrategie als Ausdruck des "totalen Krieges"', in Kettenacker (ed.), *Ein Volk von Opfern?*, pp. 27–47.

51 Rolf-Dieter Müller (unter Mitarbeit von Florian Huber and Johannes Eglau), *Der Bombenkrieg 1939–1945* (Berlin 2004).

52 Roger Chickering, Stig Förster and Bernd Greiner (eds), *A World at Total War: Global Conflict and the Politics of Destruction, 1937–1945* (Cambridge 2004).

53 A pathbreaking example of this combination of military and social history is provided by Jörg Echternkamp (ed.), *Die deutsche Kriegsgesellschaft 1939–1945*, vol. 1: *Politisierung, Vernichtung, Überleben*, and vol. 2: *Ausbeutung, Deutungen, Ausgrenzungen* [vol. 9, 1–2 of *Das Deutsche Reich und der Zweite Weltkrieg* (Munich 2005)].

54 Mary Nolan, 'Air Wars, Memory Wars', *Central European History*, 38 (2005), 7–40. For tentative beginnings of such comparativisation of the themes, see Horst Boog (ed.), *Luftkriegsführung im Zweiten Weltkrieg. Ein internationaler Vergleich* (Herford-Bonn 1993). For further comparative perspectives, see Peter Dines and Peter Knoch, 'Deutsche und britische Erfahrungen im Bombenkrieg 1940–1945', in Dieter Brötel and Hans H. Pöschko (eds), *Krisen und Geschichtsbewußtsein. Mentalitätsgeschichtliche und didaktische Beiträge. Peter Knoch zum Gedenken*

(Weinheim 1996); Rainer Ohliger and Rainer Münz (eds), *Diasporas and Ethnic Migrants. Germany, Israel and Russia in Comparative Perspective* (Oxford 2001); Haug von Kuehnheim, *Flucht und Vertreibung. Europa zwischen 1939 und 1948* (Reinbek 2004); Thomas Urban, *Der Verlust. Die Vertreibung der Deutschen und Polen im 20. Jahrhundert* (Munich 2004); Norman Naimark, *Fires of Hatred: Ethnic Cleansing in Twentieth Century Europe* (Harvard 2002); Eric Weitz, *A Century of Genocide: Utopias of Race and Nation* (Princeton 2003).

55 Micha Brumlik, *Wer Sturm sät. Die Vertreibung der Deutschen* (Berlin 2005).

56 Achatz von Müller, 'Passionsspiel mit Hintersinn', *Die Zeit*, 3 February 2005.

57 Andreas Hillgruber, *Zweierlei Untergang* (Munich 1986).

58 On Walter Kempowski's ambitious project see www.kempowski.de.

59 Harald Welzer, Sabine Moller and Karoline Tschuggnall, *'Opa war kein Nazi': Nationalsozialismus und Holocaust im Familiengedächtnis* (Frankfurt am Main 2002).

60 On the discourse of 'normalisation' and the emergence of a new patriotism after reunification see Stefan Berger, *The Search for Normality: National Identity and Historical Consciousness in Germany since 1800* (2nd edn, Oxford 2003).

Select Bibliography

1 Works of historiography, general cultural history, literary history and psychology dealing with or significantly touching on issues of German suffering and/or its post-war reception.

Paul Addison and Jeremy A. Crang, *Firestorm: The Bombing of Dresden, 1945* (London 2006).

Pertti Ahonen, *After the Expulsion: West Germany and Eastern Europe, 1945–1990* (Oxford 2003).

Stephan Aust and Stephan Burgdorff, *Als Feuer vom Himmel fiel: Der Bombenkrieg in Deutschland* (Hamburg 2003).

Sabine Behrenbeck, 'Remembering the Victims of Violence in Germany', in Richard Bessel and Dirk Schumann (eds), *Life after Death: Approaches to a Cultural and Social History of Europe during the 1940s and 1950s* (Cambridge 2003).

Wolfgang Benz (ed.), *Die Vertreibung der Deutschen aus dem Osten: Ursachen, Ereignisse, Folgen* (Frankfurt am Main 1995).

Götz Bergander, *Dresden im Luftkrieg: Vorgeschichte – Zerstörung – Folgen* (Würzburg 1998).

Stefan Berger, *The Search for Normality: National Identity and Historical Consciousness in Germany since 1800* (Providence 1997).

Günter Böddeker, *Die Flüchtlinge. Die Vertreibung der Deutschen im Osten* (Munich and Berlin 1980).

Stefan Braese, 'Bombenkrieg und literarische Gegenwart', *Mittelweg*, 36:1 (2002), 2–24.

Micha Brumlik, *Wer Sturm sät. Die Vertreibung der Deutschen* (Berlin 2005).

Hans Brunswig, *Feuersturm über Hamburg* (Stuttgart 1978).

Bundesministerium für Vertriebene, Flüchtlinge und Kriegsgeschädigte (ed.), *Dokumentation der Vertreibung der Deutschen aus Ost-Mitteleuropa*, 8 vols (Bonn 1953–62).

Bundesministerium für Vertriebene, Flüchtlinge und Kriegsgeschädigte (ed.), *Dokumente deutscher Kriegsschäden. Evakuierte, Kriegssachgeschädigte, Währungsgeschädigte. Die geschichtliche und rechtliche Entwicklung*, 5 vols (Bonn 1958–64).

Stephan Burgdorff and Christian Habbe, *Die Flucht: Über die Vertreibung der Deutschen aus dem Osten* (Hamburg 2002).

Thomas Childers, '"Facilis descensus averni est": The Allied Bombing of Germany and the Issue of German Suffering', *Central European History*, 38 (2005), 75–105.

Birgit Dahlke, '"Frau komm!" Vergewaltigungen 1945: Zur Geschichte eines Diskurses,' in Birgit Dahlke, Martina Langermann and Thomas Taterka (eds), *LiteraturGesellschaft DDR: Kanonkämpfe und ihre Geschichte(n)* (Stuttgart 2000), pp. 275–311.

Jürgen Danyel (ed.), *Die geteilte Vergangenheit: Zum Umgang mit Nationalsozialismus und Widerstand in beiden deutschen Staaten* (Berlin 1995).

James M. Diehl, *The Thanks of the Fatherland: German Veterans after the Second World War* (Chapel Hill, 1993).

Helmut Dubiel, *Niemand ist frei von der Geschichte: Die nationalsozialistische Herrschaft in den Debatten des Deutschen Bundestags* (Munich 1999).

Jörg Echternkamp, 'Von Opfern, Helden und Verbrechern: Anmerkungen zur Bedeutung des Zweiten Weltkriegs in den Erinnerungskulturen der Deutschen 1945–1955', in Jörg Hillmann and John Zimmermann (eds), *Kriegsende 1945 in Deutschland* (Munich 2002), pp. 308–9.

Richard Evans, *Lying about Hitler: History, Holocaust and the David Irving Trial* (London 2002).

Sascha Feuchert (ed.), *Flucht und Vertreibung in der deutschen Literatur* (Frankfurt am Main 2001).

Georg W. Feuchter, *Der Luftkrieg* (Frankfurt am Main 1964).

Thomas C. Fox, *Stated Memory: East Germany and the Holocaust* (Rochester 1999).

Ole Frahm, '"Ein deutsches Trauma?": Zur Schamlosigkeit Deutscher Opferidentifikation', *German Life and Letters*, 57:4 (2004), 372–90.

K. Erik Franzen, *Die Vertriebenen. Hitlers letzte Opfer* (Munich 2002).

Norbert Frei, *Adenauer's Germany and the Nazi Past: The Politics of Amnesty and Integration,* trans. Joel Golb (New York 2002).

Norbert Frei, *1945 und Wir: Das Dritte Reich im Bewußtsein der Deutschen* (Munich 2005).

Jörg Friedrich, *Der Brand: Deutschland im Bombenkrieg 1940–1945* (Munich 2002).

Jörg Friedrich, *Brandstätten: Der Anblick des Bombenkriegs* (Munich 2003).

Astrid von Friesen, *Der lange Abschied: Psychische Spätfolgen für die zweite Generation deutscher Vertriebener* (Gießen 2005).

Elke Fröhlich, *Als die Erde brannte: Deutsche Schicksale in den letzten Kriegstagen* (Munich 2005).

Peter Glotz, *Die Vertreibung. Böhmen als Lehrstück* (Munich 2003).

A. C. Grayling, *Among the Dead Cities: Was the Allied Bombing of Civilians in WWII a Necessity or a Crime?* (London 2006).

Olaf Groehler, *Geschichte des Luftkriegs* (Berlin 1975).

Olaf Groehler, *Bombenkrieg gegen Deutschland* (Berlin 1990).

Volker Hage, *Hamburg 1943* (Frankfurt am Main 2003).

Volker Hage, *Zeugen der Zerstörung. Die Literaten und der Luftkrieg* (Frankfurt am Main 2003).

Geoffrey H. Hartmann (ed.), *Bitburg in Moral and Political Perspective* (Bloomington 1986).

Louis Ferdinand Helbig, *Der ungeheure Verlust. Flucht und Vertreibung in der deutschsprachigen Belletristik* (Wiesbaden, 3rd edn, 1996).

Jeffrey Herf, *Divided Memory: The Nazi Past in the Two Germanys* (Cambridge, MA, 1997).

Andreas Hillgruber, *Zweierlei Untergang. Die Zerschlagung des deutschen Reiches und das Ende des europäischen Judentums* (Berlin 1986).

Historikerstreit: Die Dokumentation der Kontroverse um die Einzigartigkeit der nationalsozialistischen Judenvernichtung (Munich 1987).

David Irving, *The Destruction of Dresden* (London 1985).

Graham Jackman, 'The End of a Taboo? The Experience of Bombing and Expulsion in Contemporary German "Gedächtniskultur"', *German Life and Letters*, 4 (2004), 343–55.

Peter Jahn (ed.), *Stalingrad Erinnern: Stalingrad im deutschen und im russischen Gedächtnis* (Berlin 2003).

Annette Kaminsky (ed.), *Orte des Erinnerns: Gedenkzeichen, Gedenkstätten und Museen zur Diktatur in SBZ und DDR* (Leipzig 2004).

Lothar Kettenacker (ed.), *Ein Volk von Opfern? Die neue Debatte um den Bombenkrieg 1940–45* (Berlin 2003).

Christoph Kleßmann, Hans Misselwitz and Günther Wichert (eds), *Deutsche Vergangenheiten – eine gemeinsame Herausforderung: Der schwierige Umgang mit der doppelten Nachkriegsgeschichte* (Berlin 1999).

Michael Klundt (ed.), *Heldenmythos und Opfertaumel: Der Zweite Weltkrieg und seine Folgen im deutschen Geschichtsdiskurs* (Cologne 2004).

Hubertus Knabe, *Tag der Befreiung? Das Kriegsende in Deutschland* (Berlin 2005).

Helmut König, *Die Zukunft der Vergangenheit: Der Nationalsozialismus im politischen Bewußtsein der Bundesrepublik* (Frankfurt am Main 2003).

Anja Kruke (ed.), *Zwangsmigration und Vertreibung – Europa im 20. Jahrhundert* (Bonn 2005).

Ulla Lachauer, *Ostpreußische Lebensläufe* (Reinbek 1998).

Pieter Lagrou, 'The Nationalization of Victimhood: Selective Violence and National Grief in Western Europe, 1940–1960', in Richard Bessel and Dirk Schumann (eds), *Life after Death: Approaches to a Cultural and Social History of Europe during the 1940s and 1950s* (Cambridge 2003), pp. 243–57.

Eric Langenbacher, 'Changing Memory Regimes in Contemporary Germany?', *German Politics and Society*, 21:2 (2003), 46–68.

Eric Langenbacher, 'The Return of Memory: New Discussions about German Suffering in World War II', *German Politics and Society*, 3 (2003), 74–88.

David Clay Large, '"A Beacon in the German Darkness": The Anti-Nazi Resistance Legacy in West German Politics', *Journal of Modern History*, 64 (suppl.) (1993), 173–86.

David Clay Large, *Germans to the Front: West German Rearmament in the Adenauer Era* (Chapel Hill 1996).

Hilke Lorenz, *Kriegskinder. Das Schicksal einer Generation* (Berlin 2003).

Charles Maier, *The Unmasterable Past: History, Holocaust, and German National Identity* (Cambridge, MA, 1988).

Harold Marcuse, *Legacies of Dachau: The Uses and Abuses of a Concentration Camp, 1933–2001* (Cambridge 2001).

Gilad Margalit, 'Der Luftangriff auf Dresden: Seine Bedeutung für die Erinnerungspolitik der DDR und für die Herauskristallisierung einer historischen Kriegserinnerung im Westen', in Susanne Düwell and Matthias Schmidt (eds), *Narrative der Shoah: Repräsentationen der Vergangenheit in Historiographie, Kunst und Politik* (Paderborn 2002), pp. 189–208.

Elke Mehnert (ed.), *Landschaften der Erinnerung: Flucht und Vertreibung aus deutscher, polnischer und tschechischer Sicht* (Frankfurt am Main 2001).

Robert. G. Moeller (ed.), *West Germany under Construction: Politics, Society, and Culture in the Adenauer Era* (Ann Arbor 1997),

Robert G. Moeller, 'Deutsche Opfer, Opfer der Deutschen: Kriegsgefangene, Vertriebene, NS-Verfolgte: Opferausgleich als Identitätspolitik', in Klaus Naumann (ed.), *Nachkrieg in Deutschland* (Hamburg 2001), pp. 29–58.

Robert G. Moeller, 'Remembering the War in a Nation of Victims: West German Pasts in the 1950s', in Hanna Schissler (ed.), *The Miracle Years: a Cultural History of West Germany 1949–1968* (Princeton 2001), pp. 83–109.

Robert G. Moeller, *War Stories: The Search for a Usable Past in the Federal Republic of Germany* (Berkeley 2001).

Robert G. Moeller, 'Sinking Ships, the Lost *Heimat* and Broken Taboos: Günter Grass and the Politics of Memory in Contemporary Germany', *Contemporary European History*, 12 (2003), 147–81.

Robert G. Moeller, 'Germans as Victims? Thoughts on a Post-Cold War History of World War II's Legacies', *History & Memory*, 17:2 (2005), 147–94.

Rolf-Dieter Müller, *Der Bombenkrieg 1939–1945* (Berlin 2005).

Norman Naimark, *Fires of Hatred: Ethnic Cleansing in Twentieth Century Europe* (Harvard 2002).

Heinz Nawratil, *Vertreibungsverbrechen an Deutschen. Tatbestand, Motive, Bewältigung* (Munich 1984).

Thomas W. Neumann, 'Der Bombenkrieg: Zur ungeschriebenen Geschichte einer kollektiven Verletzung', in Klaus Naumann (ed.), *Nachkrieg in Deutschland* (Hamburg 2001), pp. 319–42.

Bill Niven, *Facing the Nazi Past* (London and New York 2002).

Mary Nolan, 'Air Wars, Memory Wars', *Central European History*, 38 (2005), 7–40.

Ines Reich, 'Geteilter Widerstand: Die Tradierung des deutschen Widerstands in der Bundesrepublik und der DDR', *Zeitschrift für Geschichtswissenschaft*, 42 (1994), 635–43.

Peter Reichel, *Politik mit der Erinnerung: Gedächtnisorte im Streit um die nationalsozialistische Vergangenheit*, revised edn (Frankfurt am Main 1999).

Peter Reichel, *Vergangenheitsbewältigung in Deutschland: Die Auseinandersetzung mit der NS-Diktatur von 1945 bis heute* (Munich 2001).

Peter Reif-Spirek and Bodo Ritscher (eds), *Speziallager in der SBZ. Gedenkstätten mit 'doppelter Vergangenheit'* (Berlin 1999).

Oliver Reinhard, Matthias Neutzner and Wolfgang Hesse, *Das Rote Leuchten: Dresden und der Bombenkrieg* (Dresden 2005).

Klaus Rainer Röhl, *Verbotene Trauer: Ende der deutschen Tabus* (Munich 2002).

Hans Rumpf, *Das war der Bombenkrieg. Deutsche Städte im Feuersturm* (Oldenburg 1961). [Translated as *The Bombing of Germany* (London 1963).]

Frank Schirrmacher (ed.), *Die Walser-Bubis-Debatte* (Frankfurt am Main 1999).

Heinz Schön, *Die 'Gustloff'-Katastrophe: Bericht eines Überlebenden über die größte Schiffskatastrophe im zweiten Weltkrieg* (Stuttgart 1984).

Helmut Schmitz, *On Their Own Terms: The Legacy of National Socialism in Post-1990 German Literature* (Birmingham 2004).

Walter Schmitz (ed.), *Die Zerstörung Dresdens: Antworten der Künste* (Dresden 2005).

Michael Schwartz, 'Vertreibung und Vergangenheitspolitik: Ein Versuch über geteilte deutsche Nachkriegsidentitäten', *Deutschland-Archiv*, 30 (1997), 177–95.

Heimo Schwilk and Ulrich Schacht (eds), *Die selbstbewußte Nation* (Frankfurt am Main 1994).

W. G. Sebald, *Luftkrieg und Literatur* (Munich 1999). [Translated as *On the Natural History of Destruction* (New York 2003).]

Arthur V. Sellwood, *The Damned Don't Drown: The Sinking of the Wilhelm Gustloff* (Annapolis 1973).

Max Seydewitz, *Zerstörung und Wiederaufbau von Dresden* (Berlin 1955).

Max Seydewitz, *Die unbesiegbare Stadt: Zerstörung und Wiederaufbau von Dresden* (Berlin 1956).

Staatliche Kunstsammlungen Dresden (ed.), *Dresden: Bekenntnis und Verpflichtung* (Dresden 1985).

Henning Süssner, 'Still Yearning for the Lost Heimat?: Ethnic German Expellees and the Politics of Belonging', *German Politics and Society*, 2 (2004), 1–26.

Arno Surminski et al. (eds), *Flucht und Vertreibung* (Hamburg 2004).

Stuart Taberner, *German Literature of the 1990s and Beyond* (Rochester 2005).

Frederick Taylor, *Dresden: Tuesday, 13 February, 1945* (London 2004).

Philip Ther, *Deutsche und polnische Vertriebene* (Göttingen 1998).

Malte Thießen, 'Gedenken an "Operation Gomorrha": Zur Erinnerungskultur des Bombenkrieges von 1945 bis heute', *Zeitschrift für Geschichtswissenschaft*, 53 (2005), 46–61.

Gregor Thum, *Die fremde Stadt: Breslau 1945* (Munich 2003).

Gerd Ueberschär and Rolf-Dieter Müller, *1945: Das Ende des Krieges* (Darmstadt 2005).

Thomas Urban, *Der Verlust: Die Vertreibung der Deutschen und Polen im 20. Jahrhundert* (Munich 2004).
Walter Weidauer, *Inferno Dresden: Über Lügen und Legenden um die Aktion 'Donnerschlag'* (Berlin 1966).
Harald Welzer, Sabine Moller and Karoline Tschuggnall, *'Opa war kein Nazi': Nationalsozialismus und Holocaust im Familiengedächtnis* (Frankfurt am Main 2002).
Thomas Widera, *Dresden 1945–1948: Politik und Gesellschaft unter sowjetischer Besatzungsherrschaft* (Göttingen 2005).
Edgar Wolfrum, 'Zwischen Geschichtsschreibung und Geschichtspolitik. Forschungen zu Flucht und Vertreibung nach dem Zweiten Weltkrieg', *Archiv für Sozialgeschichte*, 36 (1996), 500–22.
Edgar Wolfrum, *Geschichtspolitik in der Bundesrepublik Deutschland: Der Weg zur bundesrepublikanischen Erinnerung 19481990* (Darmstadt 1999).
Alfred M. de Zayas, *Anmerkungen zur Vertreibung der Deutschen aus dem Osten* (Stuttgart 1986).

2 Literary works and (auto)biographies dealing with or significantly touching on the issue of German suffering.

Anon., *Eine Frau in Berlin* (Berlin 2003). [Translated as *A Woman in Berlin* (London 2005).]
Heinz Czechowski, *Auf eine im Feuer versunkene Stadt* (Halle/Leipzig 1990).
Tanja Dückers, *Himmelskörper* (Berlin 2003).
Gertrud von le Fort, *Am Tor des Himmels* (Wiesbaden 1954).
Dieter Forte, *Der Junge mit den blutigen Schuhen* (Frankfurt am Main 1995).
Gerd Gaiser, *Die sterbende Jagd* (Munich 1959).
Günter Grass, *Im Krebsgang* (Göttingen 2002). [Translated as *Crabwalk* (New York 2003).]
Durs Grünbein, *Porzellan: Poem vom Untergang meiner Stadt* (Frankfurt am Main 2005).
Ulla Hahn, *Unscharfe Bilder* (Munich 2003).
Christoph Hein, *Landnahme* (Frankfurt am Main 2004).
Reinhard Jirgl, *Die Unvollendeten* (Munich 2003).
Hermann Kasack, *Die Stadt hinter dem Strom* (Frankfurt am Main 1948).
Walter Kempowski, *Der rote Hahn: Dresden im Februar 1945* (Munich 2001).
Walter Kempowski, *Das Echolot: Abgesang '45, Ein Kollektives Tagebuch* (Munich 2005).
Otto Erich Kiesel, *Die unverzagte Stadt* (1949; reprint, Hamburg 1973).
Alexander Kluge, *Neue Geschichten: Hefte 1–18 ⟨Unheimlichkeit der Zeit⟩* (Frankfurt am Main 1978), pp. 33–110.
Gerd Ledig, *Vergeltung* (Frankfurt am Main 1956). [Translated as *Payback* (London 2003).]
Renate Meinhof, *Das Tagebuch der Maria Meinhof. April 1945 bis März 1946 in Pommern – Eine Spurensuche* (Hamburg 2005).

Hans-Erich Nossack, *Der Untergang. Hamburg 1943* (Frankfurt am Main 1948). [Translated as *The End. Hamburg 1943* (Chicago 2004).]

Karl Otto, *Leuchtendes Erbe* (Lengefeld 1956).

Eberhard Panitz, *Die Feuer sinken* (Berlin 1960).

Eberhard Panitz, *Meines Vaters Straßenbahn* (Halle/Leizpig 1979).

Hildegard Maria Rauchfuß, *Wem die Steine Antwort geben* (Halle 1953).

Willy Peter Reese, *Mir selber seltsam fremd. Die Unmenschlichkeit des Krieges. Russland 1941–1944* (Düsseldorf 2005). [Translated as *A Stranger to Myself* (New York 2005).]

Arno Schmidt, *Aus dem Leben eines Fauns* (Hamburg 1953). [Translated as *Scenes from the Life of a Faun* (London 1983).]

Botho Strauß, 'Anschwellender Bocksgesang', in Botho Strauß, *Der Aufstand gegen die sekundäre Welt* (Munich 1999), pp. 55–79.

Uwe Timm, *Am Beispiel meines Bruders* (Köln 2003). [Translated as *In My Brother's Shadow* (London 2005).]

Ulrich Treichel, *Der Verlorene* (1998). [Translated as *Lost* (London 2000).]

Martin Walser, *Die Verteidigung der Kindheit* (Frankfurt am Main 1991).

Martin Walser, *Ein Springender Brunnen* (Frankfurt am Main 1998).

Martin Walser, *Tod eines Kritikers* (Frankfurt am Main 2002).

Bruno Werner, *Die Galeere* (Frankfurt am Main 1949).

Friedrich Wolf, *Heimkehr der Söhne* (Berlin 1946).

Max Zimmering, *Phosphor und Flieder: Vom Untergang und Wiederaufstieg der Stadt Dresden* (Berlin 1954).

Index